THE WORLD'S RELIGIONS: THE RELIGIONS OF ASIA

The World's Religions:

The Religions of Asia

ROUTLEDGE

London

First published in 1988
as part of The World's Religions
Reprinted in 1990
by Routledge
11 New Fetter Lane, London EC4P 4EE

Printed in Great Britain by Mackays at Chatham

ISBN 0-415-05815-5

Contents

1. Introduction
Friedhelm Hardy 1
2. Philosophical and Religious Taoism
Bulcsu Siklós, School of Oriental and African Studies, University of London 10
3. Mazdaism ('Zoroastrianism')
Julian Baldick 20
4. The Classical Religions of India
Friedhelm Hardy 37
General Remarks on the Religious History of India 39
Vedic Religion 43
The Renouncer Traditions 50
Epic and Purāṇic Religion 72
Mahāyāna Buddhism and Buddhist Philosophy 95
Hindu Philosophies and Theologies 105
Later Jainism 114
The Esoteric Traditions and Antinomian Movements 117
5. Śaivism and the Tantric Traditions
Alexis Sanderson, Oriental Institute, University of Oxford 128
6. Modern Hinduism
Glyn Richards, University of Stirling 173
7. Sikhism
C. Shackle, School of Oriental and African Studies, University of London 182
8. Theravāda Buddhism in South-East Asia
W.J. Johnson, Wolfson College, University of Oxford 194

9. Buddhism and Hinduism in the Nepal Valley
David Gellner, St John's College, University of Oxford 207
10. Buddhism in China
Bulcsu Siklós 224
11. Buddhism in Japan
Bulcsu Siklós 236
12. The Religions of Tibet
Tadeusz Skorupski, School of Oriental and African Studies, University of London 247
13. Buddhism in Mongolia
Bulcsu Siklós 279

Index 287

1 Introduction

Friedhelm Hardy

In one sense, there are innumerable religions in Asia. Some of these are tribal religions, belonging to relatively small social groups which so far have resisted an integration into wider cultural and social structures. Others are folk religions, relatively amorphous practices and beliefs which underlie the more structured 'high religions'. But in a different sense, only three or four religions are of primary importance, both in terms of the complexity of their beliefs and of their geographical spread. Thus Christianity found a home in south-western India from the earlier part of the first millennium CE. From the late fifteenth century, a succession of colonial powers and missionary activities gave rise to sizeable Christian communities in other parts of India and in Asian countries like the Philippines, Vietnam, Sri Lanka and China. But far greater has been the impact of Islam. From the seventh century CE onwards, it created a whole string of Islamic countries (Iran, Afghanistan, Pakistan, Bangladesh, Indonesia, Malaysia) and also acquired numerous followers in countries like India, central Russia and China. Nevertheless, both Christianity and Islam belong historically to the Near East, and in spite of their presence further east, they changed relatively little of their basic, 'semitic', character. Thus it is primarily Buddhism followed by Hinduism which appear as the older and truly 'Asian' religions.

From its original home in India, Buddhism spread into all the neighbouring countries, and from there further afield to Central Asia, Mongolia, China, Korea, Japan, Indonesia and Indo-China. Its history in India itself was complex, and often three 'phases' are distinguished to which three different types of Buddhism correspond. Depending among other things on the period during which a particular Asian country came to know of Indian Buddhism, one of these types was adopted.

Buddhism itself (along with a much lesser known parallel movement, Jainism, which remained restricted to India) evolved out of an older religious cosmos. The latter developed in the course of the centuries a whole spectrum of concrete expressions and, commonly summarised as 'Hinduism', has influenced the majority of Indians over more than three millennia. In medieval times, Hinduism influenced the whole of Indo-China and Indonesia extensively. It was Islam that eliminated these influences (except for the small enclave of the island of Bali), just as it put an end to Buddhism in India, Iran, Central Asia and Indonesia.

Although Buddhism and Hinduism have played an essential role in the 'national' histories of most Asian countries, only occasionally did they develop into 'national' religions. Tibet is perhaps the best-known example of such a fusion of the religious with the political; Sri Lanka and, to some extent, Japan can be added to the list. But in most cases, Hindus and Buddhists (Jains etc.) lived together in the same political system. It is possible to get glimpses of such a multi-religious situation from modern Nepal for instance. Moreover, the expansion of Buddhism (and to some extent, of medieval Hinduism) was primarily due to missionary and mercantile activities without military and 'colonial' aspects.

For a variety of reasons, other Asian religions deserve to be mentioned. Thus of considerable historical interest is Mazdaism (often styled Zoroastrianism). On the basis of linguistic similarities between a whole range of languages (including Greek, Latin, Old Slavonic, Old Germanic and Sanskrit), scholars reconstructed an original Indo-European language. It appears that, in the prehistoric past, the people speaking that language broke up into various groups and gradually moved into a variety of regions. One such group (called the Indo-Iranians) moved eastward, there, in its turn, to split up further: some entered Iran, and others continued their journey towards the east, to settle in north-west India. Whilst the group that entered India is associated with the oldest form of Hinduism, the immigrants into Iran developed Mazdaism which remained prominent in that country till the arrival of Islam. The Parsees of modern India are the descendants of refugees from Islamised Iran.

With Shamanism and Taoism, we can still catch some glimpses of religious practices and beliefs which belong to a world unaffected by the religions ultimately deriving from Indo-Iranian sources. On the other hand, a religion like Sikhism represents a relatively modern offshoot of Hinduism with Islamic features in its background. Even more recent is a whole range of religious developments which in part are due to modern, Western stimuli. The 'new religious movements' of Japan have particularly attracted scholarly attention. But it would be a serious mistake simply to contrast these modern developments with fixed systems (like Buddhism). The history of all these ancient religions is extremely dynamic; they constantly change, partly by interacting with the many folk religions upon which they have imposed themselves as a more complex superstructure. To enter into the spirit of the Asian religions means to realise this dynamism.

During the last two hundred years or so, much information about, and many impressions of, the East have accumulated in our own culture. Inevitably, a fair number of stereotypes and unquestioned assumptions have crystallised in our perception of those other cultures. 'The mysterious East' is a commonly used expression in which these various preconceptions are gathered together. The word 'mysterious' is sometimes used to suggest 'incomprehensible', alien to such an extent that our own way of thinking cannot cope with it. If this were true of the East, the implications for what human nature is would be catastrophic, for it would suggest that different groups of people cannot actually relate to each other in a meaningful, namely human, manner. But if we consider the case of language as a parallel here, such a drastic position becomes unnecessary. An unknown language sounds extremely strange and incomprehensible, but so far no language has been discovered which cannot be learnt by an outsider. Some languages may be more difficult to learn than others, but in principle human speech is culturally transferable. In other words, no group of people which has a language in common is essentially isolated from other such groups with different languages. The onus would be on the person putting forward the theory of the Eastern incomprehensibility to prove that religion constitutes a case totally different from that of language.

But even if the Eastern religions were in principle 'comprehensible', they still could be 'mysterious' in the sense of being 'irrational'. In fact, this is probably the more frequent implication when we hear about the mysterious East. Again this is an assertion loaded with implied assumptions about human nature. It implies that only some people (in this case naturally us) are logical, systematic in their thinking and coherent. Other people do not possess such mental qualities, and not reason, but emotion (or something else) remains as the only means of comprehending the mystery. This particular understanding of the East is found not only in its critics, but also in its admirers. Rationality is to some the culmination of human existence, and to others the fundamental evil of Western society. Since the East is seen not to be rational, it cannot be regarded as fully developed in human terms (as the critics would see it), or it must be applauded as far more perfect (as the admirers would postulate). This is a remarkable consensus of opinion, at least as to the fundamental assumption, in whatever way it may then be evaluated. But is it true? Superficially, it is very easy to construe real-life situations (let us say, for a situation-comedy) where the Eastern reaction indeed appears incomprehensible and irrational. Take the following example. A tourist enters an Indian restaurant and asks the waiter: 'Isn't there any food here?' Imagine the answer to be 'Yes, sir.' Naturally we would find it very logical that the tourist should sit down at a table and wait for his meal to arrive. Nothing happens. The waiter has disappeared, and no food appears. The tourist begins to fidget, and finally shouts for service, the waiter reappears and answers once again 'Yes, sir!' to the question whether there isn't any food in the place. Repeat this a few times, and you have a comedy. But you have not proved that the East is irrational. All that we can say is that either the waiter does not use the English word 'yes' accurately, or that the tourist does not know how to interpret an Indian 'yes'. The Indian languages do not actually possess a word that corresponds to our 'yes'. They possess words of negation and affirmation. So all the waiter does when he replies 'yes' is to agree with our tourist. 'You are quite right: there is no food here.' Once this is realised, the whole scenario spontaneously turns into a perfectly rational affair. The confusion is merely due to the premisses by which the word 'yes' is used and understood.

On a more serious note it is still possible to make a similar point. It can be shown without difficulty that Eastern logic is identical to ours; the differences lie in the premisses of Eastern thought. Any system of thought is based on a set of axioms—fundamental facts that are regarded as so totally self-evident that they are not reflected upon and usually carried along as unconsciously made assumptions. It is here where the differences lie. The fact that a culture does not normally spell out such premisses, and that most of its members would not even be able to do so when asked, lies at the centre of the 'Eastern mystery'. Yet the logic which is then brought into operation is precisely the same as ours, but does not appear as such because of the dislocation of the premisses. Let us look at some examples to illustrate this in greater detail.

We take it utterly for granted that a thing is identical with itself. A chair is a chair, and nothing else. Moreover, such a self-identical object is a constant which we can insert into propositions. For example, 'this chair is brown and made out of oak wood.' We would be very loath to question any of this. To scrutinise it further would seem to be an extreme form of hair-splitting. And yet, empirically speaking, such a premiss is questionable, at least to the extent that it ought to force us to acknowledge that our premiss actually implies a decision about how we want to look at reality. Empirically, the chair is a most transient object. It comes about through the gluing together of various pieces of wood, taken from trees that have grown out of tiny seeds, and even if no fire or woodworm or any other destructive agent came near it, its life-span as a 'chair' is infinitesimally smaller than the life-span of the universe. The decision that we have made is to abstract from the transience (as defined above) and pretend—for totally legitimate, pragmatic reasons—that a chair is a chair. But a different decision could be made, which includes the element of transience in the basic understanding of what an object is. In that case, we are less likely to encounter propositions about 'objects', and more likely descriptions in terms of processes (the growth of trees, the joining together of different bits of wood and the gradual disintegration of this union). It is still possible to make perfectly logical statements about chairs, statements that need not make explicit the process characteristics of objects. But it is not difficult to imagine a situation comparable to the one envisaged above in the restaurant, in which talk about chairs can easily give rise to amazing misunderstandings. The 'uncomfortable chair' of one person may well be the 'pain-inflicting process stimulated by a temporarily solidified mass of transient phenomena' of another person (including some Western philosophers). Now why anybody would want to come up with such a perception of reality (and this kind of talk about it) depends on many other factors. It is needless to add that such factors fall squarely into what we call the Eastern religions.

Let us pursue this for a case where 'identity' is a crucial issue in the human destiny: the self-identity of the person. It is only through looking at the unusual or abnormal that we become aware of the implicit assumptions in our own culture. The schizophrenic appears to consist of more than one 'person'; alcohol can 'bring out a different person'; drugs can cause altered states of consciousness. But in all these cases our culture has decided to regard them as unimportant in relation to the definition of a person. In all three examples something is happening that ought not to. The 'real' person is disturbed or interfered with. Now let us turn to Asia. Here we find it culturally accepted that a person may leave his body. Thus the shaman roams about freely and enters the bodies of animals and other human beings. Or the body of one person is used by another being, in the cults of possession. Or the meditator experiences embodiment as an animal or a different human being. Or the same meditator experiences a widening of his self-awareness: the conventional boundaries surrounding the 'I' are removed and the 'I' plunges into a far more comprehensive reality. Some of this is directly observable to others, like a possessed person, through whom a different being speaks and acts. In other cases, the rest of society has to rely on the testimony of the person experiencing it. As in the example from the Western context, a decision as to the validity of such experiences for the definition of personhood has to be made. The fundamental difference between East and West here is simply that Asia has accepted such phenomena as issues worth discussing and reflecting upon and does not discard them as 'abnormal'. It is clear that regardless of how precisely a religion may sort matters out, the very fact of deciding to accept any of these experiences as a valid source of insight must have far-reachng consequences for the formulation of human destiny.

Let us look at another example. It is probably fair to say that our traditional view of the world regards it as an object lying outside ourselves. In religious terms it is a creation out of nothing and thus, ultimately, of no real concern in the relation between God and man. To the extent that Christianity has formulated this as a dogma it has explicitly identified it as an axiom. The East knows of no such thing as creation out of nothing. The world tends to be accepted as a factually given entity, like man. From this follows logically the assumption of a very intimate connection between man and the world. Within the world can be found a rhythm, a structure or pattern (e.g. the *Tao* or the *Dharma*) which is decisive for man's own destiny and fulfilment. Religion spells out how to harmonise one's individual being with this universal rhythm. Aspects of this have been labelled 'fatalism' by certain Western observers. Yet when this term is required to denote more than merely a somewhat placid personality type, content with accepting things as they are, it does not do justice to this view of the world. Wherever we find the belief in such a cosmic rhythm, it goes along with the assumption that 'ordinary' man has not yet achieved his harmonising with it. Thus he must do something: he is called for action. He is faced with a definite choice, and it is his choice alone. Even when the past is brought into this conception, as in certain ways predetermining the current life, it is never seen as preventing the essential actions asked for. Man remains in control of his destiny, at least where it is supposed to matter most. Moreover, the cosmic rhythm is often envisaged as containing undreamt-of powers which can be used by the man who knows how to get at them. Whether Taoist or Tantric, the pursuit of such powers guided by religion can certainly not be regarded as 'fatalistic' (or, for that matter, as 'world-negating' or 'spiritual').

Such a premiss of a cosmic rhythm implies another important difference from traditional Western thought. We are used to looking at the world as containing good and evil as objective entities, as universal, cosmic forces. Historically, this derives from the Judeo-Christian tradition, which in turn, some claim, may have been influenced by Mazdaism (Zoroastrianism). The powers of goodness are with God, and evil is associated with the devil. This type of binary, objectifying thought is alien to the religions further East. Objectively, there is only the world with its inbuilt rhythm and structure. As long as, subjectively, man harmonises himself with this rhythm, he does what is 'good'. The evil experienced in life is the price paid for there existing many beings who do not join into this rhythm. Such an ethical neutrality of the world in relation to man can become particularly disconcerting for a Western observer when it presents itself in a theistic form. We are so strongly accustomed to link the concept of God with that of ultimate 'goodness' that a 'neutral' God is inconceivable. Yet it is equally rational to argue that, given the nature of God as Absolute, by definition he must transcend whatever categories and attributes our contingent human mind can come up with.

We may conveniently continue this exploration of premisses by staying with the theme of theism. It goes without saying that for us religion has to do with God, or at least with gods. If we stick by this definition, a considerable amount of material found in Asia must be excluded, because there is no God here, and often not even gods. That sometimes, in a rather uncritical manner, the concept 'god' was applied to entities like the Japanese *kami* or the Indian *deva*, is another story. By themselves, the *kami* or the *deva* do not necessarily offer us the concept of 'god'

On the other hand, if we say that religion has to do with the ultimate, that it provides a transcendental reference point and guides man towards his fulfilment, then we have no problem here. Theism then reveals itself as a particular mode of envisaging or concretising this transcendental. Whether it is Buddhism, or Jainism, or Taoism (the traditional trouble-makers in the philosophical discussion about the nature of religion), they all provide us with such transcendental pointers: human destiny comprises more than the monolinear process of birth, life and death. That the charge of nihilism could have been made against these religions has actually nothing to do with the mysterious premisses of Eastern religious thought, but is merely due to our insufficient factual knowledge about these religions.

For the same reason, the existence of true monotheism has not been brought properly into focus. Certainly for India (and a case could perhaps be made also for Amida Buddhism in China and Japan) we must acknowledge monotheistic religion. Details on these will be found in the section on the Indian religions, and at this point we may simply note that behind our conventional term 'Hinduism' a great variety of truly monotheistic systems are hidden. From this emerges the rather important general conclusion that the contrast West : East is not one of monotheistic : polytheistic (or whatever). The phenomenon of monotheism allows us also to learn something further about the hidden premisses that make our understanding of the East so troublesome. Wherever the concept of an absolute God is found, his definition as a 'person' implies assumptions about certain characteristics that inhere in this 'person'. Inevitably, the way such characteristics are envisaged derives from human experience. Thus God is a 'he'; he is the 'father'. Moreover, a relational element may be introduced: God is the Father relating to the Son through the love personified in the Holy Spirit. In essence, Indian theism does the same, but makes decisions about how to concretise such characteristics which differ considerably from what we are used to in the Judeo-Christian tradition. Given the fact that about half the human population is female, it is perhaps not all that surprising to find that from the fertile religious ground of India a 'she' has also emerged as God. And instead of choosing the father–son relational model, India tends to use the husband–wife model. Such choices may appear strange to us (and may even shock us initially because of the love-life explicitly acknowledged through the husband–wife relationship), but they are not 'mysterious'.

Thus what has been suggested here so far is the possibility of detecting a level of (usually unconsciously made) premisses or axioms which provide the foundation for sometimes extremely complex edifices of viewing the world and man's destiny in it. Moreover, it has been suggested that it is not necessary to postulate a different kind of logic or rationality at work in such edifices, when they appear in different civilisations. The initial choice as to which premiss to adopt (for example, is God a 'he' or a 'she'?) concerns logical alternatives, whatever the motivation behind a particular choice may be. Again, the manner in which from a set of such chosen premisses a whole religious system is developed appears to follow the same logic and reasoning, for example when 'grace' is associated with the female side of the deity. Thus at least in principle the religions of the East do not present unassailable obstacles to our comprehension.

In practice, things are obviously more difficult and it might perhaps be of some use to look at a few examples of this kind of difficulty. We are not now talking about fundamental things like 'premisses' of thought, and have moved to a far more superficial level, the level of practicalities. Initially, the world of the East was indeed 'mysterious' for the simple reason that little factual information was available. Naturally, when during the last two hundred years or so an increasing amount of information became available, attempts were made to bring some order into this material. Phenomena that appeared related were grouped together under a common heading, the 'isms', and the whole began to make much more sense. Terms like Taoism, Buddhism, Hinduism, evolved as useful tools for surveying the rich Asian religious scene. But, however useful they may be, certainly the specialist remains aware also of how imperfect, tentative and inefficient they still are. They are no more than temporarily put-up pointers, in need of constant revision and improvement. The need for this has nothing to do with the mysteries of the East and is entirely due to our own imperfect factual knowledge. But unfortunately, our 'isms' have taken on an independent existence as well. They have moved outside the confines of academic discourse and have entered into the parlance of society at large. This has meant that here for instance 'Hinduism' is now understood to be 'the same sort of thing as Islam etc.' But in reality, a term like 'Hinduism' denotes a very large cluster of 'religions' each of which by itself would be 'the same sort of thing as Islam'. It is here where perhaps the most common justification for the belief in the mysterious and irrational East lies. Let us stay with 'Hinduism' to demonstrate this. With great effort a fair amount of factual knowledge has been acquired by the student. Thus from the rather over-full pigeon-hole labelled 'Hinduism' he knows that there is a belief in Viṣṇu (a male personal god). He also knows that there is a belief in *brahman* (an impersonal world-soul). He finally knows that there is belief in meditation as achieving final fulfilment. Since all this comes out of the same box marked 'Hinduism', he quite appropriately attempts to correlate these pieces of information. But however hard he may try, the puzzle simply does not fit. His more polite reaction will be to speak of the mysteries of the East. Similarly, in addition to his knowledge of Viṣṇu he may pick up information about the belief in Śiva (like Viṣṇu, a male personal god). The logical conclusion would be to say that 'Hinduism' is polytheistic, because a number of gods are believed in. But what has actually been done here is comparable to some Martian's attempt to formulate a logically coherent explanation of religion in Britain, by drawing information indiscriminately from the different churches, chapels, mosques, synagogues, etc. In other words, the bits and pieces of the puzzle can be put together, but in a coherent way only if we accept that they do not all belong to a single 'mysterious' religion, which we call 'Hinduism'. The seeming chaos can be turned into order, but only in the form of many ordered wholes. Naturally, what has been said here about Hinduism applies also to many of the other Asian religions.

There is one final observation that might be felt to be useful in our struggle with the incomprehensible East. Anybody acquiring a knowledge of Eastern religious material constantly repeats the question: 'what does this mean?' In itself this is a perfectly legitimate question. The problem lies in the way that a possible answer is perceived. In the Semitic traditions, religion has defined itself consciously and rigorously. Every component of its complex edifice is carefully explained, in terms of its meaning, through the system as a whole. Institutionalised 'authority' acts as the final arbiter in cases of doubt or ambivalence. But this kind of centralised meaning-definition is simply absent in the East. An enormous number of religious symbols are handed down from generation to generation, but their meaning and significance may vary greatly, depending on the individual context in which they occur. The implication of this is that the search for what religious symbols actually mean to the religious individual becomes troublesome and laborious. But there is nothing irrational or confused in this.

'Mysterious East' has one further connotation: it is perceived to be attractive, challenging, inviting exploration and pleasurable. Nothing could be further from the intentions of this present exploration than the desire to prove that such a perception is inaccurate or inappropriate. All that has been suggested here is a bit of commonsense and a lot of patience—patience when trying to fit the pieces of the puzzle together, and patience in waiting for the specialists to keep on adding further information. We are far from having acquired all the pieces of all the puzzles. Once upon a time, the East appeared as a devastating, deadly threat (and the connection of the Mongols with supposedly peaceful Buddhism is worth exploring in this context). There is no need to perceive the 'challenges' that have been spoken of here in this vein. For some it might be an exciting discovery to find a God who is a 'she'; to others it might enhance their understanding of a God who is a 'he'. Some might derive great comfort from the discovery of monotheism as far away as India or Japan; others might deepen their belief in devotion in view of beliefs about meditationally gained altered states of consciousness. But there is no threat here, only the possibility of interesting insights.

2 *Philosophical and Religious Taoism*

Bulcsu Siklós

In a sense it is inappropriate to treat the two totally separate phenomena of the title under the single rubric of Taoism. Philosophical and religious Taoism share the use of the word *tao* and not very much else—most of Lao-tzu's recommendations were and still are blatantly ignored by followers of religious Taoism. The latter term itself has come to be used as a blanket title denoting everything recognisably 'religious' in China which was not obviously Confucian or Buddhist, when it is perhaps best defined in antithesis to China's age-old indigenous 'popular' religion. To counter the insidious influence of the latter was the prime concern of the early followers of the Way of the Heavenly Masters.

The Philosophical Taoism of Lao-tzu and Chuang-tzu

Lao-tzu and his eponymous classic, also known as the *Tao Te Ching*, are both equally obscure and shadowy. Ssu-ma Ch'ien, who was author of the *Shih chi* (Historian's Records) and wrote in the first century BCE, some three centuries after Lao-tzu, is as much in the dark about him as we are today. Ssu-ma Ch'ien tells us that Lao-tzu was a native of the state of Ch'u, that his family name was Li, that he was a court archivist, that he met Confucius (551–479 BCE) and that, dissatisfied with the state of the Chou dynasty, he wandered westwards through the pass at Han Ku where he was persuaded to write a summary of his philosophy by the Keeper of the Pass, Yin Hsi. All of this is apocryphal; indeed there is no real reason to assume that there ever was a Lao-tzu or that the *Tao Te Ching* is the work of one man; nevertheless there is no harm in continuing to call the author or authors 'Lao-tzu'. The division of his work into two books, the *Tao Ching* and the *Te Ching*, gave it its alternative name. There is no reason to believe that this division goes back further than the first century.

Early Chinese is not grammatically difficult—if anything it is too simple and ambiguous—but the interpretation of a text like the *Tao Te Ching* is often a matter of *ad hoc* hermeneutics, with an end result far removed from the author's original intentions. It would be hard enough to glean the meaning of many sections of the *Tao Te Ching* even if the text were not rife with abbreviated characters, and if it were punctuated. One would think that the very obscurity of Lao-tzu's *magnum opus* would have deterred translators, but that has not been the case. It is often said that only the Bible has been translated into English more often.

Here are two versions of the opening lines of the *Tao Te Ching*:

> The way that can be spoken of
> Is not the constant way:
> The name that can be named
> Is not the constant name.
> The nameless was the beginning of heaven and earth;
> The named was the mother of the myriad creatures.
>
> (TTC I:1, tr. D.C. Lau, 1963)

> Lodehead lodehead-brooking: no forewonted lodehead
> Namecall namecall-brooking: no forewonted namecall.
> Having-naught namecalling: Heaven-Earth's fetation
> Having-aught namecalling: Myriad mottling's mother.
>
> (TTC I:1, tr. P.A. Boodberg, 1979)

The character *tao* (道) is composed of two elements (a head/person 首 and to walk/go 辵), and has the basic meaning of 'way' or 'road'. By extension it has the meaning of a 'ruled district/province', the more abstract sense of 'the (virtuous) way' or 'doctrine' and the verbal meanings of 'to enact a law', 'to state', 'to tell' and 'to instruct'. The word *tao* is thus by no means the exclusive property of Taoism—most early Chinese philosophers, Confucius included, made ample use of it, usually in the sense of an ethical code of some sort. In early popular religion tao signified the power or ability to perform magical feats, as well as the power of kings whose authority often rested on such magical skills. It was by following the order or principle of the world, apparent in the daily, monthly, seasonal and yearly alternations of *yin* and *yang*, the 'feminine' and 'masculine' principles, that the ruler came to possess tao. Perhaps it was the inclusion of that strangest of books, the *I Ching* (Book of Changes), among the canonical books of the Confucians that prompted early philosophical inquiry into the tao underlying the 64 hexagrams representing pure yang, pure yin and all the various intermediate states.

Lao-tzu used the word 'tao' provisionally, as can be noticed in the above passage. He seems to have considered his tao to have been twofold, nameable and unnameable, the unnameable being the 'constant' tao, the fundamental principle behind the named tao which produces the universe ('heaven and earth') and all beings ('the myriad creatures'). This interpretation is somewhat at variance with what Lao-tzu seems to be saying, where the nameless tao is actually responsible for the creation of the universe. We should not worry ourselves overmuch—it should be stressed that commentators, both Chinese and Western, ancient and modern, have differed in their interpretations of these and the following terms. Lao-tzu sometimes calls the nameable tao 'Being' and states (XL) that Being was produced by Non-being, which in turn is symbolised by the Mysterious Female (the nameless tao in its fecund aspect) and the Valley Spirit (the nameless tao in its void aspect). The terms *yu* and *wu*, 'being' and 'non-being' could also mean 'having' and 'having-not', referring to the presence or absence of perceptible features in each.

Lao-tzu unifies both taos under the rubric *hsüan*, 'the Obscure', which really seems to hit the nail on the head. All this is perhaps best summed up in Lao-tzu's own phrase:

> The way begets one; one begets two; two begets three; three begets the myriad creatures.
>
> (TTC XLII:93)

This sentence itself, expressing a slightly different point of view from those of the opening section already quoted, has given many commentators considerable trouble, contradicting as it does the general yet perhaps naïve concept of the tao as the One. (This misinterpretation led Catholic translators of the Bible into Chinese to translate 'God' by 'tao'.) Chuang-tzu in particular refutes this interpretation—in any case the word tao is uncountable—and there is surely no way of reconciling the concept of tao and its various manifestations to the Western ideas of universals and particulars. This is very reminiscent of the way in which the Neoplatonist Damascius held to the doctrine of the unnameable principle behind all nameables (in contrast to, say, Plotinus, for whom the One was the highest principle).

So how does the tao—the unnameable tao—appear to the mystic?

> As a thing the way is
> Shadowy, indistinct.
> Indistinct and shadowy,
> Yet within it is an image;
> Shadowy and indistinct,
> Yet within it is a substance.
> Dim and dark,
> Yet within it is an essence.
>
> (TTC XXI:49)

Although the sage has access to the tao via meditation and trance, Lao-tzu never indicates that the experience is ecstatic (or rather, enstatic) or involves any feeling of union or any experience of light or totality or any of the other typical signs of mystical achievement.

Meditational and breathing exercises, and perhaps sexual techniques, are of use to the sage wishing to attain the tao:

> When carrying in your head your perplexed bodily soul can you embrace in your arms the One
> And not let go?
> In concentrating your breath can you become as supple
> As a babe?
> Can you polish your mysterious mirror
> And leave no blemish?
>
> When the gates of heaven open and shut
> Are you capable of keeping to the role of the female?
>
> (TCC X:24)

In this poem, the term *p'o* or 'bodily soul' (the *yin* 'soul' which descends into the earth at death, as opposed to the *yang* 'soul', the *hun*, which ascends to heaven) comes to have the meaning of 'semen' according to the commentators. Likewise the 'gates of heaven' are glossed as the mouth and nostrils. It is only because everything produced by the tao—the nameable tao, heaven and earth, the myriad beings—returns to the tao that it is possible for the sage to attain the tao prematurely.

If we can ignore, perhaps unfairly, Lieh Yu-k'ou's *Lieh Tzu* (the extant text of which is based on a version some 600 years later than the author's presumed dates (fourth to fifth centuries BCE), and which is of dubious authenticity), the other early Taoist work to have survived is the *Chuang Tzu* of Chuang Chou (fourth century BCE). Once again the author is often called by the name of his work. Biographical details of Chuang-tzu's life are few and far between, and are perhaps even thinner on the ground than in Lao-tzu's case. The difference between the two authors is considerable, not necessarily philosophically but stylistically. Where Lao-tzu is lofty and mysterious, obscure and even humourless, Chuang-tzu is worldly, lively, playful and, above all, human:

> A man was terrified of his shadow, and disliked his footprints. Intending to get rid of them, he started running, but the more often he raised his feet as he ran, the more the number of footprints became, and however fast he ran, his shadow still followed him. Telling himself that he was not going fast enough, he ran faster and faster without stopping, until finally he was exhausted and dropped dead. Foolish man, if he had stayed in the shade, he would have had no shadow; if he had been still, there would have been no footprints.

How different is this to Lao-tzu's

> I do my utmost to attain emptiness;
> I hold firmly to stillness.
>
> (TTC XVI:37)

A lot of the energy expended on the dozens of translations of Lao-tzu's work would have been better spent on the *Chuang Tzu*.

There are two aspects of Chuang-tzu's thought which are worth emphasising, though one is hardly doing justice to him by ignoring other aspects such as his emphasis on spontaneity. Firstly, Chuang-tzu advocates a type of relativism based on what might be termed a 'meta-view' encasing various linguistic and conceptual terms. As we have seen, Lao-tzu was also aware of the limitations of language in describing the tao—indeed the recognition of this limitation could be regarded as a hallmark of true mysticism—but this finds far fuller expression in the *Chuang Tzu*. Secondly, Chuang-tzu wrestles with the problem of what it is exactly that controls mental activities such as perception, and thereby parallels the tao in its controlling aspect. For the controller of mental activities Chuang-tzu uses the term *hsin*, originally meaning 'heart' (the organ), but also translatable as 'mind'. Locating the essential core of man at the heart is not, of course, exclusively Chinese. The *hsin* was also a valve for the tao, a double mirror which reflected both the tao and the external world indiscriminatingly, much as the mirror-like wisdom of the *dhyānibuddha* Akṣobhya reflects the Buddhist *tathatā* or 'suchness'.

The works of Lao-tzu and Chuang-tzu exerted considerable influence in literary, court and academic circles, and indeed continue to do so in the Far East of today. In the West, Lao-tzu's conception of tao in particular has been grist to the mills of numerous thinkers, self-styled mystics, academics and, more recently, of those wishing to compare 'Eastern mysticism' with the ideas of modern physics.

Despite all this, the Taoism of Lao-tzu and Chuang-tzu never became a religion as the term is commonly understood. There was no room for faith, prayer, ecstasy, a priesthood, no way of involving the ordinary man, and no way of truly accommodating government, authority or conventional morality. It was the way purely of the solitary sage, the anchorite possessed of superior wisdom (*ming* or 'light') who achieves everything through the superficially paradoxical technique of 'not-doing' (*wu wei*), through not interfering with the natural order. *Wu wei* does not mean total abandonment of activity. Rather, it is a way of rolling with the punches, as it were; or, even better, not even being there when the punch is thrown. Strictly speaking, the Taoism of Lao-tzu and Chuang-tzu should have no place in this book.

Religious Taoism

There exists another type of Taoism which involves a variety of religious features; 'Taoism' will henceforth be used here to denote this religious material. This Taoism is an oddly assorted mixture of beliefs and practices with very little in common at first sight. A firm definition is however possible—all modern Taoist schools, however disparate their practices, recognise the primacy of the first *T'ien shih* or Heavenly Master, Chang Tao-ling (*fl*. 126–45 CE) and the revelations received by him, even if they do not venerate the present Heavenly Master. By this definition (proposed by M. Strickmann, in Welch and Seidel (1979), pp. 123–92) alchemy, breathing techniques, meditation, yoga and so forth are seen not necessarily as Taoist arts but as methods, often pre-existing ones, adapted for use by Taoists and hence only admissible into the body of Taoism when practised by Taoists conforming to the above criterion. This definition is useful mainly because, as pointed out in the introduction, Taoism becomes Taoism through contrast with the indigenous religious practices of ancient China from which certain methods were borrowed and certain practices (for example, sacrifice) very strongly rejected.

From a very early period, the primary concern of the Taoist has been the attainment of a state usually called immortality. Unification with the tao is concomitant with the achievement of a state transcending putrefaction and death, but many Taoists seem to have interpreted this not in the purely spiritual sense of Chuang-tzu but in a totally literal sense. The term *hsien*, meaning an 'immortal', originally might well have referred to Philosophical Taoists who had taken Lao-tzu's anchoretic injunctions to heart.

Numerous different types of immortality could be attained. One could become an immortal on our plane and simply inhabit a perfected body here on earth, or, perfected, one could depart bodily to higher realms; if death was somewhat premature, one could descend to the palaces within the earth to continue one's studies or actually to become the contents of an other-worldly athanor wherein one's body would be forged into one conforming to transcendent standards. This last process is very reminiscent of the trancic dismemberment and 'reassembly' undergone by shamans throughout North Asia, especially as there are indications that the prospective Taoist immortal merely died a 'temporary death' (*chan ssu*) during which his alchemical transformation took place. It is perhaps from experimentation with fungal, herbal and mineral means to achieve this state of temporary death that the later obsessions with the alchemical process developed, as well as the search for miraculous herbs and mushrooms, and the fabulous mountains and islands on which they were said to grow.

The human body is a microcosmic model of the universe, and, as such, can be affected by drawing on the powers of the external world. The body contains three Cinnabar Fields (*tan t'ien*), respectively located in the head, heart and just below the navel. These Cinnabar Fields imprison the Three Maggots or Worms, which can only be set free by their host's death. It is thus in their interest to hasten the ageing and death processes, which can in fact be halted if the practitioner abandons consuming the grain, meat and wine on which the Worms feed, and consumes only such herbal and mineral preparations as can hasten the Worms' demise. The meditative absorption of deities symbolising the tao (the deified Lao-tzu among them) into the Cinnabar Fields from their abodes in the Big Dipper also lengthens the practitioner's life and keeps the Worms at bay.

Alchemy has already been mentioned in its role as the means by which elixirs of immortality could be obtained, but, just as in Europe, the true alchemist, the practitioner of Internal Alchemy, looked down on the humble 'puffer' trying, often unsuccessfully, to concoct his potions. Using meditative procedures the internal alchemist imitated the external alchemical process by creating cinnabar in his lowest Cinnabar Field through uniting the sexual energy with the subtle aspect of breath, and then ascending from the resultant chaotic stage (comparable to the stage of blackness and putrefaction in European alchemy) to a stage where the Yellow Flower finally blossomed and rendered the adept perfected. The components of cinnabar (mercuric sulphide, HgS) are exactly those which form the basis of the stages of the Lesser ('mercury') and Greater ('sulphur') Works of European alchemy. The end result was also conceived of in a more external sense as the Mysterious Embryo, rebirth into which would enable the adept to escape his inexorably ageing body and join the ranks of immortals in any one of many heavens.

The *fang shi* or court 'magicians' of the Ch'in and Early Han periods (230 BCE–24 CE) seem to have been the forerunners of the Taoists proper. The Han dynasty itself was founded with the assistance of a magician who claimed to have received instructions from a manifestation of Lao-tzu, and later on official cults were established to honour the deified Lao-tzu as well as certain other deities who were to become part and parcel of everyday Taoist worship. Of prime importance were the *wu ti* or Five Emperors, symbolising any group of five (the Five Elements: wood, fire, earth, metal and water, or the Five Organs: liver, heart, spleen, lungs and kidneys, for example). Many of the aphorisms of the *fang shih*, as well as cosmological theories and methods for commanding the spirits are to be found in the *T'ai-p'ing Ch'ing-ling shu*, the Great Peace General Command Book, a text revealed by the spirits to a semi-legendary figure, Yü Chi, which became the basic handbook for many later groups and which also influenced Chang Tao-ling (*fl*. 126–45), the founder proper of Taoism.

Chang Tao-ling was by all accounts extremely well read in the Classics, and expressed an interest in alchemy, perhaps dating from the time he arrived in Szechuan—alchemy in general seems to have been a primarily southern and western Chinese affair. His disciples were required to pay a tax of five bushels of grain to his administration (hence the Confucian derogatory term for the sect, Wu-tou Mi-tao or Five Bushels of Grain school), an administration which Chang Tao-ling and his grandson and successor Chang Lu established very much on classical lines, following Lao-tzu's recommendations, among others.

Yü Chi's writings also inspired a certain Chang Chiao to establish another movement, this time one which was militant in the extreme and made the fatal error of actively trying to overthrow the by now sickly but not yet impotent Han dynasty. The Way of Great Peace, as it was known, was soundly suppressed for its pains, while its followers were renamed the Yellow Turbans after the headgear they wore to their deaths.

With the increasing influence of Buddhism during the North–South Period (265–581), the best minds of China had to come to grips with some of the best that India could offer in the way of philosophy, cosmology and personal salvation. The Religion of Numbers, as the Chinese termed the—to them—arcane lore of Śākyamuni, inspired several major changes in Chinese (and, more specifically, Taoist) religious practice. That linchpin of Chinese thought and morality, filial piety, was extended to cover all sentient beings through the Mahāyānist idea that all living beings throughout the universe had at some time been the parents of every other being. As a practical manifestation of this, increasing influence came to be laid on burial practices, ensuring a smooth transition for the deceased from this life through the intermediate state to a favourable rebirth. All the Taoist orders came to consider the newly created, Buddhist-inspired liturgies of the *San Tung* (Three Arcana), the first Taoist Canon, as basic to their practice.

The sect which seems to have been most influenced by Buddhism, and the founding of which dates from this period of strong Indian influence is the Mao Shan or Shang Ch'ing (Highest Purity) sect, based on a series of revelations received by Yang Hsi in *c.* 364 from several immortals, and notably from a manifestation of a perhaps legendary woman, Wei Hua-ts'un (251–334?). The Mao Shan sect was essentially monastic and much more concerned with contemplation than with collective worship. Mao Shan treatises in general show considerable Buddhist influence, yet the prime Taoist concerns with immortality and internal alchemy are still predominant. Eschatologically, some see a reflection of Maitreya, the coming Buddha, in the idea or the *Hou sheng* or Coming Sage who will at some future date, after the extermination of all evil, establish *t'ai p'ing* (Great Peace) on earth.

During the Sui and T'ang Dynasties (581–905), Indian Buddhist Tantrism reared its mysterious and colourful head(s) in China. Taoism responded by incorporating a vast selection of *mudrās* (hand gestures) and pseudo-Sanskrit *mantras* (spells, or potent formulas) into its liturgical corpus. Public ritual started increasing in popularity at the expense of meditation, one result of which was the increasing fragmentation of Taoism. T'u Kuang-t'ing (842–926) is worthy of note as being the last truly ecumenical master of ancient Taoism. The rise of sectarianism continued unabated during the Sung and Yüan periods (960–1341), a phenomenon that may be seen as akin to that of the Reformation—though, not atypically, the rivalry was less intense than in Europe, perhaps because the differences were ritual or methodological rather than doctrinal, and frequently stemmed merely from a Taoist response to new developments in Buddhist practice. It should not be thought, however, that the relationship between Taoism and Buddhism was as rosy as may be gathered from this short survey. Debate was often acrimonious in the extreme. The founding of the North Chinese Ch'üan Chen sect in particular was an obvious effort to match the rigorous, simple yet effective techniques, both meditational and monastic, of Ch'an (Zen) Buddhism. It is commonly stated that Ch'an itself was influenced by Taoism to no small degree, especially in its attachment to spontaneity and in its—theoretical—rejection of scriptural authority and outward form. However, these practices belong to the repertoire of the 'Philosophical Taoist', and are as far divorced from religious Taoism as they are from more ritualised Buddhist schools such as T'ien T'ai.

The old sects still continued to function, often in revitalised form, or under different names. The Cheng I sect was not much more than the officially sanctioned continuation of the Heavenly Master sect. Also during this period the imagination of Taoists was captured by Buddhist Tantrism, not in its Indian form this time, but in its seemingly more demoniacal Tibeto–Mongol form as practised by the Yüan court. Various sects arose, all specialising in different versions of what is known as *lei fa* or Thunder Magic, a technique whereby the energy of a thunderstorm is absorbed by the practitioner through breathing techniques, *mudrās* and *mantras*, and is then employed to light the inner fire of the alchemical furnace or to exorcise evil. Members of certain sects, notably the Shen Hsiao, were often accused of abusing the powers thus gained and not following strict canonical rules. Indeed, the Shen Hsiao is still regarded as somewhat unorthodox.

Official patronage of Taoism continued through the Ming period (1368–1644). The present Taoist Canon, the *Tao-tsang*, was first printed in the reign of Cheng-t'ung in 1447 in some 1,100 volumes, unbelievably enough a considerable reduction in size compared to earlier versions. The tripartite division of the Taoist Canon is reminiscent of the *tripiṭaka* of the Buddhist Canon, but, strictly speaking, the division corresponds more to the Three Vehicles of Buddhism, i.e. Hīna-, Mahā- and Vajra-yāna.

Sectarianism was gradually brought under control in the Ming and Ch'ing periods (1644–1911) by issuing licences to all practising Taoists once they had learnt the canonical registers and one particular brand of Thunder Magic. This of course just led to an increasing dichotomy between the 'official' orders and proliferating local orders which were in effect practising illegally. Taoism lost considerable influence under the generally pro-Buddhist Ch'ing, though it is doubtful whether its stock was as low as is commonly thought, especially as true Taoist practice found today in Taiwan and Hong Kong seems to be refined, sophisticated and based very much on old canonical standards.

Bibliography

Lao-tzu *Tao Te Ching*, translated with an introduction by D.C. Lau (Penguin, Harmondsworth, 1963)

Boodberg, P.A. *Selected Works of Peter A. Boodberg* (Berkeley, 1979)

Saso, M. *The Teachings of Taoist Master Chuang* (Yale University Press, New Haven, 1978)

Welch, H. *The Parting of the Way—Lao Tzu and the Taoist Movement* (London, 1958)

—— and Seidel, A. (eds.) *Facets of Taoism* (Yale University Press, New Haven, 1979)

3 Mazdaism ('Zoroastrianism')

Julian Baldick

Mazdaism, the principal religion of pre-Islamic Iran, counted approximately 30,000 adherents there in the 1970s, and had about 87,500 followers, known as the Parsees, in India, Pakistan and Sri Lanka in 1976. The faith is characterised by an emphasis upon a struggle between Good and Evil. It is of interest not only in its own right, as manifesting a complex mixture of archaic and variegated ingredients, but also for the study of the gods and legends of many peoples, from Ireland to India. Another source of interest is the spectacular methodological progress made in this field, particularly on the continent of Europe, during the last fifty years, which has given new life to the history of religions.

One must pay attention to the methods used by the specialists, since Mazdaism is one of the more difficult religions of the world to investigate. The original sources are few, extremely corrupt and largely incomprehensible. As a result scholars have come to widely divergent conclusions, so that the student risks bewilderment. Because Mazdean texts lend themselves to the most diverse interpretations, we are forced to concentrate upon the logic displayed by modern writers in their reconstructions, in order to determine which are the more convincing. We need not take seriously anyone who claims to know 'what actually happened' among the ancient Iranians.

The terms 'Mazdaism' and 'Mazdean' will be used here, in line with modern international practice, and as corresponding to the terminology of the worshippers of Ahura Mazdā, the 'Wise Lord', who appears as the chief (and to some as the sole) god of the religion. Since non-British writers use this terminology in works available in English it seems inappropriate to keep the old-fashioned words 'Zoroastrianism' and 'Zoroastrian', formed after a European version ('Zoroaster') of the name of the alleged founder, Zarathushtra, a figure whom scholars now tend to date to around 1000 BCE. Such usage would be comparable to speaking of

'Mahometanism' instead of the correct and now universally accepted 'Islam'.

In approaching Mazdaism it is important to bear in mind that because of its archaic, 'fossilising' character it presents features which go back to the Indo-Europeans, the linguistic ancestors of a variety of peoples in Asia and the West. Owing to the scantiness of Iranian and Mazdean materials we are obliged to resort to comparisons with the religions of other nations. Much disagreement has surrounded the question of where the Indo-Europeans originally lived, but now it is considered to have been somewhere in south Russia or Siberia.

Even fiercer controversy has raged around the theories concerning Indo-European religion propounded by the French scholar Georges Dumézil. In Mazdean studies the quarrels have been bitter, but here Dumézil has found the support of many specialists. This is not surprising, since it was largely from the Mazdean scriptures, the Avesta, that he reconstructed the alleged 'threefold ideology of the Indo-Europeans'.

The Indo-Europeans, he claims, maintained that society should be organised into classes according to three 'functions': 1. sovereignty, linked with religion in its magical and juridical aspects; 2. war; 3. fertility, in its economic and erotic aspects. These 'functions' inspired the mythology expressed in the Indo-European languages. Now we may observe that this does not get one very far in studying Greek or Indian religion, given the enormous inventiveness of the Greeks and Indians, who quickly submerged their Indo-European heritage in a rich flowering of legends. But the ancient Iranians do not appear to have produced much more than an ideoloy of this kind. They expressed it in their religious texts and national epic, and put it into practice, maintaining a rigid class system until it was broken by Islam.

We must now turn to a sub-group of the Indo-Europeans, the Indo-Iranians, when they were in their original homeland, before dividing and migrating as Indians to India and as Iranians to Iran, possibly between 2000 and 1500 BCE. Here reconstructions are completely theoretical, and belong almost entirely to the field of historical and comparative linguistics. The Indian and Iranian materials certainly present many religious features in common, but these have given rise to much academic dispute, notably concerning the various deities and the 'structures' to which they might be assigned.

The view which has prevailed for most of the twentieth century, but has been impressively challenged, is that the Indo-Iranians worshipped two kinds of gods, seen as opposing one another: on the one hand, gods called *daēva-* by the Iranians and *deva-* by the Indians, and on the other hand gods called *ahura-* by the Iranians and *asura-* by the Indians. As a result, the first class were to be demoted to the status of demons (*daēvas*) by the Iranians; the second class, in this theory, were similarly demoted to the status of demons (*asuras*) by the Indians. The work of demotion on the Iranian side is credited to the alleged founder of Mazdaism, Zarathushtra, who is supposed to have made Ahura Mazdā the sole or chief god, and 'reformed' the old Iranian religion.

This conventional theory is weak and would now appear to be obsolete. In any case, since it presents a hostility between two classes of gods in Indo-Iranian times, the idea of a later 'reform' is unnecessary, as was pointed out by the late Marijan Molé: the *daēvas* could have been demoted to the status of demons by a natural development, as opponents of the venerated *ahuras*, without the intervention of a 'Reformer'.

That this theory 'is false from beginning to end' has been argued by a distinguished British linguist on the Indian side, Thomas Burrow. He points out that it is absurd to say that a class of gods called the *asuras* were demoted into demons. For the individual Indian beings titled *asura-* were never so demoted, and so it is ridiculous to claim that the *asuras* as a class were demonised. Besides, it is wrong to speak of an original class of gods called *asura-* in opposition to gods called *deva-*. The term *asura-*, meaning 'lord', was probably used by the Indo-Iranians as a name to denote the original Indo-European sovereign sky-god, who appears as Jupiter among the Romans, and as Dyaus in the earliest Indian hymns, where the name is combined with the title *asura-*. In these hymns *asura-* is a designation for some higher gods. The term, as the Indian evidence shows, came to mean 'demon' by a gradual process of development, but the gods remained gods. On the Iranian side the sovereign sky-god presumably continued to be called 'Ahura', a name which was to form part of the combined designation 'Ahura Mazdā' ('the Wise Lord'). As for the Iranian use of the term *daēva-* as 'demon', it probably results from contact with the Indians as the latter stopped on their long migratory process towards India. The Iranians would have seen some of the Indian gods, unfamiliar to themselves, as demons. Thus some individual deities on the Indian side are named as demons in Mazdaism.

Burrow's argument has been accepted by the leading Italian specialist in Mazdean studies, Gherardo Gnoli, while the principal German specialist, Helmut Humbach, has reached similar conclusions. So instead of explaining things with reference to an original Indo-Iranian state of affairs, the scholars are now moving to a context of later contacts between Indians and Iranians. We may observe that in this perspective also no 'Reformer' is needed.

At this point we must consider some hard evidence: an inscription. It seems that some Indians, instead of making their way towards India, went to the Near East, where the names of some of their gods are preserved in an inscription of around 1380 BCE. Since the same names appear together in the earliest Indian hymns, we have the first attested 'structure': 1. Mitra and Varuṇa; 2. Indra; 3. a couple called the Nāsatyas. Dumézil claims these as representing his triad: religious sovereignty, war and fertility.

These gods have been connected with the most archaic, and in the usual view the oldest part of the Avesta (the Mazdean scripture) namely the Gāthās, hymns attributed to Zarathushtra himself. Differing dates have been proposed for Zarathushtra, but nowadays academic opinion seems to be crystallising in favour of *c.* 1000 BCE, in the prehistoric period. The language and style of the Gāthās closely resemble those of early Indian hymns. In these Gāthās Ahura Mazdā is extolled, and is surrounded by six Entities, elsewhere called the 'Holy Immortals' and viewed as archangels. Dumézil has argued that these six Entities are old Indo-Iranian gods reappearing in disguise: the five gods of the inscription plus a goddess, called on the Indian side Sarasvatī, who corresponds to all three 'functions', but especially to fertility. He establishes the correspondences as follows in Table 3.0, notably in accordance with the material elements associated with the Entities by Mazdean literature:

Table 3.0

Indian Deity	**Entity**	**Material Element**
Mitra	Good Thought	Cattle
Varuṇa	Order (or Truth)	Fire
Indra	Power	Metals
Sarasvatī	Devotion	Earth
Nāsatya I }	{ Health	Water
Nāsatya II }	{ Non-Death	Plants

This correspondence is demonstrated by various arguments external to the Gāthās, and also by counting the frequencies with which the Entities are mentioned or associated with one another within the Gāthās. This method has the advantage of avoiding the difficulties posed by the incomprehensibility of the Gāthic verses themselves.

Dumézil's analysis has been accepted by many specialists and rejected by others, who took offence at the suggestion that their cherished 'monotheistic Reformer' had dishonestly slipped the old gods in under new names. We need not take so simple a view of things. Dumézil has observed that there are unresolved questions. Does the name 'Zarathushtra' cover the ideas of a man or a group? Was there one reform, two or a long series? We may feel that such a series could be better termed a 'development'. For Dumézil's work is really still enclosed in the traditional academic reconstruction, in which Zarathushtra rejected an old polytheism, established monotheism, and then had his work undone by unfaithful successors, who brought back the old gods (under their own old names). In this tale of a founder betrayed by succeeding priests we may perhaps see another illusion of Protestant scholarship. The evidence seems rather to suggest not so much a replacement of polytheism by monotheism, with the subsequent restoration of polytheism, but more a development into a continuing henotheism, that is a belief in one god without abandoning belief in others, but giving them less attention. The old Iranian gods continued to be worshipped under their old names, but subordinated to Ahura Mazdā and his 'Entities'.

It would appear, then, that if we no longer need the idea of a Reform, or a denunciation by Zarathushtra or others of old gods common to the Indians and the Iranians, Dumézil's theory of a correspondence between the Entities and the Indian gods needs some adaptation if it is to be preserved. Presumably the answer would be that the *functional properties* of old Indo-Iranian deities, deities corresponding to but by no means always identical with those found on the Indian side, have been transformed into the Entities. At any rate we may agree that it is correct to concentrate not so much upon the names of gods and Entities, but rather upon how a god or Entity works.

We must now consider the Gāthās themselves and the question of Zarathushtra's existence. As regards the Gāthic hymns, recent research on the continent of Europe has brought scholars to conclude that their character is above all a liturgical one. It is undoubtedly correct to concentrate upon comparison with the early Indian hymns, and this is the conclusion to which such comparison leads.

British work in this field, however, has been of a biographical and moralistic kind. It has been well summarised by the American scholar R.N. Frye: 'For W.B. Henning and his school it seems that one should understand Zoroaster as a meticulous thinker who carefully chose his words, and acted in an eminently rational manner. His language too was grammatically correct, though later corrupted, and he behaved as proper prophets should.'

It must be borne in mind that Henning accepted the traditional date for Zarathushtra: 258 years before Alexander the Great (336–323 BCE). His argument was that nobody would invent '258'. He failed to notice that it had been produced by subtracting 42 years of Zarathushtra's life from 300.

Ideas put forward by Mary Boyce have remained highly controversial. Her dating of Zarathushtra successively to *c.* 1000, 1500, 1700–1500, 1400–1200 and 1400 BCE has not prevented her from recounting how he lived, received revelations and visions, organised his community, and established its rituals. She is the first Western specialist to take Mazdean legend as a serious source for Zarathushtra's life. Her method has been to project back into the past all later doctrine and practice, and then claim that she has shown the continuity of Mazdaism, which she has taken for granted as her starting-point. The academics have reacted with heavy irony, notably with regard to her presentation, as historical fact, of veneration of purely imaginary Indian and Iranian deities.

The moralistic tradition of the British school has been continued by specialists in America, who have produced 'metaphorical' interpretations of the Gāthās. Thus 'a fertile cow and a steer' is seen as a metaphor for 'the good vision' and Zarathushtra. Plants represent the believers, and the pasturage 'peace and freedom'. This has been greeted with derision from French and Belgian scholars, and a rebuke from Humbach.

The best arguments concerning Zarathushtra were presented by Molé. He observed that the diversity of academic opinions about Zarathushtra (a witch-doctor, a politician, a prophet and so on) showed the impossibility of reconstructing his personality. Since the Gāthās are liturgical texts, it is dangerous to try to extract historical information from them. When they refer to alleged incidents and people these may be real or legendary. Nothing proves that Zarathushtra composed the Gāthās. It is impossible to determine whether he existed or not. Translations of the Gāthās are highly speculative and influenced by a traditional academic picture of Zarathushtra as resembling an old-fashioned image of a prophet of Israel. This is based on later legend, imbued with Judeo-Christian and Islamic influences. Zarathushtra in the Gāthās appears as an archetypal priest.

Against Molé, it has been claimed that ancient Greek authors speak of Zarathushtra as a real person. But this is of no historical value: they are writing centuries after the Gāthās. Molé seems right in pointing to the most obvious parallel to Zarathushtra: Orpheus, the mystical founder of the Greek religion of Orphism, with whose name hymns were also associated. Also against Molé, it has been said that the Gāthās have a 'unity of tone and subject' which proves the historicity of Zarathushtra. But scholars who differ on everything else come close to agreeing that out of the 238 stanzas of the Gāthās almost 190 are incomprehensible. So what weight can be given to such a subjective opinion?

We must now consider what can be found in the Gāthās. In spite of assertions by the Anglo-American moralistic school that they provide an 'ethic' it is difficult to see what this is. To pray for good fortune for one's family and bad fortune for one's enemies hardly seems ethical.

The Gāthās are permeated by the praise of Ahura Mazdā, the 'Wise Lord'. There are bad gods, *daēvas*. Beneath Ahura Mazdā there is a Holy Spirit, Spenta Mainyu, and an Evil Spirit, Angra Mainyu. The text is clear enough, the specialists have pointed out, to show that Ahura Mazdā is *not* identical with the Holy Spirit, as Mazdaism later believes. So in the Gāthās we do not have an absolute dualism, but rather an opposition of two spirits beneath a sovereign god. The evidence suggests henotheism, belief in one god while not denying the existence of others. It seems unwise to assume that we have monotheism here. The Gāthās do not mention another leading god of Mazdaism, Mithra (the Indian Mitra), but it would appear unfounded to imagine that he is one of the bad gods, the *daēvas*. Since the

Gāthās are hymns to Ahura Mazdā, there is no reason to expect Mithra to be mentioned, let alone to take absence of mention to imply condemnation. Such an unwise assumption has accompanied the idea that Zarathushtra's unscrupulous successors brought back Mithra and the other old gods in betrayal of the 'Founder'.

This idea has dominated discussion of other hymns in Mazdean scripture, which show the worship, not just of Ahura Mazdā and the Entities, but of other gods as well. These are all called part of the 'Younger Avesta', although some of them could be of the same period as that of the Gāthās. The so-called 'Younger Avestan' dialect may be as old as the Gāthic one. Some of these non-Gāthic hymns are certainly extremely old. Burrow dates some to before 900 BCE. If they are not so old as the Gāthās, they can be taken to contain earlier materials. The usual interpretation is that they represent the return of the old gods, readmitted but only in a subordinate position. Such a view is just as hypothetical as that which posits an inner core of believers faithful to the Gāthās and Ahura Mazdā alone. It is important to avoid calling the non-Gāthic gods 'pagan' gods. This term is no longer acceptable in the history of religions. With regard to Mazdaism it seems all the more misleading and absurd as the traditional academic reconstruction appears to be collapsing.

Let us briefly mention some of these gods. Mithra (the meaning of whose name has been much disputed, 'contract' still seeming the best translation) is to be venerated alongside Ahura Mazdā (like Mitra alongside Varuṇa among the Indians). Verethraghna, 'Victory', we shall also encounter again. Aredvī Sūrā Anāhitā, 'Moist, Mighty, Immaculate', is seen by Dumézil's followers as representing the three functions—fertility, war and religious sovereignty—in her name, but also, like the Entity 'Devotion', corresponding in particular to that of fertility.

Other deities are Apąm Napāt, 'Offspring of the Waters', who has an Indian counterpart of similar name, and has been convincingly linked with the Roman water-god Neptune and the Celtic Nechtan; Haoma, a plant corresponding to the Indian Soma, and now considered to have been a hallucinogen, the preparation and consumption of which are central to the Mazdean liturgy; and Ātar, 'Fire', the veneration of which is the most famous aspect of Mazdaism, with the distinctive fire-temples of the Mazdeans leading the Muslims to call them 'fire-worshippers'.

Another feature is constituted by supernatural beings called the Fravashis. They are both the guardian angels and the higher souls of the faithful. They survive after death to be venerated by the living. They participate in battles against demons on a cosmic level, on the side of Ahura Mazdā, and in the terrestrial fighting of the believers. In general, they correspond most closely to the Valkyries, the martial maidens of Norse mythology.

We must now pass on to the historical period, and the great Persian Empire of the Achaemenid kings, which lasted from *c.* 550 to 330 BCE. Here our sources are scanty and unreliable. The most used is the Greek writer Herodotus (*c.* 485–425 BCE), famous not only as the so-called 'Father of History' but also as the 'Father of Lies'. It is difficult to see what credence can be given to this author, who in matters of Persian religion is demonstrably ignorant and misleading in the extreme. Priority must be given to the oriental materials. The inscriptions of the Persian kings themselves give a one-sided, official propagandist picture. Archaeology gives us altars, sculpture and also inscribed tablets relating to expenditure, which are by far the best source.

The empire of the Persians was preceded by that of another Iranian people, the Medes. Of these six tribes are mentioned by Herodotus, notably the Magi, a name which is also that of the priests under the Persians. This obviously leads to speculation that the Magi might originally have been a specialised priestly tribe among the Medes. That the Medes had a fire-cult and altars in temples, and a holy mountain with rooms for priests or pilgrims, is known from archaeological evidence. One surviving fire-altar clearly could not have been used for the everlasting fire characteristic of Mazdaism. Further reconstruction of Median religion is entirely speculative.

After the Medes we come to the Persian Achaemenid kings themselves, and the vexed question of whether they were followers of the religion attributed to Zarathushtra or not. A vast amount of ink has been spilt for and against. The best answer is one given by Frye, that this is a false problem, and anachronistic, since it wrongly assumes the existence at that time of a modern concept of a Mazdean religion. It would seem better to speak of 'Mazda-worship' rather than 'Mazdaism' in this period, since there is no sign of a fully-fledged system of beliefs or an organisation of believers.

The founder of the empire, Cyrus (560/559–530 BCE), is not someone of whose religious activities much can be said. In Babylonia he did homage to the Babylonian god Marduk and expressed the wish that a variety of lesser gods should intercede on his behalf. The sculptural evidence shows that he had his palaces in Iran decorated with reliefs of Assyrian magical figures. We know that his policy was to allow the various peoples of his empire to follow their own religions.

Darius I (522–486 BCE) has left inscriptional evidence of his feeling of indebtedness to Ahura Mazdā (much repeated and emphasised) and his hostility to the Lie. But by the Lie he appears to mean his enemies, and by the Truth his own power. He says that he was helped by Ahura Mazdā and 'the other gods that are'. Much has been made of his failure to mention other gods by name, but tablets show that in his reign and that of Xerxes (486–465 BCE) the state paid for the worship by Iranian priests of Mithra and non-Iranian deities, as well as employing them in the cult of mountains and rivers. Again, everything points to henotheism.

Xerxes is known to have destroyed the temples of some gods. He did this in Babylon to the cult of Marduk, and in an inscription he says that he did it to *daivas* (false gods). Again, scholars are divided as to who and where these were. He mentions his personal worship of Ahura Mazdā. As in the case of Darius, this is hardly surprising: since Ahura Mazdā is a sovereign god, it is only natural that a sovereign should concentrate his worship upon him. It has been claimed that a 'Zoroastrian' calendar was adopted by the Achaemenid court in this reign or not long after, but this too has been much disputed.

Artaxerxes II (405/4–359/8) mentions Mithra and the goddess Anāhitā along with Ahura Mazdā in his inscriptions. Much has been made of this, and also of the fact that he erected statues of Anāhitā, identified with the Greek Aphrodite. But it would be unwise to draw any conclusions by way of contrast with the previous absence of Mithra and Anāhitā from royal inscriptions, as we have seen.

Exaggerated claims have been made for alleged Iranian influences on Greek philosophy during the Achaemenid period. Classical scholars accept very little of what has been attributed to ancient Greek thinkers to support this. To project later Mazdean time-speculation ('Zurvanism') back into the Achaemenid period and then claim that it inspired Greek interest in Time is anachronistic: probably the inspiration went in the reverse direction. Similar excessive claims, sometimes now disproved, have been made for Iranian influences on Judaism, Christianity and the Roman religion of Mithraism.

The conquest of the Achaemenid Empire by Alexander the Great (336–323 BCE) was to bring centuries of domination by Greek culture, and a rupture of continuity in Iranian civilisation. This has proved a considerable embarrassment to modern writers subsidised by the Iranian monarchy in order to emphasise such continuity. For Iran itself we have no evidence about indigenous religion in the period of Alexander's successors, the Seleucids. A colourful attempt has been made to find a spirit of Mazdean resistance to the Greek yoke, by redating apocalyptic texts to this period. In works of this kind, in which prophecies of impending liberation are repeatedly revised after they have failed to be fulfilled, it is indeed normal to find literary strata of earlier generations. But in the absence of external corroboration one must be doubtful here.

In the third century BCE an Iranian people, the Parthians, came to the fore. They were gradually to displace the Seleucids in Iran, and ruled until the third century CE. Of religion under the Parthians again very little is known. It may have been in their period that the final portions of Mazdean scripture were composed, since these mention Greco-Roman measures in contrast to Iranian ones in the earlier parts of the Avesta. In these later portions we find plenty of details relating to ritual purity and the utmost severity towards sexual licence. It is not clear when the Avesta was first written down, but it was certainly after a very long period of oral transmission.

The veneration of Greek deities, identified with Iranian ones, was popular. Of particular interest is an inscription in what is now Turkey, which appears to give striking support to Dumézil's theories. As in the Indian inscription of *c.* 1380 BCE, we find listed first the two sovereign gods, Ahura Mazdā, identified with the Greek Zeus, and Mithra, identified with Apollo, Helios and Hermes; then the war-god Verethraghna, identified with Heracles and Ares; finally, 'my all-nourishing fatherland Commagene', where the function of fertility is evident enough.

Other aspects of Iranian religion in the Parthian period are the everlasting fire, known from a classical source to be associated with the monarchy, as later in Iran; and temples dedicated to Anāhitā, in whose honour prostitution was practised. But there is no evidence of any official religion in the shape of Mazdaism as we later know it or any formally constituted sect thereof.

In the third century CE a new dynasty, that of the Sassanians, took power and ruled until the Arab conquest in the seventh. This dynasty controlled a large and powerful empire, and under it Mazdaism came to fruition as an official, established state religion. But this process of establishment took a long time, and it was only in the sixth century that it was actually completed.

Study of Mazdaism as it emerges in this period is complicated by a phenomenon called 'Zurvanism', which, following Frye, we can see as time-speculation in Iranian form. Some scholars have seen this as a separate sect or indeed as a religion in its own right, but in recent years it has become more normal to see it as a tendency or even just as a popular myth.

In the Avesta there is already a minor god called Zurvān, 'Time'. According to Damascius (sixth century CE) it was reported by Eudemus of Rhodes in the late fourth century BCE that the Iranians believed the first principle to be either Time or Space. This first principle would either have given rise to Ahura Mazdā and the Evil Spirit directly or to light and darkness before them. In the third century CE the new religion of Manichaeism calls its supreme god Zurvān, which shows the exalted position now occupied by the deity, as does his occurrence in proper names. Obviously, under the Parthians veneration of Time had become important in Iran, as it had in the West. During the Sassanian period Christian writers speak of a myth in which Zurvān is the original father of Ahura Mazdā and the Evil Spirit, and attack it as the essential dogma of Iranian religion. But afterwards, in the Islamic era, it is condemned by the Mazdeans and virtually disappears except for traces discovered by modern scholars.

Various theories have been put forward to explain this. There has been an unfortunate use of the words 'orthodoxy' and 'heresy'. It must be remembered that the emerging Mazdaism was, like ancient Roman religion, essentially a set of rites. As in Rome, it was a matter of 'doing the done thing' and honouring the gods, while plenty of Greek philosophical ideas were absorbed. In such a perspective what a man believes about the original source of the gods will not get him labelled a 'heretic', whereas in Christianity such speculation about God will. Now to the Christian writers of the Sassanian period the myth of Zurvān, a god who offers sacrifice in order to have offspring, is absurd and disgusting, and consequently splendid material to use to discredit their opponents. Accordingly they present it as the central doctrine of the Mazdeans. For later, Muslim writers, who were apt to invent a 'heresy' at the slightest pretext, people who believe in the myth of Zurvān have to constitute a separate sect. From this it is only a short step to the reconstruction of a modern Christian scholar, with a Mazdean 'orthodoxy' confronting a 'Zurvanite heresy'. In this perspective an original (but imaginary) Mazdean 'orthodoxy' is replaced by 'Zurvanism' in the Sassanian period only to reimpose itself under Islam.

Shapur I (240–72 CE) is of interest as the patron of Mani (d. *c.* 274), the founder of Manichaeism, a religion which grew out of the Gnostic movement, characterised by its emphasis on a hidden knowledge reserved for an elite. Manichaeism, like Christianity, was an international religion; Mazdaism, like Judaism, was a national one. Shapur I calls himself 'Mazda-worshipping', but attributes his successes to the aid of 'the gods' in general and lays stress upon the cult of them. Since the most important Mazdean priest of the ensuing period speaks of 'Ahura Mazdā and the gods' in inscriptions, the materials point to henotheism.

After Shapur I's death Mani was executed and the Mazdean priesthood increased its power. Its leader, Kerdir, has left fascinating inscriptional evidence of a journey which he made into the next world. This is undoubtedly characteristic of shamanism, the magical religion of Central and North Asia, and perhaps shows a practice surviving from the Iranians' original homeland.

The reign of Shapur II (309–79) has sometimes been seen as establishing a kind of Mazdean 'orthodoxy', but it would appear that on the contrary Mazdaism itself was not firmly established as the state religion until the sixth century CE. On the other hand, the conversion of the Roman Empire to Christianity led to severe persecution of Christians in Iran, who were seen as belonging to the enemy. In the fifth century they proclaimed their independence from Western Christianity, but this did not prevent an unsuccessful attempt by the Persian Empire to impose Mazdaism upon its Christian subjects in Armenia.

At the end of the fifth century we must note the remarkable movement led by the reformer Mazdak, celebrated for socialistic or communistic tendencies. Mazdakism (with a 'k', not to be confused with the main-line Mazdaism) has usually been seen as a gnostic religion, founded some time before and growing out of Manichaeism. Against this Molé has argued that it was a sect of Mazdaism. But when we have an account by a Muslim who met Mazdakites and had read their writings, the doctrines are not Mazdean but undoubtedly Manichaean, maintaining that the first principle was Light, which had been partially transmuted into darkness. Moreover, it seems that their faith was called 'the joyous religion' in direct opposition to the Mazdean self-appellation 'the good religion'. Mazdak himself gained the favour of the king Kavad (488–531), who seems to have used the movement to break the power of the greater nobles. But at the end of Kavad's reign Mazdak was executed and his followers persecuted. Apparently it was in a reaction to his movement that the monarchy, now closely allied with the lesser nobility, collaborated with the priesthood to make the Mazdean religion the firmly established faith of the empire. This was done by Khusro I (531–79). He allowed Mazdean priests to persecute Christians, while he himself acted as a patron to Greek philosophers. He declared that Mazdaism, while not the only path to truth, was self-sufficient, and vigorously repressed religious teachings that he did not like.

There was a rise in conversion to Christianity (notably from the more privileged classes) in the last century of Sassanian rule. Khusro II (590–628) had a Christian wife and was devoted to St Sergius, but persecuted Christians when his territories were invaded by the Roman emperor. The intolerant character which Mazdaism now possessed, along with its insistence on class distinctions, undoubtedly weakened the Sassanian realm, as did the antiquated and national character of the religion, which was unable to compete with faiths campaigning for recruits and offering universal truths in contrast to its preoccupation with rituals and taboos. In 642 what remained of the Persian Empire's army was destroyed by the conquering Arabs, and in 651 the last Sassanian king was killed. Iran was now to be taken over by the rising religion of Islam.

We must briefly turn to the general characteristics of Mazdaism in the Sassanian period. Here Dumézil's principal disciple in this field, Jacques Duchesne-Guillemin, has argued that four divinities dominate the scene, Ahura Mazdā, Mithra, Verethraghna and Anāhitā. Since the goddess Anāhitā represents fertility, he points to a correspondence with the inscriptions of the Indians and Commagene noted above. Moreover, the Sassanians insisted on the division of society into classes: priests, warriors and a class representing the economic aspect of fertility (cultivators, craftsmen and merchants), along with a new class of bureaucrats.

The Arab conquest of the seventh century CE and the subsequent Islamicisation of Iran produced a complete reversal of fortunes for Mazdaism, as Michael Morony has well shown. From being the proud masters of society, the Mazdean priests were to become desperately defensive inferiors. Under the Sassanians they had been the guardians of privilege, with religious observance being the hallmark of social distinction, and a lowly estate in this world seen as foreshadowing a poor place in the next. Since riches were seen as good, the asceticism of Manichaeism was viewed as evil. Now the rise of Islam brought converts to the new religion, as well as more conversions to Christianity. There were economic incentives to turn Muslim: discriminatory taxation, and the prospect of employment in the army and bureaucracy. From being persecutors, the Mazdeans now became victims of persecution. Muslim rule also brought new movements of a libertine and insurrectionist character, aimed largely against the Mazdean clergy as linked with the old nobles. Various aspects of Mazdaism would be attacked in these religious uprisings, in which Islamic and Manichaean elements were put together in a common hostility to the traditional ideology of the nobility. Moreover, now that the Mazdean priesthood could no longer itself exercise repressive powers, it had to resort to moralising instead. The priests now had to come to terms with poverty and exalt its virtues. They had to face the economic realities of living with non-Mazdeans and soften their insistence on ritual purity.

It was against this background that the main Mazdean texts in Middle Persian were composed in the ninth and tenth centuries CE. The language of the Avesta (Mazdean scripture) had long since died, and the Mazdeans now had very little idea of what was meant by it. The Middle Persian translations of the Avestan texts are so bad that on their own they are enough to destroy the myth of the so-called 'continuity' of Mazdean teachings. In argument with the Muslims the Mazdeans now proclaimed an absolute dualism, with Ahura Mazdā identified with the Holy Spirit, and consequently balanced by the Evil Spirit. This was in contradiction with the original Gāthic position, in which Ahura Mazdā was above both Spirits.

This absolute dualism has been seen as a 'restored orthodoxy', after a 'heretical' period in which Zurvān, Time, was venerated as supreme. It would seem, however, as Morony well observes, that there never had been or was to be a doctrinal 'orthodoxy'. The Mazdeans found it convenient, in discussion with Jews, Christians and Muslims, to minimise their worship of divinities other than Ahura Mazdā, explaining that they were merely objects of veneration rather than gods. So in dialogue with Jews and Christians they tended to present themselves as monotheists. Often, in other contexts, they seemed to formulate their opinions in henotheist, polytheistic or dualist ways. Why a dualist one in answer to Islam?

The answer is perhaps to be sought in the atmosphere of controversy within Islam, from the eighth to the tenth centuries, about how a good God allowed evil in the world, and in the circumstance that the Muslims generally presented God as the Creator of all actions, even evil ones. To this the Mazdeans had an excellent answer in absolute dualism: there are two first principles, one good, one evil. To be sure, this view seems to have existed before Islam, but now it was to be remorselessly emphasised as the simplest and clearest answer to Muslim propaganda.

In this perspective the condemnation of 'Zurvanism', the tendency to venerate Time as the first principle, is entirely understandable. In the context of argument with Muslims this exaltation of Zurvān would have been an embarrassment in debate, weakening, obscuring and complicating the Mazdeans' clear-cut dualist case. Moreover, the old myth of Zurvān, a god sacrificing in order to have a child and then getting two, would have appeared an obscene absurdity in the Middle Eastern interfaith polemic of the ninth and tenth centuries CE.

Although these Mazdean writings of the early Islamic period undoubtedly contain plenty of much older materials, one has to allow for both priestly 'filtering' and Muslim influences. The latter would appear to be evident in the Middle Persian legend of Zarathushtra himself. At any rate plenty of Judeo-Christian traditions had been at work in the 'biography' of Zarathushtra, presented as a prophet. Here the late Jean de Menasce did well to speak of the difficulty of determining the figure's historicity.

Of the greatest interest in this literature is the story of a Mazdean called Artā Virāf, who takes a hallucinogen, goes into a period of apparent death, and visits heaven and hell. This state of apparent death is a further indication of the influence of shamanism, previously observed in the extraterrestrial journey of the priest Kerdir.

Also of interest is the continuing emphasis on incestuous marriage, a phenomenon attested beyond a shadow of doubt in Mazdean and non-Mazdean sources, contrary to nineteenth-century attempts to deny its previous existence. It is indeed noteworthy that this practice continued for so long under Muslim rule, before being replaced, sometime after the eleventh century, by cousin-marriage, and was considered in detail in the Mazdean literature of the early Islamic period, as meritorious and to be encouraged, whether children were to be expected or not. We are given evidence that women were forced against their will to marry their brothers and fathers, although the agreement of the bridegrooms was necessary.

Finally, we may note the emphasis in this literature on the division of society into four classes and the activities thereof, explicitly set out: in the priesthood, religion, education and justice; in the warrior class, horse-riding and foot-soldiering; in the peasant class, breeding and commerce; in the artisan class, preparation of bread and other food.

There were still plenty of Mazdeans in Iran in the tenth century, but at this time an important emigrant community established itself in India. The Mazdeans of India were to be known as the Parsees. Meanwhile, in Iran, Islamic influences continued to make themselves felt in practice and belief. Mazdean influences on Islam, on the other hand, have been much exaggerated. Elements such as 'the wine of the Magi [the Mazdean priests]', when found in Muslim mystical poetry, are literary motifs of a libertine or symbolic character, and do not indicate transmission of Mazdean ideas. The 'Oriental' philosophy of Suhrawardī (d. 1192), often cited to show continuity with the Iranian past, shows only a minimal acquaintance with Mazdaism.

Various sources, in succeeding centuries, show the difficulties faced by the Mazdean communities in Iran and India: persecution and enforced conversion to Islam, and ignorance among Parsees of their own religion, owing to the difficulty of communication with their Iranian counterparts, seen as the fount of authority. There was to be increased emigration from Iran to India, where attempts to combine Mazdaism with other religions and Greek philosophy, under the guise of a mystical unity, met with considerable success in the seventeenth century.

In the eighteenth century the great and intrepid French pioneer Anquetil Duperron discovered the Mazdean scriptures and introduced them to Europe. Unfortunately an absurd fit of pique among British orientalist led them to reject his materials as forgeries. But from then on it was possible for the Parsees, via European scholarship, to rediscover their own religious heritage, as the linguistic study of the Avesta partially rescued it from the confusion produced by the Middle Persian interpretations.

This rediscovery was assisted by a remarkable change of fortune among the Parsees. British rule, by freeing them from the Muslim yoke, gave them an opportunity to enrich themselves by finding favour with, and adapting themselves to, the new masters. They did this with immense dedication and success. The grateful British responded by adopting a markedly uncritical attitude towards the Parsees. This was in stark contrast to the lack of esteem usually displayed by the British rulers towards their other subjects.

The leaders of the newly-enriched Parsees, complaining of the ignorance and backwardness of their priests, set about encouraging the study of their religion. When a European scholar informed them that Zarathushtra was a monotheist they gladly accommodated themselves to what appeared a convenient position. Meanwhile modernist reformers were instrumental in what Christine Dobbin has called 'the largely successful struggle of the Parsi community to emancipate itself from the despotic authority of the community's heads'.

The economic success of the Parsee merchants in the nineteenth century has been attributed to a religious inspiration inherent in Mazdaism, and comparable to the 'Protestant work ethic'. Against this it may be said that religious and ethnic minorities generally tend to enrich themselves when not impeded by artificial restrictions. The Parsees' success was to be reversed when the Hindus acquired the necessary skills.

On the other hand, the subsequent decline of the Parsees can be partly attributed to a new phenomenon. At the end of the nineteen century some Parsees were much influenced by the Theosophical movement of Helena Blavatsky (1831–91), and decided that everything in the Avesta had a secret, inner meeting, reserved for themselves as an elite. It would seem that, like their European counterparts, they were trying to defend their privileged social position against rising competition, and sought to camouflage insufficiency of information and reasoning powers by a claim to wisdom naturally possessed or directly vouchsafed. These Theosophical Parsees found a natural ally in their priests, who have usually found employment by ingratiating themselves with wealthy patrons, and consequently tended to be lacking in knowledge and intellect. In an ideology which conferred enormous mystical powers on the syllables of their texts the priests found a welcome weapon against the menace of rationalism.

The twentieth century has seen a sharp fall in the fortunes of the Parsees. Obviously, the end of the British Empire was a major reason for the decline of its collaborators. The Parsee population has sunk in numbers, leading to considerable academic investigation, largely inconclusive, into the causes of low birth- and marriage-rates. The discovery of the widespread extent of poverty among fellow-Parsees has greatly surprised and shocked their wealthier co-religionists.

Meanwhile, the fortunes of the Iranian Mazdeans followed a different pattern from the eighteenth century to the present day. The chaos of eighteenth-century Iran, with its horrific massacres, was particularly severe in its consequences for them, and brought yet more enforced conversion to Islam and emigration to India. In the nineteenth century discriminatory measures were particularly oppressive, and hampered economic activity. However, in the second half of the century Parsee and British intervention created new opportunities for Iranian Mazdeans to leave village life for urban, professional careers. Thus in the twentieth century they continued to rise in the social scale, with a consequent decline in Iranian Mazdaism itself. For just as in the Muslim world in general Westernisation and economic progress have brought a decline of Islam within the ranks of the middle classes, so too Iranian Mazdaism has wilted before an impatient, progressive younger generation.

A highly romanticised picture of Mazdaism in modern Iran has been painted by Boyce, in an uncritical attempt to show that little had ever changed, and to suggest that there had been few differences of opinion within the community. Fortunately Michael Fischer has demonstrated that the reverse is the case: plenty of rites and legends have been taken over from the Muslims, and the feuding between Iranian Mazdeans has been particularly bitter. A large number of them were so appalled by the reactionary mindlessness of their elders that they left the faith for the new religion of Baha'ism.

The Islamic revolution of 1978–9 in Iran has naturally produced plenty of worries for the Mazdeans, who had been prospering under the monarchy now overthrown. Since the monarchy had glorified Iran's Mazdean past in contrast to Islam, there were now, not surprisingly, to be some unfortunate excesses directed against them.

Returning to the history of Mazdean studies in the West, we may note that at the moment the most exciting and impressive work is being done by Philippe Gignoux, who has pointed the way to future improvements by concentrating on the anthropology of northern Eurasia. This gives us three significant parallels with Mazdaism, attributable to influences upon the Iranians in their original homeland: 1. the important and original significance of the *bones* as constituting the source of life itself (perhaps it is to this reason that one may attribute the source of Mazdaism's method of disposing of the dead: exposing the corpse on the 'Towers of Silence' for the bones to be picked clean by dogs or vultures—a practice usually explained by the need to avoid polluting earth or fire with dead matter); 2. the presence of a multiplicity of souls within a single human being; 3. extraterrestrial journeys, accompanied by the use of psychotropic drugs and a state of apparent death.

In general, it may be said that Mazdaism strongly resembles other national religious traditions in its ritualism, in its forgetting of its original significations and in its conservatism. This conservatism, however, should not be seen as absolute, nor should it be confused with 'continuity': the original elements were to be combined in different patterns, and were modified by enormous accretions. The latter had to come from the outside: from Greek philosophy and other religions. But to learn from others is hardly discreditable.

Mazdaism's insistence on the primordiality of Evil is a salutary antidote to the modern myth of man's natural innocence. But its attribution of all that is bad to a demonic Other has discouraged self-criticism and provided an excuse for repression in the manner of twentieth-century states. Its emphasis on class distinctions, accompanying the loss of its empire, is of particular interest with regard to Britain today.

Further Reading

The Cambridge History of Iran, vols. 2–4 (Cambridge University Press, Cambridge, 1975–85)
Dumézil, Georges *The Destiny of a King* (University of Chicago Press, Chicago, 1973)
Duchesne-Guillemin, Jacques *Symbols and Values in Zoroastrianism* (New York, 1966)
—— *Religion of Ancient Iran* (Bombay, 1973)
Morony, Michael '*madjūs*' in *The Encyclopaedia of Islam*, 2nd edn
Zaehner, Robert Charles *The Dawn and Twilight of Zoroastrianism* (Weidenfeld & Nicolson, London, 1975)
—— *The Teachings of the Magi* (Sheldon Press, Oxford, 1976)

4 The Classical Religions of India

Friedhelm Hardy

Preface to Chapters 4–13

The religious situation in India has been infinitely more complicated than conventional labels like 'Hinduism' or 'Buddhism' suggest. On the one hand, a typological analysis will have to distinguish a wide spectrum of essentially different religious attitudes and expressions; on the other hand, such types appear frequently in 'Hindu', 'Buddhist', etc. garbs. The present chapter on **The Classical Religions of India** attempts to present this typological differentiation, along with its considerable overlap between different traditions. Instead of dividing the material artificially into 'Hinduism', 'Buddhism', etc. or simply presenting conventional norms put forward by some representatives of these traditions, it describes what is actually found there.

Vedic Religion (pp. 43–49) looks at the oldest documented type of religion. Brought into India by the Āryas, it has interacted in many ways with other indigenous traditions, offering points of reference not only in later Hindu religions, but also in those cases where it is consciously rejected.

The Renouncer Traditions (pp. 50–71) share certain typical assumptions which distinguish them from Vedic ritualism. While the Upaniṣads attempt a new synthesis, both Jainism and Buddhism reject such a possibility and replace rituals by asceticism and meditation.

A further component emerges as *Epic and Purāṇic Religion* (pp. 72–94), which introduces monotheism and devotion to the Hindu traditions. In Buddhism too, at least comparable features emerge as part of the Mahāyāna (pp. 95–104).

As well as the great range of religious practice described, India developed sophisticated modes of reflection by utilising philosophical and theological tools that allow a tradition to rationalise and justify its premisses. Whilst such modes have a more overtly Buddhist,

Hindu and Jain orientation, they remain nevertheless embedded in an overall Indian intellectual pursuit. (*Mahāyāna Buddhism and Buddhist Philosophy* (pp. 95–104); *Hindu Philosophies and Theologies* (pp. 105–13); *Later Jainism* (pp. 114–16)).

Finally, any account of the classical Indian religions must take note of religious developments that either place themselves above the mainstream or that reject the latter outright: *The Esoteric Traditions and Antinomian Movements* (pp. 117–26) attempts some assessment of these.

The remaining chapters of Part Four of *The World's Religions* describe further aspects already touched on in this chapter, and in particular the developments of the classical Indian religious tradition inside and outside the sub-continent. Not all areas on the typological spectrum described earlier have been studied to the same extent. Some, like the esoteric traditions (popularly known as 'Tantrism') have only very recently become the object of serious scholarship and a special study of **Śaivism and the Tantric Traditions** (Chapter 5, pp. 128–72) has been included to explore this subject in greater detail.

The classical heritage of the Indian religions has, over time, been broken up into more self-contained entities. This process has been the result of a variety of factors.

The influx of Western ideas gave rise to conscious reflections, for instance in India, on the Hindu traditions—a **Modern Hinduism** (Chapter 6, pp. 173–81) has to be placed now alongside the continuing older traditions.

From within the antinomian movements the Sikhs developed a very specific and distinct self-awareness which makes it possible to treat **Sikhism** (Chapter 7, pp. 182–93) as a separate religion.

Forms of Buddhism were taken to many other Asian countries, and once established there, developed along relatively self-contained lines. **Theravāda Buddhism in South-East Asia** (Chapter 8, pp. 194–206) explores this process for an early transplant from India. In the cases of **China** and **Japan**, and then **Tibet** and **Mongolia** (Chapters 10–13, pp. 224–85), we are dealing with two later stages of Indian Buddhism. On the other hand, **Nepal** (Chapter 9, pp. 207–23) has preserved a situation that in some respects corresponds to that of the classical India before 1200 CE when Hindus and Buddhists were still living side by side within one society and culture.

General Remarks on the Religious History of India

India, the land to the east of the river Indus, must have held great promise for anybody living in the arid regions of Central Asia or the mountains of what is today Afghanistan. Fertile and rich in natural resources, green and full of wonders, it exerted an irresistible attraction to the nomads roaming through the semi-desert to its north-west. But if it meant an earthly paradise, it was well guarded: in the north, the Himalayas, and in the north-west the Hindu Kush mountains provided an almost impenetrable barrier. Yet during the more than three thousand years of Indian history, time and again peoples managed to enter it. Although it is certain that neither the Arabian Sea, nor the jungles of the north-east acted as complete barriers, from the point of view of the religious history of India up to the colonial period, the influx of peoples from the north-west was decisive. Thus Indian religious history begins with the arrival of nomads who called themselves the Āryas, the 'noble ones', sometimes around the middle of the penultimate millennium BCE.

But it was not an empty country the Āryas entered. Other peoples were already living there, who had to be conquered or pushed into less desirable regions. Filled with an aggressive spirit and superior in terms of arms and military tactics, the Āryas appear not to have found this difficult. Yet they may not have been directly responsible for the disappearance of a much older civilisation, which had flourished along the river Indus (and is known accordingly as 'Indus Civilisation'). Perhaps an inner decay of this culture made it possible for the Āryas to move south. Very little of what the archaeologist has unearthed throws light on the religion of this unknown people, and nothing can be inferred from it, as far as the later Indian religions are concerned.

The spread of these Āryas and their culture and religion over the region took hundreds of years. Soon after 1000 BCE the Aryan heartland had shifted to the region around what is today Delhi, and less than five hundred years later the country along the more eastern part of the Ganges river had become the Āryāvarta, Aryan homeland. The third century BCE witnessed Aryan culture establishing itself further south in the

Deccan, but it took almost a millennium for it to settle properly in the extreme south (from the sixth century CE).

What will be discussed in the following pages as the Indian religions are all the result of the interaction, in a vast number of different ways, of the Aryan heritage with local and regional traditions. In most cases, the latter are extremely difficult to identify, particularly for the earlier period—historical documentation on the whole has been produced by the Aryas alone. But what scholars have discovered during the last few decades about non-Aryan cultures and religions in India adds up to enough evidence to reject the claims that we are dealing here with a homogenous and continuous, monolinear history of religious phenomena. Sometimes very fundamental transformations occurred as a result of regional influences.

Where does our evidence for this hypothesis derive from? First, there is the presence of linguistic groups which do not belong to the Indo-European Sanskrit and its subsequent developments (or to the languages in the north-west which derive from, or are related to, Old Iranian). Of primary importance here are the Dravidian languages. The term was coined by Bishop Caldwell (who even suspected that the Hebrew words for some of the exotic articles brought to Solomon were of Dravidian origin—an assumption that today looks rather far fetched). The major languages in this group are spoken in South India: Tamil, Telugu, Kannada (or Kanarese) and Malayalam (which is the mother tongue also of the 'Syrian' Christians in Kerala). But outside the south many other peoples also speak Dravidian languages, for example in the more inaccessible regions of central and eastern India. The presence of a Dravidian language, Brahui, in modern Pakistan, is perhaps the most convincing evidence for an earlier pan-Indian Dravidian presence. Furthermore, we have other peoples speaking languages which either link them with those spoken in Burma, Thailand, Kampuchea (the Mon-Khmer languages, with their most important Indian representative Santali), or with Tibet and China. Finally, as a curiosity may be mentioned Burushaski high up in the Himalayas (in Hunza) for which scholars have found no link to any other known language. The continuation of linguistic autonomy of a great variety of peoples in the country can be taken as a symptom of their relative autonomy also in terms of culture and religion.

Closely related to this is a second aspect. At least in one case we still possess a corpus of literature (in Tamil) which goes back to the very beginning of the Common Era. It documents for the extreme south a culture which is as yet hardly influenced by the north. The Tamils drew for centuries on this so-called *caṅkam* literature to express their perception of Hinduism. For instance, the Āḻvārs and Nāyaṉārs, and the *Bhāgavata-Purāṇa*, bear witness to the extent of this southern transformative power.

A third aspect is important here; this could be called 'incomplete' or 'multiple' history. Whilst we are used to thinking in terms of historical processes, say the French Revolution or the Industrial Revolution, which affected Western society to such an extent that (in degrees) nobody was left out of them, the case in India has been different. Whatever major historical events took place (the invasion of the Āryas, or of the Hūṇas in the fifth century CE, the conquest of most of the country by Muslims, or Portuguese and British colonialism), they only had a very limited effect on the Indian peoples at large, and it tended to take centuries before even this effect reached its peak. The result of this is that even today in India we can find (a few) people who belong to the Stone Age in terms of their lifestyle, and, at the other extreme of the spectrum, nuclear reactors. What lies in between is enormously variegated. In reality we ought to speak therefore of many histories of India.

All this meant, in terms of Indian society, that many groups of people, who spoke different languages, belonged to different histories and practised different religions, over a period of hundreds of years learnt to live together and interact socially. At the same time, the mere scale of such social differentiation must have been perceived as a threat to the sense of identity of the individual group within such an amorphous whole. Whilst modes of social interaction and of sharing cultural and religious elements thus evolved, modes of maintaining a separate identity were also established. Conventionally, these two sides of the same coin are treated together under the heading of the 'caste system'. But the social reality of India has been far more fluid and flexible, with enormous regional and historical variations. Of particular interest in the present context is the role of religion. Though almost always blamed for the negative sides of the so-called caste system, religion has in fact frequently played a very positive role by setting up new social structures designed to overcome certain repressive or discriminatory aspects of the social conventions.

In one sense, the history of the Indian religions could be described as the process of infusing the Aryan heritage into the whole of India. Except for the tribes (of which there exist even today quite a number, involving millions of people), most Indians were affected by this—though they may then have strongly reacted against it. This Aryan heritage itself, symbolised by 'the Veda' and the brahmin, did not however remain constant in the course of history. This latter aspect is almost totally ignored by the representatives of such a—very traditional—approach to Indian religious history. In different regions and social milieux, these symbols underwent considerable transformations and modifications. One could be tempted to describe the function of the brahmin as that of a 'clearing-house': he receives religious material and returns it in a form that bears the stamp of his style and values. The Purāṇas are perhaps the most typical expression of this process.

In another sense, the history of the Indian religions dissolves into a large number of separate histories, according to individual traditions, cultural-linguistic regions, and social groups and milieux. The conventional labels of 'Buddhism', 'Jainism' or 'Sikhism' neither exhaust the (very large) range of the traditions we can identify outside the most unhelpful title of 'Hinduism', nor do they, for the most part, even define proper 'religious systems'. The section on Sikhism, which has evolved as perhaps the most self-contained of these 'isms', will illustrate this particular approach. Two further sections will demonstrate to what extent even in relatively small regions (Kashmir and Nepal) the religious scene is differentiated and yet witnesses the constant interaction of these variegated traditions.

In a third sense, writing the history of the Indian religions could mean first, to establish some kind of typology of the religious content, of fundamentally distinct expressions of the religious, and then, secondly, to trace the documentation of each of these types. Now precisely because of the 'multiple history' mentioned above, each subsequently documented type adds to, but does not replace, the previous ones. The sections on traditional Indian religions follow this approach, and thus it is not necessary here to elaborate on it. The four basic types which became documented at subsequent stages are: ritualism, mysticism, devotionalism and antinomianism. Systematic reflections on them appear from the last millennium BCE onwards. Both our four types and also the structures of thought found in the reflective traditions cut right across the conventional four labels of 'Hinduism', 'Buddhism', etc. Further initial confusion is created by the fact that, in real life, the four different types are almost always mixed up with each other, in endless forms. For example, devotion to God combines with a set of ritual practices and daily meditational exercises.

From among the four basic types of the religious, 'antinomianism' (usually under the title of 'Tantrism') has in particular attracted popular interest. Reliable and critical scholarship on this material is, on the other hand, the least readily available. In view of this situation, more space has been given to the 'esoteric traditions', 'Śaivism in Kashmir' and 'the Religions of Tibet', than could perhaps be justified otherwise.

During the nineteenth and early twentieth centuries Indians on the one hand reacted to the influx of Western ideas and criticisms (see the separate section on this). Already this reaction involved a new type of reflection on the religious heritage (e.g. what were the 'scriptural authorities' for the 'orthodoxy' of temple worship). On the other hand, Westerners also showed curiosity and interest in the Indian religions, thereby further stimulating this new type of self-reflection. Now traditionally the Indian religions had evolved their own modes of self-reflection and conceptualisation (see on this in particular the sections on Buddhist and Hindu philosophies, and on Śaivism in Kashmir). Whatever was still known of this older conceptualisation (it tended to be Śaṅkara's Advaita-Vedānta more than any of the others), was offered to the enquiring West(erner), along with *ad hoc* 'explanations', which represent more the questioner's own prejudices than the informant's factual and critical understanding. 'The Hindu Trinity', 'idol worship' and indeed 'Hinduism' are samples of this process.

Vedic Religion

Whatever the religions may have been which were practised by the other peoples of ancient India, the documented religious history of the sub-continent begins with the arrival of the Āryas in the north-western regions. Hindus and Western scholars agree that a corpus of scriptures, known as the Veda ('[sacred] knowledge') and associated with those ancient Āryas, forms the basis of all subsequent developments of Hinduism. But it is important to realise that what either group means by this differs fundamentally.

In the Hindu understanding, the Veda consists of eternally existing (however that may be defined by individual schools) sacred scriptures. These are 'revealed' at the beginning of each cosmic age to seers (*ṛṣis*) who 'see' the Veda and teach it orally to their disciples (who thus 'hear' it). From this mode of transmission, the Veda is also known as *śruti* (lit. 'hearing'), a term denoting primary, ultimate revelation. Moreover, Vyāsa, one of the primordial sages, is regarded as the compiler of these scriptures, putting them together as a definitive corpus. This consists of four main traditions (Ṛg-, Sāma-, Yajur- and Atharva-Veda) which in turn are divided into four genres (Saṃhitā, Brāhmaṇa, Āraṇyaka and Upaniṣad). This corpus constitutes the highest religious authority and pervades all forms of Hinduism, however variegated they may appear on the surface.

But for the scholar, this monolithic block of 'the Veda' falls apart into chronologically different stages and socially separate layers of a literary development that may have lasted for perhaps as long as a thousand years. The latter half of the second millennium BCE has emerged as the most likely period for the beginnings of Vedic literature. For such a date there are few other documents of comparable bulk in the history of religion anywhere else in the world. Yet here we are dealing with religious documents in an unusual sense, for these are not written sources (like, for example, Sumerian cuneiform tablets). The Veda is primarily an oral literature, but transmitted across the centuries in such a meticulous manner that very little change or distortion has occurred.

Frequently, the term 'Veda' (or 'Vedas', for the four traditions Ṛg-, Sāma-, etc.) is used in a more restricted sense. Instead of denoting the entire corpus, it excludes the latest of the genres, that is the Upaniṣads. To speak of 'Vedas and Upaniṣads' has indeed certain advantages, for it highlights the major differences between the earlier hymns and the later Upaniṣads. The latter group of texts reflects a type of religion which is very different from early Vedic ritualism.

The centre of the religious practice of the Āryas was the sacrifice: rituals performed around and through the fire. The symbolism and the motivation behind such sacrifices can without difficulty be derived from the theme of 'hospitality', an important element in nomadic life all over the world. Thus the sacrifice is a meal, but it is shared not only between members of a group of Āryas, but also with beings of a different order called *devas*. The sacrificial meal aims to establish bonds of loyalty and mutual responsibility between men and *devas*. But who are those *devas*? To determine what 'deva' here means is almost identical with defining Vedic religion—a task which scholarship is far from having completed. Certainly these *devas* are 'beings' of some kind; they are normally invisible to the human eye, possess individual names and many personal characteristics. They are more powerful than man, and in many ways interfere in his life, both in a positive and negative manner. They can be addressed by man, be propitiated and requested to grant specific favours. Yet at the same time, they also manifest a puzzling association with natural phenomena, such as fire, rain, thunderstorm, etc. In these contexts, they are more like 'things' or 'events'. But if we acknowledge that we are dealing here with an archaic form of thought which does not yet make a clear conceptual distinction between a 'person' and other forms of agents observable in nature, at least this ambiguity need not cause undue problems. How the different *devas* are perceived, in their individuality and their interaction among themselves and with man, constitutes the perception which Vedic man had of himself within the world. Moreover, such a perception would provide the theory (however unconscious it may have been) underlying the sacrificial practices. Thus the *devas* are non-human forces at work everywhere in the world which can to some extent be manipulated through ritual means.

But there is one further problem here: the Sanskrit word *deva* is etymologically related to the Latin *deus* and the Greek *theos*, a fact that produced the conventional translation of *deva* as 'god'. The description of the *devas* offered above makes it clear to what an extent the *devas* are 'natural' beings and not 'supernatural'. To derive an understanding of Vedic religion from the nature of the *devas* alone would thus be very misleading. In fact, early scholars went even further and thought they had discovered suggestions here as to the 'origin of religion' itself. The strong association of the *devas* with natural phenomena was seen as evidence that nature, when 'personified' and 'deified', gives rise to religion. Yet logically the concept of 'god' itself cannot be derived from, only projected upon, natural phenomena. Moreover, the link between *deva* and *deus/theos* was also developed in a different direction, but again without yielding fruitful results (at least as far as an understanding of Vedic religion in its own right is concerned). In this case, the common linguistic heritage from the Indo-European past was seen as the paradigm also of a common religious past. This may well have been the case, and the reconstruction of it is certainly an exciting enterprise in its own right. But as a religious system, Vedic religion developed its identity precisely because it moved away from that common heritage. Sanskrit *agni* (fire) may be related to the Latin *ignis*, and the Greek god Ouranos may reveal some similarities with the *deva* Varuṇa. But the insights into Vedic religion from such correlations are extremely small.

The *devas* themselves makes up a motley crowd. Attempts at counting them by listing different proper names have almost reached the figure 1,000. Most of these are male, with only a few and insignificant female *devas*, that is, *devīs*. However, only a few *devas* are really central to Vedic religion. Not surprisingly, the sacrificial fire itself, under the name of Agni, is one such *deva*. Through him man communicates with the other *devas*, for offerings addressed to them are handed over to him. Similarly, since the dead are cremated, Agni conveys people into the dark and rather nebulous realm of Yama, the *deva* of death. And it is Agni who carries the nourishment to the ancestors (*pitṛs*, literally 'fathers') living in that realm. To provide this nourishment regularly (through the monthly *śrāddha* ritual) is the primary duty of any son. But the sacrifice is not just a conveyance of food. It also involves the production and offering of a liquid called *soma*, which is the material manifestation of the *deva* Soma. No definite conclusions about the identity of the plant from which the juice was derived have been reached by scholars. But it is clear that the liquid extracted from it possessed hallucinogenic properties. In this strictly controlled ritual context, a portion of the *soma* was also drunk by the human participants. The degree to which this has any bearing on the kind of poetry which was produced for these rituals has not yet been ascertained.

A very different kind of *deva* is Indra. He is the most frequently invited guest to the sacrifice, and in the way he is described we can see many features of the aggressive, conquering Āryas themselves. Then there is Varuṇa, a much less transparent figure. Both he and Indra are associated with the natural order, Indra using his valour to remove obstructions to it and Varuṇa supervising the actions of man and punishing any transgressions. It has become customary to list even in the shortest catalogues of Vedic *devas* two further figures, Viṣṇu and Rudra/Śiva. The reason for this is that *devas* of those names acquire central importance at a later stage in the history of Hinduism. But in the Vedas, they play a very marginal role.

There cannot be any doubt that Vedic religion had its mythology—traditional stories about *devas* and their past deeds—but our understanding of it is very imperfect. This has to do with the nature of our sources. Besides the offerings of food and of *soma*, the sacrifice involved recitation of poems addressed to the *devas*. An invitation to come and join the meal is expressed in such a poem, usually dedicated to one particular *deva* or a smaller group of them. These poems also flatter the *deva(s)* because of heroic deeds done or grand qualities like liberality. Suggestions are made as to the rewards desired by the sacrificer for his efforts. Given this literary form, we cannot expect a coherent narrative of whole myths; we find only sporadic fragments and allusions. Judging from later literature, it would appear that such fragments did not actually derive from one single, coherent mythology and that many different versions were current at the time. The freedom of poetic imagination and mythological inventiveness must have been considerable.

From an unknown date onwards, such poems composed for the sacrifice began to be collected, initially within priestly families as treasured heirlooms. Eventually such collections were put together as one bulky corpus, which now constitutes the main part of the Ṛg-Veda (*ṛc*, *ṛg*: hymn). In addition to the 'recitation' (performed by the *hotṛ*-priest), a much more musical mode evolved which became associated with another class of priests, i.e. the *udgātṛ*. No new poetry was created for this, and thus the Sāma-Veda contains mostly material already found in the Ṛg-Veda. Very different material was collected in a third corpus, the Yajur-Veda. Here we find the sacrificial formulas, and, depending on the recension, also the details of ritual acts, which made up the ritual function of the *adhvaryu*-priests.

These three Vedas thus arose from the functional differentiation within the priesthood responsible for the Vedic fire-sacrifice. But there is a fourth collection, the Atharva-Veda. In the first half at least we find material of a very different kind, which may well be contemporary with the early hymns of the Ṛg-Veda. 'Popular religion' is perhaps the best label to describe it. Rituals are presented to us here which do not involve the *devas* at all and which are perceived to be effective merely through their accurate performance, joining the correct verbal formulas to the appropriate ritual action. No professional priest is necessary, and the results aimed for are even more down-to-earth than that which the fire-sacrifice is supposed to yield (for example, winning the love of a woman).

This presence of two rather different religious-ritual traditions in the same society is interesting; it might also have had implications for the subsequent developments. For we notice that in the course of time the *devas*—after all very unpredictable and free agents—become less and less important and the sacrifice itself moves into the centre of the religious view of the world. In terms of underlying rationale, such a view is comparable with what we find in the Atharva-Veda. Thus at least hypothetically one might be able to speak of a transfer of popular ideas on to the hieratic sacrifice. But what is clear is that in the course of time the structure of the sacrifice became enormously complicated. Consequently a whole specialist literature evolved which dealt with these ritual details (adding accounts of the origin of rituals etc.). These sometimes very lengthy texts were called the Brāhmaṇas. At a certain stage, a third genre was formulated, the Āraṇyakas. It seems that, for reasons of their particularly powerful and thus potentially dangerous nature, certain rituals could only be performed in the forest (*āraṇyaka*: belonging to the forest), away from house and home. Material on these was collected outside the Brāhmaṇas.

The amount of textual material that has been discussed by now is quite staggering. For in the course of time, the three types of priests differentiated further into more than a dozen separate 'branches' (*śākhās*), each one with its own independent Brāhmaṇa (and Āraṇyaka). In this form it has been handed down from generation to generation. That texts which in print fill many hundreds of pages should be learnt by heart *in toto* is by itself an amazing achievement of human memory. That it should be done with almost perfect accuracy is sheer genius. We can infer this accuracy among other things from the fact that the type of language found here corresponds to what linguists would expect historically, that the grammar is consistent over the whole corpus and that different versions agree essentially. To achieve such precision, various devices were invented. Thus the texts were learnt not just once (that is, as actually recited), but many times over: having them split up into separate, individual words, arranging the words in various patterns of *ba*, *dc*, etc. That such dedication, over many years of study, should be shown to this material, clearly suggests that the Vedas themselves had acquired extreme religious status.

What does all this add up to in terms of religion? In the past, Vedic religion has often been described as 'polytheism', to which a second evolutionary stage, called 'henotheism' was added. This concept derives from a stylistic peculiarity found in many Vedic hymns, where one *deva* is addressed with the attributes (and names) of many other *devas*. Whilst this second presumed stage is of limited significance, 'monotheism', which scholars postulated as the third and final evolutionary stage of religion, did not grow out of the Vedas at all. Instead, the development took a different direction. Thus instead of pursuing the discussion of the *devas* further, it seems preferable to listen in to the discussions which the ancient Indians themselves had about these matters. For indeed the Vedic Indians did ask questions about the nature of man and the world and about what principles ordered and governed them. Already at an early stage, a concept *ṛta* evolved which denoted some cosmic order or harmony. Varuṇa in particular was its guardian, acting as the agent of retribution for any infringement of *ṛta*. This suggests that behind the multiplicity of *devas*, some unifying principle, abstract and impersonal, was envisaged. Similarly we find the concept *brahman*, denoting at this early stage a particular 'sacred', cosmic power. In fact it was this power which accounted for the efficacy of the sacrifice, since it was located within the brahmin priest, and that in turn because he had absorbed it by learning the Vedas. Such conceptions were then developed along much more conscious, searching lines. A great interest in the world, in the laws governing it and in its origin and structure, came to the fore. The sacrifice was used as a major conceptual model for exploring these issues. A search began for the one principle underlying and controlling all other forces in the world. For, and this appears to be the motivation, if this one could be controlled or manipulated ritually, total control over the world and man's destiny could be gained. In a large number of 'creation myths', a whole spectrum of suggestions of such a one principle is made. What better way to demonstrate the power of the one over the many than to show how out of the one the many evolved? Well-known examples are Vāc (Speech, that is the Vedas), Skambha (the cosmic axis), Puruṣa ('Man', the sacrificial victim, out of whose dismembered body the world with its beings and social classes evolved). It is clear from the multiplicity of such conceptions that we are not dealing here with any kind of normative ('Hindu') account of creation comparable with what we find in the book of Genesis. But eventually all these extremely variegated speculations settled on *brahman*, a term that now also denotes the one at the beginning and at the centre of all the many things and beings that make up the universe. It goes without saying that this must have added enormously to the prestige of the priests and of their sacrifices where *brahman* was located in a very special way. All these speculations found their textual home within the Vedic literature discussed above: as Book X and part of Book I of the Ṛg-Veda, as the second half of the Atharva-Veda and in scattered form in the different Brāhmaṇas. In the light of these observations, the role of the *devas* cannot exclusively be regarded as central to Vedic religion. Neither in the perception of the sacrifice as 'automatic' nor in the way a single ultimate principle is envisaged do personal features or *deva*-figures play any decisive role.

It is often said that the Veda is to the Hindus what the Bible is to Christianity. But for all practical purposes, such a comparison is at most misleading, if not totally inappropriate. Whilst it is certainly true that any reasonable description of Hinduism would have to refer constantly to 'the Veda', it would only be slightly exaggerated to say that its actual content is irrelevant (at least as far as the hymns and the sacrificial material are concerned). The reality of the Veda is primarily conceptual. Certainly the fact that they are not a written scripture is important here. But to explain why this was not done requires a look at the social context. They were the carefully guarded 'religious knowledge' of a certain group of people, and thus not a proclamation of beliefs addressed to the whole of Indian society. Moreover, parallel to a decrease in the linguistic comprehensibility went an increase of the purely functional role of this literature. Both in grammar and vocabulary, the earlier Vedic hymns are in a pre-classical form of the Sanskrit language. In the course of time, these hymns thus became increasingly more incomprehensible, even to those people who knew classical Sanskrit or whose mother tongue was derived from it. Their style and poetic conventions and their allusive mythology also became increasingly remote and archaic. But this created no obvious problems, for as was observed above, the actual content was of no importance, once a more reflex conception of *brahman* as central cosmic power had evolved. What remained important was the learning of the hymns, for *brahman* would thereby be absorbed, and the recitation of them, for *brahman* would thereby be applied to a ritual act. The Brāhmaṇas are far more easily accessible, but their relevance for the professional priest as his handbook is a primarily practical one. Moreover, whatever new forms of religion evolved during the following millennia, none could claim to be 'orthodox', or acquire social respectability, unless some connection with the Veda could be shown, however tenuous, putative or artificial this link might be. Much of what to the uncritical observer appears as the 'continuity of the Vedic tradition' in Hinduism reveals itself at closer inspection as a secondary recourse back to the ancient past, and not as historically grown extensions.

In many other ways did the Vedas stimulate further intellectual and religious developments. A whole range of academic disciplines evolved, all of which derived from concerns connected with the Veda, and are thus known as the *Vedāṅgas*, the 'limbs' of the Veda: for example, astronomy (to determine the precise time and date for a sacrifice), grammar (to maintain the comprehensibility at least of the ritual treatises) and geometry (for the precise construction of altars). But more important, because it was of far greater general relevance, was the formulation of the ideal of a 'Vedic life'. In particular two such disciplines concerned themselves with the study of domestic rituals and with life in society. The earliest textual expressions of these subjects are the various *gṛhya-* and *dharma-sūtras* which we still find included in the repertoire of the various *śākhās*. Of particular interest here is the concept of 'dharma' (a development of that of *ṛta*). But the 'classical' view of *dharma* and thus of the orthodox, Vedic life is not merely a development of Vedic religion, but a relatively late synthesis of two very different traditions. Traceable as far back as *c.* 800 BCE, that is when Vedic literature had reached the stage indicated above, we find a very different kind of religious reality. This is the 'renouncer tradition', and we must turn to it, before pursuing the topic of the ideal religious, Vedic life.

The Renouncer Traditions

The rewards requested from the *devas* in the Vedic hymns have a decidedly this-worldly character: sons, long life, victory in battle, etc. And the motivation behind the later sacrificial system is the maintenance of the cosmic order, implying the same idea of prosperity on earth. The early section of the Atharva-Veda deals even more with the minutiae of ordinary, daily life. Behind the speculations about the One lies a quest for the one power that controls all others in this world. This emphasis on 'worldly' matters may well be due to the very shadowy and rather unattractive conception of an afterlife in a gloomy underworld.

Then suddenly a new set of concepts becomes documented, from around 800 BCE onwards. These ideas are so much at variance with what we have encountered so far that some kind of discontinuity must be assumed. Here now we find expressed a conception of transcendence, a reality beyond all limitations of space, time and matter. Moreover, this reality contrasts sharply with ordinary life which appears limited, painful and undesirable by comparison with it. In addition, the span of this 'ordinary life' is extended greatly, for a potentially unlimited chain of such existences is envisaged for each living being. This is the idea of transmigration or rebirth. Each life is the result of previous lives, and in turn conditions further lives. Nevertheless, a qualitative leap into the realm of transcendence, of liberation from transmigration, is possible. It is simply a question of knowing what causes further rebirth and what the means are of escaping from it. Here also, in the perception of such means, the discontinuity with Vedic religion is apparent. No ritual, no *deva* could ever achieve it, only 'knowledge'. From the way that this 'knowledge' is described to us, and the more explicit statements about the method we are given, it can be inferred that we are dealing with ascetically, meditationally gained 'altered' or 'higher' states of consciousness. Desire and ignorance inevitably appear as the crucial cause of rebirth, and ascetic practices coupled with meditation are advocated as eradicating them. We find shared presuppositions about the need for sexual abstinence, poverty, homelessness and a radical avoidance of harming any form of life. These constitute the 'renunciation'.

The source of such ideas is obscure, but it is extremely unlikely that the *soma*-induced state of altered consciousness has had any causal link with them. It appears to be more likely that somewhere 'outside' the Vedic tradition these religious ideas were picked up and/or cultivated by some Āryas. What precisely this 'outside' could mean is impossible to answer; local tribal religion has been suggested. But it is clear that in some sense the follower of this type of religion places himself outside Aryan society and Vedic religion. He becomes a 'renouncer'.

This brief introductory sketch has gathered together material which textually has been preserved in three very different religious traditions and therefore is normally treated under three separate headings. These are the Upaniṣads, Jainism and Buddhism. But either by assuming a straightforward continuity between the Vedas and Upaniṣads, or by treating for instance Buddhism in isolation from its context within the renouncer tradition, many important features would be distorted. On various (mainly linguistic and geographical) grounds, the earliest texts known as Upaniṣads have been dated around 800 BCE. Then there are hints that Jainism is not the original creation of the alleged founder, the Mahāvīra (of the sixth or fifth century BCE), but the remodelling of a somewhat earlier religion associated with the name of Pārśva. Thus when the Buddha taught around the sixth century BCE, he had to address himself to a centuries-old tradition. The sophistication of his teaching would support his relatively late position within the renouncer tradition.

Whilst Jainism and Buddhism rejected *in toto* the Vedic religious tradition (and thus turned 'heterodox'), the Upaniṣads appear to attempt a synthesis or compromise. But whatever the theoretical position was in relation to the Veda, in terms of social behaviour the three varieties represent one movement: the renouncer tradition which defined itself as superior to ritualism. But what was felt to be even more important by each type within this tradition was a definition in relation to the other types. There are enough traces left in the literature to catch glimpses of an extremely variegated and dynamic internal discussion, and the three contestants mentioned here are no more than the eventual 'winners'.

The Upaniṣads

The word 'upaniṣad' denotes a particular genre of texts; its literal meaning has however remained obscure. 'Intimate teaching' might be a possible explanation. These Upaniṣads have come down to us as part of a neat and tidily structured package: the Veda (as Indians would use the word). In the previous chapter it was mentioned that over the centuries each Vedic *śākhā* acquired three genres of text: a Saṃhitā, Brāhmaṇa and Āraṇyaka. To these three we must add now the Upaniṣad. Indeed many of the genuinely old six or so texts belonging to this genre are simply known by the name of the *śākhā* to which they belong (like the *Aitareya-* or *Kauṣītaki-Upaniṣad*). This applies only to the Ṛg-, Sāma- and Yajur-Veda; but the Atharva-Veda also attracted later Upaniṣads. So we end up with a clear four-by-four structure. Moreover, another fourfold pattern is applied to this, that of the four stages in a man's life (for which see below). The fourth stage, that of the 'renouncer' (*saṃnyāsī*), is correlated to the fourth genre, that of the Upaniṣad.

This is the way traditional Hinduism interprets the situation. But the very neatness of the structure raises doubts about its historical validity. In view of the general remarks made above it appears more likely that we are dealing here with material which attempts to correlate extraneous and recently accepted religious ideas with the conceptions expressed in the earlier portions of the Vedic corpus. This may be an extreme way of envisaging the situation, but whatever its shortcomings may be, it has the advantage of focusing more sharply on the central religious issues than the traditional assumption of a direct continuity.

The *Chāndogya-* and the *Bṛhadāraṇyaka-Upaniṣads* have been identified as some of the oldest, and indeed historically most important, Upaniṣads. The title of the latter, bṛhad-*āraṇyaka*, highlights that the boundaries of the genres are by no means clear-cut. Thus the Upaniṣads also contain a large number of speculations on the One, along the cosmological lines of the earlier literature. And the aim is still to 'come to know it'. But the purpose of such knowledge has changed. To 'know it' now means to achieve that qualitative leap into the realm of liberation. This is how a direct link with earlier Vedic thought could be established. In trying to define what such a transcendental reality could be, the Upaniṣads draw on the images, concepts, terms and symbols of earlier Vedic literature. Some more independent speculations around symbols like fire, water and air are also expressed, but without doubt the concept of *brahman* emerges from all this as the sole survivor. This nevertheless expanded the denotation of the term far beyond what the earlier literature meant by it. Now *brahman* was not just the 'sacred' power pervading the sacrifice and the Veda itself, and not just the One out of which the many arose, but also the One into which man merges back by achieving his liberation from the cycle of rebirths (*saṃsāra*). Moreover, *brahman* is an experiential reality, available through meditation.

In more technical terms, this appears as follows. Ordinary man finds himself in *saṃsāra*, coursing from one life to the next. What remains constant is his innermost self, his *ātman*. But this *ātman* is surrounded and in fact imprisoned, not just by the different physical bodies which are cremated after death, but also by a subtle, invisible body. This *sūkṣma-śarīra* absorbs the 'qualities' of all the actions done in a given life, called *karma*, which after the disintegration of one body germinates, as it were, a new body appropriate in view of the past actions. This is by no means restricted to human bodies; rebirth as an animal, as one of those many categories of non-human beings known to ancient Indian folklore, or as a *deva* is equally well possible. Thus whatever status the *deva* may have possessed in earliest Vedic religion, it is now brought down to that of belonging to the transient order. By eradicating *karma* and 'coming to know' *brahman*, the *ātman* can liberate itself, to become reunited with *brahman*, like the spark with the fire from which it arose. That is *mokṣa* or *mukti*, the state of liberation. The 'coming to know' itself is mentioned under different names, but eventually the common and well-known term 'yoga' becomes universally used to refer to such forms of meditation.

The older Upaniṣads still lack a systematically defined terminology and neither, for that matter, do they draw on one coherent system of thought. The imagination coupled with critical, conceptual analysis is still at work to come to terms with the transcendental experience of *brahman*. Metaphor is one commonly used means of expression. When we thus find the relationship between *brahman* and the world (including man) envisaged as that of a fire and its sparks, or of a spider and its web, it is clear that an 'ontological' dependence is suggested between two real things: *brahman* and the multiple, variegated world of phenomena. Both are real, but the many derive from and depend on the One. There cannot be any question here of the world being an 'illusion', as some forms of later Hindu thought would present it. Other metaphors tell us about the achievement of liberation. It is like the merging of different rivers into the one ocean (in which they lose their identity and name), or the pollen of many flowers that make up the honey. This clearly suggests an ultimate identity of *ātman* with *brahman*, an identity in which the former is absorbed into the latter. An expansion of the self is experienced in which the whole universe is encompassed. In this context the names of at least the two most important teachers appearing in the early Upaniṣads must be mentioned: Uddālaka and Yajñavalkya. In their teaching we encounter attempts at a more systematic exposition, which could be described as 'progressive abstraction'. Thus Uddālaka has his disciple bisect a tree's fruit, then its seed, until only an invisibly small particle remains. Yet it is here, beyond the range of the human eye, in the 'essence' of the tree, that *brahman* is present, and 'that you are' is the famous conclusion drawn from it. With Yajñavalkya we find similar instances of such abstraction. From seeing to hearing to thinking to 'true knowledge' we are led along the scale of most immediate and object-bound information about reality to its most abstract, direct and non-objective form. In a famous passage (*Bṛhadāraṇyaka* II, 4) he removes his wife's doubts about this. Once the *ātman* has reunited with that which lies at the heart of all things and all events in the world (including perception itself), it makes no more sense to speak of a subject–object relationship, and the form of awareness that is connected with such a relationship is transcended in pure, that is non-objective, consciousness. Dream appears in such explorations as a useful metaphor, and more so, as an intermediary stage between the experience of *brahman* and ordinary consciousness. For in it we can already witness a degree of demolition, as far as the ordinary relationship between phenomena in the space–time–matter continuum are concerned. Following the logic of this first transition, *brahman*, as much as the experience associated with it, then appears as altogether outside that continuum. A famous formula summarises all this by describing *brahman* through the attributes of pure being (*sat*), consciousness (*cit*) and bliss (*ānanda*). But we also detect a note of despair in all this mystical exuberance, despair about the limitations of human thought and language when it comes to grasping *brahman*. Thus *neti neti* is suggested as the most appropriate way of referring to *brahman*: all that can be said about it is 'not, not'.

What has been sketched so far is typical of the older, genuinely *śākhā*-associated Upaniṣads. But in terms of the literary history of the genre, this was merely the beginning of many further developments. Thus, still well within the BCE period, Upaniṣads were produced in which the thinking took on a more systematic form, on the basis of what would seem to be somewhat different premisses. We are in fact dealing here with early expressions of a system, the Sāṃkhya, which will be discussed further in its appropriate context, that of the Hindu philosophical traditions. Still somehow linked to *śākhās*, yet another type of Upaniṣad evolved. By now we are probably in the last few centuries BCE. In works like the *Śvetāśvatara-Upaniṣad* we encounter for the first time a type of religion that can be styled monotheistic. More on this will be found in the section on the gods and God. By now the genre had established itself as most prestigious, and a large number of further Upaniṣads was produced over the next centuries. Few religious movements resisted the attempt to point at an Upaniṣad as the final authority for their particular beliefs. Even the famous *Bhagavadgītā* of the Mahābhārata epic presented itself as 'the Upaniṣad sung by Bhagavān', although this particular claim was never accepted by the Hindu traditions. In most cases, such late Upaniṣads were nominally connected with the Atharva-Veda—another sign that this Veda played a role separate from that of the other three Vedas.

It is not known from what period onwards attempts began to be made to survey the older, originally *śākhā*-specific Upaniṣads and treat them as constituting one coherent corpus of teaching. The *Brahma-* or *Vedānta-sūtras* ascribed to Bādarāyaṇa became the most prestigious work offering such a survey. It provided the basis for the most important of the so-called six schools of Hindu philosophy, the Vedānta. But later forms of Hinduism have taken recourse to the thought of the Upaniṣads in many other ways. On the one hand linked to the Veda, and on the other hand enormously variegated in content, the Upaniṣads offered the most obvious basis for any claim of 'Vedic orthodoxy'.

In the chapter on Vedic religion, mention was made of the ideal of the orthodox, Vedic life. Taken in its most radical form, the teaching of the Upaniṣads would have to appear in direct contrast to the this-worldly ritual religion of earlier Vedic literature. Indeed, we still find traces of a conscious mockery of sacrifices to the *devas* expressed in some

Upaniṣads. The ideal of renunciation challenged all conceptions of a life, however 'pious', which included wealth, sexuality, a home and possessions. But the Upaniṣads did not just externally draw on Vedic speculation about the One and attach themselves to the Vedic *śākhās*. An internal decision was implied in this: that both religious attitudes could be combined. Eventually this was conceptualised as the four stages in a man's life (the *āśramas*), and somehow overlapping with this, as the four human goals (*puruṣārthas*). Together with the assumption of a fourfold division of society (the four *varṇas*), all this crystallised in the concept of *dharma*, a cosmic order which set the norms for human behaviour and action. Provided that a man belongs to one of the higher three *varṇas* (which means that he is a true 'Ārya'), his life should proceed in four stages. First there is a period of celibate studentship, dedicated to the study of the Vedas. Then follows marriage, enjoyment of sexuality, procreation of children and pursuit of wealth. After this, a gradual withdrawal from the world should begin, culminating in rejecting all ties with family and home and becoming a *saṃnyāsī*, a 'renouncer'. Whilst during the earlier stages Vedic ritual religion is appropriate, the quest for *brahman* along the lines of the Upaniṣads characterises the final stage. *Mokṣa* is now the only legitimate *puruṣārtha*; *dharma* (in the sense of Vedic religious activities), *artha* (pursuit of wealth) and *kāma* (sexuality) cease to be relevant. This general pattern is further differentiated according to the specific requirements made of the different *varṇas*. Thus a *brahmin*'s primary link is with *dharma* and religion, a *kṣatriya*'s with warfare, and a *vaiśya*'s with trade and agriculture. The *śūdra* is left out of all this; Vedic religion is not available to him, and only through serving the other three groups can he hope to be reborn into a *varṇa* where Vedic religion and *brahman* are cultivated. This is in a nutshell the conventional understanding of the (*varṇāśrama-*) *dharma*. A vast amount of critical, literary activity evolved around it in India. The very brief summaries of early discussions contained in the *Dharma-sūtras* were replaced by lengthy treatises, the *Dharma-śāstras*. The one attributed to Manu (from around the beginning of the Common Era?) is the most famous one. But other such treatises show that no final, positive definition of *dharma* in terms of universally accepted specific norms evolved. This remained an area of discussion and divergent views. But there are further restrictions on the application of this material to the real life. On the whole, this is normative thought, suggesting an ideal, not a social reality. As we shall see, Jainism and Buddhism reject all this outright, recommending renunciation exclusively. On the other hand, it is by no means the case that the tradition advocating *dharma* unanimously accepts the ideal of *mokṣa* or renunciation. Holding on to views from a period prior to the emergence of the renouncer traditions, many strands of the *dharma* literature advocate man's 'fulfilment' directly through the adherence to the three goals *dharma*, *artha* and *kāma* alone. Much more generally, the actual relevance even of beliefs in *saṃsāra* and *karma* was quite restricted. There is ample evidence in Hindu scriptures of later periods to suggest that such ideas were not necessarily always at the forefront of the religious consciouness.

Early Jainism

The figure of Prince Vardhamāna, who became the Mahāvīra ('great hero') and from whom Jainism takes its historical origin, leads us back into the sixth century BCE. There is evidence to suggest that at that time a religious community associated with the name of Pārśva was in existence and that Vardhamāna had some connection with it. Thus it is possible that Jainism has roots beyond the Mahāvīra in a strand of the renouncer tradition of the eighth century BCE or so. The extreme archaism of much of the teaching associated with his name would speak in favour of such an assumption. However, the history of Jainism begins with the Mahāvīra, and even in his case it is very difficult to distinguish between legend and history, and between his own teaching and that of later generations. For although the Jains possess an enormous amount of canonical and post-canonical scriptures, by their own testimony anything resembling a canon was only finalised in the fifth century CE, a thousand years after Vardhamāna's preaching.

What appears fairly certain is that in the sixth century BCE, in a region of eastern India which corresponds roughly to the modern state of Bihār, a prince called Vardhamāna renounced his life as a *kṣatriya* and householder, spent many years as a renouncer in search of liberation by exposing himself to almost impossible physical hardships, obtained the state of a Jina ('conqueror') and died after many years of preaching, at an age of at least seventy years. From this title *jina* are derived 'Jainism', for the religion initiated by the Jina, and 'Jaina' (or 'Jain' in its modern Hindi form), for his followers. The religious movement founded by the Mahāvīra has evinced a surprising continuity and coherence till the present day. Although it is today by no means as numerous and influential as it was during certain phases of its history and in certain regions of India (though never outside it), unlike Buddhism it survived the onslaught of Islam, and moreover, did not split into the great variety of different school traditions as did Buddhism. Only a single bifurcation occurred in the history of Jainism (around the first century CE), and even this effected only a relatively small area of disagreement. One branch maintained that monks must not wear any clothes—thus the title *digambara*, 'dressed in space', evolved. The other branch regarded this as excessive and allowed for the wearing of one 'white dress'—*śvetāmbara*. The latter tradition maintains that a sizeable amount of the Mahāvīra's teaching has been preserved and lists about 45, partly very extensive, scriptures as its canon. According to the Digambaras, all of the Jina's teaching has been lost in its original form and it is only available through the later writings of teachers like Umāsvāti and Kundakunda. But both believe that the tenets of Jainism derive from an omniscient being (the Mahāvīra) and thus doctrinally do not allow for any fundamental transformations and developments.

Although both Jainism and Buddhism originated in the same region of India at roughly the same time and reveal amazing similarities of detail, in essence we are dealing with very different religions. It has been suggested that this may be due to the very different personalities of the Buddha and the Mahāvīra, the latter appearing as austere, authoritarian and interested in philosophical discussion. But it is not the thought of the Upaniṣads that provides the background for that discussion; it is nature-philosophical speculation.

The Jains assume the existence of only one world system, and the archaism of their teaching reveals itself in the fact that even liberation is still located within it—at the very top of the universe. Below that are found a whole range of heavenly realms, then—as the central disc—the world of human beings, and finally subterranean realms and many layers of increasingly painful hells. This whole structure is filled with an infinite number of *jīvas*, 'souls', which except for the liberated ones at the very top are all embodied in some form or other (as *deva*, human being, animal, denizen of hells. This invisibly fine material *karma* enters the *jīva*, whenever an ordinary knowledge, power and happiness. But since eternity, the souls are caught up in *saṃsāra*, the cycle of rebirth. Here again the archaism of Jaina thought reveals itself, because the reason for the *jīva*'s entanglement in *saṃsāra*—also here styled *karma*—is actually conceived of as being loaded by heavy matter (*karma*) which pushes it downwards into the heavens, human world or even hells. This invisibly fine material *karma* enters the *jīva*, whenever an ordinary act—in thought, word and deed—is performed by an embodied being. Once inside a *jīva*, this *karma* in various degrees reduces or eliminates the innate characteristics of unlimited vision, knowledge, etc., stimulates further action by giving rise to desires and passions, and thus causes further rebirth. Later Jain scholasticism went to amazing lengths of spelling out a great variety of types of *kạrma* and their respective effects on the new embodiment. Some amount of *karma* inside a *jīva* is used up during a life-span of an individual, through his moments of happiness (positive *karma*) and sufferings (negative *karma*). But at the same time, more *karma* is thereby let into the *jīva*.

The outlines of Jain teaching on liberation are clear from this sketch: man (the other classes of embodied beings cannot do so) must attempt to ward off the influx of further *karma* by controlling all his actions, and to eliminate the *karma* already present inside the *jīva*, by burning it up, as it were. A strictly regulated ethical life followed by a check on all one's senses will weaken one's passions and desires and thus reduce the amount of *karma* flowing into the *jīva*. Ascetic practices (which in certain circumstances may go as far as starving oneself to death) serve as the fire to consume *karma* already present. Quite literally, one form of such *tapas* involves exposing oneself not just to the sun of the Indian summer, but adding to it by keeping fires burning all around oneself. When eventually the *jīva* has been cleansed by these means of all the *karma* filling it, no weight holds it down in this world of transmigration, and with its innate qualities fully realised, it moves into the realm of liberation, at the top of the universe, never to return into the world of matter.

Such an ideal is obviously designed for the full renouncer only. But in practice, allowances are made for the fact that *karma* may well prevent a full commitment to the Jain path. Thus Jainism has extended its programme to laymen and nuns, offering spiritual practices in preparation for a rebirth in which liberation becomes possible. But no allowances were made for brahmin ritualism and for the social structure and restrictions associated with it. Vedic rituals were rejected as useless, and the Jaina path was open to all, whatever their social background. With enormous zeal the Jains have from earliest times onwards developed the practical details of their spiritual path, from the moment a being becomes convinced of the truth of the Jain teaching to the achievement of final liberation. Thus for the laymen we find the five *aṇuvratas* (minor vows): not to kill, tell lies or steal, and to preserve marital faithfulness and put a restraint on possessions. *Guṇa-vratas* may be observed voluntarily: to avoid acts that could be harmful to living beings, impose restraints on one's travelling and eating, etc. The layman is brought even closer to the monastic life through the *śikṣāvratas* which involve often severe forms of fasting and sexual abstinence, all kinds of religious ceremonies and a commitment to supporting the monks.

With the monks, the *aṇuvratas* turn into the *mahāv-ratas*, the 'great vows', where marital fidelity is replaced by complete chas-tity. Many further lists of virtues to be cultivated and of spiritual practices are given. Among these, three may be mentioned in particular. The cultivation of *samiti*, 'carefulness', aims at eliminating all forms of unconscious or instinctive activity and producing a conscious awareness of everything one does. The twelve *anuprekṣās* are meditational exercises on set topics, such as the transience of beings, the impurity of the human body, the difficulty of gaining liberation and the supreme value of the Jain teaching. The practice of *parīsaha*, 'endurance', encourages the monk to become indifferent not only to relatively mild forms of tribulation like hunger, thirst, cold, insect bites and insults, but also to physical persecution and martyrdom. But everything listed so far primarily achieves merely the prevention of further *karma*. *Tapas* is the true means for the monk to burn up existing *karma*. Besides long periods of fasting, adopting painful physical postures and other means already mentioned above, *tapas* also includes meditation. However, unlike the Buddhists and also the Upaniṣads, the Jains emphasise the need for physical austerities, and it is regarded almost as a by-product that thereby mental effects (ultimately, the infinite knowledge of the *jīva*) are achieved.

This teaching is contained in the very bulky canon of the Śvetāmbaras. But even they agree that this canon no longer contains the oldest scriptures (*pūrvas*, which by both branches are associated with Pārśva).

The extant 45 or so works are gathered together in six groups (Aṅgas, Upāṅgas, Prakīrṇas, Chedasūtras, Mūlasūtras and two individual treatises). Cosmology and cosmography, with lists of the various beings populating this vast universe, are mixed with doctrinal and disciplinary matters. But many of these works illustrate a feature in which Jainism excels in later times: the telling of stories. Time and again abstract matters are given concrete application by showing how for specific individuals (legendary figures, the Mahāvīra himself, or imaginary persons) *karma* operates in real life. Most of the texts are in a form of Prakrit called by scholars Ardhamāgadhī. Though developed here as a literary language, it probably comes close to the actual language spoken by the Mahāvīra. For centuries, the Jains cultivated the Prakrits for literary purposes. Thus a slightly different Prakrit was employed by them for writing increasingly complex and voluminous commentaries on the canonical scriptures. Only towards the end of this enterprise was Sanskrit used. In turn, this commentarial literature is followed by the more systematic writings of the Jain philosophers. Umāsvāti (of the early centuries CE) is still accepted by both branches as authoritative. From his exposition of Jain teaching, two well-known schemas may be mentioned. The first is that of the five *astikāyas*, 'chunks of reality'. This consists of space, of movement (called *dharma*), of rest or obstruction (*adharma*), of the infinite number of souls (*jīvas*) and of *pudgalas* (material entities, in their smallest form *aṇus*, 'atoms'). From this list it is immediately obvious how 'realistic' or 'proto-scientific' the whole is conceived of. No world-soul (like the Upaniṣadic *brahman*) or transcendental reality outside space, time and matter is envisaged. The second schema summarises the essentials of Jain teaching on the path to liberation, in the form of the seven *tattvas* or fundamental truths. Here reality is simply divided into *jīva* and *ajīva*, the remaining four *astikāyas* which are insentient. The third *tattva* is that of *āsrava*, the 'influx' of material *karma* into the *jīva*, and the fourth (*bandha*) denotes the 'bondage' to *saṃsāra* effected thereby. With the fifth, *saṃvara* or 'warding off' of new *karma*, we enter the Jain path, to proceed with *nirjarā*, 'the removing' of existing *karma*. *Mokṣa*, 'liberation', signifies the final goal.

Jainism is manifestly a very austere religion with its emphasis on physical austerities and self-inflicted pains. At the same time, it is very rigid in its fundamental doctrinal framework. Nevertheless, in spite of these basic characteristics, Jainism has developed fully fledged cultural features, taking from and feeding back into the non-Jaina Indian cultural and religious scene. However, most of these developments belong to a later age, and thus will be taken up in a separate section below.

Early Buddhism

Another religion which grew out of the fertile ground of the renouncer tradition is perhaps the most important one in the context of Asian religious history: Buddhism, the teaching of Siddhārtha, the Buddha. There cannot be any doubt about his historicity, although the precise details of his life are lost in the jungle of later hagiographies. Still, it seems likely that he lived his long life during the sixth and fifth centuries BCE in north-eastern India, that he was of *kṣatriya* descent, that he abandoned his home and family to search for a means to liberation, that he believed he had succeeded in this at the moment of his 'enlightenment' and that he spent the rest of his life teaching others about it.

Later generations felt this to be a far too lifeless account, and a variety of 'lives' of the Buddha appeared which in ever-increasing detail filled in concrete 'biographical' incidents. Moreover, these versions widened the scope and surrounded the specific life-story with all kinds of cosmological and religious features. Thus works like Aśvaghoṣa's *Buddhacarita* and the anonymous *Lalitavistara* and *Mahāvastu* do not merely narrate a story, but spell out in popularly accessible narrative terms their individual perception of Buddhism. Naturally, when the Buddha is presented as spending his early years till well after his marriage in the utmost luxury and pleasure, this highlights the alluring charm of ordinary life. When he then, out of curiosity, explores the wòrld outside the palace walls and encounters an old man, a sick man and a corpse, in a most striking and immediate manner it is shown that ordinary life is characterised by old age, illness and death. Or when we hear that Siddhārtha tried yoga with two brahmin teachers and then practised severe asceticism which brought him to the verge of death, yet found both methods unsatisfactory, this can be interpreted as a self-definition of Buddhism in relation to other movements in the renouncer tradition. It calls itself the 'middle way' which avoids the excesses of self-indulgence and fanatical asceticism. It is not difficult to see in the latter a reference to Jain *tapas*, and in the former an allusion to the easygoing, almost corrupt pretences of self-satisfied brahmin religion. As we have seen above, there may even be some historical truth in this, for both the brahmin and the Jain concern for meditation and asceticism appear to have preceded the life of the Buddha by two or so centuries. This must have affected the interpretation of Buddhism: as a relatively late phenomenon in the renouncer tradition, it could survey the spectrum of teachings already available. And in a sense it wanted to transcend and synthesise the various alternatives that were on offer. Certainly early Buddhist teaching is more abstract and 'modern' by comparison with that of Jainism and the early Upaniṣads. The same feature makes it that much more difficult to understand.

Two key periods in the life of the Buddha attracted the attention of his followers initially. One was Siddhārtha's enlightenment (*bodhi*) which transformed him into a *buddha*, an 'enlightened one'. This event is the most central aspect of the whole of Buddhism. For not only was this the point at which Siddhārtha personally achieved liberation, not only was this the source of his insight into the nature of reality, it was also the event that propelled him into teaching and thereby offering to others the same enlightenment. The second key period is that of the last few months before his death. Its importance derives from the need of the young community to define its institutional structures. Apparently the Buddha refused to appoint a successor, claiming that just as the goal of *bodhi* was the same for all, all followers of his were the same and all decisions had to be made by them in unison. This resulted in a religious history remarkably different from that of Jainism. Whilst the latter adhered to far more rigid structures, Buddhism developed a wide spectrum of interpretations of the Buddha's teaching and also of different social groups of Buddhists advocating them. Again, this great flexibility and variety adds to the difficulties in understanding 'Buddhism'.

The reconstruction of earliest Buddhist teaching is fraught with difficulties. A large number of Indian sources relevant to this task have been lost over the centuries, and this fact would naturally strengthen claims by the sole direct survivor of ancient Indian Buddhism, the Theravāda of Ceylon (Sri Lanka) to be the only legitimate, 'orthodox' form of Buddhism. A relatively recent scholarly interest in the fragments of the Indian material which have survived, and a more critical, unbiased look at other traditions outside India, suggest that such a simplistic picture of orthodox versus distorted Buddhism will have to be altered considerably. What follows here is a tentative sketch of what in the light of this might be regarded as the earliest Buddhist teaching.

Hagiography tells us that the key theme of the Buddha's first sermon was that of the Four Noble Truths. It is not difficult to regard this schema as central to Buddhist teaching generally. Modelled on ancient Indian medical procedure, it provides a critical analysis of the human situation, investigates the causes of the 'disease', states that a cure is possible and prescribes the medicine for it. It does not, however, present any theoretical framework for its pragmatic procedure, no definition of 'what it means to be healthy' (in terms of the medical model). And whilst it emphasises very strongly that there is an illness, that is, 'suffering' (thereby giving rise to an initial appearance of depressing negativism), it regards true happiness (the liberation from this 'suffering') as a self-evident phenomenon. We shall return to this attitude at a later stage.

The First Noble Truth states that there is 'suffering' (*duḥkha*, Pali: *dukkha*). Most evidently it reveals itself in the painful events of birth, illness, old age and death. Implied in this is also the assumption of rebirth, the endlessly repeated occurrence of these events. It is further implied that all beings are involved in it, man as much as animals and *devas*. Yet outside these events life is also characterised by 'suffering': to be with what we do not want, not to be with what we want, in short, every wish unfulfilled, is *duḥkha*. To this is added one further component which makes it clear that we are not just dealing with 'aspects' of life, but with its essential nature. To be a person is identical with 'suffering'. Such a person is now analysed in terms of five major layers or interacting components, 'the elements of grasping' (*upādāna-skandhas*). On the most superficial level one could say that 'suffering' is experienced in all five, or 'in thought, word and deed'. But more is alluded to through this schema. These five components want to describe the empirical person, and that in terms spelled out more clearly in the Second Noble Truth. With that focus in mind, the picture of the 'person' would look like this. There is the physical side, the body (*rūpa*, lit. 'form'). This body is endowed with the sense-organs, and through these information about the outside world is received. But man is not a computer which mechanically absorbs data. Thus this information 'affects' him, namely acquires an affective, emotional colouring. This is *vedanā*, 'emotions'. Since the senses inform us through five different channels, offering us (affectively coloured) visual, aural, etc. data, all this is put together into one composite whole, a single mental image associated with the corresponding sights, sounds and so forth (*saṃjñā*). Moreover, all kinds of additional assumptions are made with regard to such a perceived object, partly due to the influences of past *karma*. Then the will reacts, by setting in motion an act of reaching out to acquire or enjoy the object, or to reject and destroy, depending on the decision we have made as to the positive or negative qualities of the object. All this is summed up in the term *saṃskāra*. Finally, these are not mechanical processes, for we are aware of all this and constantly impose thoughts on to them, associating them with an (autonomous) 'I'. This is *vijñāna*.

The Second Noble truth mentions the cause of suffering: we suffer because we relate to objects in precisely the manner indicated above. We 'thirst' (the keyword used in this context, *tṛṣṇā*, Pali: *taṇhā*) for the enjoyment of objects that appeal to us, and by implication hate those that do not. But there is one further implication here, which alone makes sense of this analysis: no object in human experience can actually provide the happiness we hope for when desiring its enjoyment. Thus even if every wish of ours were kept being fulfilled, we would still continue to desire more. This now implies a form of ignorance, and it is indeed through such a concept (*avidyā*) that the Second Noble Truth is expanded. Again, this 'ignorance' can be specified as concerning the understanding a person has of what he is and what he could gain from any object. This means that the acquisition of any desired object would only make sense if it could add something lasting to someone lasting. But, empirically, no such 'lasting' entities are found. All five *upādāna-skandhas* are transient (thought, *vijñāna*, appears and disappears most rapidly among them). So the whole way we react to the world and perceive ourselves is mistaken. These three interrelated ideas (desire, ignorance, incorrect conception of 'I' and 'mine') are summarised as the three *āsravas*. Because of the three *āsravas* operating in the person, life is suffering.

Now in the context of renouncer thought, this is not yet a sufficient explanation. For 'life' here implies transmigration. Can the analysis of the Second Noble Truth be applied to this idea as well? This appears to be the purpose of another schema, variously known as 'conditioned origination', 'dependent co-production', etc. (*pratītya-samutpāda*). The title is symptomatic of its abstruseness. We are given a list of twelve concepts, starting with *avidyā*, 'ignorance'. The following two, *saṃskāra* and *vijñāna*, are already known to us. The fourth, *nāma-rūpa*, denotes the person (and in that sense is synonymous with the five *skandhas*). The fifth, 'the six spheres', concentrates on the sense-organs of such a person, which are in 'contact' (*sparśa*) with the outside world. Due to this, *vedanā*, and in turn *tṛṣṇā*, arise. As the ninth element, *upādāna* is mentioned. This 'grasping' conditions *bhava* ('conception of a foetus'), birth, and—as the twelfth—old age, death, grief, lament, suffering, depression and despair. The rationale of the whole list is: if such and such a phenomenon occurs (say, 'ignorance'), then it follows inevitably that the subsequent phenomenon will also occur (thus, *saṃskāras*). Now we have encountered above a dual interpretation of the cause of suffering: as 'desire' and 'ignorance'; and both terms reappear in the list. Moreover, the list seems to refer twice to the whole person (with *nāma-rūpa* and, indirectly, 'birth'). In view of this, the following interpretation may be the most original one among the traditional analyses of the list of twelve conditions. It is first shown how rebirth occurs with the concept of 'ignorance' as starting-point; then the same processes are once again described, but with 'desire' as the focal point and with different subsequent terms. But later Buddhist traditions evolved a whole range of different interpretations. The complexity of such a description of *saṃsāra* is partly due to the fact that here once again no reference to anything lasting in the 'person' (as defined by the five *skandhas*) is made. Transmigration is described merely as a chain of interconnected, transient processes which continuously yield suffering.

The Third Noble Truth simply states that it is possible to get out of this vicious circle of constantly desiring true happiness and yet constantly being thrown back into suffering. Thus, at this point, Buddhism turns cheerful and optimistic. The Fourth Noble Truth spells out the method by which liberation can be achieved. In view of what has been said above, the principles can be predicted: the eradication of desire and ignorance. This is presented as the Noble Eightfold Path. Various interpretations of it have evolved in Buddhist reflection, but the following might be the most original. The whole is a map of the spiritual path which Buddhism is advocating. We start with that initial moment when someone hears the Buddhist teaching and is struck by how sensible it all appears. Thus he feels inclined to commit himself to it and enter the path laid out in front of him. (This would be the first two stages: correct insight and resolve.) Then follow steps on the path which are basically ethical and ascetic, clearly intended to eradicate desire. A beginning is made with 'correct speech', which is followed by 'correct conduct' (*śīla*). Buddhism has formulated four or five primary ethical rules: not to harm any living being, not to steal, not to commit sexual misdemeanour (which in the case of the monk turns into total sexual abstinence) and not to tell lies and insults. To this was added a prohibition of intoxicants. These five make up the *pañca-śīla*, 'fivefold conduct'. At a certain point, the rejection of various professions is enjoined ('correct livelihood'). For example, to make a living out of hunting or being a soldier would be irreconcilable with the ideal of not harming any creature.

After 'correct effort' the path moves out of the life of a layman into that of the fully committed Buddhist, the monk. Ethic is here complemented by meditational exercises, alluded to by 'correct mindfulness (*smṛti*, Pali: *sati*)' and 'correct meditation (*dhyāna*, Pali: *jhāṇa*)', designed to overcome ignorance. Detailed information on the structure and rationale of Buddhist meditation techniques can be found in the old scriptures. Rather surprisingly perhaps, no major differences appear in a comparison with what Hindu yoga traditions have to offer. After appropriate moral preparation, the first exercises involve the cultivation of positive mental attitudes. Then a radical awareness (*smṛti*) of all one's thoughts, words and deeds is aimed at which intends to eradicate unconscious attitudes, instincts and prejudices. In this connection may be mentioned an exercise called 'application of mindfulness' (*smṛtyupasthāna*). First the body, then the emotions and the mind (*citta*), and finally all empirical phenomena are meditated upon as transient and lacking any kind of lasting inner core. This leads over to an increase of the concentrative faculties and mental clarity, and the mind now reaches out into higher states of consciousness (*dhyāna*). Ultimately this allows for the direct perception of the Buddhist teaching as true, of the nature of reality, and of the chain of causes and effects that have resulted, after innumerable rebirths, in the current existence. Alongside these insights, the experience of true happiness occurs, for suffering has been overcome and there will be no further return into its realm. Liberation has been achieved. Whether presented to us in the hagiography about the Buddha's own enlightenment or in the texts talking about Buddhist meditation, this is the content of the culmination of the Buddhist path.

This is, in a nutshell, the teaching implied in the Four Noble Truths and, in a sense, of early Buddhism. But we have to remind ourselves that it appears within the renouncer tradition, and in fact at a relatively late stage. Thus we may assume that this teaching comments in a variety of ways on the thought available at the time and defines itself in relation to it. It clearly shares with many of the other renouncers a total rejection of the Vedic religious system. The possibility of achieving enlightenment and liberation is latent in every man, and thus Buddhism addresses itself to all. To restrict true religious knowledge to a small minority, to have an elite guard the access to it and to claim that it is available only through a revealed corpus of sacred, equally well-guarded scriptures—all this appears to Buddhism as a parody of true religion. Now given the fact that a metaphysical framework of liberation which involved concepts like '*ātman*' and '*brahman*' inevitably had ideological connotations (as shown above), this is one reason why early Buddhism would find it difficult to adopt a similar framework. Furthermore, it did not want to accept the idea of an individual, permanent 'soul' or *jīva*, as found for instance with Jainism. The observable transience of all phenomena suggested to them the absence of a lasting, inner core in man. Whatever other reasons there may have been, the Buddhists decided to take a strictly empirical and pragmatic line and reject all speculation about the nature of a soul, a self, an *ātman* or a *jīva*, as unproductive. If it makes sense to assume the all-pervasive presence of suffering, the only logical conclusion to draw from this is the need for a practical course of action. To eradicate suffering by removing desire and ignorance is the only legitimate task; to sit back and speculate would be a fatal waste of time.

The absence of any explicit teaching about metaphysical issues like the existence of a 'soul' or some such inner core in man and the nature of the state of liberation has created considerable consternation not just among Western scholars, but also among Indian thinkers outside, and indeed inside, the Buddhist tradition. In fact, it could be argued that the subsequent history of Buddhist thought is no more than a struggle to interpret this Buddhist teaching and the nature of the Buddha himself (which implies, the nature of anyone 'enlightened') more in terms of a philosophical system. But such a turn to metaphysical speculation had very practical implications for the religious life. Given the absence of any centralised authority or initial metaphysical doctrines, there was obviously enormous scope for a great variety of positions to emerge. It is here where Jainism and Buddhism differ radically.

Perhaps not surprisingly, the charge of 'nihilism' was levelled against the Buddha's teaching. But if the Buddhist goal had been to overcome suffering by plunging into a total 'nothing', it would have been easy enough for the Buddha to say so. Instead we find frequent statements in which early Buddhism explicitly distances itself from 'nihilism' (which was indeed preached by some of the renouncers). An episode is told in which the Buddha was asked directly whether he accepted the existence of a soul or not. He kept silent. Afterwards he explained himself. Had he said yes, his teaching would have been interpreted as similar to those schools of thought that postulated an eternal soul (e.g. the Jains). Had he said no, it would have made no sense to the person who had asked the question. In short, neither answer would have served any spiritual purpose. Or here is another illustration of this practical orientation. If a man were hit by a poisoned arrow, he would not waste his time asking who shot the arrow, whether he was fat or slim, what his family background was, what kind of bow was used and so on.

Instead he would try to find a doctor as soon as possible. *Vis-à-vis* the fundamental fact of suffering, not metaphysical speculation but spiritual practice is urgently required. Then we have an episode where the metaphor of a burning fire is compared to earthly existence. It can be defined in terms of its place and of the time it burns, and also of its material causes (the fuel). But once it has gone out, such qualifications cannot apply any more. By 'gone out' the contemporary audience may well have understood that it has merged back into the amorphous, latent state of the cosmological element, fire. This seems to suggest that once the Buddha (and by implication, any enlightened being) has died, all qualifications in terms of space, time, matter, name, etc. do not apply any more. Like the ocean, he has become unfathomable and unchartable. If all this meant simply 'nothing', this would be dreadfully roundabout and verbose. After all, enlightenment is a totally fulfilling experience; it implies the happiness of knowing that suffering has been destroyed, or 'blown out'. The word *nirvāṇa*, which does mean 'blowing out', need not be pressed to refer to annihilation in an ontological or metaphysical sense. It is perfectly sufficient to read it as referring to the annihilation of the three *āsravas*, that is, ignorance, etc. The very fact that such an experience is possible implies that it takes place somewhere. It can certainly not be in *vijñāna* (as defined above), the most fleeting of the *skandhas*. Where else it could be is not stated; only when we come to Mahāyāna Buddhism will attempts at answering this question be found.

By making these ideas available to others and evolving concrete structures within society, the Buddha's teaching became a religion. He is presented to us as extremely sociable, and adaptable to a great variety of audiences. Here, in his attitude towards ordinary people, the principle of the 'golden middle' is applied. He is said to have succeeded in recruiting a large following from a great variety of backgrounds. The predominant lifestyle they adopted seems to have been, at least initially, that of the homeless, itinerant mendicant. What better way of backing up one's meditations about the transience of all things than by leading such an unsettled life, which brings one in contact with all kinds of people? However, like the Jains, the early Buddhists did not insist on an either/or decision. They accepted that in many cases people would benefit from closer contact with the mendicants without actually joining them. Thus we have the category of lay followers. The most obvious difference between the two groups lies in total sexual abstinence for the mendicant and a strictly regulated sexual life within his marriage for the layman. There seems to have been a certain reluctance to allow women to 'renounce', but eventually this became possible, although such 'nuns' were always kept in an inferior position. Thus, like the Jain community, the Buddhist one consists of four components: *bhikṣu* and *bhikṣuṇī*, *upāsaka* and *upāsikā*. Whilst the laymen provide the mendicants with their, theoretically meagre, requirements (simple food, an occasional ochre robe, etc.), the mendicants in return preach the Buddha's *Dharma*—his teaching—to them, to prepare them for a full commitment to the spiritual path in a later rebirth.

From early times onwards, settled monastic life provided an institutional alternative to homeless mendicancy. This monasticism seems to have started as a result of the Indian weather. Heavy downpours during the three months of the rainy season make travelling on foot almost impossible. Thus for these three months even the mendicants remained in one place. As a result of the laymen's zeal in showing their appreciation through lavish donations towards the construction of proper edifices for these 'rain retreats', and presumably also due to the temptations of a life more comfortable than the homeless wandering, the period expanded, until in the end mendicants remained the whole year in these new homes.

Sedentary monasticism stimulated the development of monastic ethics and of rules governing the communal life. At the very basis of these rules lie the ethical presuppositions of the renouncer tradition generally. But in the emphasis on intention, as opposed to a mechanistic conception of moral behaviour (more typical of the Jains), we may well sense the influence of the Buddha. Such rules were initially formulated as the *prātimokṣa*, a catalogue or litany of monastic injunctions. It has been suggested that the *prātimokṣa* was originally linked with the fortnightly communal meetings in the monasteries, acting as the 'confessional mirror' each monk had to confront. Any infringement of the rules had to be confessed, and the appropriate penance be done. Eventually, then, a full system of monastic ethics evolved, in which each rule was elaborately defined in terms of its range of application. This then is the *Vinaya*. The more than 200 rules are divided into seven groups of graded severity. Four injunctions are essential; a violation of any of them will result in the permanent expulsion from the monastic community. They are: sexual intercourse, theft, killing and the proclamation of superhuman faculties. All remaining injunctions allow for atonement. With group seven the rules are so peripheral to Buddhist spiritual discipline that they are no more than guide-lines for good manners (like not licking the fingers while eating).

Thus the *Vinaya* inculcates ethical attitudes, while at the same time it lays down precise rules for the monk's behaviour both inside and outside the monastery. In theory the whole *Vinaya* is subordinate to two other major responsibilities: to pursue one's liberation and to preach the Buddha's *Dharma*. But given the *Vinaya*'s complexity, in practice it might well have usurped central importance in the minds of many a monk. To observe the rules would in that case have become the primary spiritual goal. It will be seen below (in the section on the Mahāyāna) that certain critics at least assumed the existence of such an attitude.

Parallel to the evolution of monasticism and a complex monastic rule went another development, namely the formulation of the Buddha's teaching. What the Buddha taught was not written down, nor was it turned into a literary corpus like the Vedas. It emerged in the context of formal and informal public addresses, to a great variety of audiences and over a long period (traditionally, forty years). It seems reasonable to assume that the Buddha did not 'compose' a totally new sermon for each of the thousands of occasions when he preached. Instead, a fair number of 'repertoire pieces' of teaching must have evolved over the years. Now many of his disciples would have listened to hundreds and thousands of such sermons (*sūtras*, Pali: *suttas*). Key ideas, recurring patterns, typical structures and such repertoire pieces must have engrained themselves deeply in their memories. Thus there is no need to doubt that even some generations after the Buddha's death the essence of his teaching, in that form, was still available, though obviously very little of it verbatim. Again, it seems likely that efforts were made at certain stages to co-ordinate and regulate the available store of such memories and weed out the inevitable apocryphal material. Yet it is highly unlikely that the whole of the Buddhist movement could remain involved in such efforts, as the generations since the Buddha passed by; the geographical spread of Buddhism was far too wide for that. What is important here is the fact that we cannot assume the existence of some 'original Buddhist canon'. Instead, there is sufficient evidence to suggest that a variety of such Buddhist canons evolved only gradually, in a variety of Buddhist communities belonging to different geographical areas. It seems that the Buddha himself laid the basis for this proliferation, by preventing the creation of a 'canon' (in Sanskrit) of his teaching. Just as the teaching was delivered in the vernacular, his disciples conceptualised it and preached it by means of their respective vernaculars. But the fact that Buddhism (and its literatures) disappeared from India around 1200 CE gave rise to a rather different impression of this situation. The only 'complete' canon that has come down to us belongs to the Buddhist tradition of Ceylon (Sri Lanka). It appears that during the third or second century BCE settlers from central north India brought their Buddhism to this island. Pali was the vernacular in which the Buddhist teaching had been retained by them, and it remained the language of Buddhist learning long after texts began to be written down. But Pali was not the Buddha's mother tongue. Fragments of other 'canons' in other Indian vernaculars testify to the existence of traditions outside the Pali one. None, however, are written in what must be assumed to have been the Buddha's native language, some form of Māgadhī.

Besides the *Vinaya* and the sermons on *Dharma*, early Buddhist literature knows of a third component, the *Abhidharma*. It grew out of reflections on the sermons and did not attempt to present itself as the direct teaching of the Buddha. Thus we are dealing here with a relatively late literary product. Earliest Buddhism refrained from presenting its teaching in any systematic or metaphysical framework. The *Abhidharma* in a sense attempts to fill this gap. It is difficult to say what its original intentions were. It could have been the need to provide structured guidance for meditation, or to justify Buddhist ideas philosophically, or simply the temptation to draw on fashionable intellectual discussions and provide a Buddhist position in them. Whatever the precise circumstances may have been, the *Abhidharma* develops a systematic view of the world, man and his destiny. The key concept is that of the *dharmas* (not to be confused with the *Dharma*, the Buddhist teaching, or the Hindu concept). The whole of reality is cut up into *dharmas*, that is the smallest possible units. As far as matter is concerned, we obtain 'form-*dharmas*', of different kinds corresponding to the different elements earth, water, fire, etc. These would be the atoms of other schools of Indian thought. But similarly emotions, volition, thinking, etc. are also dissected into 'feeling-*dharmas*' etc. Here typically Buddhist ideas are now employed. All *dharmas*, of whatever kind, are characterised by three interrelated features: they are transient, lack an inner permanent core or essence and are suffering. These are the *tri-lakṣaṇas* (triple characteristics) *anitya*, *anātman* and *duḥkha*. That anything which is transient cannot be regarded as possessing some permanent substance, and in turn cannot therefore be approached as providing true happiness—these are old Buddhist ideas. But to have it applied to all *dharmas* is new. Not only that: 'transience' itself is radically redefined. Every *dharma* lasts but a moment, to be replaced by a similar one the next moment. The three *āsravas* (naturally also made up of *dharmas*) account for this replacement and thus for continuity in time. Only one *dharma* is not conditioned in this manner, and that is *nirvāṇa*. Such ideas were developed in the various treatises which together make up the *Abhidharma* and in the commentaries on them.

These now are the three basic categories (or 'baskets', *piṭaka*) of Buddhist 'canonical' literature: *Vinaya*, *Sūtra* (also called *Dharma*) and *Abhidharma*. However, as a culture Buddhism produced a variety of further literary works which found their way into the 'canon' (in the Pali, as the 'miscellaneous section' of the *Sutta-piṭaka*). Here we find among others a collection of ethical maximes (*Dharma-pada*, Pali: *Dhamma-pada*), poems by early monks and nuns (*Thera-* and *Therī-gāthās*), stories about the Buddha's previous existences (*Jātakas*) and poems, partly very ancient, on the spiritual path (*Suttanipāta*).

So far the emphasis has been on 'learned' and monastic Buddhism. We do, however, possess evidence also for developments outside the monasteries, among the laymen of the Buddhist community. Thus with striking immediacy one of the last Maurya emperors, Aśoka, speaks to us through his inscriptions (third century BCE). The Buddhist *Dharma* to him is clearly a humanitarian ethic, a concern for the well-being of people and also of animals. No philosophy, no meditation and no monastic institutions are referred to. Besides these inscriptions, we have from roughly the same period architectural remnants, the *stūpas* (or *caityas*) of Sāñchī, Bhārhūt, Amarāvatī, and so on. In origin, a *stūpa* is a burial mound for nobles of pre-Buddhist north-eastern India. Its role in Buddhism is not well defined. Legend says that portions of the Buddha's ashes were kept on top of the hemispherical structure. In terms of normative Buddhism, a visit to these sites could be no more than a reminder of the Buddhist spiritual ideal. But there must have been at work a strong popular cult as well, which approached the *stūpa* in a different way. It is clear that acts of worship were performed here, very much like what went on in popular village religion, with offerings of flowers and incense, and with music and dance. The *Vinaya* would prohibit monks participating in these rituals. Since no literary documents about these religious practices are known (though some connection with aspects of Mahāyāna Buddhist literature has been suggested), it is impossible to say what precisely the religious content could have been. For some people participating, the Buddha may well have been like a *deva*, but the more sophisticated participants must have envisaged the nature of the Buddha and his relationship with the *stūpa* cult in some other, more typically Buddhist, manner. What is important is to realise that, from an early period onwards, Buddhism expresses itself not merely as a monastic system, but as a religion with decidedly popular aspects.

Buddhism spread over India very rapidly, and by the second or first century BCE we can assume its presence in most Indian regions (including Ceylon/Sri Lanka and what today is Pakistan). Inevitably, regional variations developed. Moreover, we have the variations in terms of monastic versus laymen's and popular Buddhism. Thirdly, there is the initial absence of a rigid authority. If one takes these three features into account, it is not difficult to envisage earlier Indian Buddhism as an extremely dynamic and multifarious religion. However, there is another side to this. Such a fluid and dynamic scene has the potential for all kinds of tensions and disagreements. Some of these must have been about doctrinal issues, others about details of the monastic discipline; some could involve an ideological struggle between monastic institutions and laymen, and yet others may well be neutral, merely regional variations observable only to the traveller. The evidence available, however fragmented and ambivalent it may be, is sufficient to show that all these dynamic developments cannot be explained merely in terms of a series of 'councils' and consequent 'schisms'.

Inevitably such variety is interpreted for us through the eyes of Sri Lankan Buddhism which naturally presents itself as the single 'orthodox' tradition. Besides, its relative isolation from Indian developments allowed it to preserve a fairly 'archaic' appearance. But it must not be forgotten that the Pali canon began to be written down only around 100 BCE, and that only around 400 CE was a final corpus and its definitive interpretation established. Of the other 'sects', we know in most cases little more than their names. Moreover, it is far from clear what the rationale of such nomenclature may have been. In many cases we may be dealing merely with titles used by a regional group of Buddhists (of whatever doctrinal and disciplinary persuasion). Sometimes such a name itself created the idea of a 'heterodox' position.

One group in central India called itself the *Lokottara-vādins*. This title has been interpreted to mean 'transcendentalists' and became associated with the idea that these Buddhists believed in a supernatural (or quasi-divine) Buddha-figure. However, one of their canonical scriptures, the *Mahāvastu*, has been preserved, and an unbiased study of the text yields a different picture. This 'life-story' of the Buddha presents him indeed as capable of deeds far beyond the potential of ordinary human beings. But then he was indeed special. As the many *jātaka* stories included in the *Mahāvastu*, and the text as a whole, make clear, he was a being who over many past existences accumulated an enormous store of *puṇya* (positive *karma*). Inevitably a person who can draw on such a store will be able to do things well 'beyond what is possible to ordinary people' (this is an alternative translation of *lokottara*).

Traditionally, the first schism occurred between the *sthaviras*, the advocates of 'orthodoxy', and monks, and the *mahāsaṅghikas*. The latter term has variously been interpreted, for instance as 'the majority' or 'those believing in a wider community' (that is including laymen). The Pali for *sthavira* is *thera*, and thus Sri Lankan Buddhism presents itself as the direct continuation of that *sthavira-* or *thera-vāda*, the 'teaching of the elders'. It does, however, acknowledge a variety of 'sectarian' offshoots from its own 'mainstream' lineage. From some of these, like the *Sarvāsti-vāda* (the 'teaching that everything exists'), some literature has been preserved. Details on most of the further varieties of the *Mahāsaṅghika* are not available. But in terms of historical importance, this whole discussion of Indian sectarian developments is relatively insignificant, when compared with a very different kind of internal argument, which eventually crystallised as the Mahāyāna and the Hīnayāna. This will be discussed in a later section.

Obviously, the spread of Buddhism was partly due to direct missionary activity: mendicants travelling far and wide and preaching the *Dharma*. But in addition we must also envisage movements of whole groups of people, on a large scale. In some instances, this may have been due to banishment on account of disputes. But in most cases this was just part of the general spread of 'Aryan' people over the sub-continent. As new Aryan kingdoms were created in 'frontier regions' (like Āndhra and Ceylon/Sri Lanka during the third century BCE or the Tamil country somewhat later), they attracted groups of immigrants, and these included Buddhists. But it was relatively rare in India for a king to profess openly to be following Buddhism; Aśoka seems to have been very much the exception. This was different in Sri Lanka, where up to the present day Buddhism has been able to enjoy the patronage of the ruling power, in an uninterrupted line.

Epic and Purāṇic Religion

With the spread of Aryan culture over the whole of India, Vedic religion could establish itself as the most prestigious superstructure for most of the social groups affected by it. But at the same time, during this expansion an enormous range of other forms of religion was encountered, which in turn stimulated new syntheses of a staggering variety. It is not easy to survey or order this mass of material. That the global title of 'Hinduism' has been given to it must be regarded as an act of pure despair. In the context of the present survey of the Indian religions, three major aspects may be distinguished very tentatively: popular theism, sophisticated systematisations and esoteric and antinomian movements. The present section attempts to explore the first aspect, whilst the remaining two will be dealt with further below. Because this popular theism has found its primary textual expression in the genre of the Purāṇas, and on a more limited scale in the Epics, it may be referred to as epic-purāṇic religion. Since the literary situation is particularly complex, it appears justified to deal with it separately at the beginning. This is followed by a discussion of the typically epic-purāṇic gods and also of the emergence of a God-concept. A third section will look at typical modes of expressing devotion to these divine beings, and at the 'Hindu' religious life generally.

The Epic-Purāṇic Literature

To say that the brahmin's role in Indian society (which naturally excluded to some extent social enclaves like the Jains and the Buddhists) was defined by taking care of the religious needs of people does not actually restrict religion itself to what the brahmin had to offer. In other words, the brahmin's religion—however prestigious and normative it may be in itself—is only one expression of ancient Indian religion. Precisely because other types of religion were current even in early Aryan society, brahmin religion remained flexible, fluid and integrative. The brahmin received and moulded all kinds of religion which thereby acquired respectability and social standing.

Where now were such other types found, who were their guardians and what was their content? Given the state of our knowledge about ancient India, such questions are not easy to answer. We may begin by shifting our focus away from the brahmin to the members of the second class (*varṇa*), the *kṣatriyas* or warriors. This may take us by surprise, for we would not immediately suspect the existence of additional types of religion in this social group. But already the Upaniṣads showed a number of cases where a brahmin approached a *kṣatriya* for information on *brahman*. And although both the Mahāvīra and the Buddha opted out of their conventional lives, they did so as members of *kṣatriya* clans. These initial considerations can be complemented by the following points.

We must imagine the political situation in northern India during the first half of the last millennium BCE to have been extremely loose and undefined. Scattered all over the region were pockets and enclaves of Aryan settlements, which were particularly dense in the area known as the Āryāvarta. This is the region between the rivers Jumna and Ganges in central north India, and somewhat further east along the Ganges. To say that Aryan society was split up into various 'tribes' would give rise to confusion, in so far as we have used the word 'tribe' to denote indigenous peoples outside the Aryan influence. To speak of 'nations' or 'states' would introduce an anachronism, since it suggests a centralisation of political control and a solidity of the political unit that began to emerge only from the fifth century BCE onwards. Perhaps the word 'clan' may be used here. Whatever the precise status of the rulers of these clans may have been, these 'kings' (*rājas*) maintained courts and a court culture. In a world that was surrounded and pervaded by non-Aryan peoples, an awareness of a common Aryan bond was cultivated by the clans, not least through marriage ties binding together different 'royal courts'. But central to our discussion is the role of the *sūta*, the royal bard.

This bard was the professional expert in epic literature, or better, epic culture. Naturally, this included an element of public entertainment; but he also conveyed learning of all kinds in subjects useful to a ruler and his court. Above all, it was an important means of maintaining the awareness of the common Aryan bond between the clans, and of spelling out the position of the dynasties in the history of the world. And it is this last mentioned characteristic which accounts for the fact that the literature which eventually evolved from these bardic performances must be considered to be one of the most important textual documents of the Indian religions, particularly Hinduism. Conventionally this literature is referred to as the Epics and the Purāṇas, but how it came about is quite a long and complicated story. The following is a tentative summary of it.

Like the Vedic literature, the performances of the royal bards were not written down, at least not for many centuries. But unlike the Vedic counterpart, we are not dealing here with fixed material that was transmitted in a meticulously accurate and verbatim form. But it was certainly not the case that every bard, at every performance, made up the whole. Instead we must assume a number of thematic cycles, each one at least in outline fixed. In addition there were 'skeleton stanzas' which the bard knew by heart and around which he could improvise his narrative. Of particular importance in the history of Indian religion were four such thematic cycles, two involving all the clans, and the other two being originally purely local. Thus we have cycle A which deals with the memories, surely partly historical, of a particularly devastating war which two rival groups of Aryan clans fought. The cause of this war was a controversy over dynastic succession, and its extremely destructive outcome left deep wounds in the people's memories. We hear about two groups of cousins, the five Pāṇḍavas (including Yudhiṣṭhira and Arjuna) and the hundred Kauravas (led by Duryodhana). The former are the rightful heirs to the kingship, but lose in a game of dice their title (and common wife) for a number of years. It is when their period of exile has come to an end that the Kauravas' obstinacy in holding on to royal power necessitates the devastating war. The Pāṇḍavas do win, but it is a painful victory in view of the large-scale bloodshed.

Cycle B was primarily concerned with the genealogies of the various Aryan dynasties and the heroic deeds of outstanding members of them. The intention here was clearly to offer the kind of reference which, in theory, should make bloodshed over dynastic disputes unnecessary. Moreover, a wider frame is provided here for the histories of the Aryan kings. Not only did the clans intermarry, but their common origins were traced back to the very beginning of the world, to the first man, Manu. This offered in turn the opportunity to deal with such religious matters as the 'creation' of the world itself, its evolution and its final destiny.

Cycle C takes us to the town of Ayodhyā (near the modern Oudh); again the central theme is that of dynastic dispute over succession. But elements comparable to those of the fairy-tale are also mixed into it. Due to a promise made by the king to one of his minor queens, his son Rāma, although the legitimate heir to the throne, has to go with his wife Sītā into exile. During this stay in the forest, Sītā is abducted by an ogre Rāvaṇa. Accompanied by an army of monkeys, Rāma marches to Laṅkā, the island stronghold of the ogre, and rescues her. Moreover, all ends well when he finally recovers his kingship.

Cycle D finally takes us to the town of Mathurā, where a vicious usurper Kaṃsa is threatening the life of the legitimate crown prince, Kṛṣṇa, who is his nephew. The latter grows up secretly in the forests among cowherds. There he reveals supernatural strength by warding off dangers from the herdsmen, and equally supernatural handsomeness which infatuates all the girls and women. Eventually he defeats the usurper in Mathurā, and various other kings in the Āryāvarta who are Kaṃsa's allies.

This simple list of four thematic cycles is merely an abstract attempt at reconstructing something like a starting-point for the extremely complex history of bardic-epic literature in India. What makes it so complicated is the fact that all four cycles have had their independent developments, while at the same time an enormous amount of intermingling and fusion between them took place. Moreover, when written versions did become available, in most cases they were random accounts, not consciously 'literary' works in which the variety of current oral versions was unified and systematised. Added complexity arises from the fact that many such 'random' versions were recorded.

Cycle A was developed along truly encyclopedic lines (a development that even around 1000 CE had not yet reached its end). As a story about human self-destructive tendencies, it implied profound questions about ethics, the role and responsibility of the king, the meaning of human life on earth, caught as it was between fate and man's own will, and about a possible significance of the bloody events in the context of cosmic history. Such questions were considered on a grand scale, and a vast array of what different religious and intellectual traditions (including, quite prominently, Buddhism) had to contribute to them was laid out. Since the war involved more or less all Aryan clans, our Cycle B could be used to provide the historical background, and inevitably an interaction between the religious material (origin of the world, etc.) took place. Material typical of Cycle C could be incorporated, since it offered a thematic parallel (exile in the forest of the legitimate crown prince and eventual victory of righteousness). Cycle D contributed even more directly, since one of the main protagonists of the Pāṇḍavas is Kṛṣṇa, the prince of Mathurā. As described so far, this grand encyclopedic synthesis became crystallised as a definite text in the form of the *Mahābhārata*, arguably the world's largest epic. A complete translation would run to over three or four thousand pages. But it is the work of many people, over a period of at least 1,500 years, and belonging to different regions. Almost drowned in this enormous mass of text is a small, originally perhaps independent, work, the *Bhagavadgītā*. Of all the Hindu scriptures, this is probably the single most important one. In it we find one of the earliest formulations of a fully fledged theology, centring around the God-figure Kṛṣṇa.

The *Mahābhārata* also acquired, perhaps around the third century CE, an 'Appendix'. The primary reason for this addition was the need felt for further information on Kṛṣṇa. Material typical of our Cycle D could be used for this purpose on a large scale. But it was not presented in isolation: Cycle B laid itself around Kṛṣṇa's life as its frame and context. Here again even 1000 CE does not appear to mark the end of the literary developments of the *Harivaṃśa* (as this 'appendix' was called). The Kṛṣṇa-figures offered by the *Mahābhārata* and the *Harivaṃśa* may be part of a coherent narrative, but in character they are very different from each other. And when Kṛṣṇa appears as one of the major God-figures of medieval Hinduism, it is the Kṛṣṇa of the *Harivaṃśa* who provided the primary inspiration for it (with the *Bhagavadgītā* providing its theology).

Our Cycle C acquired literary shape in a relatively simpler manner. Moreover, unlike the other texts spoken about so far, the *Rāmāyaṇa*, 'the story of Prince Rāma', was given sophisticated poetic expression, which in turn means by one author (at least for the bulk of the work). The Indian tradition names him as Vālmiki. His date may not be too far removed from the change into the Common Era. But this sophisticated epic does not signal the end of Rāma's own history: subsequent individual works demonstrate a process of increasing deification of Rāma (more on this aspect in the following section).

This leaves us with one last thematic cycle (our B). The Indian tradition neatly summarises the complex literary developments of this cycle in the concept of the 'eighteen great Purāṇas'. If historically the process had been so simple, we would—in the light of the observations made so far—have to speak of eighteen separate recordings of Cycle B material. Yet reality is much more complicated. An ancient core can indeed be identified: views on the origin of the world, its structure and past history, the royal dynasties and the deeds of past heroes and instructions on how to perform rites in honour of ancestors generally. Such a core is still present in many of the extant texts (though by no means in identical verbal form). But then a vast amount of more or less related material was added to such a core, in different regions, by different individuals, at different times. Even after such 'recordings' were fixed and could be identified by individual names (for example, 'Viṣṇu-Purāṇa'), they set in motion a further history of additions (not infrequently by drawing on other such textually 'fixed' Purāṇas). Although there are unlimited possibilities of what could be added to a Purāṇa, and for whatever reason, certainly from our point of view it is the enormous amount of religious material which is of interest. Kṛṣṇa and Rāma figured as heroes already in the dynastic histories typical of our Cycle B. When the 'eighteen grand Purāṇas' crystallised finally as the texts that we have now, every major and minor Hindu god or God-figure had been dealt with in this literature, sometimes on a gigantic scale.

The final products (i.e. the actual text or versions of it that we now possess) belong to different periods. Thus, for example, the *Mārkaṇḍeya-Purāṇa* and the *Viṣṇu-Purāṇa*, even with their respective interpolations, may well belong to around the middle of the first millennium CE. Others, like the *Śiva-Purāṇa* or *Brahmavaivarta-Purāṇa*, appear to be compiled as late as the middle of the second millennium. But not all this material is 'anonymous' and the product of compilers over many centuries. Perhaps the most famous of all these Purāṇas, the *Bhāgavata-Purāṇa* (ninth or early tenth century CE), must in essence be the conscious literary creation of one person (in south India). In turn, the *Devī-Bhāgavata-Purāṇa*, which in some lists replaces the *Bhāgavata-Purāṇa*, is a conscious imitation, some centuries later, of the former and comes from north-east India.

By now we have almost lost track of the bards who were originally involved in the cultivation of epic literature. Indeed, at some stage interest in purely local, dynastic and genealogical matters ceased, and topics of pan-Indian relevance (such as the origin of the world and the stories associated with the gods) began to dominate epic literature. It seems likely that this transformation went hand in hand with a shift towards brahmin involvement in the epic and purāṇic enterprise. Indications of this are, for instance, the formulation of the concept of *smṛti*, literally 'memory' but denoting in this context 'tradition' as opposed to *śruti*, 'Vedic revelation'. *Smṛti* was put forward as secondary in importance to the Vedas, and as the literature spelling out the implications of the Vedic heritage. The idea of the 'fifth Veda' for the Epics brought this literature even closer to brahmin culture. As brahmin-cultivated carriers of the story material about the heroes and the gods, and of popularly expressed philosophical and theological ideas, the Epics and Purāṇas had an enormous influence on Indian religion.

But it was not just in their Sanskrit form that the Purāṇas and Epics provided inspiration to much of Indian religion. Innumerable translations, adaptations and very free renderings into the many vernaculars enhanced the accessibility of this material. Yet that is still not the end of the story. In many ways, the classification of the Purāṇas into 'eighteen grand ones' is totally artificial. To a large extent the selection of these (and the lists even of the grand eighteen vary in part) from among a very much larger number of available Purāṇas has been arbitrary. The remainder, called Upa- or 'secondary' Purāṇas, are not necessarily more recent, more 'sectarian' or more regional than many of the 'classical' eighteen.

By now we have been discussing a literature that in print would fill many thousands of pages. Yet the Purāṇas were such a popular genre of religious literature, that the list of them ought to be enlarged by thousands of further works. These are now known as the Sthala- or 'local' Purāṇas. Each one is associated with a more or less famous temple or place of pilgrimage and narrates, amongst other things, the deeds of the relevant god in that particular locality. When discussing the temple, more will have to be said about this literature.

The Hindus are not the only participants in this enormous literary enterprise. There are some indications that the Indian Buddhists also showed interest in the genre of the Purāṇas (the *Mahāvastu* could be classified like this); but the Jains developed their versions of the Epics and Purāṇas into a whole literature of grandiose proportions. More will be said about this in a later section under the heading of the Jain *Mahāpurāṇa*.

In summary then it must be stated that an exploration of the Epics and Purāṇas does not allow for easy short cuts. These are not just twenty or so texts of minor religious significance, but actually imply a whole literary history of enormous textual proportions. These works were of such popular and widespread influence that even today in many a South Asian country the stories of Rāma, Kṛṣṇa and the Pāṇḍavas constitute some of the most famous themes of various art forms. Although the old Hinduism in many of these countries has been superseded by Islam or Theravāda Buddhism, epic and purāṇic heroes still figure not just in the various literatures, but also in dances and in the puppet theatre.

The Hindu Gods and God

Conventionally, Buddhism and Jainism are characterised as 'atheistic'. We have seen how misleading such an attribute can be, since our concept 'atheism' denotes not merely the absence of a God-figure, but also a conscious rejection of anything transcendental. For Hinduism the case has been slightly more complicated. In some perceptions, it has been similarly called 'atheistic'. In other perceptions, and this is perhaps the more common one, it is labelled 'polytheistic'. The term 'polytheism' acknowledges the presence of a God-figure in a religious system, but in the plural. Thus it is said that Hindus worship many such beings we call God. But obviously this implies a very profound difference in the understanding of what such a 'God' could be. Thus how could he be omnipotent, if he has to share his power with many other peers? As we shall see, this model of understanding theistic Hinduism is actually extremely unhelpful. This may be illustrated initially by looking at another commonly made assumption. It is often said that Hindus worship three gods, and these are in fact called the 'Hindu Trinity'. The gods involved are: Brahmā, Viṣṇu and Śiva. The first is supposed to create the world (at the beginning of each cosmic cycle), the second to maintain it in being, and Śiva, at the end of a cosmic cycle, to destroy it again. There is a certain attraction to this simple and neat conception; unfortunately, it cannot be substantiated from the religious literature. Not that texts do not talk about such a Trinity—they do, frequently. But then they add a further idea which is ignored by the proponents of the theory of a Hindu Trinity. What is added invariably implies that over and above these three figures lies a single reality. This 'one above the three' controls the activities of creation etc. Brahmā and the others, who carry out these functions, are merely manifestations of that highest being, or they relate to it in some other, equally secondary, form. That the Indian traditions evolved a very large number of interpretations of what or who this ultimate, single reality is may not come as a surprise in view of what has been said already about the dynamism and proliferation of religious conceptions in these traditions. It is an issue that deserves a more detailed exploration.

We have seen that the religious status of the Vedic *devas* is relatively undefined. The late Vedic period more consciously and systematically pursued the quest towards some overall, single principle behind the rich array of *deva*-figures. But for reasons unknown to us a dual discontinuity occurred. First, as already discussed, the renouncer traditions brought their devastating critique to bear on the whole range of *devas*. Now they are unequivocally defined as members of the natural order, beings that like ourselves move in the realm of space, time and matter. A second discontinuity occurred which has not yet attracted the same attention. What has previously been discussed as the epic-purāṇic traditions certainly knows of *devas*. But strangely enough, figures appear here about which the Vedas have either nothing, or extremely little to say (Nārāyaṇa, Kṛṣṇa, Rāma, Viṣṇu, Śiva). The central *devas* of the Vedas, that is Agni, Soma, Indra, do not appear at all, or in an insignificant role (Indra). Glimpses of local folk religion, which the Buddhist and Jain canonical literature offers us, point at a god figure Brahmā. As to the religious status of these epic-purāṇic *devas*, the contexts in which we hear about them is in most cases so unspecific that we cannot comment on this. Yet in certain instances the evidence suggests beyond any doubt that something novel has happened: the concept of a single, all-powerful, eternal, personal and loving God has emerged. This is the concept of 'Bhagavān'. And to the extent that secondary implications of the Christian concept of 'God' can be ignored (e.g. creation out of nothing), it is indeed appropriate to translate Bhagavān with 'God', without giving rise to too many confusions.

But who is this Hindu Bhagavān? At least to us as the outside observers he is not one, but many. Śiva, Viṣṇu, Kṛṣṇa, Rāma, Kārttikeya and Gaṇeśa may be mentioned as the most important Bhagavān-figures. But to speak of many Bhagavāns has nothing to do with 'polytheism', for in terms of Indian society, different groups of people have their one and only Bhagavān. That means, the concept itself is an empty slot, to be filled by concrete characteristics which then make up a specific Bhagavān-figure who serves as (the one and only) God to a given group of people. To describe this with any precision would require the methods of sociology, and not of theology. Theologically speaking, there cannot be anything over and above Bhagavān. Sociologically speaking, a society—particularly as variegated as India—can know of many such figures.

It would be extremely interesting to know the answers to two interrelated historical questions: how did the concept of Bhagavān arise, and what are the sources from which the concrete characterisations were derived? Unfortunately, our known textual documents do not offer us much information on this. The two crucial texts that so far have come to our attention suggest somewhat different answers, and that really only about our second question. The *Śvetāśvatara-Upaniṣad* and the *Bhagavadgītā* are the seminal expressions of true monotheism in India. The latter introduces us to a Bhagavān-figure, Kṛṣṇa, totally unknown in earlier, Vedic literature. Thus both the concept and its visualisation in specific form make a sudden, inexplicable appearance. The *Śvetāśvatara-Upaniṣad*, on the other hand, draws very heavily on those Vedic hymns in which a *deva* Rudra is addressed. This Rudra is called '*śiva*', which means 'benevolent', and this attribute was subsequently used increasingly as this Bhagavān's proper name. But even if we allowed for a direct continuity between the Vedic *deva* Rudra and Bhagavān Śiva, no such conceptual continuity for the concept of 'Bhagavān' itself can be derived from this. Thus perhaps one of the most exciting questions in the study of Indian religions has to be left unanswered, at least until further evidence comes to light: how, during the last few centuries BCE, monotheism arose in India.

A considerable amount of scholarship has concerned itself with the problem of the historical continuity between the Vedas and subsequent religion. This has obscured another process, of equal importance: the artificial recourse to Vedic material at a much later date. A well-known textual example is the famous *Bhāgavata-Purāṇa* (ninth or early tenth century CE). Its language is not the Sanskrit of the other Epics and Purāṇas, but an artificial recreation of the Vedic (namely pre-classical Sanskrit) language. Here is a work that by sounding Vedic claims to be Vedic in its teaching. This recourse to the Vedas for the purpose of legitimisation is already apparent in the case of the *Bhagavadgītā*. The text itself throws out many references back to Vedic ideas and figures, including a very minor one to the Vedic *deva* Viṣṇu. Since the rest of the *Mahābhārata*, an ocean in which the *Bhagavadgītā* is no more than a tiny drop, focuses on Viṣṇu, amongst other things as a Bhagavān-figure, subsequent ages sought to identify this Viṣṇu with Kṛṣṇa. It is at least possible to ask whether in the case of the *Śvetāśvatara-Upaniṣad* such a process also underlies (some of) the seeming Vedic continuity.

This is clearly an extremely important aspect of the Hindu traditions, and throws considerable light on the role the Vedas have played in their history. But it must not obscure another important process: the constant recourse to folk-religious (and even tribal) material. In a sense it is precisely because the Hindu traditions were constantly involved in drawing on non-Vedic sources, that the need for Vedic legitimisation arose. We have already encountered one illustration of this process, the *Harivaṃśa*. Kṛṣṇa plays an extremely important role in the whole of the *Mahābhārata* as a prince and primary initiator of action, and naturally as Bhagavān in the *Bhagavadgītā*. Yet his youth is left a blank here. By drawing on local, folk-religious mythology, the *Harivaṃśa* filled this blank. Scholars tend to agree that the Kṛṣṇa of the *Mahābhārata* and Kṛṣṇa the cowherd, fighting ogres and infatuating all the women and girls, historically and sociologically belong to different traditions.

Another well-known illustration is the figure of Skanda. When we consult the earlier standard Sanskrit texts, we are told that Skanda is the son of Śiva and his wife Pārvatī. Śiva was known to be such a dedicated ascetic that a demon ventured to ask that his death be at the hands of Śiva's son. Somehow the *devas*, with the primary help of Pārvatī, managed to have Śiva break his ascetic vows and procreate a son, Skanda or Kārttikeya. As initially totally separate from all this we find in the ancient Tamil-speaking south a god Murukaṉ: handsome, vigorous, fighting demons and wooing girls. This Murukaṉ now became identified with Skanda, and the two mythologies fused to a new, composite whole.

A third illustration is less well known and modern, so that we can still observe the actual process at work. In Mahārāṣṭra we find a regional god, Khaṇḍobā. Evidence suggests that we are dealing here with an originally autonomous god-figure belonging to a regional and independent religious system. But when the evidence we possess about the iconography, mythology and devotion associated with Khaṇḍobā is projected on to the time-scale, we notice that this god is increasingly brought into the proximity of Śiva and turned into a secondary manifestation of him. Yet this process is by no means complete even today.

A final example takes us back to Rāma, the hero of the *Rāmāyaṇa*. Already in south India during the first millennium CE, this prince of a 'secular' epic began to enjoy a directly religious attention (particularly through his association with Viṣṇu, for which see below). But it was in north India, during the later sixteenth century, that a cult of Rāma as Bhagavān found its textual expression in the *Rāmcaritmānas* of Tulsīdās.

These four examples are no more than illustrations of a process that has been taking place on a very large scale. Naturally it was broken up into innumerable smaller events, in different regions and different social milieux. Moreover, this process of 'integration' also involved modes in which man related to these Bhagavān-figures.

Earlier epic-purāṇic and even Vedic *devas* are still relatively few in number. The number of *deva*-figures known in tribal, folk and regional religions, all over the vast expanse of the Indian sub-continent, is practically unlimited. Such a range is staggering not just for us as the outside observers, but has always been so for the more observant Indian. It has been rather underestimated as to what extent Indian reflection itself has been at work to bring some order into, and to conceptualise, this complex situation. Some examples may illustrate this.

The approximation of Kṛṣṇa and Viṣṇu in the *Mahābhārata* has been mentioned above. One particular way of envisaging this relationship proved extremely useful and prolific. This is the concept of the '*avatāra*'. It denotes a 'descent' of Viṣṇu into the realm of space, time and matter, entirely due to his own free will (and not, for example, due to the laws of *karma*), and involves on the whole a full life cycle, from (normal) conception and birth to (natural) death. Historically (and that means around the beginning of the first millennium CE) the first *avatāra* thus to be envisaged was Kṛṣṇa. But soon it was felt that a number of other figures of religious importance could be accommodated successfully too. The history of this incorporation is complex and certainly not monolinear, nor did it ever achieve a final completion. Thus when conventionally ten such *avatāras* of Viṣṇu are mentioned, it can be regarded as no more than one, particularly successful, schema. As such it deserves a few more comments. The obvious point to note here is the plurality of such *avatāras*. We are not dealing with a single, unique event in the history of the cosmos when God incarnates himself on earth; he does so time and again. Secondly, many of these *avatāras* are not recognisably human (like the Fish, Turtle, Boar, Man-Lion). Then we notice an attempt to structure the pattern of the ten in a kind of 'evolutionary' manner: from the ocean (Fish) we gradually move to the dry land (even the Boar still jumps into the ocean). Then the movement is from not-yet-human (Man-Lion, Dwarf) to fully human (Kṛṣṇa, Rāma, Paraśu- or Bala-Rāma). Finally, with Kalki, we reach the end of time, or better, of a cosmic cycle. That this pattern is intended as a means of integrating existing religious cults is made clear not just from the fact that many of the myths told about the Boar or the Turtle are actually fully fledged creation myths, but also that in some versions the Buddha appears as an *avatāra*.

The so-called Hindu Trinity is a further illustration. Certainly, through reference to Viṣṇu and Śiva, a religious system could not just differentiate itself from the systems in which Viṣṇu or Śiva was Bhagavān, but also impose itself on to them, at least claiming, if not always succeeding in this claim, that it is their fulfilment. Better known cases are religions in which Rāma or Kṛṣṇa or the Goddess (on whom see below), or even Rudra, appear as the single, ultimate Bhagavān over and above the three *devas* of the 'Trinity'. To apply to such cases what has been learnt about the relationship between Śiva and Rudra, or Viṣṇu and Kṛṣṇa, for other contexts makes no sense, since those relationships have never been defined with universal relevance.

Perhaps because it had, historically, a 'Viṣṇuite' flavour, the concept of *avatāra* was used rather hesitantly by non-Viṣṇuite religious traditions. Yet we find many illustrations of a wider appeal, particularly in vernacular contexts which are less concerned with such subtleties. Here, for example, Khaṇḍobā may be seen as an *avatāra* of Śiva, or various goddess-figures as *avatāras* of the Goddess.

Another mode of bringing some order into the vast array of available gods reminds us of the way the ancient Greek organised their pantheon, namely through family relationships. This approach is thoroughly purāṇic, which means that it merely served as a method and not a pattern which could claim pan-Indian relevance. A particularly charming example is that of the south Indian popular god-figure Aiyappaṉ. Here in the south the worshippers of Viṣṇu and Śiva socially constitute a particularly strongly demarcated binary opposition. To link Aiyappaṉ with either Śiva or Viṣṇu would have meant a definite decision in favour of one side or the other. So the following ingenious solution was proposed: he is the son of both Śiva and Viṣṇu! The story takes us back to the time when the *devas* and the *asuras* (demons) had churned the milk-ocean and recovered the drink of immortality. The *devas* felt loath to let the *asuras* have their legitimate share, and Viṣṇu changed himself into an extremely attractive woman, to entice the *asuras* and take the nectar from them. Somehow Śiva was unaware of this, and when he saw the transformed Viṣṇu, he lusted after her.

How is all this perceived through the eyes of an individual member of Indian society? The conceptual distinction between *deva* and Bhagavān is less useful than it appears at first sight. For in most cases a particular Bhagavān-figure may look the same as a *deva*. By 'looking the same' is meant here: possessing the same external characteristics (including name) and having the same or very similar stories told about his mythical deeds. From this follows that the individual (or, in practice, far more often, the group to which he belongs, and this more frequently by birth than choice) makes a decision as to how to regard such a figure. To take Viṣṇu as an example: Viṣṇu could thus be the Bhagavān for some people, a minor manifestation of Śiva for others, a godling for a third group, possibly an evil demonic being for a fourth and Īśvara (the personal, but ultimately illusory, creator) for a fifth. But this does not mean that every single religious individual in India ends up with a Bhagavān. As we have seen already it is quite possible to be religious and not be theistic.

There is another complication here. An individual may belong to a given religious system which in terms of its own normative premisses cannot acknowledge a given figure to be Bhagavān. Yet when looking into the religious life of that individual, it might well be possible that it differs from what the norm says. Sometimes this is conceptualised in the idea that every Hindu has his own '*iṣṭa-devatā*', his personally chosen deity. There may be a kernel of truth in this, to the extent that we do find a fair amount of flexibility in some milieux. But on the whole there are considerable constraints at work as to the range of such choices. One such constraint is implicitly ideological. It has been mentioned that traditional Hinduism evolved its own ways of ordering the vast mass of god-figures available in society. Both here and when it comes to making a decision as to whether or not a given figure is Bhagavān, by no means everything available is perceived to be on an equal level. One can isolate a whole scale of values, according to which *devas* are judged. Any kind of Vedic association would be most prestigious, and below that, a role in the Epics and earlier Purāṇas. Figures outside this range acquire respectability only by subterfuge, that means, as illustrated above, by becoming 'identified' with Vedic or purāṇic gods, or acquiring a, naturally relatively late, Sanskrit Purāṇa that deals with them. Otherwise, such deities will be regarded as socially 'low' by the Hindu 'mainstream'. 'Tell me who your *deva* is and I will tell you who you are' could well paraphrase the situation.

How all this comes to life in the devotion and actual 'religion' of real people will be shown in the following section. Yet surprising though it may seem, a major chunk of material relevant under the present heading has not yet been discussed. This concerns the divine in feminine form.

The more observant reader will have noticed that on the whole the *devas* and Bhagavān figures discussed are male. Whilst from the viewpoint of the Semitic traditions this may not appear remarkable, from the point of view of the Indian religions this would be only half the story. The *devīs* and Bhagavatī, the corresponding feminine forms of *devas* and Bhagavān, still require discussion. For two reasons, this material is mentioned only at this stage. First, there is the state of scholarship which till very recently has ignored this type of religion. But, secondly, that itself is actually due to the way the divine feminine was perceived in India. For on the whole, religion involving *devīs* or Bhagavatī is not quite the same as the types knowing *devas* or Bhagavān. The difference is basically social and ideological. That means *devī*-religion must be envisaged as belonging to a 'lower' stratum of society, although, as we shall see, occasional inroads were indeed made into the 'mainstream'.

The middle of the first millennium CE marks the culmination and end of what could be called 'classical' Hinduism. Yet important new phenomena now begin to make their appearance in Sanskrit literary works. For a variety of reasons it looks plausible that we are not dealing here with 'new' phenomena as such, but with facets of the religious heritage which due to social and political upheaval succeeded in attracting the attention of literati. One such facet (on another, see the section on the esoteric traditions) is the emergence of a novel, and in various ways revolutionary, concept of a personal absolute deity: God as woman.

The crucial text is the *Devīmāhātmya*, 'the glorification of the Goddess'. This short work, of *c.* 550 couplets, found its way into one of the oldest Purāṇas, the *Mārkaṇḍeya-Purāṇa*, and this position secured its preservation and popularity. The nature of this Goddess is demonstrated here through three stories, which were taken up by later writers in endless variations and transformations and which also found visual expression in a large number of sculptures. In the first of these, an older creation myth about Viṣṇu has been transformed to show that the Goddess allows for Viṣṇu to create the world, for Brahmā to reveal the Vedas, and for all demonic obstacles to be removed. The remaining two myths refer to two instances when demons have ousted the *devas*. They are unable to fight their enemies, and it is the Goddess (variously called Ambikā, Caṇḍikā, Durgā, Gaurī) and various gruesome secondary manifestations of her (such as Kālī and Cāmuṇḍā) who by their supreme power demonstrate what puny godlings they are. The second story involves a demon in the shape of a water-buffalo (Mahiṣa), whose slaughter by the Goddess has been a particularly favourite theme in Indian art. The third myth tells us about two demon brothers, Śumbha and Niśumbha, the former of whom was passionately in love with the Goddess, but suffered cruel death through her because of his arrogant advances. On all three occasions, the text makes it clear that we are dealing with earthly manifestations of an eternal, immanent and transcendent deity, to be venerated and lauded by all beings on earth. And indeed various hymns are sung by the (male) gods, to ask her for help or to sing her praise after her victories.

A surprising number of prominent post-Gupta Sanskrit court poets produced poetic masterpieces in honour of the Goddess. Mention may be made here of two of them, Bāṇa (who composed the *Caṇḍīśataka*, in the seventh century) and Ānandavardhana (who wrote the *Devīśataka* in Kashmir, in the ninth century). Bāṇa fuses in his poem the mythical incident of the Goddess thrusting her foot down on Mahiṣa's head with an amorous situation found in conventional Sanskrit court poetry: the lover attempting to placate his beloved who is furious at some unfaithfulness of his. Through this ingenious device the whole becomes transparent for the human situation generally, in which earthly happiness and liberation from *saṃsāra* are found through submission to the Goddess, ritually expressed through placing one's head on her feet. By this logic, the demon Mahiṣa also found his salvation! Similarly Ānandavardhana envisages the Goddess, ultimately, as the apex of wisdom, mental clarity and Vedic revelation—nothing here about the theory that the feminine equals unreflecting nature! Every facet of Hindu religion is in one way or other connected here with the Goddess as its ultimate rationale and motivation.

Documents from later periods reveal to us that the triumph of the Goddess, as celebrated in the above mentioned myths and texts, had its parallel in the religious history of India, or at least, certain regions. In north-eastern India in particular, during the earlier part of the second millennium, a whole range of new Purāṇas was produced which promulgated a religion of the Goddess as infinitely superior to the traditional male gods. On the whole, no new myths evolved; instead, the vast classical repertoire was reinterpreted, in order to make transparent the final agent in them. Wherever we find greed, delusion, ignorance, violence and wherever we encounter goodness, search for truth and salvation, these are instances where the presence of the Goddess can be felt. We are dealing here with a grandiose and daring attempt to encompass everything that is an object of human experience, with all its contradictions and dynamics, within the ultimate ground of being, the Goddess. The instincts as much as the desire for more controlled and conscious actions, cruelty and kindness, which anybody can easily identify within himself, along with the variegated nature of the external reality—famine and rich harvest, poverty and affluence, war and peace, illness and health—all this derives from, and converges in, the Goddess. The final culmination of this vision was reached in Rāmprasād Sen (1718–75), a poet who composed in the vernacular Bengali moving songs of altercation and submission, accusation and devotion addressed to the Goddess (variously called Kālī, Durgā, etc.). In turn, Rāmprasād inspired a whole crowd of later poets to continue the genre he had created.

Two important questions deserve closer attention: how can we explain the rise of this religion of the Goddess, and what reactions did it provoke in other circles?

In a general way it seems possible to reflect on the historicity of religious symbols and their social concatenation. Given the major upheaval caused by the collapse of the Gupta empire, it could be argued that this external disintegration of a dominant culture allowed religious symbols—already perceived as far more significant and comprehensive in relation to the concrete human situation—to emerge from subcultures which could now replace symbols which had become outdated, elitist and too limited in their range of application. This general reflection can be linked with a more specific one. The study of rural, village, or folk religion (however one may want to style it), reveals that in these milieux cults of *devīs*, 'goddesses', are widespread, if not to say, dominant. Moreover, it is possible to reconstruct regional cults which at one time may well have centred around autonomous Goddesses. The figures of Manasā (in north-east India) and Yellammā (in the Deccan) are candidates for this. To the extent that it is possible to extrapolate from this relatively recent evidence, we may infer that already in works like the *Devīmāhātmya* popular religion has found literary expression, within the genre and the conventions of hallowed tradition. In a typically Indian fashion, such regional figures are integrated by subsuming them, as her 'manifestations', in the great Goddess.

Less speculative is the question of the reaction provoked. Here a well-known contrast between 'grassroot' and elite religion and religious value-systems can be perceived to apply. Thus much more typical of the purāṇic attitude is the dominant role of the male *devas* or of Bhagavān, who acquire *devīs* as their wives. In that subordinate role, such a *devī* may be associated with some activity secondary to his divine nature. She may then be called his *śakti*, 'power'. 'Śāktism' is the term used in the Indian conceptualisation of Goddess-religion (and it has been adopted uncritically by Western scholars). It should be clear from what has been said above that such a concept does not accurately describe the nature of Bhagavatī.

Worship and Devotion

Given that the early Āryas were a semi-nomadic people, it is not surprising to find a lack of interest in particular places or localities. The sacrifice would be performed by erecting brick altars for the occasion, and the fire could be carried from one place to the next. Similarly the different offshoots of the renouncer movement re-emphasised this mobility. Meditation and asceticism did not require specific places. However, when the Āryas established more permanent settlements in north-eastern India, along the banks of the Yamunā (Jumna) and Gaṅgā (Ganges), we witness the emergence of spatial symbols. The realm itself was conceptualised as the Āryāvarta, the country of

Aryan culture *par excellence*. Even centuries later, when the *Dharma-śāstras* attempted to systematise the details of the Hindu *Dharma*, they suggest, as the final resort in cases of disagreement between different traditions, going to the Āryāvarta and observing the behaviour of true Āryas there. Besides, individual towns were drawn into a process of mythologisation. Above all it is Benares (Vāraṇāsī) that became associated with all kinds of religious and cultural ideas. Among other places may be mentioned Prayāga (Allahabād) where the Yamunā and the Gaṅgā meet. Even where at a later stage theistic notions were superimposed on these archaic ideas (as Benares is associated with Śiva), these remain secondary. It is being in Benares and dying there and having one's ashes scattered into the river that is important (as if it were the return into the womb of a primordial 'mother', Gaṅgā). Naturally it will vary enormously how individual Hindus will conceptualise and perceive the custom of going to Benares, a custom that has attracted millions every year up to the present day. Related to this, although not connected with dying and death, are similar customs, such as celebrating the *kumbhamela* in Prayāga. In the further history of the Aryan expansion many new places emerged that attempted to emulate Benares in its appeal. Different catalogues were produced of such 'holy towns', but nothing comparable to a universally agreed-upon list has evolved. Moreover, in many cases the rationale for a town's 'holiness' is primarily theistic (e.g. in the case of Kāñcīpuram, Rāmeśvaram and Śrīraṅgam in Tamilnadu and Puri in Orissa).

Typologically in sharp contrast with early Aryan 'mobile' religion and with amorphous religious associations of towns in the Āryāvarta, are the folk religions. As the Āryas spread out over the whole of India, they encountered innumerable hunter and agricultural societies with their different religions. Given the lack of information on most of the latter, any characterisation has necessarily to be hypothetical. But from information found in early Buddhist and Jain scriptures, and on Buddhist buildings (from the third century BCE), from stray references in secular Sanskrit and vernacular literature, and also because of the 'multiple history' explained above, it becomes possible to make certain general statements. These different religions appear to be localised, which means that the objects of worship are perceived to be permanently resident in specific places. This in turn allowed for increasing complexity of the structures and modes of worship over the centuries in one and the same locality. Our earliest, indirect documentation comes from the Buddhist *stūpa*, an edifice associated with such localised cults, though presumably with a transformed, Buddhist, motivation. In these local cults generally, offerings are made in a specific place with food, water, flowers, clothes, incense, perfumes, camphor and lamps. In many cases this will also involve the slaughter of animals, and alcohol. The rites are accompanied by song, music and dancing. All this goes by the name of '*pūjā*'. The choice of the place itself may not have been arbitrary: crossroads, special trees, ponds, ant-hills, caves and springs appear to have been particularly favoured spots. Quite clearly all this presupposes the presence of one or more non-human beings in honour of whom these rites are performed. Our texts conceptualise these beings as *yakṣas*, *gaṇas*, *nāgas*, etc. But it is likely that within the relevant religious community these beings were originally conceived of as 'gods'. Presumably for ideological reasons (i.e. to emphasise their non-Vedic nature) it was difficult to regard them as '*devas*'. However, once the cults of the epic and purāṇic gods, and indeed, Gods, had gained prominence, a complex interaction with these folk-religious cults began. Existing centres of worship could be reinterpreted as abodes of such a *deva*/*Deva* (or even *devī*/*Devī*), new ones could be created by using the existing forms, and *devī*-figures could be 'married' to the newcomer, the (epic-purāṇic) Aryan *deva*.

Parallel to all this runs a trend to give concrete form to the being believed to be permanently present in a given place. Even in modern India, one can still find the whole spectrum of the various possibilities represented. At one end of this spectrum, there may be no formal sign at all, other than the conventional markings of a 'sacred place of worship' (a flag, clean earth, some line of boundary, etc.). Then we may find a stone, usually marked by a red spot on it or actually painted red. Next, the stone may be given a degree of sculpturing: chiselled-out eyes, a rough nose or mouth. When we come to Śiva religion, the stone will have the shape of a *liṅga* (often set inside a *yoni*). Particularly with the Vaiṣṇavas, but also with the worshippers of the Goddess, we reach the other end of the spectrum: full-figure sculptures with all the details of, say, folds of dress, physiognomy and jewellery. This spectrum runs parallel to a shift in the understanding: whilst the uniconic stone may serve merely to mark the presence of a formless divine being, the iconic, sculptured images tend to be interpreted as the actual 'body' of the god. Yet all this has nothing to do with 'idolatry' (a charge often levelled against this type of religion), as we shall see below.

Given that a particular cult centre enjoyed popularity in a wider region and over a longer period of time, its formal structures could develop enormous complexity. In the extreme, we may end up literally with 'temple towns' (see for example Śrīraṅgam). In fact, any traveller to India will immediately encounter Indian religion through its temples, many thousands of which—small or very large—are scattered all over the country. The temple is indeed the most prominent mode for all types of the Indian religions to manifest themselves externally.

Just as we find a logical spectrum for the representation of the divine being, the complexity of even the largest temple can be explained in terms of many such spectra. Thus one such spectrum would be: from improvised roof (say a stone placed horizontally on top of two vertical stones, protecting the central figure from the rains) to 'hut' to 'house' to 'palace'. The sacred space may be demarcated by a line drawn on to the ground, or a simple fence, or even by tall and thick walls. The entrance could be built up as an arch or even as a *gopuram*, massive towers above the heavy entrance gates. The images can multiply: as a king has his courtiers and queens, the god has his wives, attendants and the saints of the past who sang in his honour. Each one of these may acquire a separate shrine. The greater the complexity of the architectural structures, the greater is the need for maintaining contact between the god and his subjects. Thus festivals evolved during which the god is carried out from his palace and in procession blesses the town or the village. Obviously no large stone image could be used for this purpose, and thus there is a duplication of the statue in bronze or a variety of precious metals. The utensils of *pūjā* require proper, professional care in their production. Thus a flower garden provides the myriad of flowers used by the garland weavers; the food offered (used to feed sometimes hundreds of temple employees and pilgrims) has to be cooked in large kitchens and the grain stored in sizeable storerooms. Music, song and dance are institutionalised and new professional groups emerge: temple musicians and '*devadāsīs*', dancing girls, who sing and dance in front of the temple image. The god or goddess may acquire large supplies of jewellery and dresses in the course of centuries, and special strong-rooms have to be built for these. To carry heavy water vessels is one of the tasks of the temple elephants (who naturally have their own stables). For the procession, large wooden carts may be constructed. The carts of the temple in Puri were so enormous that they provided the English language with the word 'juggernaut' (from the Sanskrit name of the god taken in procession, Jagannātha, 'Lord of the Universe'). Clockwise circumambulation turns into a major walk, through halls of thousands of pillars. In terms of architectural styles, there is a marked difference between the north and the south; Kerala has preserved an altogether different style.

Alongside these trends towards sometimes staggering size and complexity went the development of ritualism. There was obviously the need to codify the innumerable daily, seasonal and special ritual ceremonies: how to bathe the images, how to dress them, how to express the devotional submission of the community to the god, etc., and also how to construct the buildings themselves. Only professionals could learn all this, and thus a number of mostly hereditary traditions arose which specialised in these matters. As in the case of the philosophical systems, such traditions developed their own metaphysics and theologies, thus providing a wider frame for this ritualism. Thus with the Vaiṣṇavas, we find for example the Pāñcarātrins (with their sizeable Saṃhitās) and the Vaikhānasas (who claim to represent one Vedic *śākhā*). With the Śaivites, a whole literature called the Āgamas evolved. As to the overall symbolic model for the temple ritual, the treatment of a respected guest provides the inspiration in more limited contexts; the whole paraphernalia of a king's court and courtly ritual, that for the larger temples.

Whatever the individual theology may be that was

developed in such traditions, it is clear that the image of the deity tended to be regarded as his or her 'embodiment'. That means, the deity itself is not the stone or the metal: by its own nature, the manifested divine is beyond such material constraints. Moreover, food offerings are not literally perceived to be eaten by the deity: the physical contact with the deity's 'body' purifies it and renders it fit for human consumption. Thus it is not justified to treat all this as 'idolatry'. Among Vaiṣṇavas, a particular theological concept evolved, that of the *arcāvatāra*. Similar to the historical 'incarnations' of Viṣṇu, we now have permanent 'incarnations' in the *arcās*, the temple images. Generally speaking, an enormous literature arose for thousands of these temples all over India which tells stories about how the god came to abide permanently in a given temple, what kind of miraculous features are associated with it and what benefits certain individuals gained from visiting the temple. These are the Sthala-purāṇas, repertoires of localised mythology.

A considerable amount of the Indian religious reality is at least to some extent connected with temple worship. This is a form of devotion very few religious movements could altogether ignore. Thus even the Jains constructed temples on a large scale, installed images of their Tīrthaṅkaras (i.e. the Mahāvīra and his predecessors) in them, and instituted *pūjā* (often by hiring Hindu *pūjārīs* for the purpose). There is no reason to doubt the presence also of Buddhist temples in India; very likely the Hindu idea of the Buddha being one of Viṣṇu's *avatāras* was developed in such a temple environment. Even radical antinomian movements that began by totally rejecting temple worship tended to end up worshipping images of their founders and saints in temples (as, for example, in the case of the Nāthas). But the religious significance of the temple varies with different groups. Thus in the strictest terms of Jain doctrine, no Tīrthaṅkara can actually embody himself in a temple statue.

But it does mean that from the viewpoint of an individual member of Indian society, he is surrounded by a (random) collection of different temples. In most cases this person will not bother to study the theologies that would be integral to each individually. He may visit many temples, for different reasons probably unique to him, and worship there. Visits of Hindus to Muslim shrines and even Christian churches are commonplace. But temples want to have an appeal beyond the immediate neighbourhood. Great efforts are made to celebrate the seasonal festivals on as lavish a scale as possible, and thereby attract large numbers of pilgrims. It is difficult to say what factors account for the popularity of certain temples; it need not be size (whch often is the direct result of visits by large groups of pilgrims). In terms of 'sanctity', there is little to choose between them, for each Sthala-purāṇa tries to make the most grandiose claims. Theologically, there is often no need at all for it, since the same Viṣṇu is encountered in all the different Viṣṇu temples. Thus we must assume a whole cluster of motives (including unconscious and random ones) to be at work here.

Visiting the local temples and going on pilgrimage are two important modes of expressing religion in concrete terms. But others may be mentioned. First there are the festivals which are annually celebrated in the homes of people (thus comparable to Christmas, etc.). Naturally they follow the traditional Indian calendar, and thus often the name itself includes the particular day. For instance, Nāg-pañcamī, a festival held in honour of the Nāgas (i.e. 'mythologised' serpents), falls on the 'fifth day' (*pañcamī*) of the month Śrāvaṇa (July/August); Gaṇeś-caturthī, in honour of the elephant-headed 'god of learning' Gaṇeśa, is celebrated on the 'fourth' day (*caturthī*) of Bhādra (August/September). Once again, given the size and variety of India and its religions, we need not be surprised to find enormous regional and social differences in what festival is celebrated and how it is interpreted. Sometimes a festival is purely regional, like the Durgā-pūjā in Bengal during the month of Aśvin (about October). But often one can recognise a common core, as in the spring festival of Holi or the autumn festival of Dīvālī/Dīpāvali. But how even such 'pan-Indian' festivals are given a religious significance depends on the area, caste and religious allegiances of people. It is therefore basically wrong to claim that 'Hindus celebrate x' and offer one such religious interpretation, as if that exhausted the subject. All that can be said is that certain festivals gave gained wide recognition all over India and may have entered into the *Dharma-śāstras*; any Kṛṣṇaite, Rāmaite, Vaiṣṇava, Śaivite, etc. symbolism of it is in most cases secondary.

A further important form of religious expression in the home (apart from domestic *pūjā* and the festivals mentioned above) is the *vrata*. These are rituals usually involving some form of voluntary deprivation (fasting, sexual abstinence, etc.), often in fulfilment of a vow (*vrata* means, amongst other things, vow). Among the higher castes, a brahmin may be employed to recite the 'story' (*kathā*) which narrates the benefits of such a *vrata* and its divine origins. Such ritualised readings of other, major religious works (like the *Bhagavadgītā*, *Devīmāhātmya*, *Bhāgavata-Purāṇa*) may also take place as part of public festivals.

Naturally, there is yoga, which does not necessarily require any external structure. However, it may well be practised as part of daily visits to a temple. A more committed approach would involve leaving the fetters of society behind and turning itinerant mendicant. Alternatively, there is the institution of the *maṭha* or *āśrama* (ashram), comparable to monasteries in the case of permanent residents, and to retreat houses in the case of temporary visitors. Yoga is not a necessary part of *maṭha* or *āśrama* life, since the more emphatic theistic traditions may not cultivate it and concentrate on *pūjā*, *bhakti* and so on instead.

More important than the external forms through which religion expresses itself is the inner content. However, this is an area which does not lend itself easily to direct scrutiny. Nevertheless, there are certain obvious misconceptions which ought to be avoided here. Thus the

Indian material makes it abundantly clear that what we would call 'theology' does not necessarily describe religious content in an integral or adequate manner. Obviously a theological system is easily recognised; moreover, it presents a religious content in a rational, accessible manner. But it would be a grave mistake to describe the whole of the Indian devotional traditions merely in terms of a set of theological systems. Often the concern of Hindu theologians has been marginal to the actual devotion with which it aligned itself. More often, religious movements did not, or not fully, conceptualise their own religious premisses. That means that what will be said in a separate section about the various philosophical and theological strands in Hinduism can, and in fact must, be regarded as an enterprise at least relatively independent of the actual devotion. The case of the Goddess mentioned above is a good illustration.

The early texts that offer us a monotheistic conception also provide the key term for the devotion associated with it: *bhakti*. For instance in the *Bhagavadgītā*, this *bhakti* denotes a fundamental loyalty to Kṛṣṇa which expresses itself through the cultivation of yoga and adherence to the established (Hindu) *Dharma*. In its highest form, it becomes 'love', and that as a mutual relationship between Kṛṣṇa and the devotee. Historically, this rather abstract *bhakti* becomes predominantly associated with temple worship: in the temple image the devotee finds most frequently the concrete divine presence to which he reacts with *bhakti*. For the first time, this is documented for south India where in the context of Śiva and Viṣṇu temples a highly ecstatic type of *bhakti* emerged. Here *bhakti* also acquires a concrete form of expression which then gains universal popularity in India: the song (to be sung by a professional, or by a group of devotees). Most frequently, it is called *kīrtan* or *bhajan*. In fact, an enormous literature evolved over the centuries in all the vernaculars and also in Sanskrit. Famous poets contributed to this store, and sometimes the genre reaches the sophistication of classical Indian poetry (as in Ānandavardhana's poem in honour of the Goddess, or Vedāntadeśika's hymns addressed to Viṣṇu). Often such religious songs were collected and turned into the sacred scripture of a particular religious community; their poets become 'saints' and receive ritual treatment. Thus in the Tamil country we have the Āḻvārs and Nāyaṉārs (500–1000 CE). Their often extremely sophisticated poems were collected in the *Divya-Prabandham* and the *Tiru-Muṟai* respectively, and these corpora were integrated into Śrī-Vaiṣṇavism and the (south Indian) Śaiva-Siddhānta. Moreover, the poetry (and devotion) of the Āḻvārs provided the basis for many passages in the famous *Bhāgavata-Purāṇa* (ninth or early tenth century). From the thirteenth century, Mahārāṣṭra had its '*sants*' (most famous among these are Jñāneśvar, Nāmdev and Tukārām), who in connection with the cult of Viṭhobā of Paṇḍharpur composed thousands of poems of a Kṛṣṇaite/Vaiṣṇavite nature. From the fifteenth century onward, the region around Mathurā attracted many pilgrims and devotees. The scenes of Kṛṣṇa's youth were 'rediscovered' by them. Many founders of Kṛṣṇaite movements settled here permanently or at least established close links with their representatives there. Some of these movements managed to formulate theologies within the Vedānta (like that of Caitanya's disciples, or of Vallabha). Many others contented themselves with the composition of vernacular poetry and provided a less rigid structure for the religious practice of their followers. Different aspects of Kṛṣṇa's life tended to be emphasised. It was his early mischievous childhood on which the Vallabhites focused, or his love for the cowgirl Rādhā, which was marked by separation, on which the Caitanyaites concentrated.

Again in the south, from the early beginning of the second millennium onwards, the cult of Rāma began to flourish. Kampaṉ's Tamil *Rāmāyaṇa* illustrates the process of deification which the epic figure of Rāma was undergoing. Closer to Rāma's home country in north India, Tulsīdās, in his *Rāmcaritmānas* (*The Lake of Rāma's Deeds*) expressed the culmination of this development by envisaging Rāma as God (i.e. Bhagavān) and not as *avatāra*.

The devotional poetry in honour of other gods and God-figures is far less well studied. Śaivite material seems to be particularly amorphous. But in eighteenth-century Bengal, Rāmprasād Sen composed *bhakti*-songs in honour of the Goddess which immediately gave rise to a popular tradition of composing, and singing, such *kīrtans*. Of an even more recent date are the popular cults of Gaṇeśa in Mahārāṣṭra and of Aiyappaṉ in Tamilnadu (to mention only two examples).

With the regional gods we often find religious 'professionals' who specialise in the ritualised recitation of poetry, stories and even plays in honour of and about, say, Yellammā (Mahārāṣṭra and south), or Khaṇḍobā/Mallāri (Mahārāṣṭra and Karṇāṭak). Of distinctive, often striking, external appearance, these professional religious performers (who belong to lower castes in most cases) can be found all over India. Their individual institution may either be hereditary, or they may have been offered at birth to a particular temple. Their devotional rituals tend to be performed in people's homes or on the street, and this is another feature which adds to the 'random' availability of many different religious cults and institutions in any one locality.

Thus, for most individuals in Indian society, the religious life expresses itself through domestic *pūjā* and *vratas*, visits to temples and *maṭhas*, singing *bhajans* or *kīrtans*, celebrating the popular festivals, patronising wandering performers and consulting *svāmīs* or gurus. Only a small part of this variety has been codified in the *Dharma-śāstras*, like the 'sacraments', *saṃskāras*, of higher castes—the sacred thread ceremony, marriage, etc. Some aspects may have acquired a strong textual, theological and institutional basis. But most of it has been handed down loosely from generation to generation and has been developed by individual groups.

By now it should be clear how many 'random' factors actually determine an individual's religion. In addition, there are strong family and caste traditions of allegiance to a particular form of religion. Yet there remains ample scope for the individual in his choice of what he relates to among the many things on offer in his society. Moreover, we must not ignore the important role of charismatic figures. These may be itinerant mendicants, people associated with a temple or a *maṭha*, or religious 'amateurs'. More often than not, they are performers of some kind, gifted poets or singers or story-tellers. Their role may simply be to combine entertainment with edification, to perform rituals, or to advise on spiritual matters. But sometimes their charisma is powerful enough to create new social structures, by bringing together whole groups of families (and individuals) in a new form of religious allegiance. Since the scale of personal, religious commitment varies enormously in India, it is very difficult to decide when such a new structure ought to be called a 'sect' or a 'religious system'. Criteria developed in the West simply do not help here. Where such a new movement is consciously antinomian, it is relatively easier to identify it. The majority, nevertheless, tend to regard themselves as 'orthodox', which given the purely functional role of the Vedas can mean a wide range of things. But one point is clear: we are dealing here with one aspect of social dynamism which contradicts any rigid conception of the Indian 'caste system'. Social structures, orthodox or antinomian, created by such charismatic figures, very frequently override existing caste barriers, and in turn may give rise to new castes themselves.

To acknowledge these flexible aspects of traditional 'Hinduism' is not the same as uncritically accepting fashionable ideas about 'tolerance'. Any religious leader, however much he may emphasise his 'orthodoxy' and display 'orthopraxy', inevitably challenges others. In fact the heavy emphasis on proving one's orthodoxy (in the most elaborate case, by writing a Sanskrit commentary on the *Bhagavadgītā*, the *Vedānta-Sūtras* or the *Bhāgavata-Purāṇa*) evinces the existence of pressures in Indian society to conform. And the history of Hinduism does know of violent interreligious struggles. Thus the much advertised 'tolerance' is a matter of degree and form; it may express itself in areas where the Western traditions have not shown it.

The enormous variety of religious expressions we have observed in this exploration of epic and purāṇic religion is due to the fact that the 'Hindu' can express his religion spontaneously, whilst drawing on a wide spectrum of given symbols and models. The absence of any centralised practical and doctrinal authority has been mentioned above. But all this does not mean that India did not reflect on its own religious realities. It has been pointed out above how such reflections are expressed in mythical symbols (the 'Trinity', the *avatāras*, etc.) But over and above this level of reflection, India produced a most imposing tradition of philosophical and theological enquiry, on the basis of the religious realities mentioned so far. Historically, Buddhists, Jains and Hindus shared, in their own specific ways, in this enterprise. It is time for us to turn to these developments.

Mahāyāna Buddhism and Buddhist Philosophy

When Buddhism disappeared from India around 1200 CE, inevitably its Indian literary sources also vanished. What was not directly destroyed during the Muslim pillaging of the monasteries disintegrated in the course of time, since nobody was left who could, or wanted to, copy out the manuscripts. Thus the Buddhist community in Sri Lanka became practically the sole custodian of ancient Indian Buddhist material. Indeed the Chinese and the Tibetans made an enormous effort to translate Indian Buddhist literature, and thus, at least in this form, a very sizeable amount of Indian material was saved. However, these translating activities took place during later periods of Indian Buddhist history and concerned themselves on the whole with the materials prevalent at that time. All this had the following result for the traditional Western perception of Buddhism. From China and Tibet forms of Buddhism were known that appear to differ quite radically from that found in Sri Lanka. Since the latter had preserved archaic Indian material, and also quite naturally presented itself as 'orthodox' Buddhism, the types found in China and Tibet tended to be regarded as 'late', as transformations and distortions, almost beyond recognition, of an original Buddhism. The 'Mahāyāna' or 'Northern Buddhism' and the 'Vajrayāna' were seen as successively later developments, to contrast with the 'Theravāda' or 'Hīnayāna' as the original stage. Theism, ritualism, nihilism, magic, obscenity—such have been the labels applied to Northern Buddhism; in themselves, they reveal an interesting diversity of interpretation. Basically for two reasons, such a view of Buddhist history in India now requires drastic reinterpretation.

First, not everything had been lost or destroyed; manuscripts (though often in a fragmentary state) of Buddhist Sanskrit texts were discovered in areas (such as Nepal, Kashmir and Central Asia) where the climate (both literally and socially) was more favourable to the preservation of this fragile material. Secondly, a critical exploration of this literature (usually with the help of Chinese and Tibetan translations) has begun to yield interesting insights. Thus in many cases very complex works (which in that form may belong to, for example, the fourth or fifth century) reveal themselves as crystallisations of a long literary development, metastructures incorporating sometimes very old material (perhaps as old as the second century BCE). This now means that we are dealing here with chronological parallels to much of Pali Canon material preserved in Sri Lanka, and not with necessarily much later stages. Indications have been given above how this would affect our understanding of earlier Indian 'sectarianism'. But here we have to look at a far more fundamental division, that of the Theravāda (or Hīnayāna) versus the Mahāyāna. In fact, it might well be possible to go so far as to regard these two major strands as parallel developments out of the common core of 'original Buddhism'.

Considerable effort has been spent on trying to identify a particular region of India, or a particular Buddhist community, as the original birthplace of the Mahāyāna. The two main contenders have been north-western India and the Āndhra country in the south. However, such a quest has not proved particularly useful. Early Mahāyāna in itself is not easily defined, and the model of a one-point origin appears not to be appropriate. By looking at the earliest identifiable material in extant Mahāyāna literature, a variety of themes emerges, and it seems best to regard these as documenting a dynamic discussion within Indian Buddhist communities, which eventually crystallised as a 'revivalist' movement all over the country. Institutions surrounding the (non-monastic) *stūpa* cult, and the role of the *dharma-bhāṇaka* (lay preacher?) have been suggested as possible points of departure for Mahāyāna teaching.

Let us first look at this literature. Sanskrit appears to have been used by Indian Buddhists at a relatively late period. After all, there were strong ideological and practical reasons speaking against this. Initially scholars thought that the popular Mahāyāna works were written in a 'corrupt' form of Sanskrit. By now however it is clear that under the cover of 'corrupt' Sanskrit one or more vernacular languages are hidden, often superficially Sanskritised. Thus this is material comparable to Pali, another representative of such vernaculars. A fair amount of the oldest literary strata that can be reconstructed consists of small, self-contained poems on the spiritual life; fragments of dramatic plays may be recognised, and inevitably there are many *jātaka* tales. At least in terms of logic, if not strictly in terms of history, the next stage was that such early material was gathered together and set within an overall narrative frame, initially still in the vernacular. The 'sermon' (the *sutta*, Skt. *sūtra*) served as the literary model for such a frame. The intention of this device is clear: to present these ideas as the actual teaching of the Buddha, delivered by him on a specific occasion and in a specific place. Further developments then included a linguistic transformation; the old vernacular material is preserved, but now provided with a Sanskrit 'translation'. Other expansions involved the elaboration of the frame-story (sometimes to a very great extent), the addition of further material of similar kind and reflections of a particular work on its own religious significance, and indeed ritual treatment, as 'sacred text'. The outcome of all this was that hundreds of such (Mahāyāna) *sūtras* evolved, a few of which obtained a bulk of hundreds of pages of text individually. Much of it has actually been preserved in Chinese and Tibetan translations. On the whole it is *sūtras*, of which Indian originals have been preserved, which are the better known ones. Here may be mentioned the *Lotus-Sūtra* (*Saddharma-puṇḍarīka*), *Pure-Land-Sūtras* (*Sukhāvatī-vyūha*, shorter and longer), *Diamond-Sūtra* (*Vajracchedika*), *Laṅkāvatāra-Sūtra* ('delivered in Laṅkā'), *Sūtra of Golden Light* (*Suvarṇabhāsottama*), *Jewel-Heap-Sūtra* (*Ratnakūṭa*) and *Flower-Garland-Sūtra* (*Avataṃsaka* or *Gaṇḍavyūha*). The *Perfection-of-Wisdom-Sūtras* (*Prajñā-pāramitā-sūtras*) make up a miniature literature of their own. The oldest version is the one in 8,000 *granthas* (a counting unit of 32 syllables); the verses (called *Ratnaguṇasaṃcayagāthā*) which accompany that prose text may be even earlier. Later versions reach up to 100,000 *granthas* (the size of the *Mahābhārata*), and yet later ones reduce the bulk once again, as in the *Heart-Sūtra* (*Hṛdaya*) of only a few units. Among those with lost Indian originals may be mentioned the *Sandhinirmocana-sūtra* ('explication of the mysteries' might be the meaning of the title), the *Vimalakīrti-nirdeśa-sūtra* (which deals with the instructions given by the rather antinomian Buddhist layman Vimalakīrti), the *Śūraṅgama-samādhi-sūtra* and the *Āryā- Śrīmālā-sūtra* (in which Queen Śrīmālā figures as teacher). From this brief literary survey it must be evident that the greatest obstacle to an accurate understanding of the Mahāyāna is simply the enormous bulk of its literature, with its as yet barely charted history of a thousand years.

The rise of the Mahāyāna could perhaps be described by reference to a tension well known also in other religious movements: that between institution and charisma. Earliest Buddhism maintained a spontaneous link between spiritual perfection and social interaction by being an itinerant movement. But consequent upon the development of settled monasticism, the emphasis had to shift. The distance between monks and laymen had to increase, the elaborate rules must have absorbed a considerable amount of spiritual energy, and the ultimate goal itself moved further and further away into some distant future existence for the individual. In the formulation of the goal itself, that is *nirvāṇa*, the (philosophically realistic) *Abhidharma* appears to have developed, in certain instances, a relatively negative and sometimes perhaps even nihlistic conception. Certainly its 'monolinear' approach to spiritual progress (which allowed for no more than individual and separate streams of continuity) reduced the possibility of spiritual achievement through personal interaction. Furthermore, the grander the image became that was presented of the Buddha, and the more enormous the store of his personal *puṇya* and its consequent 'superhuman' potentials became in the stories of his life, the less immediate and ordinarily repeatable became his enlightenment.

This appears to characterise the perception of institutionalised Buddhism by at least certain segments of the Buddhist community. A reaction set in which in a variety of ways criticised individual aspects, or in fact the whole, of the Buddhist establishment. Attempts were made to restore the Buddhist teaching to its charismatic origins, and in that sense it may be possible to speak here of a 'revivalist' movement.

The following may convey some impressions of the ideas put forward by the 'revivalists'. The Buddha brought back into the world the medicine that cures the suffering of humanity: his *Dharma*. Transmitted from generation to generation, it must be spread to as many people as possible, to put an end to their *duḥkha.* Thus for someone to receive it and not to pass it on and administer it is a fundamental breach of the Buddha's intentions. Moreover, the spreading of the *Dharma* cannot simply be a mechanical act. Every human skill must be involved, searching for and applying the most appropriate means to communicate it in different contexts to different kinds of people. The concept of 'skilfulness in means' (*upāya-kauśalya*) evolved which denotes the mode in which the *Dharma* is dynamically transmitted through history and infused into society. Even the different types of Buddhism that existed in India were interpreted as expressions of the Buddhas' skilfulness in means. 'Rationalist' interpreters of Buddhism have found it difficult to accept the belief in many past Buddhas and in Buddhas found in many other world-systems. But we are dealing here in principle with a universal Buddhist idea and not a specifically Mahāyāna conception. Thus time and again in cosmic history Buddhas arose to reinstitute the *Dharma*. And, in fact, our present aeon will witness the appearance of one future Buddha, Maitreya. All that the Mahāyāna did, apart from developing such ideas further, was to derive from it its emphasis on the social responsibility (*karuṇā*, 'compassion') of the individual recipient of the *Dharma*.

But this could also be developed into another direction. Given the belief in the existence of many past Buddhas, in the accumulation of vast amounts of *puṇya* over endless periods, and in the existence of many cosmic realms other than our own world, a cult like that of the Buddha Amitābha (or Amitāyus) could 'logically' develop. The names of this Buddha mean 'possessing unlimited light' and alternatively, 'unlimited life'. Whether or not this Buddha-figure is derived from some Iranian god, does not affect his role and function in one branch of the Mahāyāna. On the other hand, it is important not to read back into the Indian understanding of Amitābha developments that took place in China and Japan, where the 'Amida' form of Buddhism became extremely popular. The Indian conception could be summed up as follows. Here is a past Buddha who through his enormous amount of merit could actually create a world-system ideally suited for the achievement of enlightenment. Ordinary human beings could become reborn in that world due to the merit acquired from worshipping Amitābha.

The Sanskrit name of that ideal world is *Sukhāvatī*, 'the blissful one'; other names are: 'The Pure Land' and 'The Western Paradise'.

Yet another very different line is pursued by a further segment of the early Mahāyāna. It concentrates its attack of institutionalism on certain implicit assumptions made in the monastic life. Ingeniously it uses ancient concepts, but redefines them. The key term here is that of 'emptiness' (*śūnyatā*). The pursuit of spiritual perfection in the monasteries implies certain 'realist' (in a philosophical sense) assumptions. There it is taken for granted that there is virtue, the Buddha, *nirvāṇa* and the process of personal continuity. Now the question is asked in what sense such items can be said to 'exist'. As to the nature of the person (including that of the Buddha), earliest Buddhism had already been teaching that it is *anātman* (or *śūnya*), lacking an eternal core or individual essence. In the *Abhidharma*, this had been generalised: all *dharmas* are *anātman*. But, these critics point out, to strive through many lives towards *nirvāṇa* actually means to ignore such fundamental facts. Thus instead of conceiving of a 'monolinear' progress through time, from *saṃsāra* to *nirvāṇa*, what ought to be envisaged is a 'qualitative leap' of insight—corresponding to the Buddha's own enlightenment. This qualitative leap beyond *nirvāṇa*, or outside both *saṃsāra* and *nirvāṇa*, is styled the 'supreme enlightenment' (*samyak-sambodhi*), or the 'perfection of wisdom' (*prajñā-pāramitā*). What has created particular difficulties for early interpreters of such ideas is the fact that '*nirvāṇa*' here has actually undergone a conceptual transformation. In early Buddhism, it may well have denoted a state of realisation which transcended the realm of *duḥkha*. Now it is used to denote merely the end of *duḥkha*. Another term created similar difficulties: 'emptiness'. Originally it denoted little else than the lack of an *ātman*. However, the *Abhidharma*, and the subsequent Theravāda philosophies which derived from it, used *anātman* as one of the three characteristics of all *dharmas*. Implicitly or explicitly, these *anātman dharmas* were regarded as momentarily real (and, in that sense also, any sequence of *dharmas*, their continuity in time, had to be seen as 'real'). At this point we have come back to the critique levelled by the proponents of the emptiness teaching against the 'realist' trends of the monastic life. Developing ideas originally formulated in the schema of the 'conditioned origination', they state that nothing which is 'conditioned' can be regarded as 'real' (in the sense of possessing autonomous existence or essence). To take an example of ordinary life: we can perceive of 'cows' only by virtue of there being non-cows (such as horses, pigs, etc.). 'Cows' are thus 'conditioned'. When this approach is pursued to the highest level of abstraction, even *nirvāṇa* (as perceived in institutionalised spirituality) is 'conditioned' by *saṃsāra*, and vice versa. Neither can therefore be regarded as possessing autonomous reality. Both are 'empty'. This does not now imply that what is 'empty' is 'nothing'. Myriads of phenomena are there, for us to perceive, including our own 'persons'. But none of these *dharmas* possesses an ontological status which could be denoted by terms like 'real', 'unreal', etc.

All we can say is that they are empty, because they are conditioned. At this point, what earlier on has been called a 'qualitative leap' can be defined in more precise terms. If all *dharmas*, including *saṃsāra* and *nirvāṇa*, are empty (*śūnya*), it becomes possible to speak of *śūnyatā*, 'emptiness' as the common ground of all *dharmas* (and the term *dharmadhātu*, 'root of *dharmas*', is indeed found). *Śūnyatā* is ultimate truth, all *dharmas* make up the realm of relative truth. This realisation of *śūnyatā* is the qualitative leap beyond *saṃsāra* and *nirvāṇa*. It is however important to keep in mind that such ideas are not primarily intended as 'philosophy'. They are an attempt to back up logically the spiritual programme put forward, and the critique levelled against the striving for personal perfection and *nirvāṇa*. The true spiritual path aims at the realisation of emptiness in all phenomena, including the Buddha, his teaching, *nirvāṇa* and virtue. This is the supreme enlightenment and the perfection of wisdom. But clearly *śūnyatā* is not something outside, or separate from, the *dharmas*. Thus, whilst the traditional, institutional approach aimed at leaving *saṃsāra* behind in the realisation of *nirvāṇa*, a dialectical attitude is suggested here. The 'perfection of wisdom' can only occur within the realm of the *dharmas*. This dialectic is now given a particular application. The realm of relative truth is, as earliest Buddhism has taught, the realm of suffering, *duḥkha*. Any insight into its fundamental nature cannot now ignore the (relative) reality of *duḥkha* and of suffering beings. The very insight into this is experienced as stimulating an active drive towards making the medicine of the Buddha's teachings available. This is conceptualised as the 'perfection of compassion', *karuṇā-pāramitā*.

Mahāyāna literature refers to the type of Buddhist it criticises by means of the term *śrāvaka*. This is the person who receives the *Dharma* externally and makes use of it purely for personal spiritual advancement towards *nirvāṇa*. Contrasted with him is the *bodhisattva* who aims at the 'qualitative leap' of 'supreme enlightenment' and combines the pursuit of wisdom and compassion. Again, the terms '*bodhisattva*' and 'perfection (*pārami*[*tā*])' are ancient Buddhist. Popular *jātaka* literature is filled with stories depicting the Bodhisattva (that is, the Buddha-to-be in past existences) cultivating the perfection in various virtues. It is not difficult to see how the Mahāyāna could derive its generalised *bodhisattva* concept from this. Besides *śrāvaka* and *bodhisattva*, we find contrasting terms denoting the different spiritual programmes. What has been characterised here as the 'revivalist' movement presented itself as the 'Mahāyāna' and labelled the *śrāvaka* tradition the 'Hīnayāna'. Our understanding of these terms is not as clear as one would wish for. Possibly the most original meaning of *yāna* is that of a '[spiritual] road'. A contrast could be construed between a 'broad' or 'high' (for *mahā*) road and a 'narrow' or 'low' (*hīna*) one. But *mahā* could also denote 'large', in the sense of incorporating more. This 'more' in turn may refer to an enhanced role of laymen, or to the claim frequently made of being the all-embracing, culminating form of Buddhism (thereby actually including the *Hīnayāna* as a lower stage). Alternatively, *yāna* has been interpreted as denoting a 'vehicle'. Whilst it is clear that '*śrāvaka*' and 'Hīnayāna' are used as derogatory terms, it is not clear whether 'Hīnayāna' referred to any specific institution or Buddhist community. More likely the term was originally intended as a critique of generally prevalent attitudes.

What has been sketched so far can relatively safely be regarded as fairly early Mahāyāna teaching. There are however further aspects which have as yet evaded a more precise chronological location within Mahāyāna history. Thus a considerable amount of material is concerned with the glorification of particular meditational exercises (called *samādhis*) and the specific insights and 'miraculous' powers gained through them (e.g. the *Samādhirāja-* and *Śūraṅgamasamādhi-sūtras*). Then we find reflections on the actual 'locus' of supreme enlightenment. Given that man lacked an inner, autonomous core, it seemed preferable to locate the ultimate spiritual experience in some real beyond the individual. In this connection the concept of the *tathāgatagarbha*, 'the seed of all Buddhas', is developed. Enlightenment is perceived as a potential (the 'seed') latent in all men and, moreover, as ultimate reality which in some sense gave rise to the world of phenomena. Or again, a closer relationship between the realm of *dharmas* and the perceiving mind was established. An ultimate insight into the nature of reality could only be regarded as 'achieving' anything (i.e. liberation) by virtue of reality itself being 'mental'. We can move away from the realm of suffering not by changing our perception of *saṃsāra* and so on, but by realising that—quite literally—they are no more than figments of our imagination. Another very different aspect of the Mahāyāna is the development of ritualism in connection with specific Bodhisattva and Buddha-figures. Once again legend and myth are busy elevating particular figures to objects of worship and veneration. Conceptually, the '*trikāya*' evolved as an attempt to provide a systematic exposition of this. Reality is envisaged here as 'three levels' (or 'realms', lit. 'chunks, bodies'). There is the realm of the phenomena (*nirmāṇa-kāya*), with its Buddhas in 'flesh and blood'. Then there is the realm of the highest truth (*dharma-kāya*), ultimate Buddhahood, emptiness, and at the same time the seat of the eternal *Dharma*. In between these two is a third (*sambhoga-kāya*), a heavenly realm filled with Buddhas such as Amitābha and Bodhisattvas like Avalokiteśvara.

From all these different trends it becomes clear that both in its beginnings and during its later history the Mahāyāna was a multifarious movement, mirroring the dynamism of the 'sects' of both the Indian Theravāda and Mahāsāṅghika. But the Mahāyāna expressed itself not merely through its enormous *sūtra* literature. On the basis of the latter, far more systematic philosophical and scholastic traditions arose. Some of this speculation found expression in further *sūtras* (see, for instance, the minute scholasticism about the spiritual career of a *bodhisattva*, divided into ten stages or *bhūmis*, found in the *Daśabhūmika-sūtra*, or the lengthy catalogue of *samādhis* in the *Gaṇḍavyūha-sūtra*, or the *tathāgatagarbha* theory formulated in the *Āryā-Śrīmālā-sūtra*). But on the whole it was in identifiable philosophical schools and by individual thinkers that these more systematic trends occurred.

One of the earliest figures to emerge is Nāgārjuna (second century CE?) He became the founder of the school of the Mādhyamika. His main concern was to place on a philosophical foundation the teaching of 'emptiness' as lying 'in between' (*madhyama*) the 'real' and the 'unreal'. Perhaps to the following century belonged Sāramati who created a system very different from that of Nāgārjuna. One truly 'real' is assumed here, a cosmic self-luminous Mind which due to extraneous impurities projects, as it were, the world of phenomena. Such ideas influenced Maitreyanātha (*c.* 300 CE?), who developed the idea of a cosmic mind further, while he tried, at the same time, to eradicate the blatantly substantialist views of Sāramati. It has been suggested that Maitreyanātha was the actual founder of the second grand school of Mahāyāna philosophy, the Vijñāna/Vijñaptimātra ('Consciousness-Only'), also called Yogācāra. Better known representatives of this school are Asaṅga and the (senior) Vasubandhu (both fourth century CE).

In a sense, Mahāyāna philosophy reached its culmination during the fourth and fifth centuries CE. Indeed it continued for centuries after this period (e.g. in the famous Nālānda in eastern India and in Kaṭhiavār in the west). But fundamentally new ideas were not produced any more. The religious focus shifted to other areas (which will be discussed in the section on the esoteric traditions.) The various philosophical schools that continued elaborated on the details of existing thought and attempted various syntheses of different trends. Thus out of the combination of ideas found in the Yogācāra and Sautrāntika (a Hīnayāna school) evolved the epistemological school associated with the south Indian Diṅnāga (fifth/sixth century CE). Whilst certain followers of the Mādhyamika school (like Buddhapālita, fifth century, or Candrakīrti, seventh century) restricted themselves to elaborating on Nāgārjuna's arguments and substituting a more satisfactory logic for them, others went further and attempted a synthesis with Yogācāra thought. Among these may be mentioned Bhāvaviveka of the sixth century. These different attitudes to the thought of Nāgārjuna gave rise to considerable controversy within the Mādhyamika, and two branches are distinguished: the *Prāsaṅgikas* (restricting their efforts to demonstrating the impossibility of all positive propositions) and the *Svātantrikas* (who were prepared to accept the more positive line of the Yogācāra teaching). With all these thinkers, Mahāyāna thought had entered into a philosophical discourse of enormous complexity and technical acumen. It would be impossible to discuss the details of this material here.

But whilst the philosophers were busy refining their systems, and whilst in other areas the esoteric traditions were influencing

Buddhist religious life, a much more popular strand continued. This was an increasing trend towards a devotionalism centred around specific grand Bodhisattva-figures. Avalokiteśvara appears to have been particularly popular, as some late *sūtras* (like the *Kāraṇḍavyūha*) and late additions to older ones (particularly to the *Lotus-Sūtra*) demonstrate. We also find figures like the 'goddess' Tārā being worshipped.

All the various forms of Mahāyāna Buddhism, with its different literary works, were taken up by the Chinese, and through their mediation transmitted to other Asian countries, like Korea and Japan.

How did the 'Hīnayāna' deal with all these developments? In one sense it attempted to keep abreast in the philosophical discussion that was going on under the banner of the Mahāyāna. Thus it created its own systematic expositions. But in another sense, it simply closed itself off against the attack of the Mahāyānists. We must not forget that from an early date onwards the 'Hīnayāna' became fragmented into many different 'sects', 'schools' and communities, scattered over a very large area. Thus it is impossible to expect a concerted and generally co-ordinated response to Mahāyāna philosophical critique. Instead we find in various individual schools separate attempts at developing traditional beliefs and practices into coherent philosophical systems that could rival, as far as the sophistication of its analysis was concerned, with its Mahāyāna competitors. Best known among these is the school of the Sarvāstivāda, which appears to have spread from Mathurā all over northern India and to have found in Kashmir one of its most important strongholds. In the (junior) Vasubandhu (fifth century) this school's thought reaches its culmination. Historically, however (as the title of Vasubandhu's main work itself bears out: *Abhidharma-koṣa*, 'Treasure of the *Abhidharma*'), the thinking is primarily an elaboration on the older *Abhidharma* and thus cannot positively relate to Mahāyāna metaphysics with its open or implied critique. More nebulous is our information on another school, that of the Sautrāntika (associated with the names of Harivarman, third century CE, and the same Vasubandhu of the fifth century, through his own commentary on his *Abhidharmakoṣa*). The contrast between the Sarvāstivāda and the Sautrāntika has been described as that of philosophical realism versus nominalism. 'Sarvāsti-vāda' itself means the 'teaching that claims "everything exists"', and refers to the belief in the reality of all *dharmas* (including the past and future ones). The Sautrāntikas, on the other hand, rejected such ideas and proposed a merely nominal reality for many *dharmas*. Since '*nirvāṇa*' was included among the latter category, the school may well be described as nihilist. *Nirvāṇa* here is, ontologically speaking, 'nothing'. Both because treatises of the Sarvāstivāda and the Sautrāntika became known relatively early in the West, and also because its teaching draws on seemingly archaic ideas, such Hīnayāna ideas tended to influence Western interpretation of Buddhism as such.

When we turn to Sri Lankan Theravāda, we also find here for the same period (the fifth century or so) attempts at systematising the religious thinking on the basis of the *Abhidharma*. Buddhaghoṣa, particularly through his treatise *Visuddhimagga* (Pali, 'Path of Purification') produced the culminating works here. But in many ways the radical extremes of the Sarvāstivādins and Sautrāntikas are avoided by him.

Buddhist philosophy, particularly Mahāyāna thought, may be regarded as leading intellectually in India for a number of centuries. There is nothing really comparable, in terms of sophistication, on the 'Hindu' side till the seventh century or so. When such systems emerge (and that means not merely dealing with religious issues in a general sense, but presenting themselves as consciously 'Vedic'), they reveal many traces of Mahāyāna ideas and of the Buddhist philosophical method generally.

Hindu Philosophies and Theologies

For a variety of motives, the Indians have shown, from an early period onwards, a considerable interest in a more systematic analysis and understanding of the world, man and religion. 'Systematic' denotes here an analytical, logically coherent and wide-ranging approach, carried out through increasingly sophisticated and carefully defined methods. Whilst it is possible to maintain a distinction between philosophy and theology in principle, the overlap and interaction between these two disciplines has been far greater in India than in the West. This is partly due to the fact that 'religion' here need not involve the concept of a personal absolute, and partly there was the need perceived by many thinkers to present their teaching within an 'orthodoxy' and 'orthopraxy' which at least nominally had Vedic authority. Thus purely philosophical systems tended to be expanded through references to religious matters. And even in cases where their premisses were directly based on religion, no concept of 'God' was necessarily involved. To describe them as 'theologies' would emphasise this religious concern, though it would be misleading, if it were associated in all cases with a *theos*, 'God'.

Traditionally, the whole arena of Hindu speculation has been conceptualised as the 'six (orthodox or Hindu) *darśanas*'. The word '*darśana*' itself denotes a 'vision' or a 'conception' of the world and man's destiny in it; it therefore fuses observation with religious practice. But for a number of reasons, the schema is extremely unsatisfactory. It was formulated at a late stage of the Indian history of thought when most of the thinking listed in it had already lost its relevance to live discussion. It obscures basic distinctions between very different types of systematic thought and their different motivations. It restricts the range of what India produced in the form of critical thought, and ignores all aspects of a historical development and interaction. Moreover, Hindu thought has not been an isolated and self-contained tradition, for over hundreds of years Buddhist philosophy, particularly that of the Mahāyāna, played a leading role in India and necessitated 'Hindu' reactions to it.

When we turn to the individual members in the group of the six *darśanas*, some further general comments are necessary. Already the later portions of the *Ṛg-Veda* demonstrate a great interest in a systematic analysis of the world. More than intellectual curiosity is involved here, for this knowledge is perceived as power, ultimately the power to control one's own destiny and, in the Upaniṣads, to reach out for liberation. Two trends may be distinguished even at this early stage: a proto-scientific (sometimes even mechanistic) approach, and attempts to create a metaphysic for 'mystical' experiences. In addition, ancillary disciplines were developed that served as tools for both approaches. But as always in India, such neat logical distinctions get considerably blurred in real life. In this context it is important to note that these forms of intellectual activity developed their own institutional structures. Professional school traditions evolved, where specific teaching was handed down and elaborated over the centuries. The primary core of such traditions would vary enormously. But given that at least to the professional within any of these traditions it made up 'his whole life', we need not be surprised to find that these cores were expanded and surrounded by a metaphysical framework. Sooner or later, every philosophical school tradition attempted to offer a 'deeper meaning' of its subject matter. Presumably this was primarily intended as a religious conceptualisation internal to the tradition, for the professional representatives. But it may well have been directed also towards society at large, justifying itself in this manner. However, what society made of it is yet another affair. It might adopt the whole package, core discipline and metaphysical framework (as was certainly the case of the Vedānta), or ignore the metaphysics and restrict itself to what the tradition had to offer in practical terms (as seems to have been the case frequently with the *Yoga-* and *Nyāya-darśanas*). Moreover, what precisely constituted a 'metaphysical frame' for a core discipline varied with time. At the beginning, this might be no more than reflections on *saṃsāra* and *mokṣa*. Theistic and 'mystical' matters evolved only later as topics to be considered. The schema of the six *darśanas* abstracts from all this and pretends that all six traditions can be lined up parallel to each other.

Let us begin by exploring the developments in the 'proto-scientific' strand of Indian speculation. Probably the most impressive results were reached, at an early period, in the area of language. They were motivated by the need to preserve the older form of the Sanskrit language that itself was rapidly changing and in fact developing various vernacular 'mother tongues'. At first sight, language consists of an unlimited number of words, put together as sentences. At closer analysis, the number of words reveals itself as finite (say, a hundred thousand). Modifications to a word (the morphemes) show themselves to be far more limited, and also suggest the existence of different types of words (verbs, nouns, adjectives, etc.). In turn, a 'root' can be abstracted from this, to which the various morphemes are added. Thus what results from such an analysis is a system consisting of

1. a catalogue of all roots, 2. sets of morphemes and 3. an account of how to combine the two. Such a system was indeed produced; its final form is associated with the name of Pāṇini and belongs to the fifth century BCE. It is presented in the form of about 4,000 formulas (called *sūtras*), systematically arranged and incomprehensible without the explanation of the commentaries.

In its own right, grammar could hardly claim a place in an account of the Indian religions. But Indian thought perceived a close affinity between language and the world, and in addition applied the methods and the principles of analysing it to other areas. As to the affinity with the world, whole metaphysics evolved. Language in the abstract (this may be called the Vedas or *śabda-brahman*, the *brahman* of words) possesses eternal, autonomous being. It then generates its concrete structures, actualises itself through the spoken word and gets concretised in the objects corresponding to the words. Thus to study the world means to study its words, and, beyond that, language in its prototypal form; language is the avenue towards the transcendental. Such ideas were expressed in various forms and traditions, including the Mīmāṃsā and the school associated with the name of Bhartṛhari. Rather different usage is made of this conception in the esoteric traditions.

As far as the method is concerned, both in approach and in the presentation of its results parallels to other areas of enquiry were perceived. Here was an ideal example of ordering an amorphous and seemingly infinite set of phenomena, by reducing this 'chaos' to a limited set of primary factors and the rules governing their combination and interaction. Obviously this could be applied to the whole world of human experience. From an early period, Indian thought envisaged four or five primary elements that made up all material forms (earth, water, fire, air and possibly ether). Correlations of these five to the five human sense-organs (eye for sight, etc.) were attempted (earth being an object for all five, ether—as carrier of sound—only for the ear). At an early date, forms of atomism emerged which postulated that matter (i.e. the elements) consisted of four or five types of innumerable atoms. To account for 'life', that means for example organic growth, movement, the healing faculty of the human body, perception and consciousness, the existence of a 'soul' or 'life-principle' (often called *jīva*) was postulated. Elements, *jīvas*, and space and time which made up the continuum within which matter and life occurred, tended to be regarded as eternal. On the basis of this raw material, whole cosmological systems could be built which described not just the outside world but also the nature of man. It is quite possible that sometimes such systems carried a conscious mechanistic intention, directed against more 'mystical' or transcendentalist forms of thought. But one of the earliest expressions of this approach is Jain philosophy, and as we have seen, this system is clearly intended to explain how in Jain terms liberation from *saṃsāra* comes about. The Buddhists made much more tentative use of this material, in their *Abhidharma* (from the third century BCE onwards). On the Hindu side, the most typical representative is the *darśana* Vaiśeṣika. As a full metaphysical programme with its (in this case very negative, almost nihilistic) teaching on liberation, it has had relatively little influence. However, one of its achievements was the development of the concept of the 'categories', which along with its cosmology had far wider impact. Reality is now perceived not simply as made up of various 'things', but different types of entities. Thus a substance is distinguished from its attributes which can only occur in conjunction with it. Transformations of substances inhered by attributes are seen as movement, a third category of being. Objects and beings are not discrete entities, but share common characteristics. Thus 'cow' refers to a whole set of animals that all have the same attributes. On the other hand, a category 'difference' (*viśeṣa*, from which perhaps the system derived its name) distinguishes 'cows' from 'horses'. Finally, the sixth category is even more abstract, since it refers to the relation between the other five. It is inherence, as for example an attribute inheres in a substance. Buddhist thought reacted very strongly against this kind of view of reality; it basically rejected the concept of autonomous substance.

Out of a concern for debating techniques arose an interest in the structures of human thought and reasoning, and in their relationship with language. Eventually this crystallised as the *Nyāya-darśana*, which at a still later stage added a kind of theistic frame to its teaching. Often the Nyāya and Vaiśeṣika were regarded as complementary and thus fused into one.

The scholastic study of the ancient Vedic ritual treatises revealed all kinds of contradictions and variations between different branches of the tradition. Thus complex and sophisticated methods of exegesis evolved. This was linked with speculation on the Vedas themselves as the authority for these rituals, and on *Dharma* (according to which these rituals had to be performed) and its role in society. This gave rise to another *darśana*, that of the Mīmāṃsā.

Originally at least, these systems of thought tended to bypass the issues that were raised in the Upaniṣads: *saṃsāra* and *mokṣa*, the *ātman* and *brahman*, and 'altered states of consciousness'. Jainism drew directly on 'proto-scientific' thought to present its own views within the renouncer tradition, and the Buddhists initially refused to put up any kind of systematic, metaphysical account, and even in the *Abhidharma* presented a very idiosyncratic view of the same proto-science. The earliest attempts within the 'Hindu' tradition to deal with such matters centrally still bear the mark of 'proto-scientific' thought, and it may be argued that differences from the actual teaching found in the Upaniṣads are due to this impact. Anyway, the *darśana* Sāṃkhya addressed itself directly to the questions of *saṃsāra* and liberation. A very idiosyncratic cosmology was suggested, in which all phenomena other than the eternal and individual souls (called *puruṣas*) are derived from one ultimate substance, *prakṛti*. The latter consists of three aspects (*guṇas*, qualities or components) *sattva*, *rajas* and *tamas*. Since the latter unequivocally means 'darkness', the other two are most easily explained as 'dust' or 'haze' (*rajas*) and 'brilliance, light' (*sattva*). Because of these three different ingredients, *prakṛti* time and again evolves increasingly 'gross', material forms. The result is a view of the person consisting of a body (made up of five subtle elements—which carry the *karma* after a person's death—and the corresponding gross elements); five senses and five primary faculties of movement; a 'mind' (*manas*). All these are regarded as evolved out of *ahaṅkāra*, the sense of 'I', and the latter in turn grows out of *buddhi* (intellect) which itself is the first stage in the differentiation of *prakṛti*. A *puruṣa* is fettered by this whole structure, but internally unaffected by it. By locating most aspects of the empirical person in the realm of *prakṛti*, it becomes almost impossible to say anything at all about the nature of the *puruṣa*, for even thought and consciousness are still part of *prakṛti*. The intention seems here to be to prevent any kind of action (even a mental one) being associated with the *puruṣa*—an extreme form of the belief in *karma*. In ordinary circumstances (namely in *saṃsāra*), the *manas* feeds into the 'self-awareness' (*ahaṅkāra*) all kinds of false ideas, which are derived from the contact of the senses with their corresponding objects in the material world. By systematically removing the *guṇas rajas* and *tamas* from the whole structure, the *ahaṅkāra* can be purified. Moreover, it is possible then to influence the *buddhi*, which at the moment of deepest insight realises that its own nature is evolved from *prakṛti* and that there exists a fundamental difference of the *puruṣa* from anything connected with *prakṛti*. At this moment the link between *puruṣa* and *prakṛti* is severed, and unimpeded by *saṃsāra* the *puruṣa* achieves liberation.

The Sāṃkhya is a difficult system to interpret. The oneness of all being of the Upaniṣads is maintained here only to the extent that all phenomenal being is unified in *prakṛti*. But the *puruṣas* are very many and remain so even in the state of liberation; there is no *brahman* into which they merge. To what extent the purification of the *buddhi* is regarded as a purely 'intellectual' affair has also been a problem, and to what extent we are actually dealing here with meditational exercises in the form of yoga. Certainly historically, the Sāṃkhya aligned itself very closely with the *Yoga-darśana*. This link itself is problematic, for it has been suggested that the earliest text of the *Yoga-darśana* indicates a metaphysics very much at variance with that found in the later commentaries which all appear to project Sāṃkhya ideas on the *sūtras*. What is important here is the fact that Indian traditions have looked on the *Yoga-sūtras* as the classical account of yoga meditational exercises.

The rationale of these are clear. After preparations of a general ethical and moral kind (*yama*, that is avoiding negative actions like lying and stealing, and *niyama*, that is cultivating positive virtues like contentedness and endurance), the technical side of yoga can begin. This involves the choice of a place conducive to inner quiet and a bodily posture that allows for comfort, relaxation and concentration (*āsana*). A new rhythm is imposed on one's breathing intended to slow down and calm our mental processes (*prāṇāyāma*). Our faculty to filter out sense data that are accidental in a given situation is consciously developed further (in *pratyāhāra*, withdrawal of the senses from their objects). Now follow the inner yogic exercises. *Dhāraṇā* (concentration) seeks to increase the length of time a thought can focus on a particular mental object, and thereby to increase its penetrating powers. 'Meditation' (*dhyāna*) develops this further towards a merger between the meditating mind and its object, and this culminates in *samādhi*, where full mental clarity and an ultimate insight into the nature of reality are achieved. Naturally this achievement is seen as constituting liberation (*mokṣa*).

The *sūtra* (or a similar device) constitutes the formal expression of all these types of teaching. But unlike the Buddhist *sūtra*, the word refers here to extremely concise formulas which are incomprehensible without a commentary. Such explanations tended to be given orally and are therefore not available to us. Even in those cases where literary commentaries were produced, frequently they have not come down to us. This then made it possible for later commentators to read all kinds of interpretations back into the enigmatic *sūtras*. In the case of the sixth of the *darśanas*, the Vedānta, this is particularly apparent.

When discussing theistic and 'mystical' matters, the Epics and earlier Purāṇas used concepts derived from, or related to, the Sāṃkhya system. Even a group of relatively early Upaniṣads resorted to the Sāṃkhya for their speculative material. Although what can be recognised as 'Sāṃkhya material' does not quite correspond to the classical formulation of the system (as found in Īśvarakṛṣṇa's *Sāṃkhyakārikās* and its commentary *Yuktidīpa*, both fifth or sixth century CE), it can by no means be said that we are dealing here with an integral systematisation of the thought of the earliest Upaniṣads. In fact, a systematic metaphysic which could conceptualise *saṃsāra* and *mokṣa* in terms of *brahman* and *ātman* was developed only at a relatively late date. A concept of the 'transcendental experience' of *brahman* was not easily formulated against the background of other philosophical schools. The *Brahma-* or *Vedānta-sūtras* ascribed to Bādarāyaṇa (possibly fourth/fifth century CE) are the earliest known attempt to systematise the teaching of the early Upaniṣads. In turn they served as the scriptural authority for the whole of the *Vedānta-darśana*. 'Vedānta' itself means 'end of the Vedas' and denotes the Upaniṣads, as the Veda's final portion. Thus by its very title this system claims the highest Vedic authority. But from the critical outsider's point of view, the systematisation offered by Bādarāyaṇa is no more than one way of analysing the wide spectrum of Upaniṣadic thought. Moreover, it contains a major unresolved tension. While the cosmos is envisaged as a real transformation (*pariṇāma*) of *brahman*, the liberation of the *ātman* is seen as a monistic merger into *brahman*. Later commentators had to decide which of these two positions to adopt for a fully coherent framework.

Thus Gauḍapāda (in his comments on the *Māṇḍūkya-Upaniṣad*, *c.* seventh century CE) interpreted the world of phenomena as a purely illusory imposition (*vivarta*) upon the universal Mind (equivalent to *brahman*). But it was the south Indian Śaṅkara (between 650 and 750) who through his commentary on the *Brahma-sūtras* established the classical exposition of this approach. He proposed two levels of reality (or 'truth'), an empirical and an ultimate one. The world of the phenomena is explained as the effect of universal ignorance (*avidyā*) upon pure consciousness (*brahman*); individuality as the effect of (individual) ignorance on the *ātman* which in essence is identical with *brahman*. From the ultimate point of view, *brahman* is the sole real. *Avidyā* cannot possess separate, autonomous existence. This dependent relationship between *brahman* and *avidyā* is styled *a-dvaita*, 'non-dual'. Since *brahman* alone possesses true being (*sat*), Śaṅkara cannot accept the existence of a Bhagavān. Thus the God-figures of Hindu religion are conceived of as ultimately illusory aspects of *avidyā*. Overtly in Gauḍapāda, and still implicit in the structure of Śaṅkara's thought, are many Buddhist influences, particularly from the Mahāyāna. But by identifying, for instance, Mind-Only with *brahman*, not only does the Vedānta turn substantialist; it also becomes consciously Vedic, that is Hindu, and anti-Buddhist. Of somewhat doubtful historical value are the accounts that have Śaṅkara imitate the Buddhists by also founding a variety of monastic orders. But monasticism certainly did develop in the tradition of the *advaita-Vedānta*. The increasingly subtle discussion of the precise relationship of *brahman* with *avidyā* (or *māyā*, 'illusion') gave rise to a number of further schools.

The non-classical Sāṃkhya of the Epics, Purāṇas and some Upaniṣads knows of Bhagavān over and above *prakṛti* and the *puruṣas*. In Śaṅkara's system, there was no place for such a figure. But by drawing on the popular devotion to Viṣṇu current in South India at the time (i.e. the tradition of the Āḻvārs), and on theological ideas found in the Pāñcarātra, Rāmānuja (twelfth century CE) created a blatantly monotheistic system. He also applied the cosmological realism of Bādarāyaṇa to the relationship between *brahman* (who is Viṣṇu here) and the *ātman*. The universe, with its beings and its material objects, is as it were Viṣṇu's body. For their existence they depend totally on him (thus again this is *advaita*), and they are his real external expression—he is 'differentiated' into, or 'qualified' by, them (*viśiṣṭa*). Thus the system known as the *viśiṣṭādvaita*. Later theologians (like Vedāntadeśika, thirteenth/fourteenth century CE, and his contemporary Piḷḷai Lokācārya) focused on the problematic relationship between the operation of Viṣṇu's grace and human merit. Eventually, Śrīvaiṣṇavism, that is the religious movement of the *viśiṣṭādvaita*, split into two branches. One side maintained that in no way could human merit (acquired through virtue and religious works) be a condition for Viṣṇu's saving grace. As the cat simply grabs its kitten at the moment of danger and carries it off to safety, Viṣṇu simply comes and saves. The other branch insisted that by this logic either everybody should be in the state of salvation, or Viṣṇu would be a cruel lord. At least in some small measure man must make himself ready to receive the divine grace, as the baby monkey must at least hold on to its mother's neck in order to be carried into safety.

The period between the thirteenth and the sixteenth centuries witnessed the formulation of many further theistic varieties of the Vedānta. Madhva (thirteenth century) formulated a strictly dualistic system, with Viṣṇu as *brahman*. Even in the state of liberation, the soul does not lose its individual identity. Nīmbārka (before the sixteenth century), Vallabha and Caitanya's disciples, particularly Rūpa and Jīva Gosvāmī (all sixteenth century) focused on Kṛṣṇa as *brahman*. It is impossible here to provide further details on all these theological developments within the Vaiṣṇava or Kṛṣṇaite Vedānta.

A commentary on the *Brahma-sūtras* was one of the most prestigious ways of formulating a theology and thereby establishing the orthodoxy of a religious system. But theologies were created in India in many other ways; the example of the *Devīśataka* by Ānandavardhana has already been mentioned in a previous chapter. Thus alongside the Pāñcarātra, the Śaiva Āgamas had also been transmitted from north India to the south. Against the background of the earlier Śaiva mystics (the Nāyaṉārs), a theology was developed on the basis of the Āgamas which is called the Śaiva-siddhānta. Meykaṇṭaṉ, Aruḷnanti and Umāpati (1200–1300 CE) are some of the more important theologians involved in this; they all wrote in the vernacular Tamil. The devotionalism derived from the Nāyaṉārs added features in the south which made the system look rather different from its earlier namesake in Kashmir. In a similar manner, Pāñcarātra ritualism acquired a devotional dimension through the Āḻvārs and Śrīvaiṣṇavism.

Theism and mysticism (in the sense of meditationally gained 'knowledge') are, however, not the only areas to which this type of critical and systematic thought was applied. The materials typical of the esoteric traditions (about which more will be said in following sections) also became the object of philosophical investigation. Kashmir was particularly fertile in the production of such systems.

From these various observations it should have become clear that, in spite of the enormous spectrum of different views contained in the labels of the Vedānta, and of the 'six systems' generally, Hindu religious speculation does not restrict itself to these traditions. As far as the religious content of this speculation is concerned, a similar variety and flexibility presents itself. Man may be envisaged as capable of achieving his own liberation (through meditation, or through rituals which in turn may be exoteric or esoteric); or he may be regarded as totally dependent on divine grace, or a subtly balanced combination of both views may be proposed. Attempts may be made to gather together the totality of all that exists in one ultimate unity, or irreconcilable and unfusable differences of categories of reality may be perceived to persist even on a fundamental level, or again, combinations of both positions may be proposed. The possible varieties are unlimited, and over more than a millennium Hinduism has formulated a large number of them. That such intellectual dynamism was possible is due to a number of factors: a particular interest of Indian society at large in such matters and its readiness to support its institutionalised forms, but perhaps most of all, the absence of any central and all-embracing doctrinal authority. Naturally, the emergence of ever new religious teachers and movements made the formulation of ever new systems necessary.

Later Jainism

The apparent austerity of Jainism was complemented by a considerable culture-forming power, at least in certain regions of India and during certain periods. Moving from Gujārāt and Rājasthān southwards in the western half of India, via Mahārāṣṭra and Kārṇāṭaka. and ending in Tamilnadu, we travel through regions which at some time or other during the last two millennia have been strongly influenced by the Jains. Thus many of the various languages spoken in these regions were actually moulded by Jains as vehicles of literary expression. The Jain literature in Tamil, Kannada and Gujarati in particular is of staggering size. Besides, the Jains continued cultivating Prakrit (in its Māhārāṣṭrī form), frequently resorted to Sanskrit and made ample use of Apabhraṃśa (a literary language derived from an early medieval vernacular of the Gujārāt/Rājasthān area). Northern Mahārāṣṭra can be regarded as a very rough dividing line between the Śvetāmbara and Digambara branches, the latter belonging to the southern part.

In the south, Jainism flourished during almost the whole of the first millennium CE, though much later works were still produced in Tamil. In Gujārāt the Jains began to dominate the political and cultural scene towards the close of the first millennium CE, and, though suffering heavily from Islamic persecution, have maintained their prominence till the present day.

In the history of Tamil literature, the Jains are not only known for their ancient moralistic classics (like the *Tirukkuṟaḷ* and *Nalāṭiyār*). They also cultivated a large amount of local, originally secular, folklore and epic material. The best-known work in this category is the epic *Cilappatikāram* (perhaps of the fifth or sixth century CE). The year 892 CE saw the completion of another major literary enterprise. Began by Jinasena, continued by his disciple Guṇabhadra and finished by the latter's disciple Lokasena, under the title of the *Mahā-Purāṇa* (*Ādi-* and *Uttara-Purāṇa*) a grandiose vista of world history and the role of the Jaina saviour-figures in it was expressed in the prestigious Sanskrit. To the many later works dealing with these themes and written in various vernacular languages must be added, on the Śvetāmbara side, Hemacandra's *History of the 63 Great Men* (written in Sanskrit in the twelfth century in Gujārāt). On a gigantic scale Jainism has produced here its own version of the epic and purāṇic literature. Starting therefore with the origins of our present cosmic age, the figure of Ṛṣabha is presented as the Jain culture-hero, who not only made the Jain teaching available to our aeon, but also instituted social structures and so on. Twenty-three further such *tīrthaṅkaras*, religious founders, followed after him, the penultimate being Pārśva and the last one, the Mahāvīra. Alongside these figures, twelve universal emperors (*cakravartins*) are mentioned (three of whom also count as *tīrthaṅkaras*). In addition, from the Kṛṣṇa and Rāma stories were developed three series of nine Vāsudevas (equivalent to Kṛṣṇas), anti-Kṛṣṇas and Baladevas (equivalent to the Kṛṣṇas' half-brothers). These are the 63 heroes. By telling the life-stories of all these, the Jains could not only incorporate the material which also found expression in the *Mahābhārata*, *Rāmāyaṇa* and earlier Purāṇas; they could also draw on and develop a vast store of other stories, myths and legends.

Generally, the Jains were the great tellers of religious stories in India. This literature, obviously intended for the edification of lay people, is vast. In endlessly variegated form the key tenets of Jainism are shown to apply to a person's life: the pernicious effects greed and lust, hatred and violence have on subsequent existences. From among this almost unsurveyably large range of material, the story of Yaśodhara may be singled out because of its particularly frequent and sophisticated treatment; perhaps best known is the *Yaśastilaka-campū* of Somadeva, 959 CE. Because king Yaśodhara had permitted the 'sacrifice' of a cock made of dough, for many further existences he had to pay for this minimal act of violence by suffering the utmost cruelties.

Without apparently suffering a loss of their essential teaching and religious identity, the Jains adopted a variety of other features from their environment. Although in terms of their teaching the veneration of images cannot make any sense, the Jains took to temple building on a large scale. Images of the *tīrthaṅkaras* have been installed, *pūjā* is being performed and hymns full of the spirit of *bhakti* are sung. The *tīrthaṅkaras* in the state of *mokṣa* may not be addressable through these forms of devotion. But as well-intended pious acts these religious expressions are generally acknowledged to produce merit. But in fifteenth-century Gujārāt—possibly under the influence of Muslim ideas—a Jain layman, Loṅkā Śāha, founded a movement (the Sthānakavāsins) in opposition to the widespread Śvetāmbara acceptance of temple worship.

Given the extent to which Jain doctrine had been formulated from early times, it was far more difficult for the Jain philosophers to participate in the discussions and trends that dominated the Indian scene. What was developed over the centuries as the *syādvāda*, the 'teaching that [things] may be [this, or may be that]', must be regarded as a primarily defensive device. This means that there are always a whole range of possible viewpoints (a list of seven evolved) from which any item can be approached. No single statement can thus encompass the whole truth. However, a thinker like Kundakunda (a Digambara from the Deccan, perhaps fourth century CE) showed that adjustments to the current trends in Buddhist and Hindu thought were possible. The archaic emphasis on the materially conceived *karma* as the cause of *saṃsāra*, and the corresponding cultivation of physical modes of eradicating it, stood in stark contrast to most of Hindu and Buddhist thought. Where these did not focus on 'ignorance' as the cause of *saṃsāra*, and on meditation as the primary spiritual practice, they emphasised devotion, *bhakti*, and the role of divine grace. Kundakunda made 'ignorance' (*ajñāna*) the primary cause of *saṃsāra*. By distinguishing now a level of relative from that of ultimate truth, he argued that only on the former does the soul (*jīva*) appear to be active, and thus appear to be generating further *karma*. On the level of ultimate truth, the *jīva* merely perceives its own nature, and that as totally distinct from everything material. To realise this is, according to him, liberation. Such a new focus, away from *tapas* towards meditation (which naturally is the means for the *jīva* to realise the ultimate truth), was also made use of in a different context. Although the Jains on the whole did not participate in the 'tantric' developments to be mentioned in the next chapter, or merely externally adopted the usage of certain *mantras* and *yantras*, we do find traces of an antinomian attitude similar to that of the nominally Hindu *sants*. Apabhraṃśa works like the *Paramappapayāsu* (end of first millennium?) attack external religious practices (including the adherence to labels like 'śvetāmbara' and the inferior role of women in religion) and advocate the cultivation of inner spiritual values and of 'knowledge'.

It is very difficult to compare the role of Jainism with that of Buddhism in the context of the Indian religions. Given the almost total disappearance of Buddhist literature from India, it is impossible to assess the cultural face of Buddhism during the period studied here. Yet this itself may suggest a hint of an explanation. Possibly Buddhism suffered so much worse under the hands of the Muslims because it had far less contact with its lay populace—because it lacked the 'cultural face' Jainism consistently developed.

The Esoteric Traditions and Antinomian Movements

It was roughly the middle of the first millennium CE that witnessed the emergence of a whole new branch of religious literature. This consists of texts which tend to call themselves 'tantras'. It is not just the original meaning of the word 'tantra' which is disputed and far from clear. The nature of the material itself found here is still extremely obscure and its critical study has only just begun. The chapter on 'Śaivism and the tantric traditions' will summarise the results of current scholarship as far as material from Kashmir is concerned. Here some general comments will be made. Precisely because little critical study of the esoteric material has been available till very recently, all kinds of claims and global assessments by popularist writers could be made. Thus a concept 'Tantrism' (with the related adjective 'tantric') has gained great popularity, with its implied assumption that we are dealing here with a well-defined and coherent system of religious ideas and practices. But in reality, no such systematic coherence exists throughout the vast literature of the Tantras.

Historically speaking, it seems possible to explain the literary emergence of esoteric material by reference to the changed social and cultural circumstances in northern India after the collapse of the Gupta empire. A 'normative' and intellectual superstructure collapsed which made it possible for religious undercurrents to rise to the surface and find literary expression. It seems extremely unlikely that a new type of religion itself originated during this period. Indeed, externally not much is actually 'new' here. For most of the material found, earlier parallels could be cited. If anything, it is the combination of such material that is novel. Furthermore, it is the attitude and the purpose behind its application which are expressed now in a literary manner.

The term 'magic' is frequently used to describe or define the material found in the Tantras. But this is not a useful approach. It is in no way possible either to set up objective criteria for what features distinguish 'religion' from 'magic', or to reduce the enormous spectrum of religious activities in India to such a simplistic polarity. For example, the *mantra* is a particular combination of syllables (which may or may not have a direct linguistic meaning). Knowing it and reciting it is universally regarded as an act of actualising the particular power latent in the *mantra*. But Vedic hymns consist of '*mantras*', the worship of God in the temple is accompanied by *mantras* and yogic meditation may well be accompanied by the muttering of them. Yet in all three cases it is hardly possible to regard this as 'magic' or 'esoteric', or to ignore the distinctions between these three types of religion. However, if a person actually believes in the existence of an all-powerful God and then expects to gain personal access to that power directly through the recitation of the appropriate *mantra*, then this must be regarded as a fourth type. To call it 'magic' will still obscure those cases in which the practice has a consciously expressed transcendental objective ('to achieve liberation'). 'The tantric approach' will be used here as the term to refer to the type of religion which pursues the objective of gaining 'power', for whatever reason.

The following could be put forward as a very tentative general framework within which this type of religion could be assessed. Man lives in a universe which is pervaded by all kinds of forces. Many of them are destructive and threatening, others relate in a more positive manner to his life. What conventional society has on offer as the means of controlling these forces is believed to be limited and restrictive as to the realisation of man's full potential. There is, however, a knowledge available which the more adventurous and mature person can draw on and thereby improve that realisation radically. But it is esoteric, well guarded by a secret tradition. With the help of this esoteric knowledge it becomes possible to expose oneself to even the most dangerous and powerful of such universal forces and not just survive, but actually control them and absorb them for one's own fulfilment.

Such a global description implies various important features. The world-view is that of ordinary people, not that of the philosopher or theologian. The value-system of ordinary society is maintained. For example, a potentially fatal force is still perceived as such here. But by means of the esoteric knowledge it is now possible to come in contact with precisely the taboo areas shunned by ordinary society because of these dangerous forces. Finally, just as this knowledge itself, so its application remains a secret affair. Clearly we are dealing here with a form of antinomianism, but because of its secret nature it must be distinguished from other types (which are discussed below) which publicly reject certain conventional assumptions about what is 'dangerous' or forbidden. Naturally, in real life there will be a fair amount of overlap and fusion, but at least conceptually the differences of these types of antinomianism ought to be maintained.

When such ideas were given literary expression (however secret the texts themselves may then be kept), it became possible to draw upon the mainstream of the Indian intellectual scene. That means that the whole store of the philosophical and theological discussion could be utilised for the conceptualisation of this religion. Particularly prominent were the advaita-Vedānta, Śaiva theology, and the Mahāyāna, and that also means that typically 'Hindu' and typically 'Buddhist' formulations evolved. Yet the presence of mainstream terminology and concepts must not be mistaken for an intrinsic relationship between the tantric approach and other forms of Buddhist and Hindu religion.

Thus there are at least three layers that have to be distinguished. They are not just historical, but also social. At the basis, we have the 'raw material' upon which then the 'tantric approach' is imposed. This in turn was given metaphysical interpretation and thus linked with Buddhist and Hindu thought.

Attempts to define 'Tantrism' through catalogues of its 'raw material' necessarily fail, because all items of such a list are more or less Indian universals. *Mantras* and *yantras* (or *maṇḍalas*), powerful strings of syllables and combinations of visual patterns, are all-pervasive in Indian religion. So are *mudrās,* particular gestures of the hands and fingers, and *pūjā*, the rituals employed to propitiate, venerate or worship powerful non-human beings. The concept of *śakti* ('power'), abstract or personalised (particularly as a 'goddess'), occurs frequently in monotheistic and other systems of thought. Certain elements are socially restricted, which means they are 'natural' and legitimate for some classes of society, but not for others. Among these may be mentioned the consumption of meat and alcohol and the celebration of orgiastic fertility festivals (like Holi), Inevitably the concern for 'purity' of some classes of society necessitates the (legitimate) existence of other classes that remove (and thus handle) 'impurity'. Finally, certain phenomena would probably universally be regarded as taboo, like acts of wilful killing or the consumption of bodily excretions (faeces, urine, spittle, vomit, etc.), particularly of another person. All this is perceived not as objectively 'bad' (or even 'impure'), but as subjectively harmful and destructive.

To understand how the 'tantric approach' deals with this situation, it would be of primary importance to define the social position of the *tāntrika*. Unfortunately, little direct information on this is available, and we have to rely on the whole on inference. But given the fact that we are dealing with actual texts in Sanskrit (however incorrect it may be in some cases) and that certain rituals can be analysed as conscious and systematised acts of breaking social taboos, it appears appropriate to locate this position somewhere above the tribals, peasants, artisans and villagers generally, with whom some of the features (like alcohol, meat, 'impurity') occur naturally. For only from the vista of 'middle class' (or better, of higher castes) certain practices could appear as 'taboo'. Though it is useful for a social identification of the 'tantric approach' to concentrate on the breaking of taboos, this is obviously a far too limited overall definition. Certain types of ascetics have been suggested as more original practitioners of tantric rites.

At the heart of this religion lies the pursuit of power. Thus by drawing the right diagram (*yantra* or *maṇḍala*) and reciting the appropriate *mantras*, powerful beings can be brought down into the centre of the *maṇḍala* (or into the person himself). *Pūjā* may then be offered, and that could mean to oneself as the seat of that power which has been made to enter the body. Furthermore, many forces normally perceived to be dangerous can be invoked and/or treated ritually through items equally perceived to be dangerous: blood, alcohol, etc. The setting itself could be a realm ordinary people would never enter, in particular the cremation ground, and that during night-time. Although of no such overall importance in the Tantras themselves, one particular ritual has dominated the imagination of many Western writers on the subject. These are the five M's—a ritual involving five features which all begin with the letter *ma* in Sanskrit. At the beginning, there is *mada*, alcohol, consumed by the participants. Then there are dishes of *matsya* (fish) and *māṃsa* (meat). This is followed by *mudrā*, which in this context probably does not refer to gestures of the hand, but to a particular dish perceived as an aphrodisiac. Finally, there is *maithuna*, sexual intercourse. A host of interpretations have been proposed for this; moreover, there is enormous variation as to the precise context and the concrete details. Particularly when envisaged as practised in a cremation ground at night by male and female members of a secret cult who are not married to each other, it is not difficult to see in it a ritualised breaking of taboos. Powers are utilised which according to ordinary perception are so dangerous that they are kept 'taboo', that is, outside one's own person and realm. Moreover, the organisation of the ritual itself could suggest a progressive stimulation of sexual energies towards the final climax. But given the ritual context, such a climax is not perceived as merely physical. A force is released or realised which can be used for spiritual purposes.

How all this may work (whether specifically the five M's or any other such rituals) depends on many factors, which include theories of a quasi-physiological nature. Accordingly, we may find that ejaculation is prevented. Whilst emission of semen is regarded as 'waste' of energy, the ritualised intercourse rechannelises this energy, pushing it upwards a (nominal, i.e. non-physiological) duct. This is part of a more comprehensive model, which itself may be found in a wide range of contexts (including 'mainstream', post-classical yoga). Two primary, complementary powers are located inside the human body, one in the head and the other at the base of the spine. By activating the lower one, pushing it upwards and letting it unite with the top one, an initially 'diffuse' person can become integrated and in total control of all his faculties. Alternatively, the union of man and woman can be explained as achieving a fusion of powers that normally occur only separately.

Any application of the tantric approach to the practical raw material implies some specific conception of its rationale and mode of operation. Whilst in principle it may not be impossible to establish a chronological scale of such conceptions, in practice only the more advanced levels of this conceptualisation are available to us. In other words, with the present state of scholarship these religious practices only make sense to us when they are spelled out within a known metaphysical framework. As indicated above, such a framework is not fixed or unique; a variety of very different traditions may be employed in different contexts. In Hindu environments, a whole array of associations around the concept of '*śakti*' can be made use of. Philosophically, an in itself immutable and passive absolute can be envisaged as active (for example, as creating, maintaining and destroying the world) by envisaging *śaktis* inhering in it. Theologically, this may be concretised as Śiva and his goddesses, his *śaktis*, or as Kālī and her 'powers'. The tantric approach may now present itself as the concrete, ritual means of personally realising the unity of Śiva and his *śaktis*, of establishing individually the union of the absolute with the world of phenomena. In different words, liberation within the world can thus be achieved. Generally, the links with Śaivism are quite pronounced in tantric literature, and Śaivite symbolism and terminology is ubiquitous. But often it is not Śiva, but Kālī, who appears at the centre of such systems. Moreover, there are examples of a Vaiṣṇava and Kṛṣṇaite character. The Bengal Sāhajīyas draw heavily on the Kṛṣṇaism to which Caitanya gave shape in the sixteenth century, and from the twelfth century south Indian Śrīvaiṣṇavism knows a *Lakṣmī-Tantra*, a work quite popular in the official temple worship of the Pāñcarātra.

More complex is the Buddhist application of this material. But even here it is possible to correlate the intentions with standard Buddhist ideals. Late popular Mahāyāna Buddhism may have venerated Bodhisattvas and Buddhas on a large scale, but, in terms of Mahāyāna metaphysics, these could never be regarded as 'objective' realities or beings. Instead, they shared with all other phenomena the basic characteristic of being 'empty'. Particularly with the help of a model like that of the *trikāya* it was possible to emphasise the emptiness of all Buddha- and Bodhisattva-figures, while stating their 'reality' on the level of phenomenal existence. On this level, worship in temples and prayers addressed to them made sense. To proceed further and manipulate such figures ritually was in fact far less 'sacrilegious' than in a monotheistic Hindu system. For on the plane of absolute truth, no omnipotent absolute being can be envisaged. Moreover, the evolution of specific Bodhisattva- and Buddha-figures, with their mythologies, was a special development out of the original ideal that every good Buddhist should be a *bodhisattva.* The tantric approach allowed for precisely such an identification between the individual person and the—artificially projected—image of a (mythologised) Bodhisattva. As to the breaking of taboos, it could be argued that any view of the world that maintains as absolute a division of the respectable versus the forbidden is still limited and, in fact, characterised as fundamental ignorance. All phenomena are relative, because they condition each other. Ritually breaking taboos is a concrete way of transcending the level of the conditioned. Finally, the grand ideal of the Mahāyāna is the union of the perfections of wisdom and compassion. Now just as in Hindu contexts the conception of two complementary forces could be presented in Tantric contexts as the union of Śiva and *śakti*, Buddhism could envisage it as the ritual concretisation of the union of *prajñā* and *karuṇā*.

But in some ways, the Buddhist conceptualisation of the tantric approach differs fundamentally from the Hindu varieties. Thus it does not break any metaphysical taboos; there is no clash here between the conception of an omnipotent highest reality (say Bhagavān Śiva) and its tantric manipulation. That means, in its intentions tantric Buddhism is not esoteric, is not the alternative to an insufficient and mistaken mainstream religion. It simply presents itself as an easier, more efficient means of achieving standard Buddhist ideals, through methods that are appropriate for a feeble and decadent age. Thus when we sometimes find this form of Buddhism described as a third '*yāna*' (most often, 'Vajrayāna'), this is not really parallel to the critical self-definition of a Mahāyāna *vis-à-vis* the Hīnayāna. Tantric Buddhism applies the abstract insights of Mahāyāna thought to concrete, ritualised practice.

The tantric approach is not uniform in other respects as well. By no means all applications can be called religious in any sense of the word. Often quite practical aims are being pursued: increase of wealth, power (in a political or economic sense), victory in military matters, health, etc. As far as the latter aim is concerned, there is an overlap with an enormously complex and variegated range of material which all deals with 'healthy living' and curing diseases. This includes the use of drugs, elixirs, medicines, yoga and sexual practices. In such contexts we may well encounter the ideal of 'liberation' expressed as 'bodily immortality'. Secondly, where the tantric rituals are envisaged as operating on some internal aspect of the person, say mental or meditational, it was logical to internalise the ritual itself with its concrete, physical utensils, or present the latter through innocuous substitutes. A traditional classification of left- and right-hand Tantra refers to this possibility. Only the left-hand variety would physically and literally execute the rituals; the other variety obviously ceases to be truly antinomian.

Tantric Buddhism dominated the Indian scene during the last few hundred years of Buddhist presence in the sub-continent (until *c.* 1200 CE). China took in pre-Tantra Buddhism, and acted as a kind of filter when tantric material began to appear for a brief period. Only a minute amount of tantric materials was taken over, to become the Chen-yen (Japanese: Shingon) school. Tibet on the other hand encountered Buddhism during the flourishing phase of its tantric expression, and it is fundamentally this type of material which was translated and preserved in the Tibetan Canon (where hundreds of Tantras can be found). The Tibetans adopted tantric Buddhism not as an already fixed system, but as a still dynamic affair, and they actively continued the conceptualisation of the tantric approach in terms of Mahāyāna thought. But it would be unrealistic to assume that the north Indian Buddhist 'universities', where tantric Buddhism was cultivated, received from many Asian countries students and endowments merely because of the lofty ideal of achieving supreme enlightenment. As a system of gaining 'power', in a variety of senses, it had an attraction far beyond the strictly religious realm. The same applies to tantric Hinduism. Here the history has continued up to the modern time, although the practice of left-handed rituals must be assumed to have become extremely rare, if ever it played a significant role among non-ascetics. The boundaries between more abstruse forms of yoga, medicine, alchemy, *pūjā* and right-hand *tantra* have become almost totally blurred during the second millennium CE.

In some senses related to, and in other senses radically different from, the tantric approach is another component of the Indian religious scene. This may be called the 'antinomian movements'. What links them with the material discussed so far is a conscious rejection of certain socially accepted taboos, and of a belief in the efficacy of official religion. What is different is the rejection of any external expression of religion, including the forms of tantric ritual. Moreover, this antinomianism expresses itself publicly, without resorting to clandestine alternative or additional practices. Again, it is easy enough to draw conceptual distinctions; in reality the differences are blurred, particularly in the case of the 'right-handed' *tantra*, which has become 'domesticated'.

Such antinomian movements have occurred in most regions of India over most of its history. The following observations can do no more than provide a very general characterisation of these movements. While it is inevitable that every religion creates its own external forms of expression, the antinomian critics point out that a mere adherence to such outside manifestations cannot be regarded as 'true religion'. Institutionalisation allows for ossification: the inner life has died away, while the shells of outer form remain. Rituals, sacrifices, temple worship, yogic postures, social structures, sacred language, nocturnal tantric rites in cremation grounds—these and many similar phenomena may all be practised in a purely external, mechanical manner, without a commitment to an inner purification. Moreover, they may act as obstacles to the live religious realisation.

No study of the Indian religions would be accurate which did not pay attention to the permanent dynamism of evolving such forms (as signs of religious expression) and criticising them when they are perceived to have lost the life they are meant to contain. A classic example is obviously early Buddhism. Already here we see many factors at work which time and again during the following centuries generate similar antinomian attitudes. The Buddha quite consciously rejected 'Brahmanism', with its restrictive claim that only a minority of the population could have access to 'true religion', that the latter was contained in the Vedas, and that only the brahmins could be the legitimate guardians and ritual functionaries of this religious reality. The Mahāyāna in turn reacted against institutionalised forms of a slightly later Buddhism. In the course of the centuries, other areas of attack can be identified in 'Hinduism': its temple worship, folk rituals, forms of esoteric yoga and indeed tantric practices. What is set up as the live alternative is an inner religion that produces a real change in the person, non-ritualistic expressions, a fluidity that avoids solid and permanent structures (both literally and metaphorically), usage of the vernacular directly accessible to all members of a society and democratic and non-elitist social structures. The last mentioned point has often been called 'attack on the caste system', but this label is not very useful, for on the whole the attack was restricted to aspects of the social system which were discriminatory in religious matters alone. Generally it did not affect features like marriage or economic status. In terms of metaphysics, we can find time and again Buddhist undercurrents at work (for instance, in some of the Tamil Cittars). With the Mānbhāvs of Mahārāṣṭra some Jain influence might be detected. Advaita-Vedānta with its conception of oneness of all beings could be applied, and radical forms of monotheism (around Śiva or Viṣṇu) also produced antinomian movements. Frequently, commonsense and arguments derived from what resembles our 'proto-science' are used to demonstrate the meaninglessness of rituals etc. In northern India, after the gradual permeation of society by Islamic ideas, Sufism in particular (itself a potentially antinomian phenomenon) began to interact with the traditional Indian attack on ossified religion. The arrival of Western ideas about religion and democracy added a further theoretical basis for antinomian attitudes. In many cases at least, what has conventionally been described as 'reform Hinduism', with the West priding itself in having provided the inspiration, ought to be regarded as modern representatives of the age-old antinomian dynamism.

The information on antinomianism during the first millennium CE is relatively sparse; a separate section deals with various Śaivite movements that can still be identified. Towards the last few centuries of this millennium, the Apabhraṃśa language established itself as a lingua franca over wide areas of northern India. Derived from various local vernaculars, it produced a literature which included antinomian strands. Thus we have from this period Saraha's *Dohākośa*, a work that officially would belong to Tantric Buddhism, but in terms of its ideas is perhaps more typical of the antinomianism discussed here. The religious realisation is *sahaja*, 'innate' in man, and will occur 'spontaneously', once all external and ossified religious forms have been removed. The Jains also expressed similar ideas in works like the *Pāhuḍadohās* and *Paramappapayāsu*.

From around the thirteenth century, a more pronounced regionalism emerges, with the return to the actual contemporary vernaculars. Various antinomian movements were directly involved in this linguistic and literary change. Thus during the twelfth century, in what is today the state of Kārṇāṭaka, originated the Vīra-Śaivite or Liṅgayite movement, with Basavaṇṇa as its primary instigator. Monotheism (with Śiva at the centre) provided the metaphysical framework, but by attacking temple worship, brahmin rituals and the restrictions of the caste system (which in this particular case seems to have included the 'secular' side as well, i.e. marriage), the Liṅgayites are clearly antinomian. A large store of religious poetry in the vernacular Kannada (Kanarese) was produced by Basavaṇṇa and other poets like Allama-prabhu and the poetess Mahādevīyakka. The thirteenth century witnessed in neighbouring Mahārāṣṭra the rise of the Mānbhāvs (Mahānubhāvas) to whom Cakradhar gave its structure. This movement is characterised by a pronounced anti-Vedism and emphasis on asceticism. At a later stage, it developed the concept of the five Kṛṣṇas (which includes Cakradhar, the Hindu figure of Kṛṣṇa and the central deity, Parameśvara). It produced a sizeable literature in Marāṭhī. Both movements have continued up to the present day; the Liṅgayites in particular, with five million followers in 1959, constitute an important influence in Kārṇātaka. In Tamilnadu, Śrīvaiṣṇavism under Maṇavāḷa mā muṉi (fifteenth century CE) derived from the total submission to Viṣṇu's saving grace an alternative social structure which discarded all the paraphernalia of 'orthopraxy'.

In many other instances, less well-defined movements occurred. Thus in the Tamil-speaking region, we find a whole string of individual poets (from well back in the first millennium CE onwards), who are called Cittar (from Sanskrit Siddha) and who all share certain typically antinomian ideas. Northern Buddhism also knows of a series of Siddhas (which includes Saraha mentioned above). The theoretical centre of Siddha religion is at least the cultivation of *siddhis*, 'miraculous' powers gained through esoteric yogic practices. Closely related are the Nāthas who all over northern India have produced a more clearly defined movement. From Bengal must be mentioned the Bāuls, whose poetry has had a considerable impact on Bengali thought and religion. Here the interaction between Sufi and antinomian Hindu ideas is particularly strong, and indeed members of both religions join the (loosely defined) movement which still exists today.

Finally, in the Hindi-speaking regions of northern India we find another string of individual antinomian poets, the Sants. In most cases, these 'saints' did not create religious institutions as permanent frames for their ideas. Often from humble origins and also from Muslim backgrounds, they sang their religious songs on the market-places and by the roadside. Their deity is ultimately ineffable and beyond all human comprehension and conception. Thus they refer to it indiscriminately as Allah, Rām, etc. Divine saving grace is available everywhere; by purifying the heart and removing the obstacles of external religious forms, man can open himself up for it. Perhaps the most famous individual among the *sants* is Kabīr (fourteenth century). But it was Gurū Nānak (fifteenth century) and his nine successors who created a well-defined religious organisation within the overall framework of the sant tradition. This is the religion of the Sikhs (on which see the separate section pp. 182–93).

As an example of the continuity of the antinomian movements well into the nineteenth and twentieth centuries may be mentioned Nārāyaṇa-guru. He belonged to a relatively low caste of Kerala, but managed to acquire the Sanskrit learning which on the whole had been restricted to the highest castes. Not only did he make the teaching of Advaita-Vedānta available to his own caste-fellows by transposing it into the vernacular Malayalam language. From its teaching on the oneness of all beings he also derived a social programme that challenged established modes of religious practice.

No discussion of antinomian movements in India would be complete without a reference to the further histories of such movements within the context of Indian society. They all may set out to challenge society at large, in a variety of ways. But most end up once again contained within the overall social fabric, for example as yet another caste or caste-cluster. Internal hierarchies and status symbols evolve which produce a new form of stratification. The spontaneous religious poetry in the vernacular of the past poets gets collected and turns into a 'sacred scripture' (often no longer comprehensible due to linguistic changes in the community). Hagiographies of the grand saints of the past are produced, and often Sanskrit is resorted to in order to define the belief-system within the framework of the Vedānta. Temples are erected and modes of *pūjā* are developed, not just in honour of the central deity, but also of the images of the past saints (often regarded as incarnations of the deity). Even such *sants* who refused to create institutional structures for their religious message may be drawn into this development. Thus around the figures of Kabīr and Ravidās religious movements arose long after their deaths. Yet it would be a mistake to regard this return to external forms of expression simply as the reassertion of some ultimately static reality. The continuous emergence of new antinomian movements maintains a dynamism, and however formalised individual movements may become in due course, something genuinely new may well be added to the whole. For example, the way Mānbhāvs venerate Kṛṣṇa in their temples, Sikhs deal ritually with their Sacred Book and even the Jains worship at temple images of their Tīrthaṅkaras, is something new which cannot be subsumed under some general and fixed heading 'Hindu temple worship'.

Further Reading

Bechert, H. *Buddhismus, Staat und Gesellschaft in den Ländern des Theravāda-Buddhismus*, 3 vols. (Frankfurt/Wiesbaden, 1966–73)

—— and R. Gombrich (eds.) *The World of Buddhism* (Thames & Hudson, London, 1984)

Bhattacharyya, B. *Introduction to Buddhist Esoterism*, 2nd edn (Varanasi, 1964)
Brockington, J. *The Sacred Thread* (Edinburgh University Press, Edinburgh, 1981)
Carrithers, M. *The Forest Monks of Sri Lanka* (Oxford University Pres, Delhi, 1983)
Collins, S. *Selfless Persons—Imagery and Thought in Theravāda Buddhism* (Cambridge University Press, Cambridge, 1982)
Conze, E. *Buddhist Thought in India* (Allen & Unwin, London, 1962)
—— *A Short History of Buddhism* (Allen & Unwin, London, 1980)
Dasgupta, S. *A History of Indian Philosophy*, 5 vols. (Cambridge University Press, 1922–49)
Dasgupta, S.B. *An Introduction to Tantric Buddhism* (Berkeley, 1974)
Dayal, H. *The Bodhisattva Doctrine in Buddhist Sanskrit Literature* (Kegan Paul, London, 1932)
Dhavamony, M. *The Love of God According to Śaiva-Siddhānta* (Oxford University Press, Oxford, 1971)
Edgerton, F. *The Beginnings of Indian Philosophy* (Allen & Unwin, London, 1965)
Frauwallner, E. *Geschichte der indischen Philosophie*, 2 vols. (Otto Müller, Salzburg, 1953 & 1956)
—— *Die Philosophie des Buddhismus*, 3rd edn (Akademie-Verlag, Berlin (GDR), 1969)
Foucher, A. *The Life of the Buddha* (Middletown (Con.), 1963)
Gombrich, R. *Precept and practice—Traditional Buddhism in the Rural Highlands of Ceylon* Clarendon Press, Oxford, 1971.
Gonda, J. *Vedic Literature* (Harrassowitz, Wiesbaden, 1975)
Gupta, S., D. Hoens and T. Goudriaan *Hindu Tantrism* (Brill, Leiden, 1979)
Hacker, P. *Prahlada—Werden und Wandlungen einer Idealgestalt*, 2 vols. (Steiner, Wiesbaden, 1959)
Hardy, F. *Viraha-bhakti—The Early History of Kṛṣṇa Devotion in South India* (Oxford University Press, Delhi, 1983)
Hawley, J.S. and D.M. Wulff (eds.) *The Divine Consort—Radha and the Goddesses of India* (Berkeley Religious Studies Series, Berkeley, 1982)
Hiriyanna, M. *Outlines of Indian Philosophy* (Allen & Unwin, London, 1967)
Jaina, P.S. *The Jaina Path of Purification* (Motilal Banarsidass, Delhi, 1979)
Keith, A.B. *The Religion and Philosophy of the Veda and Upanishads* (Harvard University Press, Cambridge, Mass., 1925)
O'Flaherty, W.D. *Asceticism and Eroticism in the Mythology of Śiva* (Oxford University Press, London, 1973)
—— *Hindu Myths* (Penguin Books, Harmondsworth, 1975)
Rahula, W. *What the Buddha Taught*, 2nd edn (Gordon Fraser, Bedford, 1972)
Ramanujan, A.K. *Speaking of Śiva* (Penguin Books, Harmondsworth, 1973)
Sangharakshita, B. *A Survey of Buddhism* (Shambala, Boulder (Colorado) and Windhorse, London, 1980)
Schubring, W. *The Doctrine of the Jainas* (Motilal Banarsidass, Delhi, 1962)
Schumann, H.W. *Buddhism—An Outline of its Teachings and Schools* (Rider & Co., London, 1973)
Sontheimer, G. *Biroba, Mhaskoba und Khaṇḍobā* (Steiner, Wiesbaden, 1976)
Spiro, M.E. *Buddhism and Society—A Great Tradition and its Burmese Vicissitudes* (New York, 1970)
Vaudeville, C. *Kabīr*, vol. 1 (Clarendon Press, Oxford, 1974)
Williams, R. *Jaina Yoga* (Oxford University Press, London, 1963)
Zaehner, R.C. *Hinduism* (Oxford University Press, London, 1966)
Zvelebil, K. *The Poets of the Power* (Rider & Co., London, 1974)

5 *Śaivism and the Tantric Traditions*

Alexis Sanderson

The term Śaivism here refers to a number of distinct but historically related systems comprising theology, ritual, observance and yoga, which have been propagated in India as the teachings of the Hindu deity Śiva. A Śaiva is one who practices such a system. To understand the term to mean 'a worshipper of Śiva' or 'one whose deity is Śiva' is less precise; for a Śaiva may well be a worshipper not of Śiva but of the Goddess (Devī). Though she is commonly represented as the consort of Śiva and, theologically, as that god's inherent power (*śakti*), it is none the less the defining mark of certain forms of Śaivism that she is seen as transcending this marital and logical subordination.

The scriptural revelations of the Śaiva mainstream are called Tantras, and those that act in accordance with their prescriptions are consequently termed Tantrics (*tāntrika*). The term *tantra* means simply a system of ritual or essential instruction; but when it is applied in this special context it serves to differentiate itself from the traditions that derive their authority from the Vedas (direct revelation: *śruti*) and a body of later texts that claim to be Veda-based (indirect revelation: *smṛti*). This corpus of *śruti* and *smṛti* prescribes the rites, duties and beliefs that constitute the basic or orthodox order and soteriology of Hindu society. The Tantrics however saw their own texts as an additional and more specialised revelation (*viśeṣaśāstra*) which offers a more powerful soteriology to those who are born into this exoteric order. The Tantric rituals of initiation (*dīkṣā*) were held to destroy the rebirth-generating power of the individual's past actions (*karma*) in the sphere of Veda-determined values, and to consubstantiate him with the deity in a transforming infusion of divine power.

The Śaivas were not the only Tantrics. There were also the Vaiṣṇava Tantrics of the Pāñcarātra system, whose Tantras, considered by them to be the word of the deity Viṣṇu, prescribed the rituals, duties and beliefs of the devotees of Vāsudeva in his various aspects (*vyūha*) and emanations (*vibhava*, *avatāra*). In addition to these two major groups of Tantrics there were Sauras, followers of Tantras revealed by the Sun (Sūrya); but while we have access to a number of Vaiṣṇava Tantras and to a vast corpus of Śaiva materials, the Saura tradition is silent. An early Śaiva Tantra (*Śrīkaṇṭhīyasaṃhitā*) lists a canon of 85 Tantras of the Sun, but not one of these these nor any other Saura Tantra has survived.

The production of Tantric revelations was not limited to those who accepted the supernatural authority of the Vedas. It went on, though on a much smaller scale, among the Jains, while the Buddhists added an enormous Tantric corpus to their canonical literature during the period *c.* 400–750 CE. By the end of this period the system of the Tantras, called 'the Way of the Diamond' (Vajrayāna) or 'of Mantras' (Mantrayāna), was generally recognised among the followers of the Greater Way (Mahāyāna) as the highest and most direct means to liberation (*nirvāṇa*), and its esoteric deities were enshrined in the monasteries as the high patrons of the faith. The Tibetans, who received Buddhism at this stage of its development, preserve, in the Tantric section of their canon, translations from the Sanskrit of almost 500 revealed texts and over 2000 commentaries and explanatory works. Of these more than three quarters concern Tantras of the most radical kind, those of the Higher and Supreme Yogas (*Yogottara-tantras* and *Yogānuttara-tantras*).

All these Tantrics were similarly related to the traditional forms of religion, the Buddhists to the monastic discipline and the Vaiṣṇavas and Śaivas to Vedic orthopraxy. They were excluded by the traditionalists because they went beyond the boundaries of these systems of practice. But the Tantrics themselves, while excluding these exclusivists, included their systems as the outer level of a concentric hierarchy of ritual and discipline.

In those communities in which it was possible or desirable to add to the exoteric tradition this second, more esoteric level, there might be forms of the Tantric cult in which this transcendence entailed the infringement of the rules of conduct (*ācāra*) which bound the performer of ritual at the lower, more public, level of his practice. Thus some rites involved the consumption of meat, alcohol and other impurities, even sexual intercourse with women of untouchable castes (*antyaja*). These practices originated as part of the magical technology of certain extremist orders of Śaiva ascetics. They passed over into the married majority; but when they did so, they survived unrevised only in limited circles. The general trend—and this was also so in the case of Tantric Buddhism—was to purify the rites by taking in everything except the elements of impurity. This left the essential structure intact: one worshipped the same deity, with the same complex of emanations or subordinate deities, *mantras*, deity-enthroning diagrams (*maṇḍalas*), and ritual gestures and postures (*mudrās*). The spread of the Tantric cults in Indian religion is largely the history of this process of domestication and exotericisation.

The followers of these cults, even in their undomesticated form, should not be seen as rebels who rejected a ritualised social identity for a liberated cult of ecstasy. This popular view of Tantrism overlooks the highly-structured ritual contexts (Tantric and non-Tantric) of these un-Vedic practices. A person who underwent a Tantric initiation (*dīkṣā*) was less an anti-ritualist than a super-ritualist. He was prepared to *add* more exacting and limiting ritual duties to those which already bound him. Indeed he has much in common with the most orthodox of Hindus, the *śrauta* sacrificer, who transcended the simple and universal domestic rites prescribed in the secondary scripture (*smṛti*) to undertake the great rituals of the primary and more ancient revelation (*śruti*). Though the *śrauta* and the Tantric occupied the opposite ends of the spectrum of Hinduism they shared the character of being specialists of intensified ritual above the more relaxed middle ground of the *smārtas* (the followers of *smṛti*). This similarity is carried through into their doctrines of liberation from rebirth (*mokṣa*). Both the *śrauta* tradition articulated by the Bhāṭṭa Mīmāṃsakas and the Tantric represented by the Śaivas stood apart from the mainstream by holding that the mere performance of the rituals prescribed by their respective scriptures is a sufficient cause of final liberation (see pp. 159ff.). It is this ritualism which largely accounts for the rapid decline of the Tantric traditions in recent decades. The complex obligations and time-consuming rituals which the Tantric takes on for life can hardly be accommodated within the schedule of the modern employee.

Un-Vedic though it was, the Tantric tradition was destined to have a far greater influence than the *śrauta* on the middle ground. While the *śrauta* tradition all but died out, the Tantric came to pervade almost all areas of Indian religion. The distinction between the Vedic and the Tantric in religion continued to be crucial, and it was drawn in such a way that the Tantric continued to be the tradition of a minority; but what was called Vedic here was essentially Tantric in its range of deities and liturgical forms. It differed from the properly Tantric principally in its *mantras*. This became the chief formal criterion: in Vedic worship (*pūjā*) the actions that compose the liturgy were empowered by the recitation of Vedic *mantras* drawn from the *Ṛgveda* and *Yajurveda* rather than by that of the heterodox *mantras* of the Tantras. At the same time these de-Tantricised reflexes of Tantric worship were non-sectarian. While properly Tantric worship was more or less exclusive, being emphatically centred in a particular deity, Vedic domestic worship was inclusive. Its most typical form is the *pañcāyatanapūjā*, the worship of the five shrines, in which offerings are made to the five principal deities, Śiva, Viṣṇu, Sūrya, Gaṇapati and the Goddess (Devī). The scriptural authority for these neo-Vedic rituals was provided by the indirect revelation (*smṛti*) and in particular by the ever-expanding Purāṇas, though the exact text of worship is generally a matter of unascribed tradition. Such worship is therefore called *smārta* ('*smṛti*-based') or *paurāṇika* ('Purāṇa-based'), or, where the properly Vedic or *śrauta* tradition is completely absent, simply *vaidika* ('Veda-based'). Its form in a particular community is largely the product of the history of the various Tantric traditions within that community. An example of this will be given below, when we consider the religion of medieval Kashmir (see pp. 169–72).

What follows falls into two parts. In the first I present Śaivism on the evidence of what survives, mostly unpublished, of its earliest scriptural sources. In most of this material the domestication of which I have spoken above has yet to begin. We shall therefore be looking in the main at traditions of Śaiva asceticism. Here the married man (*gṛhastha*) is altogether absent or at best subordinate. In the second part (pp. 158–72) we shall consider what happened to these traditions when they were domesticated. Our evidence here is the literature of the Śaiva community of Kashmir from the ninth century onwards.

This second body of texts is our earliest datable and locatable evidence for the Śaiva traditions. How much earlier than these Kashmiri works the scriptures to which they refer were composed cannot be decided yet with any precision. At best we can say that the main body of these early Tantras must have been composed between about 400 and 800 CE. To this we can add some relative chronology. We know even less about where these Tantras were composed or about the areas within which they were followed. However I incline to the view that when these traditions became the object of sophisticated Kashmiri exegesis between the ninth and thirteenth centuries they were widely represented throughout India. It is certain that the Kashmiri and the Newars of the Kathmandu valley looked out on much the same distribution and interrelation of Śaiva Tantric cults at this time, and it is highly probable that each community inherited these traditions independently by participating in a more widespread system, which may have included even the Tamil-speaking regions of the far south of the subcontinent.

The Kashmiri exegesis considered in the second part is a local tradition of much more than local impact. In a very short time it was acknowledged as the standard both in its theological metaphysics and in its liturgical prescription among the Śaivas of the Tamil south. This was the case in the Śaiva Siddhānta (see pp. 159–60), the Trika (see pp. 160–4), the Krama (see pp. 164–7), and the cults of Tripurasundarī (see pp. 156–7) and Kubjikā (see pp. 154–6). Consequently, while the Hindu culture of Kashmir declined in influence and vitality after the thirteenth century with large-scale conversion to Islam and periodic persecutions, the Tantrics of the far south continued the classical tradition, and through their many and outstanding contributions to Tantric literature guaranteed it a pan-Indian influence down to modern times. These southern and subsequent developments are unfortunately beyond the scope of this essay.

The Atimārga and the Mantramārga

The teaching of Śiva (*śivaśāsana*) which defines the Śaivas is divided between two great branches or 'streams' (*strotas*). These are termed the Outer Path (Atimārga) and the Path of Mantras (Mantramārga). The first is accessible only to ascetics, while the second is open both to ascetics and to married home-dwellers (*gṛhastha*). There is also a difference of goals. The Atimārga is entered for salvation alone, while the Mantramārga promises both this and, for those that so wish, the attainment of supernatural powers (*siddhis*) and the experience of supernal pleasures in the worlds of their choice (*bhoga*). The Atimārga's Śaivism is sometimes called Raudra rather than Śaiva. This is because it is attributed to and concerned with Śiva in his archaic, Vedic form as Rudra (the 'Terrible'), the god of wild and protean powers outside the *śrauta* sacrifice. It has two principal divisions, the Pāśupata and the Lākula.

The Pāśupata Division of the Atimārga

The ascetic observance (*vrata*) which is this system's path to salvation is the Pāśupata. It bears this name because its promulgation is attributed to Rudra as Paśupati (the 'Master [*-pati*] of the Bound [*paśu-*]'). Paśupati is believed by the followers of this tradition (the Pāśupatas) to have appeared on earth as Lakulīśa by entering and re-animating a brahmin's corpse in a cremation ground. Thus yogically embodied he gave out the cult's fundamental text, the *Pāśupata Aphorisms* (*Pāśupatasūtras*). Our principal source for the detail of the tradition is Kauṇḍinya's commentary on this text. It has been suggested on slender evidence that this commentator belongs to the fourth century. The Pāśupata cult itself, at least that form of it which derives itself from Lakulīśa, is at least two centuries older.

The Pāśupata observance (*pāśupata-vrata*) was restricted to brahmin males who had passed through the orthodox rite of investiture (*upanayana*), which gives an individual access to his Veda and full membership of his community. The stage of life (*āśrama*) from which such a brahmin became a Pāśupata was irrelevant. He might be a celibate student (*brahmacārin*), a married home-dweller (*gṛhastha*), a hermit dwelling in the wild (*vānaprastha*), or a peripatetic mendicant (*bhikṣu*). Transcending this orthodox classification he entered a 'fifth' life-stage, that of the Perfected (*siddha-āśrama*).

The final goal of the Pāśupatas was the end of suffering (*duḥkhānta*). It means just this, but was also conceived positively as the assimilation of Rudra's qualities of omniscience, omnipotence and so forth at the time of one's death. This was the state of final liberation and it was to be achieved through four stages of discipline. In the first the ascetic lived by a temple of Śiva. His body was to be smeared with ashes and he was to worship the deity in the temple by dancing and chanting, boisterous laughter (*aṭṭahāsa*), drumming on his mouth (*huḍḍukkāra*), and silent meditation on five *mantras* of the *Yajurveda*, the five *brahma-mantras* which in course of time would be personified as the five faces of Śiva.

In the second stage he left the temple. Throwing off all the outward signs of his observance he moved about in public pretending to be crippled, deranged, mentally deficient or indecent. Passers-by being unaware that these defects were feigned spoke ill of him. By this means the Pāśupata provoked an exchange in which his demerits passed to his detractors and their merits to him. By acting in this way he was simply making unorthodox use of a thoroughly orthodox principle. He was exploiting his ritual status as one who had undergone a rite of consecration (*dīkṣā*) to initiate an observance (*vrata*); for in the *śrauta* system one bound by the observance (*vrata*) consequent on consecration (*dīkṣā*) for the Soma sacrifice was similarly dangerous to anyone who might speak ill of him.

Purified by this period of *karma*-exchange, the Pāśupata withdrew in the third stage to a remote cave or deserted building to practise meditation through the constant repetition of the five *mantras*. When he had achieved an uninterrupted awareness of Rudra by this means, so that he no longer required the support of the *mantras*, he left his place of seclusion and moved into a cremation ground to wait for death. While previously the Pāśupata had begged for his sustenance he now lived on whatever he could find there. This fourth stage ended with his life. Entering the stage of completion (*niṣṭhā*) with the falling away of his body and the last traces of suffering, he was believed to experience the infusion of the qualities of Rudra. The cause of this final liberation was not thought to be any action of his, but simply the grace or favour of Rudra himself.

The Lākula Division of the Atimārga

The second division of the Atimārga, that of the Lākula ascetics, developed from within the original Pāśupata tradition. It accepted the authority of the *Pāśupata Aphorisms* and maintained both the *mantras* and the basic practices of its prototype. However, its special discipline required a more radical transcendence of Vedic values. After his consecration (*dīkṣā*) the ascetic

> should wander, carrying a skull-topped staff (*khaṭvāṅga*) and an alms-bowl fashioned from a human cranium. His hair should be bounded up in a matted mass (*jaṭā*) or completely shaved. He should wear a sacred thread (*upavīta*) [the emblem of orthodox investiture (*upanayana*)] made from snake-skins and he should adorn himself with a necklace of human bone. He may wear nothing but a strip of cloth to cover his private parts. He must smear himself with ashes and decorate himself with the ornaments of his God. Knowing that all things are Rudra in essence he should

hold firmly to his observance as Rudra's devotee. He may eat and drink anything. No action is forbidden to him. For he is immersed in contemplation of Rudra, knowing that no other deity will save him.

Niśvāsatattvasaṃhitā (MS), ch. 4.

Here the ascetic took on a more radical aspect of Rudra's nature as the outsider within the Vedic religion. He became Rudra the brahmin-slayer. For it is ruled in orthodox sources that one who is guilty of this terrible crime may exonerate himself only if he removes himself from society for twelve years, lives in a cremation ground and carries the skull-bowl (*kapāla*) and the skull-staff (*khaṭvāṅga*) when he goes forth to beg for food. Thus the Lākula's observance, generally called that of the skull (*kapālavrata*), is also known as that of exile, 'of those that are outside the world' (*lokātītavrata*). It is also referred to as the Greater Pāśupata Observance (*mahāpāśupatavrata*). While the Pāśupata ascetic's outsideness was limited to the system of life-stages (*atyāśramavrata*), the Lākula skull-bearer was to abandon the more basic notion of the pure and the impure.

The Kālāmukha ascetics who are known from many south Indian inscriptions from the ninth to thirteenth centuries were part of this Lākula division of the Atimārga. Doxographic material from this region records among their practices bathing in the ashes of the cremated (their milder predecessors had been content with the ashes of cow dung), eating these ashes and worshipping Rudra in a vessel filled with alcoholic liquor. This mode of worship was common in the rituals of the Kaula Śaivas (see pp. 679–89), but there is no reason to think that it was connected here as there with rituals involving sexual intercourse. It appears that these followers of Rudra the solitary penitent were bound by strict vows of celibacy.

The Lākulas had their own canon of scriptures concerned with both theology (*jñāna*) and ritual (*kriyā*), the eight *Authorities* (*Pramāṇas*). Of these nothing survives but their names and a single quotation from one of them, the *Pañcārtha-Pramāṇa*, in the works of the Kashmiri Kṣemarāja. For their doctrines we have an account of Lākula soteriology and cosmography in the *Niśvāsatattvasaṃhitā* quoted above, and a few scattered discussions in later Śaiva sources from Kashmir. From this we can see that the Lākulas had already developed most of the detailed hierarchy of worlds (*bhuvanādhvan*) which characterises the later Mantramārga. The Lākula ascends to his salvation through a succession of worlds, each governed by its own manifestation of Rudra. The highest of these is the world of the Rudra Dhruveśa. Reaching this he attains liberation, a state of omniscience void of activity.

In the closely clustered systems which form the Mantramārga the soul of the initiate is raised through such a world-hierarchy at the time of his consecration. The difference is that the hierarchy has been further extended. It contains that of the Lākulas, but adds a number of new worlds above Dhruveśa's. The Lākula cosmos was itself the outcome of such a process of extension. For immediately below Dhruveśa is the world of the Rudra Tejīśa. This was the final goal of the Vaimalas, a superseded group about whom our surviving sources tell us little but this. Further down the scale are the worlds of the Rudras Kṣemeśa and Brahmaṇaḥsvāmin. These were the cosmic termini of two other obscure Pāśupata groups, the Mausulas and the Kārukas.

The Mantramārga

It is clear that the cosmos of the Mantramārga grew out of that of the Atimārga by the same process of competitive extension which set the Lākulas above the Vaimalas, and the Vaimalas above the Mausulas and the Kārukas. And there are other continuities between the two Paths in the fields of ritual, iconography, *mantras* and observances (*vrata*). However, in spite of these continuities, there is a fundamental difference of character between the two main branches of the Śaiva tradition. While the Atimārga is exclusively liberationist, the Mantramārga, though it accommodates the quest for liberation, is essentially concerned with the quest for supernatural experience (*bhoga*).

This difference might be thought to correspond to that between the aspirations of the original ascetics and the newly admitted married householders. On the contrary, it corresponds to that between two varieties of ascetic. For in the Mantramārga it is the ascetics who are principally concerned with the attainment of powers, the path of liberation being largely the domain of the men in the world; and it is the methods by which power may be attained that are the main subject matter of the Mantramārga's scriptures. The gnostic home-dwellers, who would come in time to dominate the Mantramārga, are here the unmarked category of aspirant. They are defined by the fact that they do *not* involve themselves with the concerns which generated not only the greater part of their texts but also the system's internal diversity. For it was for the sake of the power-seeker that there developed the extraordinary variety of rites, deities and *mantras* which sets the Mantramārga apart from the purely gnostic Atimārga.

The history of the expanding hierarchy of the Rudra-worlds shows that the Mantramārga is later than the Atimārga. None the less, the dichotomy between the liberation-seeking and the power-seeking forms of Śaiva asceticism is more ancient than the present corpus of Mantramārgic texts. The latter contain more archaic strata at which the superior deities of the developed Mantramārga give way to the earlier Rudra. If we compare these text-elements with the Rudra cult of the Atimārga, we see that the dichotomy which underlies the later form of the division is between a solitary and celibate Rudra in the Atimārga and a Rudra associated with bands of protean and predominantly female spirits in the background of the Mantramārga. In the fully developed and diversified Mantramārga this association is but one aspect of that with feminine power (*śakti*) conceived more universally. It is this association which most obviously marks off the Mantramārga from the *śakti*-less Atimārga. We shall see that within the Mantramārga the major divisions correspond to different representations of this association.

The Tantras of the Śaiva Siddhānta

While our evidence for the Atimārga is very sparse, the Mantramārga can be studied in an enormous body of Sanskrit texts. The scriptures of the Mantramārga fall into two groups. On the one hand is the well-defined and relatively homogeneous canon of texts (the ten *Śiva-Āgamas*, the eighteen *Rudra-Āgamas* and attached scriptures) that constitute the authority of the tradition known to itself and others both in the scriptures and later as the *Śaiva Siddhānta*. On the other hand is a much more diverse, numerous and variously listed body of revelations known as the scriptures of Bhairava (*Bhairava-Āgamas*) or collectively as the Teaching of Bhairava (*Bhairavaśāstra*).

The Śiva forms of both are visualised as skull-bearing denizens of the cremation grounds. In the Śaiva Siddhānta, however, the god lacks the aura of terrifying and ecstatic power which is emphasised in his manifestations in the tradition of Bhairava ('the Fearsome'). Similarly, while the concept of feminine power (*śakti*) is found throughout the Mantramārga, it tends in the Śaiva Siddhānta to move away from personification as the Goddess or goddesses towards metaphysical abstraction. It is seen here principally as the creative power of the male Deity, manifest in the cosmic and soteriological process and embodied in his *mantra*-forms. In the daily ritual of the initiate the deity is worshipped, like the Rudra of the Atimārga, without a female consort. Linked to this is the purity of the mode of his worship. There is none of the offering of alcoholic drinks, blood and meat that typifies the rituals of the rest of the Mantramārga, with its greater emphasis on feminine and transgressive power.

The Tantras of Bhairava: Kāpālika Śaivism

The Tantras of Bhairava, so called because they take the form of his answers to the questions of the Goddess (Devī, Bhairavī), have been variously listed and classified in different parts of the corpus. The classification given here corresponds, I believe, to the main structure of the Śaiva tradition outside the Śaiva Siddhānta at the time when the Kashmiri began their work of post-scriptural systematisation in the ninth and tenth centuries.

Within these Tantras there is a primary division between those of the Seat of Mantras (Mantrapīṭha) and those of the Seat of Vidyās (Vidyāpīṭha). The latter are either Union Tantras (*Yāmala-tantras*) or

Power Tantras (*Śakti-tantras*). Within the latter one may distinguish between the Tantras of the Trika (or rather of what was later called the Trika) and material dealing with cults of the goddess Kālī. Tantras which teach the cult of Tumburu-bhairava and his four sisters (Jayā, Vijayā, Jayantī and Aparājitā) are fitted into this scheme as a third division of the Vidyāpītha. But this is artificial. It accommodates a tradition whose importance had been superseded by that of the Mantrapīṭha (the cult of Svacchanda-bhairava) to the extent that it was no longer part of the main structure. No more will be said of this minor tradition here.

Figure 5.1: The Structure of the Mantramārga

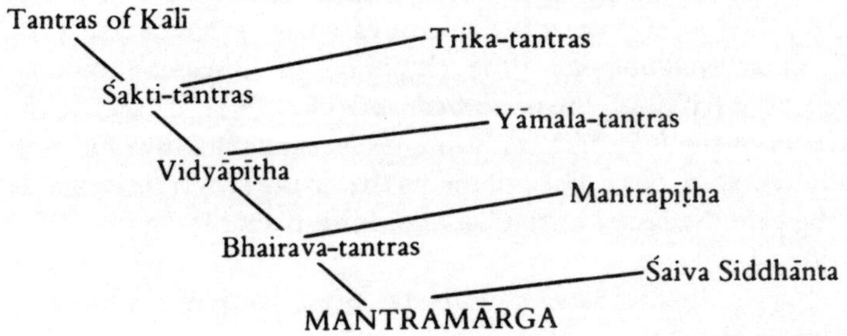

This arrangement is hierarchical. Whatever is above and to the left sees whatever is below it and to the right as lower revelation. It sees itself as offering a more powerful, more esoteric system of ritual (*tantra*) through further initiation (*dīkṣā*). As we ascend through these levels, from the Mantrapīṭha to the Yāmala-tantras and thence to the Trika and the Kālī cult, we find that the feminine rises stage by stage from subordination to complete autonomy.

The Mantrapīṭha and the Cult of Svacchandabhairava

At the beginning of this ascent is the Seat of Mantras (Mantrapīṭha). This term expresses the fact that this group of Tantras emphasises the masculine, while in the Seat of Vidyās (Vidyāpīṭha) it is the feminine that predominates (the nouns *mantra* and *vidyā*, which both signify the sacred sound-formulas, being masculine and feminine respectively).

The basic cult of the Mantrapīṭha is that of Svacchandabhairava ('Autonomous Bhairava') also known euphemistically as Aghora ('the Un-terrible'). White, five-faced (the embodiment of the five *brahma-mantras*) and eighteen-armed, he is worshipped with his identical consort Aghoreśvarī, surrounded by eight lesser Bhairavas within a circular enclosure of cremation grounds. He stands upon the prostrate corpse of Sadāśiva, the now transcended Śiva-form worshipped in the Śaiva Siddhānta.

The traditions of the Bhairava Tantras are Kāpālika, the basic form of their ascetic observance being that of the skull (*kapālavrata/mahāvrata*). The difference between this and the Lākula form of this observance is largely a matter of the basic difference of the Mantramārga stated above. The term Kāpālika is reserved here for this Mantramārgic segment of the Śaiva culture of the cremation grounds.

This Kāpālika background is evident from the iconography of the divine couple. Worshipped within an enclosure of cremation grounds they themselves wear the bone ornaments and brandish the skull-staff (*khaṭvāṅga*) of the Kāpālika tradition. None the less these features are not emphasised here to the extent that they are in the Vidyāpīṭha. Though the *Svacchandatantra*, which is the authority for this cult, teaches the worship of certain secondary forms of Svacchandabhairava such as Koṭarākṣa ('the Hollow-Eyed') and Vyādhibhakṣa ('the Devourer of Diseases'), which, being visualised as terrifying, gross-bodied and black, are closer to the standard Bhairavas of the Kāpālika tradition, Svacchandabhairava himself, the deity of daily worship, has milder elements that make him transitional in type between the calm Sadāśiva of the Śaiva Siddhānta and the gods of the Kāpālika mainstream.

In the Śaiva Siddhānta, Śiva (Sadāśiva) was worshipped alone. In the Mantrapīṭha he is joined in worship by his consort as the personification of *śakti*. Iconically she is his equal. But the larger ritual context shows that she is still subordinate. Her feminine presence is not reinforced by secondary goddesses in the circuit (*āvaraṇa*) that surrounds the couple. Furthermore Svacchandabhairava is worshipped alone after he has been worshipped with his consort. His appearance with Aghoreśvarī is his lower form.

The Vidyāpīṭha

With the ascent to the Vidyāpīṭha the Śaiva entered a world of ritual in which these last restraints on *śakti* dissolved. He was consecrated in the cults of deities who presided in their *maṇḍalas* over predominantly female pantheons, and who passed as he ascended to the left from Bhairavas with consorts, to Goddesses above Bhairavas, to the terrible Solitary Heroines (*ekavīrā*) of the cults of Kālī.

If in the cult of Svacchandabhairava the Kāpālika culture of the cremation grounds was somewhat in the background, here it is pervasive. The initiate gained access to the powers of these deities by adopting the observance of the Kāpālikas. With his hair matted and bound up with a pin of human bone, wearing earrings, armlets, anklets and a girdle, all of the same substance, with a sacred thread (*upavīta*) made of twisted corpse-hair, smeared with ashes from the cremation-pyres, carrying the skull-bowl, the skull-staff and the rattle-drum (*ḍamaru*), intoxicated with alcohol, he alternated periods of night-wandering (*niśāṭana*) with worship (*pūjā*) in which he invoked and gratified the deities of the *maṇḍala* into which he had been initiated. This gratification required the participation of a *dūtī*, a consecrated consort, with whom he was to copulate in order to produce the mingled sexual fluids which, with blood and other impurities of the body, provided the offering irresistible to this class of deities.

The Cult of Yoginīs. Accessible from the main cults of the Vidyāpīṭha, and underlying them in a more or less constant form, is the more ancient cult of Rudra/Bhairava in association with female spirits (Yoginīs). In the Atimārga and thence in the Mantramārga the series of cosmic levels (*bhuvanādhvan*) is governed by Rudras. When the initiate passed into this subjacent tradition he found that this masculine hierarchy was replaced by ranks of wild, blood-drinking, skull-decked Yoginīs. Radiating out from the heart of the Deity as an all-pervasive network of power (*yoginījāla*), they re-populated this vertical order of the Śaiva cosmos, appropriated the cycle of time (ruling as incarnations in each of the four world-ages (*yuga*)), and irradiated sacred space by sending forth emanations enshrined and worshipped in power-seats (*pīṭha*) connected with cremation grounds throughout the sub-continent.

The goal of the initiate was to force or entice these Yoginīs to gather before him and receive him into their band (*yoginīgaṇa*), sharing with him their miraculous powers and esoteric knowledge. The time favoured for such invocations was the fourteenth night of the dark fortnight, the night of the day of spirits (*bhūtadina*); and the most efficacious site was the cremation ground, the foremost of their meeting-places. The Śiva worshipped in these rites is Manthāna-Rudra (or Manthāna-Bhairava), a four-faced and therefore secondary or archaic form. Not 'married' to the Goddess as in the cults of entry, he is rather the wild ascetic who leads the Yoginī hordes (*yoginīgaṇanāyaka*).

The cult of Yoginīs is not concerned with these protean powers only as the inhabitants of a theoretical and liturgical universe, and as goddesses enshrined in the cremation ground power-seats. For they were believed also to possess women and thereby to enter into the most intimate contact with their devotees. Of these incarnate Yoginīs some, having been conceived in the intercourse of the consecrated, are considered divine from birth. Others appear in girls of eight, twelve or sixteen who live in the vicinity of the power-seats, these being of three degrees of potency. Others are identified in untouchable women from the age of twenty-seven as Ḍākinīs and other forms of assaulting spirit.

All Yoginīs belong to the family (*kula*) or lineage (*gotra*) of one or other of a number of higher 'maternal' powers, and in any instance this parentage is ascribed on the evidence of certain physical and behavioural characteristics. An adept in the cult of Yoginīs can identify members of as many as sixty-three of these occult sisterhoods, but is most vitally concerned with the eight major families of the Mothers (*mātṛ*) Brāhmī, Māheśvarī, Kaumārī, Vaiṣṇavī, Indrāṇī, Vārāhī, Cāmuṇḍā and Mahālakṣmī. For at the time of consecration he entered a trance in which the possessing power of the deity caused his hand to cast a flower into a *maṇḍala* enthroning these Mothers. The segment into which the flower fell revealed that Mother with whom he had an innate affinity. This established a link between him and the incarnate Yoginīs, for these families of the eight Mothers were also theirs. On days of the lunar fortnight sacred to his Mother the initiate was to seek out a Yoginī of his family. By worshipping her he aspired to attain supernatural powers and occult knowledge.

The Union Tantras (Yāmala-tantras): the Cult of Kapāl'īśabhairava and Caṇḍā Kāpālinī. Above this Yoginī cult, in the front line of the Vidyāpīṭha. the first level of the ascent of Śakti towards autonomy is seen in the Union Tantras. The principal cult here is that of Bhairava Lord of the Skull (Kapāl'īśa-, Kapāleśa-, Kapāla-bhairava) and his consort 'the Furious' (Caṇḍā) Goddess of the Skull (Kāpālinī). This is taught in the twelve thousand stanzas of the strongly Kāpālika *Picumata-Brahmayāmalatantra* (MSS). In the cult of Svacchandabhairava, in the Mantrapīṭha, the secondary deities surrounding the couple in the *maṇḍala* were male and solitary. Here they are female, with subordinate male consorts in the densely populated *maṇḍala* installed for exceptional worship, and alone in the much simpler pantheon of the private daily cult (*nityakarma*).Bhairava rules these secondary deities as the unifying holder of power (*śaktimat*, *śakticakreśvara*), in accordance with the general Śaiva conception of the divine nature. But this supremacy on the iconic plane is transcended by *śakti* on that of the deity-embodying *mantras*. For the essential components of the *mantras* of the nine deities who form the core of the greater *maṇḍala* and are the pantheon of daily worship are the syllables of the *mantra* of Caṇḍā Kāpālinī: (OṂ) HŪṂ CAṆḌE KĀPĀLINI SVĀHĀ ('... O Caṇḍā Kāpālinī ...!'). Thus Kapālīśabhairava (HŪṂ), his four goddesses (Raktā (CAṂ), Karālā (ḌE), Caṇḍākṣī (KĀ) and Mahocchuṣmā (PĀ)) and their four attendant powers or Dūtīs (Karālī (LI), Danturā (NI), Bhīmavaktrā (SVĀ) and Mahābalā (HĀ)), are aspects of a feminine power which transcends the male–female dichotomy which patterns the lower revelations.

The Power Tantras (Śakti-tantras): the Cult of the Triad (Trika). Above the Yāmala-tantras are the Śakti-tantras. These contain the scriptural authority for the system that in its later Tantras is called the Trika, and also that of the esoteric Kālī cults.

In the Tantras of the Trika (*Siddhayogeśvarīmata* (MSS), *Tantrasadbhāva* (MSS), *Mālinīvijayottaratantra*) the cult of Yoginīs permeates all levels; for the cult of entry is itself a development of that tradition. The focus of the Trika is directly on the network of Yoginīs (*yoginījāla*) as the hierarchy of cosmic manifestation, from the innermost resonance of the deity's power to its gross transformations as the sense-data that populate individualised consciousness.

The Trika's system of ritual and yoga leads to liberation and power by treading the steps of this emanation in reverse. The worshipper ascends to the core within the circuits of lesser Yoginīs. This core is the triad of the goddesses, Parā (see Figure 5.2), Parāparā and Aparā, worshipped alone or with subordinate Bhairavas and visualised as enthroned on three white lotuses that rest on the tips of a trident (*triśūla*) (see Figure 5.3). This trident is superimposed in imagination along the central vertical axis of the worshipper's body so that the trifurcation rises through a space of twelve finger breadths above his head, the whole from its base at the level of his navel to this summit being identified with the series of cosmic levels from gross matter to the Absolute. The central goddess, Parā, is white, beautiful and benevolent. Single-faced and two-armed she holds a sacred text and exhibits the gesture of self-realisation (*cinmudrā*). Parāparā and Aparā, to her right and

Figure 5.2: Parā

left, are red and black respectively. Raging Kāpālika deities, they brandish the skull-staff (*khaṭvāṅga*). Externally the three are worshipped with offerings that must begin with alcoholic liquor and red meat, and on such 'thrones' as a *maṇḍala*, a square of ground prepared for this purpose (*sthaṇḍila*) or an image painted on cloth (*paṭa*) or incised on a human cranium (*tūra*).

***Figure 5.3: The outline of the* Maṇḍala *of the Trident and Lotuses* (triśūlābjamaṇḍala) *as prescribed in the Trika's* Devyāyāmalatantra**

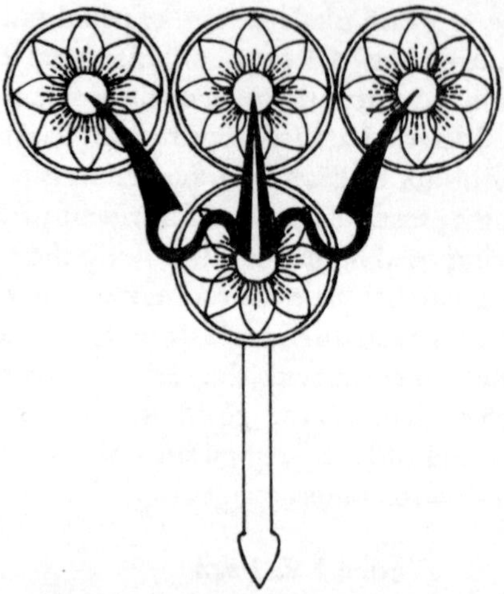

Parā has two aspects, for she is worshipped both as one of the three and as their sum and source. In this higher aspect she is called Mātṛsadbhāva (Essence of the Mothers), the summit of the hierarchy of the female powers which populate the cult of Yoginīs. Later all this would be interpreted along more metaphysical and mystical lines. Mātṛsadbhāva was read as Essence of (All) Conscious Beings ([*pra-*]*mātṛ-*) and the three goddesses were contemplated as the three fundamental constituent powers of a universe which was consciousness only. Parā was the power of the subject-element (*pramātṛ*), Aparā that of the object-element (*prameya*) and Parāparā that of the cognitive field or medium (*pramāṇa*) by virtue of which they are related, while their convergence in Mātṛsadbhāva came to express the ultimate unity of these three within an Absolute of pure consciousness contemplated as the liberated essence of the worshipper.

The Jayadrathayāmala and the Cult of Kālī. Beyond the cult of the three goddesses, at the extreme left of the Mantramārga, is the *Jayadrathayāmalatantra* (MSS). Also known as the King of Tantras (*Tantrarājabhaṭṭāraka*) it expounds in 24,000 stanzas the Kāpālika cults of over a hundred manifestations of the terrible goddess Kālī as the Destroyer of Time (Kālasaṃkarṣiṇī).

There are two main levels in the Tantra. The first, which is taught in the first quarter of the work (probably composed earlier than the rest), is that of the cult of a golden-limbed, twenty-armed Kālasaṃkarṣiṇī with five faces of different colours, that which faces the worshipper being black. Conventionally beautiful but holding such Kāpālika emblems as the skull-staff (*khaṭvāṅga*) and the severed head (*muṇḍa*), wearing a tiger skin dripping with blood, trampling the body of Kāla (Time) beneath her feet, she holds a trance-possessed Bhairava in a two-armed embrace in the centre of a vast, many-circuited *maṇḍala* of goddesses enclosed by cordons of male servant-guards and an outer ring of cremation grounds. In the elaborate form of worship both the goddesses and the guards embrace consorts. Here then is a Yāmala (Union) cult very similar to that of Kapālīśabhairava and Caṇḍā Kāpālinī taught in the *Picumata-Brahmayāmala* but centred in Kālī rather than Bhairava.

In the remaining three quarters of the text Bhairava is excluded from worship altogether. He is now just the highest of the male deities whose power Kālī transcends, the seventh at the summit of the hierarchy of the dethroned, coming above Indra, Brahmā, Viṣṇu, Rudra, Īśvara and Sadāśiva. Lying beneath her feet or dismembered to adorn her body, Bhairava suffers in his turn the humiliation which he inflicted on Sadāśiva in the Mantrapīṭha. With his fall the pantheons of worship are entirely feminised. But the femininity which remains is not that of the Yāmala systems. There *śakti* is worshipped in the form of beautiful and passionate consorts. Here the triumphant Goddess reveals herself to her devotees as a hideous, emaciated destroyer who embodies the Absolute (*anuttaram*) as the ultimate Self which the 'I' cannot enter and survive, an insatiable void in the heart of consciousness.

Typical of the conception of the Goddess in this second and more esoteric part of the Tantra is Vīrya-Kālī (Kālī of the [Fivefold] Power) (see Figure 5.4). Visualised in the centre of an aura of blinding light and contemplated as the innermost vibrancy (*spanda*) of consciousness she is black and emaciated. She has six faces and her hair is wreathed with flames. She is adorned with the severed heads and dismembered limbs of the lower deities. She rides on the shoulders of Kālāgnirudra (the Rudra of the Final Conflagration). In her twelve hands she carries a noose, a goad, a severed head, a sword, a shield, a trident-*khaṭvāṅga*, a thunderbolt (*vajra*), a ringing bell, a *ḍamaru*-drum, a skull-cup, a knife, a bleeding heart and an elephant-hide. The Rudra who is her vehicle (*vāhana*) is black on one side of his body and red on the other, symbolising the two breaths, the ingoing (*apāna*) and the outgoing (*prāṇa*), whose fusion and dissolution into the central axis of power reveals the state of thoughtless (*nirvikalpa*) awareness that holds the Goddess in its heart. The fivefold power (*vīrya*) that she embodies as 'the essence of the entire Vidyāpīṭha' is that by virtue of which the 'waveless' (*nistaraṅga*), self-luminous ground of reality projects itself as content in consciousness, and then re-absorbs this content, returning to its initial tranquility: this cyclical movement being the pulsation of consciousness from moment to moment as well as the pulsation of consciousness in cosmic creation and destruction. She passes from pure Light (*bhāsā* (1)) within the Śiva-void (*śivavyoma*), through incarnation (*avatāra* (2))

Figure 5.4: Vīrya-Kalī

as the impulse towards extroversion, to actual emission (*sṛṣṭi* (3)) of content, which appears as though outside consciousness, to her Kālī phase (*kālīkrama* (4)), in which she re-absorbs this content, and finally to the Great Withdrawal (*mahāsaṃhāra* (5)), in which she shines once again in her initial state as the pure Light. By contemplating this sequence (*krama*) in worship the devotee of Kālī is believed to realise the macrocosmic process within his own consciousness and thereby to attain omniscience and omnipotence.

In the fourth quarter of the *Jayadrathayāmalatantra* we are introduced to what the text claims to be the ultimate form of the Kālī cult. Here Mahākālī (Great Kālī) is worshipped in a black circle with a vermilion border surrounded by a ring of twelve such circles containing Kālīs who differ from her in their names but are identical in appearance. The relation of dependence between the Goddess and Śiva-Bhairava has already been transcended in the pure *śakti* cult of the higher level of this Tantra. Now even the hierarchy of source and emanations which remained within *śakti* herself is ritually dissolved, in a *maṇḍala* which expresses the perfect identity in essence (*sāmarasya*) of the Absolute and its manifestations, of the state of liberated transcendental (*sarvottīrṇa*) consciousness (*nirvāṇa*) and its finite projections, as the state of transmigratory existence (*bhava*, *saṃsāra*). Worshipped externally in orgiastic rites, the thirteen Kālīs (12+1) are to be realised internally in mystical self-experience, flashing forth as the ego-less (*nirahaṅkāra*) void through the voids of the senses during sexual union with the *dūtī*. This system known here as the Kālīkrama or Kālīkula, links this Tantra with the Krama to be described below (see pp. 151–2 and 164–7).

***Figure 5.5: The Trika's* Maṇḍala *of the Three Tridents and (Seven) Lotuses* (tritriśūlābjamaṇḍala) *with the twelve Kālīs in its centre, as prescribed by the* Trikasadbhāvatantra**

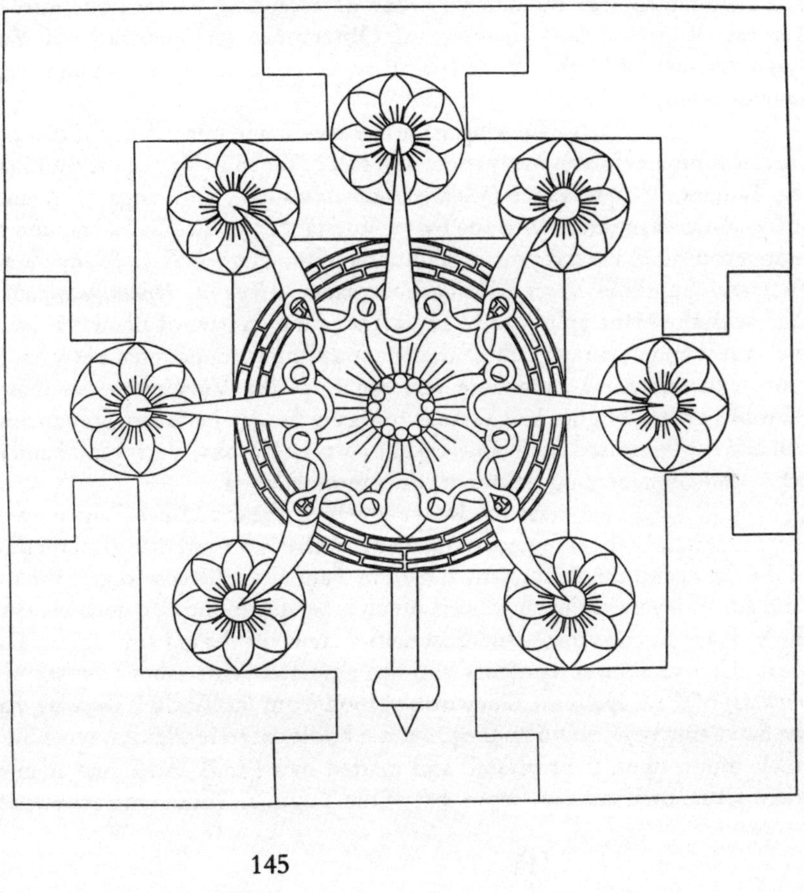

The Kālī-based Trika. The cult of the three goddesses and that of Kālī were not sealed off from each other in the manner of rival sects. The *Jayadrathyāmala* shows that the devotees of Kālī had developed their own versions of the cult of the three goddesses. The Trika in its turn assimilated these and other new and more esoteric treatments from the left. Consequently we find a later Trika stratum in which Kālasaṃkarṣiṇī has been introduced to be worshipped above the three goddesses of the trident (*Devyāyāmalatantra*). Finally there is a radical reorientation in which a system of sets of deities, worshipped in certain forms of the Kālī cult as the embodiment of the phases of cognition, is superimposed on to an elaborated version of the ancient triad as the inner structure of the point in which the three goddesses converge into the mystical fourth power, which is their interpenetration (3×3) in unity. In the centre of this convergence are the twelve Kālīs of the Kālīkrama (or Kālīkula) in their twelve circles (see Figure 5.5).

The Vidyāpīṭha and Esoteric Buddhism. By the eighth century CE the Buddhists had accumulated a hierarchy of Tantric revelations roughly parallel in its organisation and character to that of the Mantramārga. Their literature was divided in order of ascending esotericism into the Tantras of Action (*kriyā-tantras*), of Observance (*caryā-tantras*), of Yoga (*yoga-trantras*), of Higher Yoga (*yogottara-tantras*) and Supreme Yoga (*yogānuttara-tantras*).

Leaving aside the lowest and miscellaneous category we can compare the relatively orthodox cult of the mild Vairocana Buddha in the Tantras of Observance (*Mahāvairocanasūtra* etc.) and Yoga (*Tattvasaṃgraha*, *Paramādya*, etc.) with the Śaiva Siddhānta's cult of Sadāśiva, and the more esoteric and heteropractic traditions of the Higher Yoga (*Guhyasamāja* etc.) and Supreme Yoga (*Abhidhānottarottara*, *Hevajra*, *Ḍākinīvajrapañjara* etc.) with the Mantrapīṭha and Vidyāpīṭha of the Tantras of Bhairava. Just as the Svacchandabhairava cult of the Mantrapīṭha is transitional between the more exoteric Śaiva Siddhānta and the Kāpālika Vidyāpīṭha, so that of Akṣobhya in the Higher Yoga stands bridging the gap between the Vairocana cult and the feminised and Kāpālika-like cults of Heruka, Vajravārāhī and the other *khaṭvāṅga*-bearing deities of the Supreme Yoga.

At the lower levels of the Buddhist Tantric canon there is certainly the influence of the general character and liturgical methods of the Śaiva and the Pāñcarātra-Vaiṣṇava Tantric traditions. But at the final (and latest) level the dependence is much more profound and detailed. As in the Vidyāpīṭha cults these Buddhist deities are Kāpālika in iconic form. They wear the five bone-ornaments and are smeared with ashes (the six seals (*mudrās*) of the Kāpālikas). They drink blood from skull-bowls (*kapāla*), have the Śaiva third eye, stand on the prostrate bodies of lesser deities, wear Śiva's sickle moon upon their massed and matted hair (*jaṭā*). And, just as in the Vidyāpīṭha, their cults are set in that of the Yoginīs. Those who are initiated by introduction to the *maṇḍalas* of these Yoginī-encircled Buddhist deities are adorned with bone-ornaments and given the Kāpālika's *khaṭvāṅga* and skull-bowl to hold. Those who wish to do so may take on the long-term practice of the Kāpālika observance itself (Vajra-Kāpālikavrata), living in the cremation grounds, consuming meat and alcohol and offering erotic worship.

The Buddhist-Kāpālika Yoginī cult which gives these Tantras of Supreme Yoga their distinctive character and the greater part of their subject matter—indeed, they refer to themselves as Yoginī-tantras on the whole—borrows much of its detail and textual material directly from parallel Śaiva sources. Thus most of the material in the *Abhiahānottarottaratantra* and *Saṃpuṭodbhavatantra* listing the characteristics by which Yoginīs of different sorts may be recognised, and the sign language and syllabic codes with which they must be addressed (*chommā*), has been lifted with some Buddhist overwriting from such Vidyāpīṭha texts as the *Yoginīsaṃcāra* of the *Jayadrathayāmalatantra*, the *Picumata-Brahmayāmalatantra* and the *Tantrasadbhāva*.

The Kaula Reformation of the Yoginī Cult

The Yoginī cult, like the main cults of entry into the Vidyāpīṭha, was the speciality of skull-bearing ascetics removed from conventional society. It might reasonably have been expected to remain so but for Kaulism. This movement within esoteric Śaivism decontaminated the mysticism of the Kāpālikas so that it flowed into the wider community of married householders. In that of Kashmir it found learned exponents who used it to formulate a respectable metaphysics and soteriology with which to stand against the Śaiva Siddhānta.

The rites of the Yoginī cults and the fruits they bestowed were called *kaulika* or *kaula* in the texts which prescribed them, these terms being adjectives derived from the noun *kula* in its reference to the families or lineages of the Yoginīs and Mothers. Thus a Kaulika rite was one connected with the worship of these *kulas*, and a *kaulika* power (*kaulikī siddhiḥ*) was one that was attained through that worship, above all assimilation into these families (*kulasāmānyatā*).

Kaulism developed from within these Yoginī cults. It preserved the original meaning of the term *kula* and its derivatives but it introduced a new level of esotericism based on a homonym. For *kula* was also taken to mean the body and, by further extension, the totality (of phenomena), the 'body' of power (*śakti*). This last meaning neatly encompassed the original, for this cosmic 'body' was said to consist of the powers of the eight families of the Mothers. One was believed to enter the totality (*kula*) through that segment of its power with which one had a special affinity, determined as before by the casting of a flower during possession (*āveśa*).

Furthermore, these eight Mothers of the families were made internally accessible by being identified with the eight constituents of the individual worshipper's 'subtle body' (*puryaṣṭaka*), these being sound, sensation, visual form, taste, smell, volition, judgement and ego. The worshipper was therefore the temple of his deities; the central deity, out of whom these Mother-powers are projected, in whom they are grounded and into whom they are re-absorbed, was to be evoked within this temple as the Lord and/or Lady of the Kula (Kuleśvara, Kuleśvarī), as the blissful inner consciousness which is the worshipper's ultimate and trans-individual identity.

In the cults of the Vidyāpīṭha the propitiation of the deities involved sexual intercourse with a *dūtī*. This practice is continued in Kaulism. Indeed it moves to the very centre of the cult. However while its principal purpose in the Vidyāpīṭha was to produce the power-substances needed to gratify the deities, here the ritual of copulation is aestheticised. The magical properties of the mingled sexual fluids are not forgotten: those seeking powers (*siddhis*) consumed it and even those who worshipped for salvation alone offered the products of orgasm to the deities. However the emphasis has now moved to orgasm itself. It is no longer principally a means of production. It is a privileged means of access to a blissful expansion of consciousness in which the deities of the Kula permeate and obliterate the ego of the worshipper. The consumption of meat and alcohol is interpreted along the same lines. Their purpose, like that of everything in the liturgy, is to intensify experience, to gratify the goddesses of the senses.

The Kāpālika of the Vidyāpīṭha sought the convergence of the Yoginīs and his fusion with them (*yoginīmelaka*, *-melāpa*) through a process of visionary invocation in which he would attract them out of the sky, gratify them with an offering of blood drawn from his own body, and ascend with them into the sky as the leader of their band. The Kaulas translated this visionary fantasy into the aesthetic terms of mystical experience. The Yoginīs became the deities of his senses (*karaṇeśvarīs*), revelling in his sensations. In intense pleasure this revelling completely clouds his internal awareness: he becomes their plaything or victim (*paśu*). However, when in the same pleasure the desiring ego is suspended, then the outer sources of sensation lose their gross otherness. They shine *within* cognition as its aesthetic form. The Yoginīs of the senses relish this offering of 'nectar' and gratified thereby they converge and fuse with the *kaula*'s inner transcendental identity as the Kuleśvara, the Bhairava in the radiant 'sky' of enlightened consciousness (*cidvyomabhairava*).

Kaulism developed into four main systems. These were known as the Four Transmissions (*āmnāya*) or as the Transmissions of the Four Lodges (*gharāmnāya*) (eastern, western, northern and southern). Each has its own distinctive set of deities, *mantras*, *maṇḍalas*, mythical saints, myths of origin and the like.

The Kaula Trika: the Eastern Transmission (Pūrvāmnāya). The first context in which we find this Kaula esotericism is the Trika. The Kaula form of the cult of the three goddesses of the trident was well established among the Kashmiri by the beginning of the ninth century; and our first detailed exegesis of the Kashmiri Trika, at the end of the tenth century, shows that there had long existed a hierarchical distinction between the lower, Tantric form of the cult (*tantra-prakriyā*) and the new Kaula tradition. Kaula sources outside the Trika, such as the *Ciñciṇīmatasārasamuccaya* (MSS), indicate that the Kaulism of this branch of the Vidyāpīṭha is the closest to the origin of the tradition.

The basic Kaula pantheon consists of the Lord and/or Goddess of the Kula (Kuleśvara, Kuleśvarī) surrounded by the eight Mothers (Brāhmī etc.) with or without Bhairava consorts. Outside this core one worships the four mythical *gurus* or Perfected Ones (*Siddhas*) of the tradition (the four Lords of the Ages of the World (Yuganātha)), their consorts (*dūtīs*), the offspring of these couples and their *dūtīs*. The couple of the present, degenerate age (*kaliyuga*) are Macchanda (the Fisherman), venerated as the revealer (*avatāraka*) of Kaulism, and his consort Koṅkaṇā. Of their sons, the twelve 'princes' (*rājaputra*), six are non-celibate (*adhoretas*) and therefore specially revered as qualified (*sādhikāra*) to transmit the Kaula cult. They are worshipped as the founders of the six initiatory lineages (*ovalli*). At the time of consecration one entered one of these lineages and received a name whose second part indicated this affiliation. Hand-signs (*chommā*, *chomā*, *chummā*) enabled members of the *ovallis* to reveal themselves to each other (a remnant of the more elaborate code-languages [also called *chommā*] of the Kāpālika Yoginī cults and their Buddhist imitators); and each *ovalli* had lodges (*maṭha*) for its members in various parts of India. In this last respect they maintained the earlier tradition of Śaiva asceticism.

The Trika's Kaula cult added little to this matrix. It simply worshipped its three goddesses Parā, Parāparā and Aparā at the corners of a triangle drawn or visualised enclosing the Kuleśvara and Kuleśvarī of the centre. The worship could be carried out externally, on a red cloth upon the ground, in a circle filled with vermilion powder and enclosed with a black border, on a coconut substituted for a human skull, a vessel filled with wine or other alcohol, or on a *maṇḍala*. It may also be offered on the exposed genitals of the *dūtī*, on one's own body, or in the act of sexual intercourse with the *dūtī*. Later tradition emphasises the possibility of worshipping the deities within the vital energy (*prāṇa*)—one visualises their gratification by the 'nectar' of one's ingoing breath. We are also told that the seeker of liberation may carry out his worship in thought alone (*sāṃvidī pūjā*). However even one who does this must offer erotic worship with his *dūtī* on certain special days of the year (*parvas*).

The Kaula tradition of the Trika saw itself as essentialising Tantric practice. In this spirit it offered a much condensed form of the liturgy followed in the Tantra-system, emphasising spontaneity and intensity of immersion (*tanmayībhāva*, *samāveśa*) over elaborate ritual. Thus the usual preliminary purifications (*snāna*), the internal worship (*antaryāga*) which always precedes the external in Tantric rites and the offerings in the sacrificial fire (*homa*), which follow and repeat the worship of the deities, may all be discarded as superfluous. Moreover, the worshipper may advance from an initial stage in which he worships the full Kaula pantheon until eventually he worships only the central Kuleśvara.

The same condensation and intensification determines the form of consecration (*kaula-dīkṣā*). The guru opens the initiate's path to salvation and power by ritually annulling in advance whatever future experiences other than his present goal might await him at the various levels of the cosmos. He unites him with the deity at the summit of the subtle levels of the universe and then equips him with a 'pure' or divine body so that after this elevation to the immaterial plane of the deity he can re-enter the world as an initiate. In the Tantra-system of the Trika, as in all Tantra-systems, this destruction of karmic bonds involves an elaborate sequence of offerings in the sacred fire (*hautrī dīkṣā*). The initiate may be entirely passive during this process. In the Kaula system all this is achieved with minimal ritual, while the initiate is required to manifest signs of possession (*āveśa*) and is said to have direct experience during his trance of his ascent from level to level of the cosmos.

The Tantra-system with which this Kaulism is contrasted is not exactly the Trika-Tantrism of the ascetics. It is rather that tradition's domesticated form as it was practiced by the married householders from whom the Kaula Trika received its initiates. One might conclude, then, that this Kaulism, with its emphasis on possession and mystical experience, offered the married Tantric enthusiast an acceptable substitute for the intensity of the Kāpālika Tantric tradition to which he was directly linked through his deities and *mantras*, but from which he was necessarily excluded by his status as a married home-dweller.

The Kaula Kālī Cult: the Mata, the Krama and the Northern Transmission (Uttarāmnāya). After its appearance in the Trika, Kaulism next emerges in the Kālī cult. We must distinguish here three major traditions, (i) the Doctrine (Mata), (ii) the Sequence(-system) (Krama), also called the Great Truth (Mahārtha), the Great Way (Mahānaya), or the Way of the Goddess (Devīnaya), and (iii) the cult of Guhyakālī.

(i) The Mata. The Kaula Mata is rooted in the tradition of the *Jayadrathayāmalatantra*. Its essence or culmination is the worship of the twelve Kālīs, the *kālīkrama* which, as we have seen above, was believed to irradiate or possess the consciousness of the adept and his *dūtī* during sexual intercourse, obliterating the binding structures of differentiated awareness (*vikalpa*).

This Kaulism, like that of the Trika, rests upon a broader base of Tantric practice, but unlike that of the Trika this base is unrestrainedly Kāpālika. The most striking feature of this Tantric Mata is the prevalence of deities who have the faces of animals, or who have numerous such faces in addition to a principal anthropomorphic face. In the centre of its pantheon are three terrific goddesses of this second type, Trailokyaḍāmarā (Terroriser of the Universe), Matacakreśvarī (Goddess of the Circle of the Mata), and Ghoraghoratarā (She who is More Terrible than the Terrible).

Our only detailed account of the Kaula form of the Mata is the *Ciñciṇīmatasārasamuccaya* (MSS). Given there as the Kaulism of the Northern Transmission (Uttarāmnāya) it is expounded through two mystical texts of twelve and fifty verses respectively associated with the probably mythical gurus Vidyānandanātha and Niṣkriyānandanātha. In style and content these are closely related to the Kālīkrama section in the *Jayadrathayāmalatantra*.

(ii) The Krama. A much more elaborate or rather better documented Kaula system of Kālī worship is found in the literature of the Krama. The outstanding characteristic of this tradition is that it worships a sequential rather than a simply concentric pantheon. A series of sets of deities (*cakras*) is worshipped in a fixed sequence as the phases (*krama*) of the cyclical pulse of cognition (*saṃvit*). These phases are Emission (*sṛṣṭikrama*), Maintenance of the emitted (*sthitikrama*) (also called Incarnation (*avatārakrama*)), Retraction of the emitted (*saṃhārakrama*) and the Nameless fourth (*anākhyakrama*) (also called the Phase of the Kālīs (*kālīkrama*)), in which all trace of the preceding process is dissolved into liberated and all-pervading consciousness. This sequence differs somewhat from that seen below in the cult of Vīryakālī, and considerably as far as the actual deities who are worshipped in these phases are concerned. The final phase, that of the Nameless, is identical to that of the thirteen (12+1) Kālīs seen in the Mata. Indeed this set of deities is the feature which is most constant through the different forms of the Kālī cult.

The main scriptural authority for this form of the Krama is the *Devīpañcaśataka* (MSS). However there was a variant Krama tradition based on the *Kramasadbhāva* (MS). This adds a fifth sequence, that of pure Light (*bhāsākrama* (see p. 144)), to the four above. It also worships a system of sixty-four Yoginīs (also called Śākinīs) in five phases as the prelude to the cult of the Kālīs of the Nameless. In the period of the Kashmiri exegetes elements from each of these two traditions were brought together (see pp. 165–6 for the interpretation of this cycle of sixty-fourf Yoginīs). None the less there remained a permanent division in the tradition between tetradic and pentadic *krama*-worship, deriving from the *Devīpañcaśataka* and the *Kramasadbhāva* respectively.

The scriptures of this tradition considered themselves to be above the Vidyāpīṭha, and it is true that, though there are continuities with the *Jayadrathayāmalatantra*, they are more sophisticated in a number of respects. Thus the cult has *mantras* but lacks the grosser level at which the deities take on iconic form. External worship is greatly simplified and looked upon as inferior to worship in the mind, it being understood that the order of worship (*pūjākrama*) is no more than a reflection of the ever-present order of cognition itself (*saṃvitkrama*).

This claim to superiority is also expressed by the fact that the two scriptures mentioned reject the universal convention of the Bhairava Tantras which has Bhairava teach the Goddess. Here the roles are reversed. The Goddess teaches Bhairava. For she embodies what he cannot know, the cycle of cognitive power which constitutes his own self-awareness.

While on the whole it is not possible to say at present where the majority of the Tantras originated, the scriptural tradition and the Oḍḍiyāna, the Northern Seat of Power (*uttara-pīṭha*). This was in the Swat valley in what is now Pakistan, some 300 kilometres north-west of the valley of Kashmir. The same place figures prominently in the hagiographical histories of Buddhism as the major centre from which the traditions of the Yoginī-tantras (=*Yogānuttaratantras*) were propagated. With the advent of Islam and the subsequent collapse of urban and monastic culture in that region, all traces of its Tantric traditions have disappeared.

(iii) The Cult of Guhyakālī. It is a common phenomenon in the history of the Tantric traditions that such refinements as those of the Krama are quickly written into the lower, more concretely elaborated rituals which they sought to transcend. So there has flourished, from at least the tenth century to the present, a cult in which the mystical deity-schemata of the Krama are fleshed out with iconic form as the retinue of the Goddess Guhyakālī. The source of this concretisation is the Tantric tradition of the Mata. In her three-faced and eight-armed form, Guhyakālī's faces are worshipped as the three Mata goddesses Trailokyaḍāmarā, Matacakreśvarī and Matalakṣmī (=Ghoraghoratarā). Thus she is seen as the transcendent unity of that tradition. Further, in her principal form she is virtually identical with the third of these goddesses. Eight- and finally fifty-four-armed, black and ten-faced, she dances on the body of Bhairava in the centre of a cremation ground (see Figure 5.6).

The earliest datable evidence of this cult is also our earliest datable example of a Tantric ritual handbook providing detailed instructions on worship with all the *mantras* to be recited. This is the *Kālīkulakramārcana* of Vimalaprabodha, an author first mentioned in a Nepalese manuscript dated 1002 CE. This and many other practical texts of her cult have circulated and circulate still in the Nepal Valley, where she is the esoteric identity of Guhyeśvarī, the major local Goddess from our earliest records (*c.* 800 CE) to the present. The Newars, who maintain the

Figure 5.6: Guhyakālī

early traditions of the region, preserve her link with the Northern Transmission. For them Guhyakālī is the embodiment of that branch of Kaulism. Linked with her in this role is the white Goddess Siddhalakṣmī (always written Siddhilakṣmī in Nepal), one of the apotropaic deities (Pratyaṅgirā) of the *Jayadrathayāmalatantra* and the patron goddess of the Malla Kings (1200–1768 CE) and their descendants.

A version of the cult of Guhyakālī seems also to have flourished in Mithilā (in northern Bihar) on the authority of the *Mahākālasaṃhitā*. The connection with the Krama sequence-worship is very attenuated here. Though her icon is as elsewhere, she is unusual in being worshipped with a consort and one who is not a form of Śiva, as one might have expected, but the Man-Lion (Narasiṃha) incarnation of the rival God Viṣṇu. But that too has its precedent in the *Jayadrathayāmalatantra*. For in its fourth quarter that Tantra teaches the cult of a Kālī Mādhaveśvarī to be worshipped as the consort of this same Viṣṇu-form. Indeed this seems to have been a major tradition in Kashmir, for Abhinavagupta, the great Kashmiri Tantric scholar, gives this cult in his *Tantrāloka* as one of two forms of Kaulism connected with the Trika.

The Kaula Cult of Kubjikā: the Western Transmission (Paścimāmnāya). Intimately connected with the Trika is the third form of Kaulism, the cult of the Goddess Kubjikā. It is distinct from the Trika in that it adds the cult of a new set of deities, so that the Trika recedes from the front line of devotion into the ritual, yogic and theoretical body of the system. Its dependence on the Trika is revealed by the fact that much of its principal and earliest scripture, the *Kubjikāmata*, consists of chapters and other passages taken with minor overwriting from the scriptural corpus of that tradition.

***Figure 5.7: Kubjikā with Navātma on Agni, according to the visualisation text of the* Nityāhnikatilaka**

The high deity of the new pantheon is the goddess Kubjikā ('the Humpbacked' or 'Stooped'). Black, fat-bellied, six-faced and twelve-armed, adorned with snakes, jewels, human bones and a garland of severed heads, she embraces her consort Navātma ('the Nine-fold' [embodying the nine-part *mantra* H-S-KṢ-M-L-V-Y-R-ŪṂ]). He is five-faced and ten-armed. Also black, but youthful and handsome, he dances with her on a lotus which grows from the navel of Agni, the god of Fire, who lies in the centre of a lotus visualised by the worshipper in his cranial aperture (*brahmarandhra*) at the summit of an axis of brilliant light rising from the power-centre (*cakra*) in his genital region (*svādhiṣṭhāna*) (see Figure 36.7).

The tradition of the *Kubjikāmata* is *śākta*, which is to say that it is a Śaiva cult which emphasises the Goddess (*śakti*) rather than Śiva/Bhairava. In this sense all the Transmissions are *śākta*. However in the Western Tradition (Paścimāmnāya) there is a parallel system known as the Śāmbhava. It is Śāmbhava as opposed to *śākta* because it stresses Śambhu (equivalent to Śiva, i.e. Navātma) rather than *śakti* (=Kubjikā). Similarly masculinised variants existed in the Trika and the Krama. In the first there is the Kaula cult, in which Parā, Parāparā and Aparā are worshipped as the powers of Triśirobhairava (Bhairava the Three-headed); and in the second Manthāna-bhairava may take the place of the thirteenth Kālī in the Kālīkrama. This Śāmbhava system, however, was much more widely propagated. It is found in the *Śambhunirṇayatantra* (MS) and in much south Indian postscriptural literature (e.g. Śivānandamuni's *Śambhunirṇayadīpikā* (MS), Tejānandanātha's *Ānandakalpalatā* (MSS), and Umākānta's *Ṣaḍanvayaśāmbhavakrama*). It was even taken into the mainstream of the purified Kaulism propagated by the south Indian Śaṅkarācāryas of Śṛṅgerī and Kāñcīpuram, being the esoteric content of the ever popular *Ānandalaharī* attributed to Śaṅkara.

In this system Navātma also called Naveśvara or Navaka is worshipped as Solitary Hero (*ekavīra*). Alternatively the divine couple (Navātma and Kubjikā) assumes six variant forms to preside over the Six Orders (*ṣaḍanvaya-*) located in the six centres (*cakras*) along the central power-axis of the body and equated with the five elements (earth, water, fire, wind and ether) and mind (*manas*). These six levels are further populated by six series of divine couples (*yāmala*), 180 in all (the 360 'rays'), drawn from the pantheon of Kubjikā in the earlier cult of the Western Transmission.

The system of the six power-centres (*cakras*) (*ādhāra*, also called *mūlādhāra*, in the anus, *svādhiṣṭhāna* in the genital region, *maṇipūra* in the navel, *anāhata* in the heart, *viśuddhi* in the throat and *ājñā* between the eyebrows) is also characteristic of the yogic rituals of the *Kubjikāmata*. Later it became so universal, being disseminated as part of the system of *kuṇḍalinī-yoga* beyond the boundaries of the Tantric cults, that it has been forgotten in India (and not noticed outside it) that it is quite absent in all the Tantric traditions except this and the cult of the goddess Tripurasundarī. The yoga of these two traditions sets them apart from the earlier Kaula traditions of the Trika and the Kālī cult. It is noteworthy in this respect that these two newer forms of Kaulism also mark themselves off from the earlier by worshipping as their founding Siddhas Mitranātha, Oḍḍanātha, Ṣaṣṭhanātha and Caryānātha, while the Trika and the Kālī cults share the series Khageṅdranātha, Kūrmanātha, Meṣanātha and Macchandanātha also called Matsyendranātha.

The Southern Transmission (Dakṣiṇāmnāya) and the Cult of Tripurasundarī. Under the heading of the Southern Transmission the *Ciñciṇīmatasārasamuccaya* describes the cult of Kāmeśvarī (the Goddess of Erotic Pleasure), a slim, two-armed and single-faced maiden (*kumārī*) surrounded by a retinue of twelve. Eleven of these are goddesses with such appropriate names as Kṣobhinī (the Exciter) and Drāviṇī (the Melter). The twelfth is male, Kāmadeva, the Indian Eros.

This cult of erotic magic is the prototype or part of the prototype of the Kaula cult of Tripurasundarī (the Beautiful Goddess of the Three Worlds), also called Kāmeśvarī, the Goddess who is worshipped in and as the nine-triangled *śrīcakra*, red, red-garmented, garlanded with red flowers, single-faced and four-armed, carrying a noose (*pāśa*), an elephant-goad (*aṅkuśa*), a bow and five arrows (the five arrows of the Love God), and

Figure 5.8: Tripurasundarī on Sadāśiva

seated above the lower gods Brahmā, Viṣṇu, Rudra and Īśvara, on the prostrate body of a white Sadāśiva (see Figure 5.8).

The classical form of this cult remembered that it had a special link with the older Southern Transmission; but it had come to see itself as transcending this quadripartition of the Kaula traditions. It called itself the Upper or Supreme Transmission and considered the four divisions to be subsumed within it. In a later elaboration of the cult known as the Kālī-Doctrine (Kālīmata) worship of Tripurasundarī incorporated more or less artificial and inaccurate versions of the pantheons of these other systems. To these new liturgies corresponded the almost universal ascendancy of this form of Kaulism throughout the middle ages down to the present.

The cult of Tripurasundarī is certainly the latest of the traditions of the Mantramārga covered here. Its basic scripture, the *Nityāṣoḍaśikārṇava*, clings to the edge of the Śaiva canon, being known in this canon only to itself. The southerners, who took this cult very seriously—it became so powerful that it was adopted, in a purified form, by the orthodox authority of the Śaṅkarācāryas of Śṛṅgerī and Kāñcīpuram—considered it to be Kashmiri in origin. However, this is quite possibly because they failed to distinguish the scriptural tradition itself from the Kashmiri theological and exegetical system within which they received it from the north and within which they continued to work. From Kashmir itself the evidence is inadequate. The Kashmiri Jayaratha (*fl. c.* 1225–75 CE), who wrote a learned commentary on the *Nityāṣoḍaśikārṇava* (his *Vāmakeśvarīmatavivaraṇa*), refers to a long tradition of local exegesis, but we cannot conclude from his evidence more than that the cult was introduced into Kashmir at some time between 900 and 1100 CE.

Figure 5.9: Śrīcakra

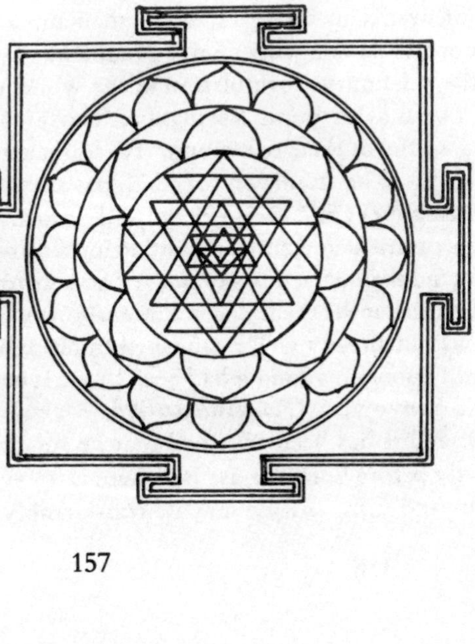

The *Nityāṣoḍaśikārṇava* is an unsophisticated text which concentrates on external ritual and on the various supernatural effects which such ritual can bestow on the worshipper, particularly in the quest for control over women. For a deeper meaning the tradition had to turn to the *Yoginīhṛdaya*. Here one could find the internal correspondences of the external elements, the metaphysical meaning of the sequence of creation and re-absorption which the deity-sets of the densely populated *śrīcakra* were believed to embody (see Figure 5.9). Thus the text of the ritual, though apparently concerned with erotic magic—the names of many of the constituent goddesses make this clear enough—could become the vehicle of ritualised, gnostic contemplation. However, although the *Yoginīhṛdaya* is scriptural in form (a dialogue in which Bhairava teaches the Goddess), there is no evidence of its existence before the thirteenth century in south India, shortly before Amṛtānandanātha (*fl. c.* 1325–75) wrote the first known commentary. Certainly it was composed when the non-dualistic Śaiva system of the Kashmiri exegesis of the Trika and the Krama had become the norm in the reading of the Kaula cults in south India, that is after *c.* 1050 CE. This is clear from the fact that it frequently echoes such popular texts of the Kashmiri tradition as the *Pratyabhijñāhṛdaya* of Kṣemarāja (*fl. c.* 1000–50).

The Post-scriptural Śaiva Traditions of Kashmir from the Ninth Century

The Common Base

From the middle of the ninth century these Tantric Śaiva traditions of the Mantramārga emerged from their scriptural anonymity into an extensive body of Kashmiri exegesis. In this literature we encounter two schools. On the left were the theoreticians of the Trika and the Krama. On the right was the staider and more Veda-congruent Śaiva Siddhānta. The doctrines of the former reached their definitive formulation in the works of Abhinavagupta (*fl. c.* 975–1025 CE) and his pupil Kṣemarāja. Those of the latter school culminated in the works of their contemporary, Rāmakaṇṭha.

The tradition of Abhinavagupta was recent. It looked back to Vasugupta (*fl. c.* 875–925 CE) and Somānanda (*fl. c.* 900–50 CE) as the founders of a new and anti-Śaivasiddhāntin movement among the learned. The Śaiva Siddhānta itself has preserved no records of its presence in Kashmir beyond Rāmakaṇṭha the Elder, a contemporary of Somānanda. We know that there was an already well established tradition in Kashmir at that time, but we do not know how long it had been there. It based itself above all on the works of Sadyojyoti (*Nareśvaraparīkṣā*, *Mokṣakārikā*, *Paramokṣa-nirāsakārikā*, etc.); and it has been assumed that he too was Kashmiri, and that he lived shortly before Somānanda. But there is no evidence that Kashmir was his home, and some that he may be considerably older.

Both schools addressed themselves principally not to the specialist seekers of powers so prominent in the scriptures themselves but to the seekers of liberation (*mumukṣu*), to those with no specific goal, who seek self-perfection through conforming to the physical and mental rituals of the Śaiva tradition. This, the unmarked category, was the sect's broad base in society, the community of married Śaiva householders. It is in accordance with this breadth that Śaivism appears in both schools not merely as a system of doctrines but first and foremost as a set of social facts independent of or presupposed by doctrine. Thus beneath the fundamental differences in theology which separate the schools there is complete solidarity in a basic faith that it is enough to be a Śaiva in a purely ritual sense, that the least gnostic (privy to special knowledge) of their common audience will attain liberation simply by being processed by the rituals of the community.

The Kashmiri Śaiva Siddhānta

The Kashmiri Śaiva Siddhānta enclosed and reinforced this exoteric base. It propagated an anti-gnostic ritualism which immunised the consciousness of the Tantric performer of ritual against the mystical and non-dualistic tendencies of the Kāpālika and Kaula left, and encouraged him to internalise without inhibition the outlook and values of non-Tantric orthodoxy.

According to Rāmakaṇṭha the scriptures of the Śaiva Siddhānta teach that salvation can only be attained by ritual. To be bound to the cycle of death and rebirth (*saṃsāra*) is to be ignorant of one's true nature, but knowledge of that nature cannot bring that bondage to an end. This is because the absence of liberated self-awareness is caused by impurity (*mala*). This cannot be removed by knowledge, because it is a substance (*dravya*). Being a substance it can be destroyed only by action and the only action capable of destroying it is the system of ritual prescribed in the Śaiva scriptures.

The rite of consecration (*dīkṣā*), through which one enters upon one's ritual obligations, destroys all the impurity (*mala*) which would otherwise be the cause of further incarnations. The daily (*nitya*) and occasional (*naimittika*) rituals which one is bound to perform after consecration cause, said Rāmakaṇṭha, the daily decrease of the impurity which the rite of consecration has left intact, the impurity which is the support of one's current physical and mental existence. But since the passage of time itself accomplishes this end, bringing one daily closer to the liberation at death which is the promised effect of consecration, it is hard to believe that this theory that ritual after consecration has a positive effect can have been in the forefront of the awareness of the Tantrics of the Śaiva Siddhānta. More compelling must have been the negative argument offered by Rāmakaṇṭha, as by the Bhāṭṭa Mīmāṃsakas, that one performs one's ritual duties in order to avoid the evil consequences of not performing them. For if one omits them, or breaks any other of the rules (*samaya*) which bind the initiate, one must perform a penance (*prāyaścitta*); and one is told that if this penance is neglected one's liberation guaranteed by the rite of consecration may be postponed by another incarnation, even by a period in hell.

The Kashmiri Trika

The Kashmiri authorities of the Trika attacked this ritualism of their Śaiva Siddhāntin contemporaries. They claimed that they had exaggerated certain tendencies in the scriptures of the Śaiva Siddhānta by means of sophistic exegesis. Thus, said the Trika, these scriptures place a greater emphasis on ritual than those of the left, but they do not go to the extent of claiming that salvation can be gained by no other means.

According to the left, the Śaiva Siddhānta contains the truth as modified by Śiva for the benefit of those not mature enough to enter the less conditioned and more demanding paths of his esoteric revelations. The extreme positions of the current Śaiva-Siddhāntin exegesis were believed to have arisen from failure to see this essential continuity of the Śaiva revelation. Thus the left attacked certain interpretations of these scriptures—and it must be said that in the main its criticisms are justified—but it never denied the efficacy of the religious practices of those who followed the prescriptions of these scriptures, even if they accepted the right's biased exegesis. The left was content to believe that the most hardened Śaiva-Siddhāntin ritualist would attain perfect liberation at death by the power of Śiva manifest in the mechanism of ritual. It drew its strength not from exclusion but from the propagation of a universally applicable *theory* of ritual. This theory promised liberation to all Śaivas while motivating ascent into the esoteric left through further consecrations in which the meaning of ritual proposed by the theory could be realised with ever greater immediacy and intensity. The culmination of this intensification is liberation, not at death but in life itself.

The left maintained that there are those who have attained this mystical transformation spontaneously or by means of gradual, ritual-less insight. Thus while the Śaiva Siddhāntins held that liberation could not be attained except through ritual, the authorities of the Trika maintained that liberation, while attainable by ritual alone (Śaiva-Siddhāntin or esoteric), could also, though more rarely, be attained by mystical experience and gnosis. Further, their theory divided the performance of ritual itself into two levels. Ritual without internal awareness would lead to liberation at death, as we have seen; but ritual could also be a means of liberation in life. Gnostic meaning encoded into the manipulations and formulas of the ritual could be so internalised through daily repetition that it would no longer require this external medium of expression in action. It could become purely mental, a ritual of self-definition in thought. The Tantric was exhorted by the left to see the sequence of ritual (*pūjākrama*) as a mirror in which he could perceive and contemplate his ultimate nature. Thereby he could attain liberation, for to be fully aware *of* this ultimate nature is to be liberated *as* this nature. By means of daily repetition he was to achieve a state of mind in which he believed that he was and always had been that which his ritual defines.

The ritualist of the Śaiva Siddhānta maintained that the scriptures taught no self beyond that of a purified and blissless individuality. For him salvation was not a merging into a transcendental godhead. It was simply that state of the eternally individual self in which its *equality* with Śiva previously concealed by the substance of impurity had become fully manifest. He did not become Śiva; he became *a* Śiva, omniscient and omnipotent but numerically distinct. Thus the Kashmiri Śaiva Siddhāntins stressed the difference between the Śiva who had never been bound, the 'original Śiva' (*anādiśiva*), and those who were Śivas through liberation from bondage, 'released Śivas' (*muktaśivas*). The latter were held to be capable of performing the five cosmic functions (*pañcakṛtya-*: creation, maintenance of the created, retraction of the created, and the binding and liberating of other selves), but to refrain from so doing because of the non-competitive spirit inherent in liberation.

Equally absolute in the Kashmiri Śaiva Siddhānta was the doctrine that matter and consciousness are entirely separate. According to Rāmakaṇṭha, following Sadyojyoti's interpretation of the scriptures, selves know and act upon a world whose existence is entirely independent of them, though it is arranged to fulfil their karmic needs. Śiva causes the entities of our universe to emerge by stimulating an independently eternal, all-pervasive, and unconscious 'world-stuff' (*māyā*). Thus are created the various spheres, bodies and faculties by means of which eternal selves can experience the effects of their past actions (*karma*) and eventually attain release from their beginningless state of bondage through Śaiva consecration (*dīkṣā*).

In the Kashmiri Trika the seeker of liberation (*mumukṣu*) is to realise through his ritual a self which breaks through these exoteric barriers of pluralism, realism and reified impurity. For the self of his worship and meditation is an absolute and omnipotent consciousness which, by manifesting contraction of its infinite powers, *appears* as separate individuals, their streams of experience, and the 'outer' objects or 'causes' of those experiences. He thinks of the three goddesses convergent in the fourth as this infinite and all-containing self, seeing their structure as that of his own consciousness. As this awareness deepens through immersion in the ritual, his individual consciousness, which is these powers contracted without change of structure, dissolves into its uncontracted prototype (cf. p. 141).

The Doctrines of Vibration (Spanda) and Recognition (Pratyabhijñā)

According to the Kashmiri Trika these doctrines of the ultimate non-plurality of centres of consciousness, of the non-existence of any reality except as projection within this all-containing consciousness, and consequently of the immateriality of impurity (*mala*), have been revealed by Śiva in all the Tantras of Bhairava. This is to say that they were read into this corpus or presupposed in any reading, for the surviving texts themselves hardly support this sweeping claim.

None the less, these doctrines are not entirely post-scriptural. For the view that the Deity is non-dual, dynamic consciousness (*saṃvidadvayavāda*, *śāktādvayavāda*) was already present at the far left of this corpus, in the literature of the Kāpālika and Kaula cults of Kālī (in the Mata and the Krama). From the middle of the ninth century the Trika, which was then permeated by the Kālī cult (see p. 146), produced theological metaphysicians who elevated these doctrines towards respectability within the Śaiva mainstream by abstracting them from their heterodox ritual context, by formulating them in a less sectarian terminology and by defending them philosophically against the doctrines of the Buddhists. This new direction began precisely during the period at which royal patronage in Kashmir started to shift from Pāñcarātra Vaiṣṇavism to Śaivism.

The first stage of this development is seen in two works of the ninth century: the *Aphorisms of Śiva* (*Śivasūtra*) and the *Concise Verses on Vibration* (*Spandakārikā*). The first was 'discovered' by Vasugupta. The second was composed by Vasagupta according to some, or by his pupil Kallaṭa according to others.

The *Śivasūtra* is too brief and allusive a work for us to be able to form a precise picture of its doctrine apart from its inevitably biased interpretation in the commentaries of Bhāskara (*fl. c.* 925–75) and Kṣemarāja (*fl. c.* 1000–50). We can see only that it sought to outline the non-ritual soteriology of an esoteric Śaiva tradition closely related to what we find in the *Jayadrathayāmalatantra* and the Kālī-based Trika.

The *Spandakārikā*, being more discursive, can be much more clearly understood independently of the commentaries. The work's fifty-two verses, offered as the key to the theology of the *Śivasūtra*, proposed that Śiva is all-inclusive reality, a single, unified consciousness, which manifests itself as all subjects, acts and objects of experience by virtue of an inherent and infinite dynamism. This dynamism, the essential nature of the Deity, was termed the Vibration-Reality (*spanda-tattva*). Liberation was to be attained by realising this vibration (*spanda*) in the source, course and end of all states and movements of consciousness.

Kṣemarāja, the author of an important commentary on this work, was probably right when he claimed that the scriptural background of this text is the Krama and the Mata with some elements of the

Trika. For the concept of 'vibration', or rather the use of this term to denote the inherent dynamism of a non-dual consciousness, which is the signature of this doctrine, is well-established in the *Jayadrathayāmala* and other texts of the Kālī cults.

The second stage of this scholarly underpinning began in the early tenth century with the *Perception of Śiva* (*Śivadṛṣṭi*) by Somānanda (*fl. c.* 900–50). While the *Spandakārikā* preserved some of the heterodox flavour of the goddess-orientated traditions of the far left, Somānanda, though he was certainly an initiate in those traditions, formulated a Śaiva non-dualism along more orthodox and rigorously philosophical lines. His pupil Utpaladeva, also a *guru* of the Trika and the Krama, gave this non-dualism its classical form in his *Concise Verses on the Recognition of the Deity* (*Īśvarapratyabhijñākārikā*). Claiming to follow his master he offered a 'new and easy path to salvation' through the recognition (*pratyabhijñā*) that it is one's own identity (*ātman*) which is Śiva, the Great Deity (Maheśvara). This transpersonal Self (*ātmeśvara*) is to be seen as that which contains all subjective and objective phenomena, holding this totality in a blissful synthesis of non-dual awareness. Through this recognition, which is forcefully defended against the Buddhist doctrine of impersonal flux, one is released from the cycle of death and rebirth (*saṃsāra*). For one's true identity is an already-liberated and never-bound 'I'-consciousness outside *time*, *form* and *location* (the three bases of (the appearance of) bondage in the continuum of transmigratory existence). This state of limitation is to be contemplated as the spontaneous play of this 'I'-consciousness. The pure autonomy (*svātantrya*) of the self expresses itself by manifesting its own 'contraction' in the form of limited centres of consciousness perceiving and acting within time, form and location, in accordance with the causal power of their acts (*karma*). Thus there arises the 'binding' appearance of essential differences between a world 'out there', a self 'in here' and other selves. Liberation is the realisation that all this is internal to the awareness which represents it as external. Consciousness thereby throws off its state of 'extrinsicist contraction', and knows itself only as the pre-relational, pre-discursive unity of manifestation (*prakāśa*) and self-cognition (*vimarśa*).

The philosophical position of Utpaladeva's Doctrine of Recognition was analysed and supported in great detail by Abhinavagupta (*fl. c.* 975–1025), a pupil of his pupil Lakṣmaṇagupta, in a commentary of the *Concise Verses* (*Īśvarapratyabhijñāvimarśinī*) and in a much longer commentary on Utpaladeva's own exegesis of his verses (*Īśvarapratyabhijñāvivṛtivimarśinī*).

The Doctrine of Recognition and the Trika

The Kashmiri Trika is known to us principally through the works of this same Abhinavagupta, particularly through his *Tantrāloka*, *Tantrasāra*, *Mālinīvijayavārtika* and *Parātriṃśikāvivaraṇa*. In the first three of these he expounds the doctrine and ritual of the Trika on the basis of the *Mālinīvijayottaratantra*. In the fourth he develops a more concentrated form of Trika worship, which focuses only on Parā, the highest of the three goddesses. Because the goddess is worshipped here as Solitary Heroine (*ekavīrā*), that is without the customary offerings to aspects and emanations, this tradition is sometimes distinguished from the Trika proper as the Ekavīra. For the same reason it is known as the Anuttara, 'that above which there is nothing'.

His exegesis of both of these forms of the Trika is based on the Doctrine of Recognition. Utpaladeva's concepts and terminology provide his metaphysical groundwork and are fed into Trika ritual. Thus, to give but one example, the phases of the worshipper's divinisation of his person with *mantras* (*nyāsa*) is required to be understood within the framework of Utpaladeva's four levels of contraction in which the self manifests itself in progressively grosser forms as the sensation-less void (*śūnya*), internal sensation (*prāṇa*), the mind (*buddhi*) and the body (*deha*).

Thus we may speak of at least three major phases in the evolution of the Trika. At the beginning are the *Siddhayogeśvarīmata* and related texts (see pp. 140–2) which teach the cult of the three goddesses alone. Then this triad is transcended and subsumed within Kālī (see p. 146). Finally we have the Pratyabhijñā-based Trika of the Abhinavagupta with its two aspects, the first being the Kālī-based cult of the *Tantrāloka*, and the second the condensed cult of Parā as Solitary Heroine.

The Kashmiri Krama

The Krama passed from its scriptural phase into chartable history with Jñānanetra *alias* Śivānanda in the first half of the ninth century. Said to have been instructed supernaturally by the Goddess herself in Oḍḍiyāna, he was the source of well-attested *guru* lineages in Kashmir and beyond. His tradition is remarkable for the theoretical structure of its ritual. It synthesised and adjusted the scriptural prototypes (principally those of the *Devīpañcaśataka* and the *Kramasadbhāva* (see pp. 151–2)) to produce a liturgy which could be thought of as the unfolding of the imperceptible sequence of cognition (*saṃvit-krama*) in the perceptible sequence of worship (*pūjā-krama*).

After contemplating various pentads as the structure of his bodily and mental existence and seeing them as emanations of a set of five goddesses representing the cycle of cognition—thus he consecrates his person as the true site of worship and seat of power (*pīṭha*)—the worshipper proceeds to a five-phased worship which enacts the progress of cognition from initial to terminal voidness. Each phase is equated with one of these same five goddesses.

In the first, that of the goddess Vyomavāmeśvarī (She who Emits the [Five] Voids), he worships the whole pentadic cycle (the

Five Voids) as condensed within the initial and eternal vibration of thoughtless consciousness.

In the second, the phase of the goddess Khecarī (She who Pervades the Void [of Cognition]), he worships the twelve Lords of the Wheel of Light (*prakāśa-cakra*). These are identified with the twelve faculties of cognition (the introvertive mental organ [*buddhi*] and the five senses) and action (the extrovertive mental organ [*manas*], speech, manipulation, locomotion, excretion and sexual pleasure). He mediates on these as illuminated by cognitive power as it moves from its initial vibration (*spanda*) in the five voids towards the extroverted representation of objects facing a subject.

In the third stage, that of the goddess Bhūcarī (She who Pervades the [Outer] Field), the constituents of the preceding phase have moved outwards and incorporated into consciousness the representation of the five external sense-data (sound, tactile sensation, visible form, taste and odour). This extroversion entails the suppression of the introvertive mental organ. Thus there are now sixteen constituents: the preceding twelve reduced to eleven and increased by five. These he worships as the sixteen Yoginīs of the Wheel of Sensual Bliss (*ānanda-cakra*).

The fourth stage is pervaded by the goddess Saṃhārabhakṣiṇī (She who Devours in Retraction). It represents the first stage in the reversion of cognitive power to its prediscursive source, the internalisation of the object of sensation that occurs in the awareness that one has perceived it. The extrovertive mental organ (*manas*) which was distinct in the preceding phase is now submerged and the introvertive mental organ (*buddhi*) re-emerges. These sixteen are increased to seventeen by the addition of ego-awareness (*ahaṅkāra*). They are worshipped as the Lords of the Wheel of Fusion (*mūrti-cakra*).

The fifth and final stage is that of the goddess Raudreśvarī (The Terrible). Here he worships the sixty-four Yoginīs of the Wheel of the Multitude (*vṛnda-cakra*). The ego-awareness which emerged in the preceding phase is represented as suddenly expanding to obliterate all that conceals the radiant voidness of the transpersonal Absolute within consciousness. This obliteration is worshipped in five stages as sixteen, twenty-four, twelve, eight and four Yoginīs.

The first sixteen of these Yoginī emanations dissolve the latent traces (*vāsanā*, *saṃskāra*) of the field of objective sensation worshipped as the Wheel of Sensual Bliss (*ānanda-cakra*). In the second stage the traces of the twelve constituents of the cognitive Wheel of Light (*prakāśa-cakra*) are obliterated. Twenty-four Yoginīs are worshipped here, because each of the twelve has two aspects, a latent and an active. In the third phase twelve Yoginīs penetrate this cognitive field with pure, non-discursive awareness. Now there remain the latent traces of the subtle body (*puryaṣṭaka*) consisting of the five sense-data (sound, etc.) and the three internal faculties (the extrovertive and introvertive mental organs together with ego-awareness). By worshipping eight Yoginīs here he enacts the elimination of these elements. The four Yoginīs worshipped in the fifth and last phase of the Wheel of the Multitude (*vṛnda-cakra*) represent the obliteration of a subtle residue which the preceding eight left untouched: the deep latent impression of the threefold inner mind and of objectivity reduced to a single, undifferentiated sensation of contact (*sparśa*).

He now worships Raudreśvarī herself as the sixty-fifth power, the non-relational ground of these sixty-four Yoginīs, consciousness in its pristine purity. He identifies her with Maṅgalā *alias* Vīrasiṃhā, the goddess incarnate of Oḍḍiyāna. He thereby equates the Krama's Absolute with the lineage of teachers, male and female, who have embodied this Absolute and transmitted it to him. For after Maṅgalā he worships Jñānanetra and then the *gurus* who descend from Jñānanetra to himself.

Finally he worships the four Sequences (*krama*), those of Emission (*sṛṣṭi-*), Maintenance (*sthiti-*), Retraction (*saṃhāra-*), and the Nameless (*anākhya-*) which pervades the three as their ground. The twelve Kālīs of this fourth sequence are to be worshipped during sexual intercourse with the *dūtī*. They are understood as the gradual withdrawal of cognitive power into Kālasaṃkarṣiṇī (Kālī the Destroyer of Time), the waveless void of the absolute Self. Here the worshipper realises the absolute autonomy (*svātantrya*) of the Goddess (Consciousness) through which she assumes the form of the universe without contamination or diminution of her nature.

Three major works of this Kashmiri Krama survive, all entitled *Mahānayaprakāśa* (Illumination of the Great Way), that of Śitikaṇṭha (in Old Kashmiri with a Sanskrit auto-commentary), that of Arṇasiṃha (MS) and the third anonymous. The last is the source of our exposition of the phases of pentadic worship leading up to that of the four Sequences.

The function of the ritual sequence of this tradition is said to be that it prepares the initiate for the non-sequential (*akrama*) intuition that will enable him to transcend it. It is designed to condition awareness with the image of its true nature, so that eventually it will provoke a spontaneous and instantaneous 'swallowing of dichotomising cognition' (*vikalpagrāsa*), the annihilation (*alaṃgrāsa*) of the mechanisms of individuation and projection through which the innate (*sahaja*) purity of awareness appears *as though* it were sullied in the natural processes of ideation and perception. The worshipper is to pass through the ritual to reach the liberating conviction that absolute reality is this pure awareness, and that the phases and levels of cognition are co-extensive with it as its innate vitality. Liberation (*mokṣa*) here is the resolution of the distinction in self-perception between a transcendental or internal state of *nirvāṇa* and an imminent or external state of finite, transmigratory existence (*bhava*, *saṃsāra*).

This system of contemplative worship was not the Krama's only means of enlightenment. It believed that there were those who were capable of reaching the goal without it. For these two higher paths are described. In the first, that of Oral Instruction (*kathana*), the *guru* was to provoke the disciple's intuition through certain mystical aphorisms (*kathā*, *chummā*). The emphasis here is on sudden enlightenment (*sāhasa*). In the second path the goal was believed to be attained without any instruction, either spontaneously or through some non-verbal stimulus such as the *guru*'s glance.

Both this intuitionism and this view of ritual as a mode of liberating insight are thoroughly in harmony with the position which Abhinavagupta expounds for the Trika. Indeed in this respect the Trika was greatly indebted to the Krama. It had already accommodated important elements of this system in the second phase of its development (see p. 146). In the third phase, during which this enriched Trika was grounded in the Doctrine of Recognition, we find Abhinavagupta drawing directly on the postscriptural Krama of the lineage of Jñānanetra, adapting it as the basis of the Trika's claim to be the ultimate in Śaiva revelation. Kṣemarāja, his pupil, who offered no detailed exegesis in the Trika itself, unambiguously asserts that it is the Krama that embodies this final truth. Clearly the prestige of the Krama-based Kālī cult was widely felt in esoteric Śaiva circles. The *Manthānabhairavatantra* places it above the Trika at the summit of the hierarchy of the Śaiva traditions, allowing it to be transcended only by the Western Transmission (Paścimāmnāya), the tradition of the text itself. Another work of that Transmission, the *Ciñciṇīmatasārasamuccaya*, goes further. It gives the realisation of the Krama's Kālīs in the Sequence of the Nameless as the highest, internal worship within the cult of Kubjikā itself.

The Kashmiri Cult of Svacchandabhairava

We have seen that Śaivism in Kashmir was split between two centres of authority. On the right was the ritualistic Śaiva Siddhānta with its anti-mystical pluralism and extrinsicism. On the left was the gnostic non-dualism of the Trika and the Krama. The right saw the left as heretical while the left saw the right as the exoteric base of the Śaiva hierarchy, leading to liberation but only at death.

It might be imagined therefore that it was the tradition of the Śaiva Siddhānta which was the source of the practice of the greater part of the Śaiva community, and that the Trika and the Krama were the preserves of enthusiasts dependent on this exoteric or common Śaivism both for the candidates for these 'higher' initiations and as the form of their own more public identity in the wider society. This then would be the sense of the frequently quoted maxim of the left which requires one to be privately Kaula, publicly Śaiva and Vedic in one's social intercourse.

However, the interrelation of the traditions was more complex in Kashmir. For the Śaiva cult of the majority was not that of Sadāśiva taught by the Siddhānta, but that of Svacchandabhairava. Since the latter derived its authority from the *Svacchandatantra* of the Mantrapīṭha section of the Tantras of Bhairava (see p. 138), it was, strictly speaking, a tradition of the Kāpālika-based left. None the less, the Kashmiri practised a thoroughly domesticated form of the cult, and in the tenth century the Śaiva Siddhānta, though not its source, had taken advantage of this to bring it under the sway of its doctrines. The Śaiva Siddhānta was, therefore, the principal doctrinal authority among the Śaivas of Kashmir, at least during the tenth century.

It is hardly surprising, then, that the non-dualistic tradition of the left should have tried to oust the Śaiva Siddhānta from this position of power once it had itself attained a degree of respectability during the course of the tenth century. This vital task of establishing the authority of the new exegesis beyond the confined territory of the Trika and the Krama was accomplished by the works of Kṣemarāja. While his teacher Abhinavagupta limited himself to the exposition of the esoteric traditions in harmony with the Doctrine of Recognition, Kṣemarāja (*fl. c.* 1000–50) popularised the essential doctrine and applied it through commentaries to the cult of Svacchandabhairava and its annexes. In the first case we have such works as his *Essence of Recognition* (*Pratyabhijñāhṛdaya*) and his commentaries on two popular collections of hymns, the *Stavacintāmaṇi* of Bhaṭṭa-Nārāyaṇa and the *Stotrāvalī* of Utpaladeva. In the second case we have his elaborate analytical commentaries on the *Svacchandatantra* and the *Netratantra*.

In both of these commentaries Kṣemarāja states that his motive is to free the understanding of these texts from the dualistic exegesis that was traditional in his day. The importance of the *Svacchandatantra* has already been stated. The *Netratantra* was the authority for the cult of Amṛteśvarabhairava and his consort Amṛtalakṣmī. The worship of this pair was closely linked with that of Svacchandabhairava and Aghoreśvarī in the Kashmiri tradition, as can be seen from the surviving ritual handbooks (*paddhatis*) in use until recently among the Tantric family priests.

In purely doctrinal terms Kṣemarāja's commentaries do violence to both of these texts, at least as much as that of which the dualistic commentaries must have been guilty. Neither Tantra fits either exegetical straitjacket. In the area of ritual, however, Kṣemarāja had a clear advantage. When, for example, he attacked the then current practice of substituting water for alcoholic liquor in Svacchandabhairava's guest-offering, he was simply reinstating the text within the tradition of the Bhairava Tantras to which it properly belonged. This recontextualisation would have seemed all the more plausible in the light of the fact that when the deity-system of the Svacchanda cult of common Śaiva worship in Kashmir extends beyond its immediate boundaries, it does so not to the right and the

Śaiva Siddhānta but to the left and the goddess cults. Thus we find the *Picumata-Brahmayāmala's* Caṇḍā Kāpālinī with her eight *śaktis* (see p. 140), Kuleśvarī and the eight Mothers with the Bhairavas (see p. 149), the Kaula alcohol deity Ānandeśvarabhairava, the Trika's Parā and Mālinī (as Goddess of the Eastern Transmission), Kubjikā (as Godess of the Western Transmission), several aspects of Tripurasundarī and a number of goddesses from the *Jayadrathayāmala*.

The literature of this common Śaiva worship current in Kashmir shows that this attempt to throw off the influence of the Śaiva Siddhānta was entirely successful. How quickly this was achieved cannot be seen from the evidence so far uncovered. We can say only that the corpus of the anonymous texts of Śaiva ritual in Kashmir is completely non-dualistic in the manner defined by Abhinavagupta and Kṣemarāja, that this corpus records a tradition which must go back at least five hundred years, and that there is no trace of any Kashmiri literature in the doctrinal or liturgical aspects of the Śaiva Siddhānta after the eleventh century. But the most striking indication of its ascendency is its influence outside the sphere of the properly Tantric.

Śaiva Non-Dualism and the Non-Tantric Tradition in Kashmir

When the Pratyabhijñā-based Trika was emerging in Kashmir both the Vedic and the Tantric traditions were fully deployed. The first was active in both its *śrauta* and its *smārta* forms (see pp. 128–30), while the second could be seen not only in the various forms of Śaivism outlined above but also in the Vaiṣṇavism of the Pāñcarātra.

At some point, probably during the Muslim period from the fourteenth century, the Kashmiri *śrauta* tradition of the Kāṭhaka-Yajurvedins disappeared entirely. All that remained of the Vedic tradition were the domestic rites (following the ordinances of Laugākṣi) together with a repertoire of non-Tantric deity-worship (*devapūjā*). In Kashmir, as elsewhere, this *smārta* tradition of worship mirrors the Tantric at a safe distance. This is to say that it has borrowed Tantric deities and liturgical forms, but uses Vedic rather than Tantric *mantras* within this framework.

The Tantric Vaiṣṇavism of the Pāñcarātra also disappeared, but not without leaving behind clear evidence that it was once a powerful influence in Kashmiri religion. For the Tantric tradition mirrored in the *smārta* worship of the region is not the Śaiva as one might have expected but precisely the principal cult of the earliest scriptural Pāñcarātra, that of Vāsudeva in his form as Vaikuṇṭha (see Figure 5.10), in which a mild human face is flanked by those of his incarnations as the Man-Lion (Narasiṃha) and the Boar (Varāha), with that of the wrathful sage Kapila behind.

Thus there remained only the simple dichotomy between a *smārta* tradition influenced by the Pāñcarātra and the Tantric Śaiva

Figure 5.10: Vaikuṇṭha

tradition which, as we have seen, was itself simplified by the decline of the Śaiva Siddhānta.

It should not be imagined, however, that the non-Tantric excluded and condemned the Tantric in Kashmir. While this may have been the more usual position in the rest of India, as earlier in Kashmir itself, the evidence of recent centuries shows a more or less unified community. The Vedic tradition came to be outside the Śaiva only in the sense that the former comprised the rituals of those who had undergone the common investiture (*upanayana*) of the Brahmanical tradition but had not yet undergone or never underwent special consecration in the form of the Tantric Śaiva *dīkṣā*. Thus they were not bound by the additional and more exacting duties of Tantric worship. However, outside the special domain of ritual these brahmins were as Śaiva as the rest. Texts dealing with their duties teach side by side with non-Tantric ritual a thoroughly Tantric form of *yoga*. This is designed to cause *śakti* as macrocosmic power within the microcosm of the body (*kuṇḍalinī*) to rise from her state of latency in the region of the anus (*mūlādhāra-cakra*), to ascend through the central channel (*suṣumṇā*) imagined along the internal vertical axis of the body, to transcend the body through the cranial 'aperture of Brahmā' (*brahmarandhra*), and finally to come to rest in union with Śiva at a point twelve finger-breadths above the head (*dvādaśānta*). This form of *kuṇḍalinī-yoga* is derived, as we have seen (see pp. 155–6), from the later Kaula tradition of the cults of Kubjikā and Tripurasundarī. As for duty in the form of the cultivation of liberating knowledge (*jñāna*), this is the study of the mystical soteriology of the Trika expounded by Abhinavagupta, which is to say the practice of all but the ritual of that system.

Thus the whole society of Kashmiri brahmins had become Śaiva. It was no longer necessary, as the earlier tradition had insisted, to take Tantric consecration, thereby binding oneself to perform Tantric worship, if one wished to have access to Tantric yoga and mystical doctrine.

This separation, which enabled Tantric Śaivism to pervade the community so completely, is not a recent phenomenon. Its roots can be seen at the turn of the millennium in the works of Abhinavagupta and Kṣemarāja themselves. For it is in the essence of their opposition to the Śaiva Siddhānta that they saw ritual as a lower and transcendable mode of self-knowledge (see pp. 168–9). The rule that only those who had been consecrated and bound to Tantric ritual could attain liberation was preserved only in the letter. For the definition of consecration was stretched into the metaphorical so that it could bypass ritual in the special case of 'consecration by the deities of one's own consciousness'. This sort of thinking was justified by appealing to the authority of the most heterodox area of the Śaiva Mantramārga; but it served in the end to make a private Tantric identity accessible to all Kashmiri, while the Śaiva Siddhāntins, for all their ostentatious orthopraxy, declined and disappeared from the scene. For though the Siddhānta argued that it was pure in the sense accepted by the non-Tantric, it did not do so out of any desire to extend its domain across boundaries of ritual qualification (*adhikāra*) into the wider community. Its concern was rather to claim high social status for its adherents as a distinct and exclusive group within that community. The Śaiva Siddhānta has survived to this day in south India among an endogamous community of Śaiva temple-priests, the Ādiśaivas, as the basis of their profession and the guarantee of their exclusive hereditary right to practise that profession. It seems very probable that the Kashmiri Śaiva Siddhāntins were protecting similar rights. If they died out it may have been because centuries of Islamicisation had deprived them of their institutional base. Certainly nothing survives in Kashmir that is remotely comparable to the richly endowed Śaiva temples which continue to provide the livelihood of the Ādiśaivas in the Tamil south.

Finally, just as the esoteric Śaiva traditions in Kashmir flowed into the non-specialised brahmin majority, so when these same traditions went south they took root among the Śaiva brahmin community that surrounds the Ādiśaiva enclaves in that region. The cult of Tripurasundarī (see pp. 156–7) became particularly well established. In purely Tantric circles it was propagated within the theological system of the Pratyabhijñā-based Trika; but, much as in Kashmir, it came to pervade the wider community of Śaiva brahmins known as the Smārtas. Purged of its Kaula heteropraxy, it became there the special cult of the renunciate (*saṃnyāsin*) Śaṅkarācāryas, who are the ultimate spiritual authorities of this community. Its emblem, the *śrīcakra* (see pp. 157–8), was installed in the major Śaiva temples to assert their claim to pre-eminence even within the domain of the Ādiśaivas.

Further Reading

On Pāśupata doctrines:

Hara, Minoru 'Nakulīśa-Pāśupata-Darśanam', in *Indo-Iranian Journal*, vol. II (1958), pp. 8–32

On the Pāśupatas, Kālāmukhas and Kāpālikas:

Lorenzen, David N. *The Kāpālikas and Kālāmukhas: Two Lost Śaivite Sects* (Thomson Press (India), New Delhi, 1972)

On the doctrines of the Śaiva Siddhānta:

Brunner, Hélène, 'Un chapitre du *Sarvadarśanasaṃgraha*: Le *Śaivadarśana*', in *Mèlanges Chinois et Bouddhiques*, vol. XX (*Tantric and Taoist Studies in Honour of R.A. Stein*) (Institut Belge des Hautes Études Chinoises, Brussels, 1981), pp. 96–140

On the mysticism and ritual of the Śaiva Siddhānta:

Brunner, Hélène, 'Le mysticisme dans les āgama śivaites', in *Studia Missionalia*, vol. 26 (1977) (Gregorian University, Rome), pp. 287–314
—— *Somaśambhupaddhati*, vols. 1–3 (1963–77) (Institut Français d'Indologie, Pondicherry). See the introductions to these volumes for an excellent account of Śaiva ritual. The other traditions of Tantric worship (the Pāñcarātra, the Trika, the cult of Svacchandabhairava, etc.) differ from this only in their deities, *mantras*, *maṇḍalas*, *mudrās* and such constituents. The ritual framework is largely constant.

On the Trika and related systems:

Gnoli, Raniero (trans.), *Luce delle Sacre Scritture (Tantrāloka) di Abhinavagupta*, (Unione Tipografico-Editrice Torinese, Turin, 1972)
Padoux, André *Recherches sur la Symbolique et l'Énergie de la Parole dans certains Textes Tantriques* (Institut de Civilisation Indienne, Paris, 1963)
Sanderson, Alexis 'Purity and Power among the Brahmans of Kashmir' in Michael Carrithers, Steven Collins and Steven Lukes (eds.), *The Category of the Person* (Cambridge University Press, Cambridge, 1985), pp. 191–216

6 Modern Hinduism

Glyn Richards

Any attempt to give an account of Hinduism in the nineteenth and twentieth centuries within the compass of a short article must of necessity be selective. What I propose to do in the following essay is to select those leaders of thought who may be regarded as both inheritors of the Hindu religious and social traditions and contributors to the renewal of Hinduism and the development of modern India.

It is not without justification that Rāmmohan Roy (1772–1833) has been described as the father of modern India. His enthusiasm for reform may be attributed in part to the influence of Islamic thought and Western ideas, but, as his *Vedānta grantha* shows, he is also indebted to Vedāntic teaching concerning the unity and supremacy of *Brahman* as Eternal Being and One without a second. His defence of Hinduism against the attacks of Christian missionaries is an indication of the influence of his Brahminic upbringing and the part it played in moulding his desire to restore the religious purity of Hinduism. He endeavoured to do this through his journalistic and literary activities and through the formation of the *Brāhmo Samāj*, a society he founded in 1828 to promote the worship of the one eternal, immutable God and the rejection of image worship so characteristic of popular devotion. If the intellectual bent of the *Brāhmo Samāj* deprived it of popular appeal, it nevertheless succeeded in creating an atmosphere of liberalism and rationality in which a reinterpretation of the Hindu tradition could take place.

Roy's emphasis on logic and reason is reputed to have characterised one of his earliest Persian works entitled *Tuhfatul-ul-Muwahhiddin* (Gift to Deists), in which belief in a Creator, the existence of the soul and life after death, are claimed to be the basic tenets of all religions (though such tenets could hardly be attributed either logically or reasonably, e.g. to Buddhism). The same work dismisses as irrational beliefs in miracles, anthropomorphic deities and the efficacy of rituals in man's salvation. It was his earnest endeavour to convince his fellow-countrymen and prove to his European friends that what he called superstitious and idolatrous practices had nothing to do with the pure spirit of the Hindu religion. He was not convinced of the symbolic nature of the images worshipped and maintained that Hindus of his day firmly believed in the existence of innumerable gods and goddesses.

His opposition to idolatry is matched by his rejection of some of the social customs of Hinduism, especially suttee, the practice of burning widows on the funeral pyres of their husbands. His advocacy of the provision of education for his fellow-countrymen, particularly in mathematics, natural philosophy, chemistry and other useful sciences, was aimed at the elimination of such customs, the cultural improvement of the native population and the harmonisation of Western science and Eastern spirituality for the benefit of mankind. His pursuit of this goal justly earned him a place of eminence as one of the most creative personalities of nineteenth-century India.

A fellow member of the *Brāhmo Samāj*, whose opposition to idolatry matched that of Roy, was Devendranāth Tagore (1817–1905). It was his firm belief that the ultimate good of India would derive from the rejection of tantric and puranic myths and legends and the acceptance of *Brahman* as revealed in the Upaniṣads. He showed great enthusiasm for the purification of the Hindu religion and joined the campaign to provide free education for Hindu children. A man of sensitive spirit, Tagore in his later years inclined to mysticism and his piety earned him the title Maharishi, 'great sage'. He attracted many able young men to the *Samāj*, including Keshab Chunder Sen (1838–84), who became equally committed to religious and social reform.

Sen's enthusiasm to propagate the message of the society led him to found the *Indian Mirror* and the *Dharmatattva*, journals of religion and philosophy, and to establish branches of the *Samāj* in many parts of India. Like Roy he rejected idolatry as erroneous and superstitious, but unlike his predecessor he recognised the popular need for visible and tangible expressions of the divine and the intense love, reverence and faith manifested in the worship of images. Hence his claim that Hindus ought to be grateful for the gods and goddesses of India and the legends of Hindu mythology. His unbounded enthusiasm and vitality proved a mixed blessing to the society and schisms ensued which resulted in the founding of the *Brāhmo Samāj of India* in 1865, and subsequently the setting up of the *Sādhāran Brāhmo Samāj* in 1878 by his disenchanted followers.

Sen's close acquaintance with Christian teaching provided him with the terminology he needed to express the principles of his New Dispensation. This he refers to as equivalent to the Jewish and Christian Dispensations; as the fulfilment of Christ's prophecy; as the harmonisation of all scriptures and all religions; and as proclaiming the message of love which prohibits all distinctions between Brahmins and Śūdras, Asiatics and Europeans. Its uniqueness for him lay in its insistence on the direct, unmediated worship of God. His acceptance of the divinity of Christ and the title of Jesudās, the servant of Jesus, suggests that he completely embraced the Christian faith. In fact he considered Christ to be an Asiatic and his concept of the Incarnation is not 'once and for all' but the manifestation of God in history through great men and prophets. Christ, he claims, held the doctrine of divine humanity, which is essentially a Hindu doctrine and at one with the Vedāntic notion of man's unity with the Absolute.

Sen's belief in the providential nature of British rule would not have been shared by Dayānanda Sarasvatī (1824–83), whose promotion of Hindi as a national language was not unrelated to the development of national self-consciousness. He was fully aware of the intimate relation that pertained between language, religion and nationalism, and was convinced that political independence was the natural corollary of the restoration of Vedic ideals. It was his firm belief that the Vedas contained true revelation and were the authoritative source of the Hindu religion. Through the generosity of his followers he founded schools to teach the Vedas but this proved an unsuccessful experiment. More successful was his insistence on the place of morality in true religion and his denunciation of idol worship as contrary to the teaching of the scriptures. In his view God, being formless and omnipresent, cannot be conceived of existing in any particular object, and the evil practice of idol worship was responsible for widespread ignorance and mendacity in the country.

The *Ārya Samāj*, founded by Dayānanda in 1875, provided him with the organisation necessary to propagate his religious and social ideals. Among the rules adopted by the society, belief in God, the authority of the Vedas and the rejection of idol worship and incarnational doctrines were paramount. The duty of all members of the *Samāj* was to promote spiritual monotheism, Vedic authority and social reform. The reforms he advocated related to child marriage, widow remarriage and *niyoga.* He was aware of the problems of early widowhood and child marriage and the relation between the dowry system and female infanticide. The eradication of the practice of child marriage, he believed, would reduce the number of widows and he advocated *niyoga*, the temporary legal union of widows and widowers, as an interim solution to the problem of early widowhood. He approved of the education of both sexes, insisting that it was the basis of mutual respect between husband and wife. The best form of marriage, in his view, was marriage by choice (*svayaṃvara*) after the education of the contracting parties had been completed. Education itself should involve Hindi and Sanskrit and a case should be made for making them the medium of instruction in schools.

Dayānanda's aggressive nationalism and deep desire to lead his fellow-countrymen back to the Vedas earned him the title of the

'Luther of India', a description which is not entirely inappropriate.

Of the mystics of modern India pride of place must go to Rāmakrishna (1836–86), who from an early age is reputed to have experienced mystical trances. Though lacking formal education he possessed an abundance of native intelligence and for the greater part of his life served God at the Kālī temple at Dakshineswar. Through his association with followers of the Tantric and Vedānta schools he acquired an understanding of yogic techniques and the ways of *bhakti* (devotion) and *jñāna* (knowledge) as means of union with the divine. His personal experiences of other religious traditions, especially Islam and Christianity, enabled him to make the claim that different religions are simply different paths to the same goal. As Kālī, the Divine Mother, and *Brahman* are two aspects of the same reality so the mystical experience of Christ is at one with the mystical experience of Allah. God may be called by different names but he is one and the same. There is no necessity to choose between the formless Absolute and the personal God, for God with form is as real as God without form and the difference between them is no more than that between ice and water. The impediment to spiritual development is worldliness which is *māyā*. It is man's ignorance of his true self that causes him to become enmeshed in *māyā* in the first place, and release is attained through discrimination which recognises God alone as real and eternal. Social reform, including the elimination of caste distinctions, should derive naturally from the love and worship of God.

Rāmakrishna's disciples, of whom Vivekānanda was the most prominent, proclaimed his teaching throughout India but were more explicitly committed to social reform than their master, establishing schools, orphanages and hospitals in order to give practical expression to their religious ideals.

Another of India's mystics was Rabindranāth Tagore (1861–1941) whose views concerning the interrelation of God, man and nature would classify him as a nature mystic. The Absolute is manifested in creation and both man and nature are revelations of God. The same power that creates the universe enlightens man's consciousness and the main goal of life is to realise the Absolute through the immediate apprehension of the divine in one's own soul. Spiritual progress is achieved through a life lived in close proximity to nature, hence the rural location of Viśva Bhārati University founded by Tagore in 1921 to promote his religious and cultural ideals.

Man's kinship with nature is coupled with his identity with his fellow man. God's immanence in creation implies man's involvement with social justice and the needs of all God's creatures. In a world suffused with the spirit of God nothing can be deemed untouchable so the rigidity and exclusivism of the caste system must be rejected as contrary to the cultivation of spirituality. Similarly, the selfish pursuit of materialistic goals, which intensifies the inequality between those who have and those who have not, undermines the social system and degrades man himself. The same applies on a national level when selfishness takes the form of patriotism devoid of concern for humanity as a whole which resorts to force to achieve its ends. Concern for the nurture of the soul determines Tagore's attitude to every aspect of life and gives a marked distinctiveness to his social, cultural and religious ideals.

One of the foremost mystical philosophers of India is generally accepted to be Aurobindo Ghose (1872–1950), who, after a period of political activity in close association with Bāl Gangādhar Tilak (1856–1920), which resulted in his being jailed on a charge of advocating terrorism and violence, withdrew to the French settlement of Pondicherry where he spent forty years in study and contemplation. The fruit of those years is his philosophical system of integral yoga which he describes as Vedāntic. The essence of his system is that the Absolute by a process of involution and evolution manifests itself in, and expresses itself through, grades of reality, or levels of being, from matter to spirit. The Absolute is the starting-point of the evolutionary ascent from lower forms of matter through mind to supermind and spirit, and the involutionary descent of the spirit through supermind to mind and matter. For Aurobindo every aspect of reality is permeated by the Absolute and the veil between mind and supermind is where the higher and lower levels of reality meet. The development of divine consciousness depends on rending the veil through involution and evolution and the divine life produced manifests that fullness of spirituality which can be described as gnostic being. Because of their divine cosmic consciousness gnostic beings are able to effect the transformation of lower levels of being and the whole of nature.

What Aurobindo seeks to do in his philosophy of synthesis is to reconcile matter and mind, mind and spirit, finite and infinite, God and man. Though complex and highly esoteric in terminology his system is marked with spiritual insights which succeeded in inspiring enthusiasm among intellectuals in particular for the cultural heritage of India.

Two of the more systematic philosophers of India are Vivekānanda (1863–1902), and Rādhakrishnan (1888–1975), an acknowledged academic who was elected President of his country. Both were interpreters of Advaita Vedānta. The Vedāntic doctrine of the divinity of man is a significant tenet in Vivekānanda's teaching and one aspect of the message he proclaimed at the World Parliament of Religions in Chicago. Another aspect of his message is the essential unity of all religions and the basic oneness of existence. For Vivekānanda there is but one life, one world and one existence. God permeates all that exists from stones and plants to human beings, so the difference between one life and another is one of degree and not of kind. It would be contrary to Vedāntic teaching to claim that animals were created in order to provide man with food. Similarly, he upholds the ideal of a universal religion not in the sense of a single ritual, mythology or philosophy, but in the sense that every religion proclaims an aspect of the universal truth according to its insights. Each religion is a pearl on a string and no one form of religion will do for everyone. Religion is in essence one but diverse in application, and toleration teaches us not to look for defects in religions other than our own. The Advaitist or qualified Advaitist does not say that dualism is wrong; it is a right view, yet a lower one which is on the way to truth. So the finest pearl on the string after all, for Vivekānanda, is Advaita Vedānta!

Rādhakrishnan claims that in his philosophical writings he seeks above all to convey his insight into the meaning and purpose of life; to provide a coherent interpretation of the world; and to promote the religion of the spirit. He sees no discontinuity between human life and spiritual life or between animal life and human life since all forms of life are expressions of the divine spirit. Spiritual existence is the fulfilment of human life and the ultimate goal of the cosmic process. This means that the world is not illusory but a manifestation of the divine spirit. It depends on the immanent creative activity of God without which it would cease to be. So the reality of the world is a dependent not an ultimate reality, which is precisely what the doctrine of *māyā* seeks to convey. Knowledge of the primordial divine spirit is possible through rational analysis of empirical data, but certainty comes through the immediate, intuitive apprehension of the nature of ultimate reality which is the result of *jñāna*, gnosis, or integral insight. It is a state of ecstasy; it is what is meant by being at one with God. This is an experience common to all religions, hence the importance of learning about the basic principles of all the great religions of the world and recognising the folly of missionary activity. No one religion can claim to be exclusive; religious traditions are imperfect expressions of the essence of religion which is truth. And since all men are bound together in one spirit, a life of service and sacrifice is inevitable for those who would promote the religion of the spirit and defend the ideals of freedom and justice.

One of the most remarkable men of twentieth-century India was Mohandās Karamchand Gandhi (1869–1948). Though he resented being called a saint, since he thought it too sacred a term to apply to a simple seeker after truth, there can be no doubt that he was a 'great soul' and most worthy of the title Mahātma. Fundamental to his thought is the concept of Truth (*Satya*), the existential quest for which forms the basis of all aspects of his teaching. He is faithful to the traditions of Hinduism when he affirms the oneness of Truth and Being, Consciousness, Bliss (*Saccidānanda*), and when he describes Truth as the most significant term that can be used for God. Yet his preference for the idea of God as formless Truth does not prevent him from recognising that God is personal to those who need to feel his presence, thereby accepting the *anekāntavādin* position that reality has many forms. He acknowledges that perfect Truth is beyond man's empirical grasp and that he must hold on to such relative truth as he is able to apprehend through his understanding of the essential teaching of his own religious tradition. All religions, he claims, possess truth but no single religion can embody the whole truth since it is a human construct and therefore imperfect. This has implications for missionary activity but it does not prevent those who wish to change their religious affiliation from doing so, or others from making a plea for toleration.

The reverse side of the coin to Truth is *ahiṃsā*, non-violence, and as far as Gandhi is concerned the attainment of one involves the realisation of the other. Ends and means are convertible terms in his philosophy, but it does not mean that he is unable to conceive of situations when violent action might be justified. Like perfect Truth, perfect non-violence is beyond man's grasp and in situations of moral dilemma one must do what it is morally possible for one to do while remaining informed by the spirit of *ahiṃsā*. The same applies to *Satyāgraha*, or holding firm to Truth, which is the technique of *ahiṃsā*. Its method is conversion rather than coercion, and although it involves civil disobedience and non-co-operation it seeks to establish social justice by the power of love and gentle persuasion.

In Gandhi's thought no distinction is drawn between Truth, Reality and the Self or *Ātman* which all men share. Belief in the indivisibility of Truth and the oneness of God involves belief in the oneness of humanity. We may have many bodies but we have but one soul. These metaphysical presuppositions point clearly to the interrelation of morality and religion and imply that we have an inescapable moral obligation towards our fellow men. This is illustrated in Gandhi's emphasis on *sarvodaya*, the welfare of all, which is revealed in his concern for the status of Harijans (Untouchables) and women in Indian society. He proclaims the need for the abolition of the caste system, child marriages, enforced widowhood and purdah which were harmful to the moral and spiritual growth of the nation. Radical social changes were required to improve the lot of the outcastes and the status of women and only the restoration of the purity of the Hindu way of life would suffice to effect the changes needed.

The social, economic and political implications of Gandhi's emphasis on *sarvodaya* are far reaching. His economic policy is people-oriented and rejects developments that dehumanise and degrade people's lives, including unbridled industrialisation; his alternative educational system fosters rather than undermines the cultural heritage of the nation; and his political goal of *Svarāj*, self-rule, promotes Indian self-respect and the determination of his people to accept responsibility for managing their own affairs.

It is not without significance that Gandhi subtitles his autobiography 'the story of my experiments with Truth'. He sought to live his life in the spirit of Truth and in accordance with the religious and ethical ideals of the Hindu way of life.

One of Gandhi's most ardent admirers and enthusiastic followers was Vinobā Bhāve (1895–1983). He was impressed by Gandhi's views on the importance of indigenous languages, the plight of the poor and the need for purity in personal and public life. In the ashram at Wardha he laboured diligently to prove himself a true disciple and became one of the first *satyāgrahīs* when the civil disobedience movement began. After Gandhi's death he inaugurated the *bhūdān* movement designed to encourage wealthy landowners to donate land voluntarily to those who had none and succeeded over a period of six years in acquiring four million acres for distribution. The method he adopted was persuasion rather than coercion in accordance with the principle of *ahiṃsā*.

Another of Vinobā Bhāve's activities involved the decentralisation of government and the development of self-sufficient, self-governing village units. *Grāmrāj*, village government, was an extension of *svarāj* with each village having the power to manage its own affairs. This meant the progressive abolition of government control, (*rāj-nīti*), and the establishment of government by the people (*lok-nīti*). For Vinobā the best form of government is freedom from government and this is what he means by *sarvodaya*.

With the decentralisation of government and the development of *grāmrāj* goes the responsibility for educating people to manage their own affairs. Vinobā's concept of *nai talim* (new education) meant the introduction of a programme directed towards establishing a *vidyāpīṭh*, a seat of knowledge or university, in each village. It involved also the establishment of village industries and the recognition of the principle of social equality. In short, his new education programme was education for the whole of life.

Many parallels exist between Vinobā and Gandhi but the former developed his theories in his own way and the *bhūdān* movement was his distinctive contribution to resolving the problem of the poverty of India.

Further Reading

de Bary, Wm. Theodore (ed.) *Sources of the Indian Tradition*, vol. II (Columbia University Press, New York/London, 1958)

Embree, Ainslie T. (ed.) *The Hindu Tradition: Readings in Oriental Thought* (Vintage Books, New York, 1972)

Naravane, V.S. *Modern Indian Thought: A Philosophical Survey* (Asia Publishing House, Delhi, 1964)

Richards, Glyn (ed.) *A Source-Book of Modern Hinduism* (Curzon Press, London/ Dublin, 1985)

—— *The Philosophy of Gandhi* (Curzon Press, London/Dublin; Barnes & Noble Books, New Jersey, 1982)

7 *Sikhism*

C. Shackle

Sikhism is the most recent in origin of the recognised Indian religions. There are now more than ten million Sikhs in India (largely concentrated in the north-western state of Punjab and the surrounding areas), where they significantly outnumber the combined totals of all Indian Buddhists and Jains. As a consequence of successive waves of emigration over the past hundred years, there are also perhaps a further one million Sikhs settled in other parts of the world, the most important communities of this diaspora being found in North America and in the United Kingdom, where the numbers of Sikhs are now comparable to those of British Jewry.

Throughout its development from the time of its origins in the early sixteenth century, Sikhism has nevertheless remained closely linked to its homeland in the Punjab, where most of its holy places are located and where the great majority of its adherents still live. Most Sikhs are consequently Punjabi by culture and by language. Indeed, the word 'Sikh' itself (correctly pronounced to rhyme with 'wick' rather than with 'week') is the Punjabi for 'disciple'. Without some understanding of the general background of historical events in the Punjab, it is therefore impossible to form a proper appreciation of the somewhat complex stages of development through which the Sikh religious tradition has evolved, whether these concern its attitudes to other religions in the area, or its own remarkable transformation over time from an initial core of pacific inner-directed adoration so as to accommodate a subsequent strong emphasis upon disciplined militancy.

Guru Nanak

Guru Nanak, the founder of Sikhism, was born to Hindu parents in a village west of Lahore in 1469. For knowledge of his life we are almost entirely dependent upon the much later prose hagiographies (*janamsakhi*) which were composed in the Sikh community during the seventeenth century. Like all such pious accounts, to whose compilers minute historical accuracy is of far less concern than their principal aim of mythological glorification of their subject, they must be used with some caution as biographical records.

In very broad outline, however, the picture given by the hagiographies may be accepted, not least their frequent references to the great diversity of religious life in sixteenth-century Punjab. As one of the first areas of India to be conquered by Muslim invaders, the Punjab had for some four centuries been subject to strong Islamic influences. Ultimately subordinate to the authority of the sultans in neighbouring Delhi, Muslims had long been politically dominant, and the state authority supported the institutions of orthodox Islam and the clerics who serviced them.

By this period Islam had long since ceased to be exclusively an alien import or just the religion of a foreign ruling class. Intense missionary activity, largely the initiative of Sufi preachers with their more tolerant interpretation of Islam and often charismatic personalities, had brought about mass conversions of substantial groups of the local population. The shrines of such great Sufi saints as Shaykh Farid (1173–1265) of Pakpatan, administered by their spiritual successors, were firmly established as major centres of popular devotion.

Amongst the Hindus, too, a variety of religious traditions was to be found. While perhaps less rigidly enforced in this border region than in its heartland in the Gangetic plains, the dominant orthodoxy was that of Brahminical Hinduism, upholding the necessity for the strict observance of caste distinctions. But the claims of the Brahmins to exclusive spiritual authority had never gone completely unchallenged. The Punjab had long been, for instance, an important centre of the Nath yogis, claiming descent from the semi-legendary Gorakhnath, who inspired considerable awe by the powers they allegedly derived from the intensive practice of *haṭha-yoga* techniques.

More recently, as all over northern India, various devotional movements had come to exercise an increasing appeal. The most prominent of these movements of devotion had as their object a personalised God (*saguna bhakti*), and the most popular cults focused upon incarnations of Vishnu, especially Krishna. In these cults, which may in one sense be seen as the response of a revitalised Hinduism to the spiritual challenge presented by the political dominance of Islam, the emotional togetherness of the congregations of the faithful listening to hymns of adoration composed in easily understood contemporary language stood in sharp contrast to the hierarchical separation of castes encouraged in the traditional Sanskritic rituals performed by the Brahmins.

Finally, there were also devotional movements directed towards the worship of an impersonal God (*nirguna bhakti*), which derived from the teachings of a loosely associated group of reformers known as the Sants. Almost all of very humble caste, these Sants included the cotton-printer Namdev (1270–1350) from Maharashtra, the weaver Kabir (1440–1518) from Benares and his younger contemporary, the leather-worker Ravides. Though naturally varying in their expression, the teachings of the Sants tended to be more radical than those propounded by the personalised cults. Not only were traditional learning, rituals and caste-observances pronounced useless, but devotion to images too was regarded as an obstacle to the salvation which could only be attained by heeding the voice of God in the human heart. In their expression of this central doctrine in their vernacular verses and hymns, the Sants relied not just on vivid local imagery, but on terminology drawn both from the personal cults and from the system of yogic terms earlier developed by the Nath yogis to describe the workings of the inner spiritual process. In a very real sense, therefore, the teachings of the Sants, which were diffused by informal transmission of their compositions rather than by the sort of formalised religious institutions which they so frequently attacked in others, represent a summation of the reformist currents of medieval Hinduism, though never achieving a fully integrated expression of the constituent elements involved.

The fact that Guru Nanak was able to achieve such an integration in his teachings may be attributed in some measure to his background. Whereas the Sants had come from low castes, Guru Nanak was a member of the Khattri caste, traditionally involved in business and administration. His father was a village accountant (*patvari*), the lowest rank in the revenue administration, and when Guru Nanak himself left home, it was to be employed as the steward of a local Muslim magnate. Both the imagery and organisation of his compositions and the coherence of his teachings reflect this early professional background.

The traditional accounts provide no certain clues as to the nature of Guru Nanak's early spiritual development. As a boy and youth, he is said to have been a dreamer, little interested in worldly affairs, and even after his marriage, which resulted in the birth of two sons, and his employment as an administrator, he continued to be absorbed in matters of the spirit. His great moment of transformation is said to have occurred when he was about thirty years old and went, as was his practice each morning, to bathe in the river. On this occasion he was taken before God, and did not emerge for three days, when he came out uttering the famous words, 'There is neither Hindu nor Muslim', which are taken as the charter of Sikhism's character as a separate, third religious tradition. (They should also serve to give the lie to the common misconception that Sikhism is some sort of syncretic synthesis of Hinduism and Islam.)

This profound experience caused Guru Nanak to abandon his job and his family for an extended series of travels, traditionally depicted as a series of triumphs over all rival religious leaders, during which he was accompanied by his devoted follower, the Muslim minstrel Mardana, who would accompany the Guru's hymns.

This long period of wandering, during which the first Sikhs would have been drawn to give their allegiance to him, came to an end in about 1520, when Guru Nanak settled down on land given him by a wealthy follower at Kartarpur, where he was to be based for the rest of his life. It was during this final phase, when he resumed domestic life as the head of a religious settlement, that his teachings were ultimately refined and future guide-lines for the Sikh community's subsequent development were established. After selecting one of his disciples as his successor, Guru Nanak died at Kartarpur in 1539.

Guru Nanak's Teachings

Guru Nanak's hymns, composed in a mixture of Old Punjabi and Old Hindi, are preserved in the Sikh scriptures. His teachings, expressed in poetry of great power and beauty, are therefore far better recorded than are the circumstances of his life. As has been indicated, these place him as a religious thinker firmly within the Sant tradition of devotion to a non-anthropomorphic God on the one hand, but on the other, by the quality and coherence of the insights which they collectively reveal, as the founder of a new religion.

At the centre of Guru Nanak's theology lies the issue of how salvation is to be attained, given the inherent dichotomy between God the creator and the observer and controller of his creation, whose oneness and unknowability is continually underlined, and unregenerate man, whose psyche (*man*) is totally clouded by his false sense of a self-determined identity that can operate without reference to the will of God (called *haumai*, literally 'I–me'). The fate of such a psyche-dominated man (*manmukh*) can only be to suffer the torments of death, hell and transmigration. The solutions offered by other religious specialists, whether Brahmins, yogis, Krishna-cultists or Muslim *qazis*, are totally belied by the personal corruption of their parasitic existence, to whose criticism many of Guru Nanak's most vivid verses are dedicated.

This apparently hopeless divide can, however, be bridged. One of the most striking tributes to Guru Nanak's quality both as religious thinker and as poet lies in his adaptation of Muslim political terminology to express theological insights. So God, conceived as the ultimate ruler whose designs are in the last resort unfathomable, does in his graciousness provide the means by which his true servants may approach him. For these to be apprehended, their fidelity must first be demonstrated both by the rejection of idle asceticism in favour of the practical discipline of earning one's own living honestly and sharing its fruits with others, and by the inner discipline of opening one's heart to the inward meditation on his 'name' or divine qualities (*nam japan*, *nam simran*), both by private devotion and by participation in congregational worship, where fellow-aspirants to salvation join in listening to hymns with inner attention.

With these preconditions fulfilled, the devotee may be fortunate enough to be the recipient of the divine sovereign's look of favour (*nadar*), also expressed as being able to hear the call (*sabad*) in one's heart. In this active aspect of himself as communicator, God is usually described as the Teacher (*guru*) or True Teacher (*satiguru*). Those privileged in this way to receive the divine message, through Guru-direction (*gurmukh*), may apprehend the full significance of the divine order (*hukam*) and attain the ultimate bliss of freedom from the cycle of birth and death so as to participate in the heavenly joys of the company of saints (*satsang*), who sing in eternity at the gates of God's ineffable court the praises of his glory.

Guru Nanak's Successors

However distinguished from them by superior internal cohesion, it will be seen that Guru Nanak's teachings share with those of the earlier Sants a profound emphasis upon inward spirituality rather than the outward organisation of religious life. A vastly greater number of verses are devoted to the praise of the heavenly company of saints and to the mysterious workings of the Divine Guru in the human heart than are allotted to rules for honest everyday existence.

It was, however, important that the original nucleus of the Sikh community established under Guru Nanak's direction in his later years at Kartarpur (literally, 'City of the Creator') should be maintained and developed, if it were to achieve its purpose of creating the conditions by which the faithful on earth might aspire to the ultimate achievement of the heavenly model so powerfully set before them in Guru Nanak's hymns. The subsequent successful evolution of Sikhism along its separate way stands in sharp contrast to the amorphous character of the groups stemming from the other reformers of the time, and is to be attributed not only to the coherence of Guru Nanak's message, but also to his provision for continuing effective leadership after his death.

While Sikhism has from the beginning laid much stress on the irrelevance of caste distinctions, it appears from early lists that most of the early converts were from a Khattri background similar to that of its founder. Certainly, all the Gurus were from various sub-groups of Khattris. But the succession was not at first hereditary. Guru Nanak passed over the claims of his son Sri Chand, disqualified by his asceticism, in favour of his disciple Angad (1504–52), who in his turn chose in preference to his own sons his elderly disciple Amar Das (1479–1574), originally a Khattri convert from Vaishnavism. Thereafter the hereditary pattern asserted itself with Guru Amar Das's selection of his son-in-law Ram Das (1534–81), succeeded in his turn by his youngest son Arjan (1563–1606), the direct ancestor of all the later living Gurus (see Figure 7.1).

Figure 7.1: The Sikh Gurus

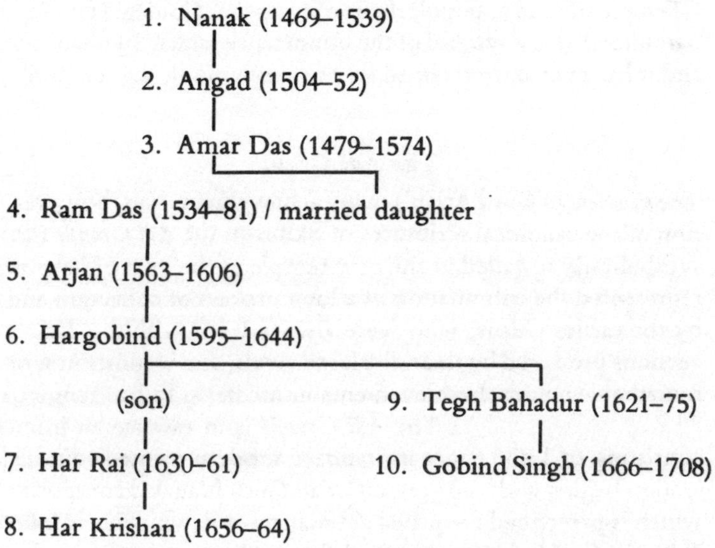

Although each succession was disputed at the time, the splinter groups founded by disappointed claimants dwindled more or less quickly into insignificance, while the institutions of the main community were developed and strengthened by the Gurus to ensure its cohesion as it grew in numbers, especially in the Punjab. The Guruship itself, conceived as an office passing from one to another successor as one lamp is lit from another (*joti jot samauna*), provided the central focus for the Sikhs. The collection of Guru Nanak's hymns was supplemented by the subsequent compositions of the later Gurus, whose spiritual identity was symbolised by their common use of the poetic signature 'Nanak'.

A network of local communities was established, each having as its centre of congregational worship a temple, corresponding to the modern Sikh *gurdwara* ('house of the Guru'), to which there might be attached a free kitchen (*langar*), symbolically open to all, regardless of caste. These local communities were organised into regions, each under the authority of the Guru's appointed representatives, responsible for transmitting his teachings and instructions and for collecting his tithe for remission to his centre.

In the early years, this centre, at which all Sikhs were expected to gather before their Guru on the day of the New Year (*Baisakhi*), shifted with each accession to the Guruship. Guru Ram Das, however, established his centre on a new site granted him at Amritsar ('Lake of Nectar'), and it was here that his son Guru Arjan completed in 1604 the construction of a great temple set in a large pool of water. This Harmandir ('Temple of God'), popularly known as the 'Golden Temple', was surely in part intended as a symbol of the importance which Sikhism could now claim, and it has ever since retained its primacy among the religion's sacred sites.

The *Ādi Granth*

The greatest of Guru Arjan's many achievements was, however, his compilation of the canonical scriptures of Skihism, the *Ādi Granth* ('Primal Book'), symbolically installed in the new temple in the year of its completion. This represented the culmination of a long process of collection and composition by the earlier Gurus, who were always faced with the dangers of heretical versions produced by their displaced rivals, and it constitutes one of the most remarkable editorial achievements in medieval Indian religious literature.

The *Ādi Granth* is in essence an immense hymnal, consisting of 1,430 pages in standard modern printed editions. A prefatory section begins with the greatest of all Guru Nanak's compositions, the *Japji*, which is prescribed for private recitation at dawn. This is followed by short collections of hymns prescribed for the liturgical offices of worship in the evening (*sodar rahiras*) and then before retiring (*kirtan sohila*). The bulk of the scripture is then arranged, in accordance with its hymnal character, by the mode (*rag*) in which the various compositions are to be performed. Within each of these thirty-one modal headings, hymns are arranged first in order of metrical length, then by author. A concluding section includes a number of miscellaneous compositions for which no place could appropriately be found under the main headings.

The language of the *Ādi Granth* naturally varies somewhat from author to author, sometimes from genre to genre, but seldom diverges greatly from the poetic idiom so memorably established by Guru Nanak. Its archaic character, whose difficulties are compounded by the conciseness of expression favoured in medieval Indian religious poetry, means that it is no longer fully approachable by Sikhs today without some special study, and much effort has gone into the compilation of commentaries and translations. The use of the sacred Gurmukhi script (a distinctive relative of the Devanagari script used to write Sanskrit and Hindi) both in the *Ādi Granth* and for modern Punjabi has, however, served to blur the distinction between the two.

The great bulk of the contents of the *Ādi Granth* naturally consists of hymns by the early Sikh Gurus. It is possible to give some idea of their relative contribution by enumerating the compositions attributed to them, although the varied length of these makes this only a rough guide. At their core, and as their major inspiration, lie the hymns of Guru Nanak (974), briefly supplemented by the scattered couplets of Guru Angad (62), and extensively restated in the hymns of his last contemporary Guru Amar Das (907). The new note first struck by Guru Ram Das (679) was developed on a collosal scale by the largest single contributor to the volume, its compiler Guru Arjan (2,218), whose enormous *œuvre* explores almost every possibility suggested by his predecessors, and includes the *Sukhmani* ('Peace of Heart') as both its most famous item and as the longest of all the hymns in the collection.

Also included in the *Ādi Granth* are a few eulogies of the Gurus by the bards attached to their courts. Much more remarkable is the incorporation of hymns by other teachers, whose works first entered the Sikh tradition in a collection compiled during the time of Guru Amar Das. Designed to demonstrate the universal truth of the Gurus' message by analogy, these included extensive contributions from Namdev (60), Kabir (541) and Ravidas (41), besides the Sufi Shaykh Farid (116). While it is subordinate in status to the *gurbani* ('Utterance of the Gurus') proper, the inclusion of this *bhagat-bani* ('Utterance of the Saints') is striking testimony to the breadth of the religious vision of the early leaders of Sikhism.

The Seventeenth Century

The seventeenth century was a time of transition, during which the Sikh community, while continuing to grow in size and importance, was substantially altered in character by the influx of converts from the farming Jat caste with more warlike traditions than the Khattris who had formed the majority of the first disciples. These changes had the dual consequence of making the Gurus more prominent politically and of increasing the suspicion with which they, as leaders of a growingly warlike sect in a region close to Delhi, came to be regarded by the Mogul emperors.

Guru Arjan himself was the first to fall martyr to this inherent tension between the Sikhs and the Mogul authorities when, following his support for an unsuccessful claimant to the imperial throne, he was executed at Lahore in 1606. His son Guru Hargobind (1595–1604) was also imprisoned by the Moguls for a time, and is credited with being the first Guru to claim both spiritual and temporal authority (*piri miri*). As a symbol of the latter he constructed opposite his father's Harmandir the Akal Takht ('Throne of the Immortal Lord'), which has ever since remained the symbolic organisational centre of Sikhism. His successor Guru Har Rai (1630–61) was driven by imperial hostility to take refuge in the hills north of the Punjab, and his son, the child Guru Har Krishan (1656–64), died in custody in Delhi.

By the time of Guru Tegh Bahadur (1621–75), the organisation of the Sikh community was thus falling into increasing disarray, since the Gurus were increasingly constrained from exercising authority over their local representatives. Guru Tegh Bahadur's own efforts at reform were ended by his execution in Delhi on the orders of the Emperor Aurangzeb. His son Guru Gobind Singh (1666–1708) was brought up by his followers in the safety of his refuge in the hills at Anandpur, though even there he was brought into increasing conflict with the neighbouring chieftains.

The Khalsa

Guru Gobind Singh, revered by Sikhs as the greatest of Guru Nanak's successors, effected a radical and lasting transformation of both the organisation and the outlook of the Sikh community by his institution of the quasi-military order of the Khalsa (a technical term used to designate land under direct imperial control, also suggesting the sense of 'Company of the Pure'), which abolished the authority of intermediate spiritual representatives and invested the community itself with ultimate power and responsibility.

The symbolic foundation of the Khalsa took place when the Sikhs gathered before their Guru on the Baisakhi festival at Anandpur in 1699. The Guru asked for five volunteers, from different castes, who were taken into a tent and apparently executed. But as they were led out, it was revealed that goats had been slain in their place, and that these heroic 'five beloved ones' (*panj piare*) were to form the nucleus of the new order of the Khalsa. Their initiation was symbolised by the administration of baptism, involving the drinking of sweetened water (*amrit*) sanctified by the utterance of prayers during its preparation and mixing with a dagger. The five disciples then in their turn administered baptism to the Guru, symbolising the transfer of authority to the community.

The code of conduct (*rahit*) expected of all initiates of the Khalsa, as laid down by Guru Gobind Singh and subsequently elaborated, emphasises both the equality of its members and the martial spirit expected of them by awarding the Rajput titles of Singh ('lion') to men and Kaur ('princess') to women, irrespective of caste origin. Also incumbent on all male members is the observance of the five outward tokens known from their Punjabi names as the 'five Ks' (*panj kakke*), including unshorn hair (*kes*), a comb (*kangha*) to hold it, a dagger (*kirpan*), a steel bangle (*kara*) and a pair of breeches (*kachh*). To these should be added the turban, which has long been the best-known symbol of the Sikh identity. The baptismal vows also include distinctive dietary restrictions, including total abstinence from the consumption of tobacco and from all meat which has not come from animals butchered by beheading (*jhatka*).

The new militant spirit of the Khalsa was given verbal expression in the hymns composed by Guru Gobind Singh. Some of these were added to those by the earlier Gurus prescribed for the three daily offices, thus a baptised Sikh is expected to add to Guru Nanak's *Japji* in his morning prayers the recitation of Guru Gobind Singh's *Jap Sahib* and ten short poems (*das savaie*). Guru Gobind Singh's compositions are collected in the *Dasam Granth* ('Book of the Tenth Guru'). While of comparable size to the *Ādi Granth*, it is much more heterogeneous in character, containing a great amount of material obviously not by the Guru himself, and has never enjoyed the same canonical status.

The status of the original scriptures was further heightened as a consequence of Guru Gobind Singh's remodelling of the Sikh community. During a brief respite from the almost perpetual fighting against the Moguls and their local allies in which much of his life was spent, and during which all his four sons were killed, he re-edited the *Ādi Granth* so as to include his father's compositions, although not his own. In this final form, the scriptures received the authority of the Guru, and consequently received the honorific title of *Guru Granth Sahib* by which Sikhs usually refer to their holy book. With Guru Gobind Singh's death in 1708, the line of living Gurus came to an end, and Sikhs have since revered the scripture which they composed as their spiritual guide. The *Guru Granth Sahib* occupies the central place in all *gurdwaras*, and elaborate reverence is paid to it in the rituals of the larger temples.

Subsequent Developments

The decentralisation of authority involved in the creation of the Khalsa inevitably brought to an end the long period of the primary theological formulation of Sikhism by Guru Nanak and his successors. But the new order proved most successful in ensuring the community's survival during the long succession of wars which followed the collapse of the Mogul Empire early in the eighteenth century, as invaders from Afghanistan battled with the local Muslim governors for control of the Punjab. Inspired by the war-cry *raj karega khalsa* ('the Khalsa shall rule'), the Sikh guerrilla bands eventually emerged victorious, and the heroic age of Sikh history culminated in the kingdom established in the name of the Khalsa at Lahore by Maharaja Ranjit Singh (1799–1839).

But while the Khalsa thus proved well able to deal with the threat to the community's existence by hostile Muslim political forces, the rapid reversion to Hinduism by many fair-weather converts following the final British conquest of the Punjab from the Sikhs in 1849 showed it had been less effective in maintaining the distinctive character of the reformist teachings of the Gurus. As was so often the case in colonial history, the loss of political power led to a period of intense self-questioning and the rearticulation of reformist ideals.

Some of the most trenchant of these mid-nineteenth-century reformers fell foul (through their excessively stated claims to spiritual authority) of the doctrine of the abolition of the living Guruship in Sikhism, and they and their followers were hence regarded as more or less heretical by the main body of Sikhs. As from Guru Gobind Singh's time, this included not only the baptised Khalsa Sikhs but also large numbers of *sahajdhari* ('slow-adopting') Sikhs who followed the Gurus' teachings and the temple rituals, but without adopting the Khalsa baptism and the discipline thereby entailed. In this fluid situation, with many families having both Hindu and Sikh members, and many temples having in the course of time fallen into the hands of hereditary quasi-Hindu administrators, it was all too evident to the founders of the main late nineteenth-century reformist movement, the Singh Sabha, that Sikhism risked being reabsorbed totally into the capacious Hindu tradition from which it had been born. An intensive programme of propaganda was accordingly instituted, directed both towards inculcating stricter adherence to the Khalsa discipline within the community, and outwardly to combating the aggressive assertion by such reformist Hindu sects as the Arya Samaj that the Sikhs were no more than heretics to be reclaimed for Hinduism.

Largely successful in their primary objectives, the reformers' campaign assumed an increasingly political emphasis with the struggle in the 1920s to assert the community's physical control over its major shrines. The British authorities at first supported the legal claims of the traditional administrators, but were eventually forced by the massive demonstrations organised by the newly formed Akali Dal ('army of the Immortal Lord') to hand control of the great temples and their massive endowments to the Sikh activists in 1925.

Contemporary Sikhism

At the centre of contemporary Sikh organisations lies the Gurdwara Management Committee, or SGPC, set up to administer the major temples in Punjab. This is an elected body, which has always been under the control of one or another group of the Akali Dal, the main Sikh political party. In keeping with the long-standing traditions of Sikhism, the SGPC is run by lay members, and the officials of the temples, whether readers (*granthi*) or musicians (*ragi*), are its paid servants, without the sacerdotal status of 'priests' in the accepted sense of the term.

In lesser temples, too, whether in the Punjab or in the diaspora, a similar pattern of management obtains, with lay members having chief responsibility for running the temple and the *langar* attached to it, for ensuring compliance to the Khalsa discipline, and if necessary undertaking the excommunication of members for grave infractions, such as the cutting of hair, or fixing penalties for lesser offences. A summary code of guidance, laying down the fundamental rules of Sikh belief, religious and personal life, was issued by the SGPC in 1946.

The evolution of Sikhism has, however, been such that its purely religious aspect is only somewhat artificially to be regarded in complete isolation from its contemporary political expression. The political activism to which the reformists' energies had become increasingly directed received further impetus through the circumstances in which the British Empire in India was dissolved in 1947. This involved the partition of the Punjab between the successor states of India and Pakistan and a massive transfer of population between the two halves of the province, with the whole Sikh population of the western districts being forced to migrate to India.

A long campaign by the Akali Dal eventually secured the establishment of the Sikh-majority state of Punjab in India in 1966. But the dream of a fully independent Khalistan ('land of the Khalsa') has continued to appeal to some Sikhs. It received further impetus from the campaign of violence instigated by Sant Jarnail Singh Bhindranwale (1947–84), a village preacher with a message of charismatic fundamentalism, and from the Indian Army's storming of Sikhism's holiest shrine, the Golden Temple complex at Amritsar, in June 1984, when Bhindranwale and his followers were killed and from the continuing subsequent repercussions of this military assault.

As has, however, been indicated by subsequent events in India and the polarisation of feeling among many sections of the Sikh diaspora, it would be unwise to disregard the appeal of the new fundamentalism in attempting any assessment of the contemporary profile of Sikhism, which continues to contain within itself the effects of the several stages of development which have gone into its making.

Further Reading

Cole, W.O. and Sambhi, Piara Singh *The Sikhs, Their Religious Beliefs and Practices* (Routledge & Kegan Paul, London, 1978)

Grewal, J.S. and Bal, S.S. *Guru Gobind Singh* (Chandigarh, 1967)

Harbans Singh *The Heritage of the Sikhs*, 2nd edn (New Delhi, 1983)

Khushwant Singh *A History of the Sikhs*, 2 vols., 2nd edn (Delhi, 1977)

Macauliffe, M.A. *The Sikh Religion*, 6 vols. (Oxford, 1909), reprinted as 3 vols. (Delhi, 1963)

McLeod, W.H. *Guru Nanak and the Sikh Religion* (Oxford University Press, Oxford, 1968)

—— *The Evolution of the Sikh Community* (Oxford University Press, Oxford, 1976)

—— (ed.) *Textual Sources for the Study of Sikhism* (Manchester University Press, Manchester, 1984)

Shackle, C. *An Introduction to the Sacred Language of the Sikhs* (University of London, SOAS, 1981)

—— *The Sikhs* (revised edn) (Minority Rights Group Report no. 65, London, 1986)

8 Theravāda Buddhism in South-East Asia

W.J. Johnson

The use of the Pali term 'Theravāda' ('Doctrine of the Elders') to define their particular school reflects the fact that the Theravādins present themselves as belonging to that branch of Buddhism which has continued to preserve the 'orthodox' or 'original' teaching of the Buddha. Less chauvinistically, the term refers to the doctrines and practices of the one monastic school to have survived from among the unknown number of Indian schools that had branched out from an original Sthaviravādin (Pali, *Theravādin*) trunk, itself the result of a schism early in Buddhist history. This survival of Theravāda is synonymous with the survival of its Pali scriptures, the only complete recension of the Canon extant in an ancient Indian language. In a wider sense, 'Theravāda Buddhism' is that form of Buddhist culture which has dominated religious, political and social life in Sri Lanka, Burma and Thailand, and, until very recently, Laos and Cambodia as well. It has been the interaction of these two aspects of Theravāda—of the 'school' with the wider culture—which has given rise to the characteristic features of the religion's history.

The history of Theravāda in India remains obscure, and perhaps impossible to extricate from the history of Buddhism in general, although it is known that it was the dominant tradition in a number of important centres in the South-east of the subcontinent, in Andhra Pradesh and Tamil Nadu. Thus at one time there were Tamils who were Theravāda Buddhists. In Sri Lanka, however, where Theravāda established itself firmly as the national religion, the historical situation is clearer. The major source for this history is the Pali verse chronicle, the *Mahāvaṃsa*, or 'Great Chronicle', written by a Sinhalese monk late in the fifth century CE. This was based on another chronicle, the *Dīpavaṃsa*, compiled a century earlier, possibly by nuns. These are, of course, essentially Buddhist histories, whose aim is to establish the inextricability of Theravāda Buddhism from Sinhalese (or Sinhala) national identity. However, their account of Theravāda after its arrival in Sri Lanka is probably broadly accurate.

According to the *Dīpavaṃsa*, the Pali Canon was taken to Sri Lanka and South-east Asia by missionaries sent out by Aśoka in the middle of the third century BCE. Although scholars are extremely sceptical about the claim for South-east Asia, there seems no reason to doubt that Theravāda made its first appearance in Sri Lanka at about this time. Whether the Canon itself arrived all at once in the heads of the first missionaries or more gradually, it is likely that the Pali commentaries (which Buddhaghosa, writing in the fifth century CE, claims Mahinda, the missionary son of Aśoka, brought with him and then translated into Sinhala) arrived over a longer period of time. It is even possible they originated in Sri Lanka itself. Certainly, additions continued to be made to the commentarial literature until about the middle of the first century CE, at which time the corpus was probably closed. It is this body of material that Buddhaghosa himself superseded in the process of translating it from Sinhala into Pali and editing it into what became its definitively orthodox form.

About half a century before the body of commentarial work had been closed, there had occurred what was probably the most significant and far-reaching event in early Theravāda history. During a period of turmoil, late in the first century BCE, when Sri Lanka was threatened by foreign invasions and famine, the decision was taken to commit the Theravāda Canon to writing. This happened between 29 and 17 BCE. Until then the Canon had been transmitted orally from generation to generation of monks. The monastic community, the Saṅgha, was the sole repository of the Buddha's Doctrine (*Dhamma*; Sanskrit, *Dharma*), and it was through the Saṅgha alone that the laity had access to that Doctrine. Perhaps it was only when it was presented with the threat of its own imminent destruction that the Saṅgha made the conscious decision that its first duty—indeed, its primary function—was to preserve the Doctrine for future generations. This decision and its consequence, the writing down of the Pali Canon, had far-reaching consequences for the nature and subsequent history of the Saṅgha itself.

As important as the Canon for the Theravāda tradition is the Pali *Visuddhimagga*, or 'Path of Purity', an original work composed in Sri Lanka in the early fifth century CE by the same Indian monk, Buddhaghosa, who edited the commentaries. This compendium of Buddhist doctrine has been the touchstone of Theravādin orthodoxy ever since. Its intended 'readership' was the monastic community, an audience reflected in the work's dual function as a summary of doctrine and a handbook for meditators. The dominant theme is the cultivation of that moral and mental purity which, allied to the necessary prerequisite of learning, together make up the practical path to enlightenment. After Buddhaghosa other monks soon wrote definitive Pali commentaries on those parts of the Canon he had left untouched, including a Pali version of the commentary on the *Jātaka* stories about the 550 previous births of the Buddha. And presently Pali subcommentaries on these works also appeared. By reverting to a classical language (Pali), Buddhaghosa and his followers effectively internationalised the Theravādin tradition. That is to say, they prepared the way for Sinhala orthodoxy to become the standard form of Theravāda Buddhism throughout South-east Asia. Such 'internationalisation', combined with the universalistic ethic expounded in Buddhist teaching, meant that Theravāda had some invaluable instruments with which both to consolidate its expansion and to renew itself in times of decline.

In the terms of its self-definition the history of Theravāda Buddhism is synonymous with the history of its monastic community, the Saṅgha, in that it is only through the Saṅgha that the teaching is preserved and handed on. Two monastic rites are crucial to the establishment and survival of the Saṅgha: higher ordination (Pali, *upasampadā*) and the fortnightly communal recitation of the Disciplinary Code (Pali, *pātimokkha*) after the confession of faults. To convey the authentic tradition of the Buddha's Doctrine, the higher ordination ceremony must be valid, and the validity of any particular ordination depends on its being at the end of an unbroken line of valid ordinations going back to the Buddha (the continuity being preserved by the presence of a quorum of monks who are themselves validly ordained). This can only be guaranteed if the monks who belong to a particular Saṅgha lead morally pure lives according to the Discipline (*Vinaya*). Such purity is ensured and expressed by the fortnightly *pātimokkha* recitation, for a monk who has committed a transgression against the Disciplinary Code may not attend and thus endorse his commitment to the Code without first having purified himself by confessing his fault. When the 'unity of the Saṅgha' is referred to, it is precisely this unanimous adherence to a single Disciplinary Code that is meant. Anything less than unanimity constitutes a split in the Saṅgha, i.e. the formation of a new sect. This is not a matter of choice: it is considered essential that every monk within an area defined by a formally established monastic boundary, or *sīmā*, should personally attend a *pātimokkha* ceremony once a fortnight. Without the prior establishment of an area of bounded monastic territory, no formal act of the Saṅgha, whether ordination ceremony or *pātimokkha*, can take place. Thus whenever the Saṅgha (i.e. 'Theravāda Buddhism') wishes to establish itself in a new region or country, it requires immediate material support from the laity in the form of a gift of land. Beyond that, it needs daily support in the form of alms, and ultimately it needs to recruit new members from the local population to sustain itself. In return for all this material support, the monks provide the infinitely more valuable gift of the Buddha's teaching, and spiritual good in general, especially merit.

From its origins in India the Saṅgha had been supported by the rich and influential. This was a pattern that developed in Sri

Lanka and South-east Asia into what is sometimes called a 'symbiotic' relationship, i.e. a mutually beneficial relationship between the Saṅgha and the ruling power or king (in essence, the chief layman). It is important to note that, once Buddhism becomes established as the religion of a nation-state such as Sri Lanka, the significance of the Discipline undergoes a substantial change. Thus if one takes the slogans 'No Buddhism without the Saṅgha' and 'No Saṅgha without the Discipline', and adds to those the further slogan, 'No Sri Lanka/Burma/Thailand without Buddhism', it becomes clear that the preservation of the Discipline, i.e. of the moral purity of the Saṅgha, is the essential component in the preservation and proper functioning of the nation. In this context, the monk, who is the embodiment or exemplar of moral purity, of Discipline, becomes a figure with public responsibility. It is no longer, if it ever was, simply a matter of cultivating his own enlightenment (although, of course, the two roles are not necessarily incompatible). Moreover, the king, as the embodiment of the state, feels that ultimately it is his duty to preserve the institutions of society, especially the Saṅgha. Much of later Theravāda history is therefore patterned by the recurrent efforts of kings to preserve or re-establish the purity of the Saṅgha, since the prosperity of the nation is ultimately seen to depend upon its moral example. The precedent for such royal interference in the affairs of what, ideally, was the self-governing Saṅgha had been set by Aśoka, who had undertaken a purification of the Saṅgha—albeit in accordance with *Vinaya* rules—in India in the third century BCE. And it was Aśoka who remained the inspiration and model for later monarchs in their dealings with the monastic community. That is to say, they saw it as their duty to defend the Saṅgha by expelling its corrupt members and, in some cases, by introducing ordination traditions from countries which were believed to have a superior variety.

Corruption of the Saṅgha has two principal aspects: luxurious living, i.e. a laxness in Discipline and thus a diminution of moral purity, and a consequent disharmony that threatens to split the unity of the community. In other words, practice by some members of the Saṅgha which diverges from the norm laid down in the *Vinaya* leads to a situation where all members do not acknowledge the same *pātimokkha* rules, and a split occurs. Given this analysis of corruption, there can be little doubt that royal patronage was itself a factor in bringing about that very decay of the Saṅgha which the kings' periodic 'purifications' were intended to reverse. For state patronage cast monks in new roles which were frequently quite at odds with the Discipline. Perhaps the most immediately obvious of these was that the monasteries became great landlords. From late in the first century BCE land grants to monks and monasteries became a frequent occurrence in Sri Lanka, so much so that monastic land-holding became a major feature of the economy, until between the ninth and twelfth centuries CE monasteries were probably the greatest landlords in Sri Lanka. And while legal fictions could be devised to justify the Saṅgha's communal involvement with property, it was more difficult to accommodate the economic business of individual monks to the Discipline, particularly the practice of inheriting personal monastic property. Inevitably the way of life of wealthy monks and monasteries came to differ substantially from the canonical ideal. Similarly, the central role of the Saṅgha in the welfare of the state led some monks into politics. Perhaps the most typical role for the monk in the Theravāda countries, however, has been that of the 'village-dwelling' scholar and preacher who, from the laity's point of view, acts as a ceremonial specialist and is often involved in astrology and medicine as well. In essence the 'village-dweller's' function is to make merit for the laity. Classically, the complementary opposite to the 'village-dwelling' monk is the 'forest-dwelling' ascetic (Pali, *āraññika*), who retires alone to pursue insight and enlightenment through meditation. But such groups of monks have always been in a small minority, following a special vocation within the Saṅgha, and have persistently been drawn back into the 'village' mode of life, which in practice constitutes the monastic norm. Their status, however, is very high since they are popularly regarded as holy or 'ideal' monks.

Sri Lanka was the first and, for the first millennium CE, the only Buddhist state. Whatever Theravāda Buddhism there was elsewhere in this period has left little trace of itself, although there is some evidence for its presence in both Burma and Thailand by the seventh century CE. However, the Sinhala-derived orthodoxy that came to dominate much of South-east Asia established itself only gradually from the late eleventh century onwards, after the rise of the monarchical states and the corresponding possibility of royal patronage. The Burmese king Aniruddha is credited with the establishment of Theravāda in upper Burma (*c.* 1057 CE) by having the ordination tradition and the Canon brought from Sri Lanka. At the end of the twelfth century a Burmese monk returned from Sri Lanka to Burma to set up a separate *nikāya* or 'fraternity', the 'Sinhalese Saṅgha', which became the main indigenous monastic tradition. And again in the fifteenth century, the reforming king, Dhammaceti, imported the ordination tradition afresh from Sri Lanka, at the same time unifying the Saṅgha and establishing a monastic hierarchy.

Theravāda probably reached Thailand via the Burmese 'Sinhalese Saṅgha' in the thirteenth century, and with the help of further injections of purity from the Sinhalese tradition gradually overcame the Mahāyāna and Hindu forms of religion which had preceded it. By the mid-fourteenth century the Sinhala Theravādin orthodoxy was also established in Laos and Cambodia—probably, in the latter case, coming from Thailand and initiating the subsequent close connection between the Buddhism of the two countries.

In Sri Lanka itself the Saṅgha was in decay during the two centuries of Tamil invasions and civil wars at the beginning of the second millennium, and it was probably during this period that the order of nuns died out. This decline was only halted with the 'purification' and unification of the Saṅgha undertaken by Parakkama Bāhu I in 1164/5. He set up a single authority structure for a national Saṅgha, headed by a monk known as the 'king of the Saṅgha' (*Saṅgharāja*), who was aided by two deputies. This kind of political organisation was imitated in Theravāda countries in South-east Asia, and in Thailand in particular it was elaborated into the institutionalised hierarchy of offices which is so evident today. The effect of this reform movement was felt in Sri Lanka until the fifteenth century, but thereafter the Saṅgha suffered an even more serious erosion of standards, so much so that the indigenous ordination tradition was lost, and between the end of the sixteenth century and 1753 it is likely that there were no true monks in Sri Lanka but only those who had taken lower ordination. Again the original export of the Sinhalese ordination tradition came to the rescue, and in 1753 it was returned from Thailand, where centuries before it had found its way, via Burma, from Sri Lanka itself. Contemporary *nikāyas* in Sri Lanka, however, belong to ordination traditions introduced from Burma in the nineteenth century.

From the nineteenth century onwards Buddhism in the Theravāda countries has had to face the pressures of colonial rule and the competition of Western ideologies. In Burma, for instance, royal patronage of the Saṅgha ceased abruptly when the country was incorporated into the British Empire in 1885. And while this did not mean the collapse of Buddhism as such, it did mean that the Saṅgha lost its organisational structure. In general during the colonial and post-colonial periods individual monks as well as the Saṅgha became deeply involved in independence and nationalist movements. In this era there has also been the periodic appearance of millenarian sects, especially in Burma, often using the expected imminent arrival of the future Buddha, Maitreya, as their point of focus. Also Western 'rationalist' interpretations have been fed back into Theravāda cultures, leading to 'modernist' movements which reject many traditional Buddhist beliefs and practices. Furthermore, the introduction of Western education and the spread of literacy have caused the Saṅgha to lose its monopoly of religious authority, and the idea has developed that each person is responsible for his own salvation, and thus for the welfare of the religion in general. Yet thanks to Buddhism's strong scriptural foundation, there have continued to be 'fundamentalist' and reform movements, even among meditators, basing themselves on the revival of scriptural knowledge. On a tragic note, two great Theravāda traditions, those in Laos and Cambodia, were brought to an abrupt halt in 1975 when the communists and the Khmer Rouge took over. In Laos the Saṅgha can now be said at the very least to have lost its traditional influence, while in Cambodia Buddhism was completely destroyed, with most of the monks being murdered. It is obviously too early to say whether these traditions will again be able to revive themselves, or to speculate as to what form such a revival might take.

What was Buddhism's relation to the pre-Buddhist or 'folk' religions it encountered as it spread throughout what are now the Theravāda nations of Sri Lanka and South-east Asia? In this respect, it should be remembered that Buddhism originated in the context of another culturally dominant religion, Brahminical Hinduism, and, more generally, in an Indian culture which, like others, held beliefs about demons and spirits as well as about 'higher' gods. Thus Hindu gods (*devas*) and demons have been part of the Buddhist world-view from its inception, and play their part in the Pali Canon. Typically, the merit acquired at Buddhist ceremonies is always subsequently offered to the gods so that they can respond with this-worldly protection. The Buddha never denied the existence of supernatural beings, he simply viewed them as irrelevant to his soteriological system for bringing about the end of suffering. Similarly, the Buddhist view of gods and spirits has continued to be that, while they may be harmful or beneficial with regard to worldly ends, they are ultimately insignificant precisely because they belong to *saṃsāra*, the world of cause and effect. Thus they are as much subject to the law of *karman* as human beings. Buddhism, however, is not concerned with worldly ends, its purpose rather being to bring that cycle of *saṃsāra* to an end. So in all Theravāda countries followers of the Buddha have retained non-Buddhist beliefs in spirits and gods. In Burma, for instance, the cults of the Nats (animistic spirits) co-exist naturally with Buddhism, since the concerns of the former are to attain material well-being and to avert danger, while the latter's interest is in moral purity, future lives and, ultimately, final release from worldly existence. Such gods and spirits are easily accommodated within the Buddhist cosmic hierarchy, governed by the law of *karman*, with the Buddha at its apex. Thus while all deities are seen to embody Buddhist values, and remain connected to all other beings, including man, by the law of *karman*, they, and the practices associated with them (such as possession), are at the same time appropriated to Buddhism with very little change in meaning. In this way Buddhism was able to spread and become a popular religion throughout Sri Lanka and South-east Asia without coming into conflict with indigenous religions. This is not to say that Buddhism, because of its ethical purity, is not itself often used magically as a protection against dangers of the present existence—but that, paradoxically, is precisely because it is not itself concerned with such particular dangers. The real religious conflict, of course, arises between different soteriologies.

So far, I have looked at some of the main themes and events in the history of Theravāda Buddhism, and little has been said about Buddhism as it is practised today. The rest of this chapter will therefore provide a sketch of some 'modern' practices. This has sometimes been called 'popular' Buddhism, but one should beware of what is often implied by such categorisations, namely, that there has been some gradual corruption or decay from a 'pure' Buddhism, or that Buddhism has become syncretistic. Modern studies have shown that from a very early period Theravāda has been nothing if not 'popular'. The religion practised in the villages of Sri Lanka and South-east Asia until very recently differs very little from what was happening 1,500 years ago, and probably very little from the practice of Buddhism soon after, or perhaps even during, the Buddha's lifetime. For the overwhelming majority of both laity *and* monks this accommodation of normative, Theravāda doctrine—of the Canonical ideal of renunciation leading to *nibbāna* (Sanskrit, *nirvāṇa*)—to the needs of life in the world is what constitutes, and always has constituted, orthodox Theravāda Buddhism.

For lay people to define themselves as 'Buddhist', it is sufficient for them to declare that they 'go for refuge' to the Buddha, the *Dhamma* and the Saṅgha (the 'Three Refuges'), and that they will abide by the Five Precepts (not to kill, steal, be unchaste, lie, or take intoxicants). However, in the Buddhist liturgical calendar there are days in the lunar month of intensified observance (*uposatha* days) when, ideally, a lay person takes the Eight Precepts. These are the basic five, with the modifications that all sexual activity is excluded, that one should not watch entertainments or use adornments, and that one should not use luxurious beds. This is close to lower ordination or novitiate (*pabbajjā*), which entails taking the Ten Precepts. The latter are the same as the Eight, but abstention from entertainments and adornments are treated as separate precepts, and an injunction against using money is added. To take the Ten Precepts it is not necessary to be ordained; indeed, since the Theravāda order of nuns is extinct, following these precepts is formally the closest that women can come to ordination. Nevertheless, there are some women who behave very much as nuns might, leading ascetic lives, either in religious communities or alone, but without the same recognition that monks enjoy. A novice (*sāmaṇera*) can enter the order at about the age of seven, and can go on to take higher ordination and thus become a monk (*bhikkhu*) at twenty. Although monks are always free to leave the Order, ordination in Sri Lanka is assumed to be for life. In other Theravāda countries, however, there is a far more flexible system of temporary ordination. And perhaps the majority of the male population in these countries has spent at least some time, however short, as a novice.

In theory, the single aim of Buddhist practice is to attain *nibbāna*, the extinction of desire and so the end to re-birth and suffering. Classically, this goal is attained by progressing via moral purity, self-restraint and the practice of meditation, to the achievement of wisdom, a path which only the monk or nun can hope to tread successfully. In practice, however, *nibbāna* has proved to be too remote, too difficult either to understand or to achieve, and thereby simply too unattractive as an immediate religious goal for the vast majority. Beyond that, the Buddhist teaching that existence is 'unsatisfactory' or 'suffering' (*dukkha*) is evidently only partially or intellectually accepted by most people: they can see or imagine states of wealth and power where suffering is outweighed by happiness and pleasure, and those states, however impermanent, still seem desirable. So the ideal goal becomes not *nibbāna* but a better re-birth, if possible as a god in heaven, or at worst in an improved station on earth. Lip-service is still paid to *nibbāna* as the ultimate goal, but it has been indefinitely postponed. Some day one may be in a position both to merit and to understand it; until then it is better to proceed by stages. Interacting with this attitude, there is the widespread popular belief that Buddhism has declined so far that it is no longer possible for men to attain *nibbāna*.

How then is one to achieve the modified goal of a better re-birth? The answer is through the acquisition of merit (Pali, *puñña*), and virtually all Buddhist religious practice, whether by laity or monks, has merit as its aim. Moreover, such merit-making is perceived as being quite compatible with doctrine, since it all contributes towards *nibbāna* in the end. It also develops psychological states, such as feelings of peace, happiness and generosity, which are in themselves mentally purifying and thus steps along the road to *nibbāna*. What is merit and how does one go about attaining it? Simply, merit is the 'karmic' recompense for good deeds which produces a better re-birth: the more merit acquired the better the re-birth. Bad action, particularly action which violates the Buddhist moral precepts, produces demerit and thus karmic retribution in the form of a worse re-birth. As understood by the unsophisticated, merit is therefore a kind of intangible spiritual 'currency' which can be reckoned and 'transferred', and which increases in proportion to the amount 'invested'. There is a well-known but uncanonical Pali verse list of 'Ten Good Deeds' which includes all the possible ways of earning merit: generosity, observing the precepts, meditation, transferring merit, empathising with merit, serving (one's elders), showing respect, preaching, listening to preaching, and holding right beliefs. The inclusion of the moral precepts in this list is, of course, a nod towards the Canon, but following them is seen principally as a way of avoiding demerit; the only way to feel certain that one is actually acquiring and increasing merit itself is to take action. The most rewarding merit-making activity is generosity (*dāna*). Principally, this means giving food and other goods to monks in exchange for religious services, chiefly preaching, presiding at funerals and the chanting of *paritta* texts (see below). Because the Saṅgha follows and disseminates the Buddha's doctrine (*Dhamma*), it is considered to be 'the supreme field in which to sow merit', the most worthy recipient of respect and donations. This, of course, runs counter to the usual reading of Buddhist ethics—that karmically it is the intention of the actor which counts in any particular deed. Here the amount of merit acquired is in direct proportion to the *perceived* spiritual worthiness of the *recipient*. There is a Burmese saying that feeding a hundred dogs is the equivalent in merit of feeding one human being, feeding a hundred laymen the equivalent of feeding one novice, feeding a hundred novices the equivalent of feeding an ordinary monk, and so on. In other words, merit-making requires the co-operation of both laity and monks, and from the layman's point of view the most important function of the Saṅgha is to provide him with the opportunity to make merit by giving, not only through daily alms but also through the monastic feeding ceremonies that accompany every important public event. Thus the everyday relationship between the Saṅgha and the lay population is typified by the invitation to monks to take part in various rituals where they can, as it were, become both the 'targets' for extensive generosity and the generators of further merit. This is clearly a long way from the ideal of the monk as world-renouncer. Ideally, the monks' major religious activities are limited to obeying the Discipline and studying the scriptures; in practice, however, most monks spend most of their time performing merit-making rituals for laymen. Yet since few monks consider *nibbāna* to be a realistic goal, such activity is in fact beneficial for them as well, for preaching and propagating the *Dhamma* is one of the ways in which they acquire merit and thus the chance of a better re-birth. This is a spiritual economy in which both parties benefit and the store of merit goes on increasing.

Nearly all public Buddhist acts are seen as occasions for mutual merit-making: the laity feed the monks, and the monks reciprocate by 'preaching'. This may take the form of sermons, or readings from texts. Traditionally, the main content of sermons is derived from the *Jātaka* collection and in particular from its preface, the *Nidānakathā*, which is the principal Theravādin source for the Buddha's biography. Another popular source is the commentary on the *Dhammapada*. The most distinctive form of preaching, however, is the formalised and often lengthy recitation of Pali scriptures known as *paritta*, literally 'protection' texts. These are essentially a magical means of bringing good luck, of improving one's health and wealth. Similarly, after every public Buddhist ceremony the merit acquired is offered to the gods so that they can reciprocate by helping in the worldly realm which is their proper sphere of influence. How merit can be 'transferred' or 'shared' in this way requires some explanation. The original context for transferring merit is probably the funerary ritual. This, quite remarkably when one considers other religions, is the only 'life-crisis ritual' at which Buddhist monks officiate (albeit simply as preachers), and thus it is the only such ritual officially sanctified by Buddhism. A week after the death the monks are formally fed, again three months later, and thereafter at annual commemorative rites. And it is on these occasions that the merit, which goes in the first place to the donor, is ritually 'transferred' to the dead person. According to the normative theory of *karman* this should be impossible: the responsibility for an individual's fate lies in his own hands—strictly speaking, in his intention or volition, which alone decides the karmic quality of his thoughts and actions, and thus settles his future. However, it is clear that people have a pressing emotional need to do something for their dead relatives, and if that contradicts the law of *karman* they are quite happy to ignore or leave unformulated that contradition. In fact the more sophisticated, especially the monks, have developed a subtle and complex justification for the 'transfer of merit' based on the doctrine that the moral weight of an action lies in its intention. The donor can *intend* to transfer his merit to somebody else (a god or a dead relative) and so, without actually losing any, acquire more. Similarly, the intended 'recipient' is given the chance to applaud or empathise with the intention of the 'donor' to share his merit, and thus the 'recipient' too can perform an action (i.e. have an intention) which makes merit. Such a rationale is clearly strained, but the whole question of merit and its transfer draws attention to another area in which there has been a shift in the perception of a classical Buddhist teaching, namely, the doctrine of 'no-self' (*anattā*). Clearly, if a man is concerned that he should have a good re-birth, and believes that his dead relatives can have merit transferred to them, then he can hardly feel in any deep sense that an individual has no lasting personality and that the only continuity between this existence and the next one is karmic. The abiding wish for the survival of some personal essence after death cancels out the counter-intuitive doctrine of 'no-self', even when lip-service is paid to it. (The question of whether many people really understand this difficult doctrine is a related but somewhat different one.) This, no doubt, is also one of the reasons why *nibbāna*, the state which requires that the 'selflessness' of the person should be fully realised, remains a deferred ideal.

In addition to those mentioned above, a number of other Buddhist practices, all connected with devotion, can be seen as opportunities to produce material welfare through the transfer of merit. However, the best motive for acts of devotion is said to be that they are part of that complex of mental training which constitutes the Buddhist path: in so far as they calm the mind they produce spiritual welfare. From very early in Theravāda history the related practices of building *stūpas*, going on pilgrimages, and worshipping relics have been commonplace. Indeed, these three activities as well as the transfer of merit have canonical authorisation (in the *Mahāparinibbāna Sutta*). *Stūpas* originated as burial mounds for the Buddha's relics. They proliferated under the belief that all enlightened beings were entitled to such tombs, eventually even all Theravādin monks. However, only *stūpas* said to contain the relics of a Buddha are worshipped. The relic may be something like a piece of bone, or it may be a part of the Buddha's 'Dharma-body', i.e. a part of scripture. *Stūpas* are thus, in one sense, 'reminders' of the Buddha; and by a relatively late classification relics were divided into body relics (such as bone, teeth or hair), objects used by the Buddha (such as begging bowls, but also the Bo tree under which he attained enlightenment) and places associated with his life, and 'reminder relics', which included statues. In one way, all sacred objects are reminders to devotees of the (dead) Buddha, bringing them psychologically that much closer to him. Pilgrimage, which is by no means an obligation for Buddhists, is mainly to *stūpas* and sites associated either with the historical Buddha or with one of the many Buddhas who are supposed to have preceded him. Such sites, supported by various myths concerning miraculous visits from Gotama Buddha, exist in all Theravāda countries. Thus it is chiefly by the doctrine of relics that Buddhist worship and the practices associated with it are justified. Yet worship remains an individual and simple affair, one in which flowers or incense are offered before a Buddha image, and some Pali verses recited, very much in accordance with its stated function as a way of purifying the mind. To put this in more general terms, while the Buddha himself is the principal object of religious emotion and the focus of devotion, it is the monks who, as 'sons of the Buddha' and living exemplars of Buddhist ideals, receive the greatest veneration. Thus the very reason for the existence of a village temple, for instance, is that it is the residence of at least one monk.

Throughout the history of Theravāda the great majority of laity and monks have practised their religion in the ways outlined above—pursuing various devotional practices and making merit for themselves and others. There have, however, certainly intermittently and perhaps always, been some monks who have concentrated entirely on the ideal practices of meditation and asceticism, and so followed the path to *nibbāna*. The tradition is probably not an unbroken one. However remote the hermitage, its monks are still dependent on the laity for food, and such is the veneration in which meditating monks are held, and so great is the potential merit to be gained from giving to them, that they are constantly in danger of being drawn back into 'village' activities, i.e. into the monastic norm of preaching and teaching. In one case in modern Sri Lanka it is necessary to 'book' a year in advance to give a group of forest-dwelling meditators a meal, so great is the demand. It is likely that a pattern was established from a relatively early date in Theravāda history whereby monks setting themselves up as meditators had to revive the tradition from written sources rather than from any living master. The classical source is Buddhaghosa's *Visuddhimagga*. There, meditation (*bhāvanā*) is described in terms of moral and mental self-discipline, the total cultivation of the individual which results in wisdom (*paññā*). That purification which leads to and is synonymous with *nibbāna* is the objective, and it is renunciation which is seen as the height of moral purity. When it actually comes to 'sitting in meditation', two techniques are prescribed: meditations for 'tranquillity' (*samatha*), and 'insight meditation' (*vipassanā*), the distinctively Theravādin form. One proceeds from the first to the second, the aim of the latter being to realise in one's own experience the psychological reality of the Buddhist doctrine that all things are impermanent, unsatisfactory, and that there is no self. Realising this truth, desire is discarded and *nibbāna* achieved. Hermitage revival movements in the twentieth century have also depended on Buddhagosa; however, there have been a number of new developments, some of them heterodox, notably the teaching of 'insight' meditation to laymen and the setting up of meditation centres.

The meditating monks who live in the forests attempt to act by the Buddha's moral code and embody the ideals expressed in his doctrine in their own ways of life. In a sense, by purifying themselves they purify the entire Saṅgha, turning it back towards its ideal past. And throughout the history of Theravāda Buddhism, it is the Saṅgha that has in turn provided the rest of the population with an ideal of civilised behaviour, an ideal which is encapsulated in the *Visuddhimagga*'s prescription to meditators: that a man should first of all wish himself well, but then he should go on and do the same for others.

Further Reading

Bechert, H. and Gombrich, R.F. (eds.) *The World of Buddhism* (Thames & Hudson, London, 1984)

Carrithers, M. *The Forest Monks of Sri Lanka* (Oxford University Press, Delhi, 1983)

Gombrich, R.F. *Precept and Practice: Traditional Buddhism in the Rural Highlands of Ceylon* (Oxford University Press, Oxford, 1971)

—— *Theravada Buddhism: A Social History from Ancient Benares to Modern Colombo* (Routledge & Kegan Paul, London, 1988)

Spiro, M.E. *Buddhism and Society, A Great Tradition and its Burmese Vicissitudes* (University of California Press, Berkeley, 1982)

9 Buddhism and Hinduism in the Nepal Valley

David Gellner

Introduction

The Kathmandu Valley is a roughly circular bowl about twenty-five kilometres in diameter set high in the Himalayan foothills. The rich black soil of the valley, and its strategic position on ancient trade routes between Tibet and India, meant that it became an outpost of South Asian civilisation from the fourth century CE onwards. The Chinese Buddhist pilgrim Hsüan Tsang (Xuan Zang), passing through the plains of India in the early seventh century, heard that the Valley possessed both Hindu temples and Buddhist monasteries close together, and that there were 'about 2,000 [Buddhist] monks who study both the Great and the Little Vehicle'. Numerous inscriptions in elegant Sanskrit and many beautiful sculptures, still today sited in temple compounds or in wayside shrines, attest to the high level of culture attained in the Licchavi period (fifth to ninth centuries CE).

Subsequently the Kathmandu Valley experienced a period of weak and decentralised government, lasting about 500 years. We know very little about the first 300 years or so, but after that there is much more evidence. Then in 1382 King Jaya Sthiti Malla ascended the throne and united the Valley under one ruler for the first time in many centuries. Although he reigned for only thirteen years his influence seems to have been profound: many of the religious and cultural practices still alive today can be traced back to his reign or to the time of his immediate successors. His descendants ruled over the Valley, which was subsequently divided into three separate kingdoms, until 1768–9, when it was conquered by Prithvi Narayan Shah, the ancestor of the present king. This was the crucial step in the establishment of the modern kingdom of Nepal, which stretches far beyond the narrow confines of the Kathmandu Valley.

From an ethno-political point of view the backbone of Prithvi Narayan Shah's dynasty was provided by the Brahmin and

Kṣatriya castes (pronounced locally as 'Bāhun' and 'Chetri' respectively). The Brahmins were priests of course, but they were also administrators, judges and landowners. The Kṣatriyas were soldiers, policemen, politicians and farmers. Still today the King of Nepal must by law come from the Kṣatriya caste. These groups, and associated untouchable service castes, are known as 'Parbatiya'. They migrated throughout the hills of Nepal, taking their language, now called 'Nepali', with them. Nepali had become the lingua franca of the hills even before the time of Prithvi Narayan Shah; now it is the national language and is fast gaining ground among the various tribes-cum-castes (e.g. Magar, Gurung, Rai, Limbu) who inhabit the Nepalese hills.

The Parbatiyas migrated also to the Kathmandu Valley, but they are not its traditional inhabitants. These are the Newars, an ethnic group defined primarily by its language, Newari. This is a Tibeto-Burman tongue but through almost two millennia of influences from the south it has absorbed a very large number of Indo-European words, especially in those contexts (e.g. religion) in which the *written* word is important. The Newars have their own caste system which, thanks to the fact that they are traditionally city dwellers, is more complex and elaborated than that of the Parbatiyas. Figure 9.1 gives a very simplified representation of it.

Figure 9.1: Newar Caste System

Newar Brahmins	Buddhist priests and monks (goldsmiths, artisans)
High Caste Hindus (administrators, businessmen, astrologers)	High Caste Buddhists (businessmen, artisans)
Farmers	
Various Artisan and Service Castes	

Untouchables

Since the establishment of modern Nepal by Prithvi Narayan Shah many Newars have emigrated from the Kathmandu Valley, their 'homeland', and become traders and shopkeepers throughout the hills of Nepal. The Newars also provide most of Nepal's artisans—carpenters, masons, sculptors, potters, coppersmiths and goldsmiths. Within the Kathmandu Valley, as is shown on the chart, they constitute a complete social system. Unlike the Parbatiyas, who are all strong Hindus very similar to those of north India, the Newars have the unique characteristic of possessing both Buddhist and Hindu religious traditions side by side, and both in a very archaic form. In general terms, much of what I shall say applies to the Parbatiyas also, especially to those living in the Kathmandu Valley. But my description is primarily of the Newars, since they are the inheritors of the Valley's ancient civilisation, a fact of which they themselves are extremely proud.

In spite of the political changes which have occurred, the Shah dynasty has maintained most of the traditions associated with that ancient civilisation. From 1846 to 1951 the Rana family of hereditary prime ministers held absolute power. They pursued a deliberate policy of isolation from British India so that Nepal knew little of the complex changes set in motion by the colonial power with its laws, factories and new ways of thinking. Modernisation has only come to Nepal in the years since 1951. So far change has been more eye-catching than thoroughgoing and the old ways still vastly outnumber the new.

Thus it is that one can see in the Kathmandu Valley a unique and ancient urban culture still functioning today. Three- and four-storey houses of brick and wood, with intricately carved windows; three- and five-storeyed 'pagoda' temples, their roofs covered with beaten copper and held up by beautifully carved wooden struts; numerous sunken water fountains in which a continuous stream of water—often brought long distances underground—flows from several carved stone ducts; public meeting-houses, wayside shelters, temples, monasteries and shrines of all sorts at every corner; the meticulous farming which gets three crops a year from irrigated fields and skilful artisan work of all kinds—all this is visible to any casual observer. Moreover, he or she cannot fail to notice a devotion to religion which overflows into festivals, fasts and rituals on almost every day of the year. Many visitors to the Valley have remarked that there seem to be almost as many temples as houses, as many gods as men.

The rituals and festivals of the Newars are, like most of their culture, extremely ancient. Some new cults may have risen to prominence, some new observances have been initiated, some new castes have emerged, but the basic structure of their religion and society seems to have remained much the same since the fourteenth century. Thanks to a combination of geographical isolation and political circumstance, the Valley avoided both Muslim rule and also (with the exception of some ill-fated visits by Jesuits in the seventeenth century and Capuchins in the eighteenth) the attentions of missionaries. Many traditions even go back beyond Jaya Sthiti Malla. The rites of the Buddhists can be traced back to the great monasteries of Bihar and Bengal in the late first millennium CE. Only here, in this little corner of South Asia, has this type of Indian Buddhism survived. Here too are forms of Tantric Hinduism which are equally ancient. The cultural conservatism of the Valley, and its temperate climate, have also meant that many ancient Buddhist and Hindu Sanskrit manuscripts, lost in the rest of South Asia, have survived here.

A Religion Based on Worship

Religion in the Kathmandu Valley is primarily a set of practices and these are all based on the idea of worship, doing *pūjā*, to a superior. Usually the superior in question is a deity, but it can also be a priest, elder or monk, someone considered to incarnate a deity, or anyone worthy of respect; and there are two popular family festivals, held on consecutive days, in which respectively one worships one's own body, for good health, and elder sisters worship their younger brothers, for long life.

The simplest worship consists simply of bowing one's head with folded hands; also indicative of respect, though not constituting worship as such, is the practice of keeping the deity or other superior on one's right hand. If offerings are made, the simplest is a few grains of rice or, these days, a coin. A more elaborate worship is made by offering a set of five things together: flowers, incense, light, vermilion powder and food (e.g. rice, sweets or fruit). To these may be added an offering of water, representing the bathing of feet, and thread tied in a circle, representing cloth. All of these offerings may be made by an individual on his own; but in rituals which require the specialist services of a priest the number of offerings increases rapidly. Some of these offerings are kept at home by each family, others may be bought at shops specialising in the sale of ritual perquisites, and some are so unusual—such as the rhinoceros meat required when performing ancestor worship—that the priest will bring along a minute quantity himself. Certain deities accept animal sacrifice: the various forms of the Hindu Goddess (e.g. the Eight Mothers and the Nine Durgās), Bhairava, Gaṇeśa and Bhīmasena. But to sacrifice an animal to high and pure deities—Mahādeva (Śiva), Nārāyaṇa (Viṣṇu), the Buddha or the Buddhist *bodhisattvas*—would be a heinous sin. However there is another class of deities, the secret or Tantric deities, who may be seen and worshipped directly only by those with special empowering initiations; while not normally receiving actual blood sacrifice they must be offered cooked meat and alcohol.

The offerings made in worship must be new and fresh—offering a half-eaten banana would be a terrible insult, and contradict the basic emotional attitude of worship, namely respectful acknowledgement of one's inferiority and, often only implicitly, a request for protection. Likewise the offering must be kept pure, that is, it must be kept away from contact with impurity, a category which, as in the rest of South Asia, includes saliva, excrement, menstruating women, dogs, leather, Untouchables, the soles of the feet and so on. When worship has been performed it is usual to receive back some of the offerings as a blessing: vermilion powder as a spot on the forehead, flowers put behind the ear (right for men, left for women), water or food—including the meat of a sacrificed animal—to consume.

A Westerner from a secular society can only be amazed at the time, energy and resources that Newars devote to their religion. Every day offerings must be made and every year hundreds of festivals are observed, some confined to a particular village or quarter of the city, others common to all Newars alike. In addition every lineage has its own deity which must be worshipped once or twice a year, as do many castes or professional groups. High-caste families have their Tantric deities requiring regular worship. There are gods for toothache, earache, smallpox and infertility, gods who will help you find things you have lost, gods whose worship can help to remove the sin of adultery. Birth, entry into adulthood, marriage, the attaining of the ages 77, 80 and 99, and death are all marked by religious observances which involve the whole family and many relatives.

Newars also have a unique and characteristic religious organisation called *guthi*: these group together a number of men usually, but not invariably, of the same caste, for some socio-religious purpose or other. Every Newar belongs to at least one *guthi*, a funeral association which takes charge of the cremation of its members. But there are hundreds of others, e.g. those responsible for the maintenance of wayside shelters, *guthis* set up to ensure the annual performance of a particular fast, or charged with the building of the cart of a popular deity, to mention only a few. *Guthis* are funded by lands and other donations, gifted either by the founder or subsequently as an act of religious merit, or by annual contributions from its members. Each year or month, depending on the rhythm of the *guthi*'s activities, a different member takes charge of its organisation. At the conclusion of his turn he must give a feast for all the members. The dishes to be served are laid down by tradition and participating in it is also a religious act, since the food is consecrated by the presiding divinity. Similar feasts are eaten by the family, and its guests, at the conclusion of every life-cycle rite, and at every important annual festival.

Underlying this efflorescence of religious activity is a complex but stable society, built on respect and hierarchy. Different castes are related to each other, just as men are related to gods, in certain fixed and traditional ways, which are re-enacted every year as inevitably as the seasons. The historian or anthropologist can detect that certain rituals have gone out of, or come into, fashion (e.g. the fast of Svasthānī, mentioned below), that the caste system is mutating and that new types of religious activity have emerged. But the Newars themselves remain extremely attached to their traditions and to the idea that they are unchanging and ought not to change.

Newar religious practices can be divided into the compulsory and the optional. The sheer quantity of compulsory observance is very slowly decreasing, but there seems to be at least as much optional religious activity as there ever has been.

Obligatory Religious Practices

Every family has its own god-room situated high and near the back of the house, i.e. as privately as possible. For the women of the house, keeping the god-room, the kitchen and the storeroom (considered the abode of Lakṣmī, the goddess of wealth) clean and briefly worshipping all the deities present, is part of their daily religious duty. That done, one person from the house, again usually female, visits the shrines of the locality, making offerings at each.

Men who have taken some kind of initiation must also perform a daily ritual: this is a lifelong personal obligation they have undertaken. Mostly this ritual consists in the recitation of sacred formulas and prayers; depending on the type of initiation and the individual's piety, it may last for anything from ten minutes to two or three hours. Until this daily worship has been performed no food may pass his mouth. The difficulty this obligation imposes means that those who take initiation are usually old or at least middle-aged. In any case neither young men, unless of the priestly castes, nor children are expected to take any great interest in taxing religious observances.

Just as cleaning the house each morning is a religious act for women, so cleaning the shrine and bathing the deity is an obligatory daily task for men who are temple-priests, either permanently or in rotation, and for those families that have established their own private shrines. In every temple of any size the first thing that occurs early in the morning is this 'regular worship' before outside worshippers may present their offerings. At the temples of popular deities huge crowds gather during which the priests recite prayers and bathe the deity. The water is then sprayed onto the assembled worshippers as a blessing. Out of simple faith and devotion this regular worship occurs, scaled down, at thousands of other small shrines and temples every day, though no one may be there to observe or bring offerings. The high and pure gods, and for the most part the Tantric deities, are the preserve of the priestly castes of the two religions—Brahmins and Karmācāryas (Hindu Tantric priests) for Hindu gods, and Vajrācāryas (literally 'master of the diamond [Vehicle]') and Śākyabhikṣus ('Buddhist monks') for the Buddhist deities. But many other deities, worshipped in common by the followers of both religions, are served by priests of other castes: Gaṇeśa shrines for instance are usually served by farmers and even the Untouchables have temples where they have the right to keep all offerings, namely those of the Mother Goddesses that ring the city and protect it from external evil influences.

Every month, calculated according to the moon's cycles, certain holy days recur: the no-moon day, the eighth (sacred to the Bodhisattva Lokeśvara), the eleventh (on which no meat may be sold, sacred to Nārāyaṇa), and the full-moon day; in the waning half of the month, there is the fourteenth (sacred to various deities); also holy are the days that the sun passes into a new zodiacal sign and initiates a new solar month (likewise sacred to the Bodhisattva Lokeśvara). On all these days religious observance brings greater merit: both men and women take greater pains with their daily worship, visit more shrines and say more prayers than usual. At large temples special rituals mark these holy days. Similarly each day of the week is holy to a particular deity, for instance Tuesday to Gaṇeśa, Saturday to Mahākāla and to many of the Mother Goddesses. On these days their shrines will be many times more crowded than on normal days.

Every year numerous annual festivals are celebrated in the home. On these days it is forbidden to eat cooked rice, the consumption of which involves mild impurity (that is why one's daily ritual must be completed before eating). Instead parboiled flattened rice, buffalo meat cooked in various ways and numerous tasty vegetable and bean dishes are eaten. But this feast occurs only after the head of the household and his wife have performed the ritual necessary to that day. The following day daughters of the household who have been given away in marriage to other families must be invited along with their children; on a few important festivals their husbands will also be included in the invitation. In this way women maintain frequent contact with their natal home, and their children come to regard their maternal uncles with special affection. Men say that they have a religious duty to feed their married sisters and daughters whenever they celebrate anything because, by marrying into another family, they have lost the right to inherit from their own parents.

In addition to the annual festivals which everyone observes there are many particular to individual areas, castes or *guthis*. People also observe their own birthdays by making offerings at various temples. Membership of most *guthis* is optional, but it is not something lightly abandoned. If one's ancestor has founded a Buddhist *caitya* (Buddhist cult object), or donated a tympanum, for example, to a temple, every year the anniversary of the donation must be marked by a reconsecration: the family priest must be called, a fire sacrifice lasting several hours (during which all participants fast) must be performed, and finally a feast served.

The various stages of life are also marked by religious ritual. Only by ritual can a house be purified after a birth or a death. These occasions implicate relatives too, so that Newars often describe how closely they are related by mentioning the degree of mourning they are obliged to observe for each other's death. During these periods of impurity it is forbidden to worship deities, except indirectly or from outside a given area. Auspicious stages of life are also defined religiously: a child's first rice-feeding is a time of great joy and the help of the gods is required to ensure its healthy growth. In later life Newar girls pass through a ceremony in which they are 'married to a *bel* fruit'; according to Buddhist priests the girls are marrying the god Kumāra, and according to Brahmins, Nārāyaṇa. The *bel* fruit is, on learned interpretations, just a witness, but for ordinary Newars these are academic matters. Ritually speaking the girl is then married, and married for life, so that even if her human husband dies she is not supposed to suffer the indignity of being a widow (in practice however high-caste women do suffer some stigma). Girls must also undergo a twelve-day rite in which they stay in a room without seeing the sun; its purpose is, it seems, to defuse the danger of their imminent menstruation. Boys pass through a single though complex rite called 'tying the loin-cloth'; for Brahmins and high-caste Hindus this also involves the donning of the sacred thread; boys of the Buddhist priestly-monk caste spend four days as a Buddhist monk. All these rites mark the transition to adulthood, so that the boy or girl is now considered a full member of his or her caste and family.

Marriage, too, is a long and complex ceremony, sanctified at every stage with worship of the gods. If an old person reaches 77, 80 or 99 years they are also entitled to a further rite which consecrates them as becoming ever more divine themselves. All members of their lineage come to show their respect and do obeisance to them. Finally death is marked by ceremonies extending over many years. Every year, at least for the first two years, and usually for many years afterwards, a deceased father receives worship and 'feeding' from his eldest son, a mother from her youngest son. The complex ceremonies performed on behalf of the dead are felt to be a great help in times of bereavement, since they give those left behind concrete measures to take on behalf of their loved one.

The higher castes, both Hindu and Buddhist, are more punctilious in observing these various life-cycle rituals than the low castes. In fact more ritual involvement in general is part of the way in which 'high' caste is defined. The life-cycle rites are seen, especially in the Hindu view, as purifying; some Buddhists tend to play down the importance of particular rites, but they, like all Newars, see the undertaking of the rules and restrictions involved in ritual in general as a sign of commitment to the religious life.

Public Festivals

The most spectacular side of Newar religion is its public festivals. These form an intermediate category between the obligatory and the optional: they must take place, and for those directly involved in organising them there is no choice; but everyone else takes part for the fun and religious merit of it.

One type of public festival involves visiting every shrine of a particular deity within the city. In Lalitpur the most popular festival of this sort is called 'The procession of [offering] light': thousands of worshippers circulate without stopping and without eating on a route laid out beforehand, visiting and making offerings to every *caitya* in the city, which takes from 5 am to about 8 pm to complete. Ten different sections of the city take it in turn to organise the festival. In the same way there are processions to every Bhīmasena shrine, to every Gaṇeśa, to every Kṛṣṇa and so on at different times of the year, events in which hundreds of people participate.

In chariot and palanquin festivals it is the god who circulates for the benefit of worshippers on a prescribed route around the town. The most famous of these is the chariot festival of the god called Matsyendranāth by Hindus, Karuṇāmaya by Buddhists and Buṃgadyaḥ by most ordinary Newars. It is also the festival with the tallest chariot and lasts longer than any other. All sections of the population observe the festival with great enthusiasm but it is perhaps the farmers who show the greatest devotion since Matsyendranātha is believed to bring the rain on which their crops depend. Chariots with huge wooden wheels are expensive and time-consuming to make so most deities circulate on a palanquin carried on the shoulders of four or more men. In these festivals different tasks are laid down by tradition for different castes. These duties are usually jealously guarded privileges, a source of pride to the groups and individuals concerned.

In most public festivals the king plays a significant role. Before 1768 each of the three major cities of the Valley, Kathmandu, Bhaktapur and Lalitpur, had its own king and he would be present as principal sponsor of the festival and guarantor of the material and spiritual well-being of the kingdom. In smaller settlements the local headman, as representative of the royal power, played and often still plays the role of 'king'. When the present dynasty established its capital in Kathmandu the kings continued to be present at some rituals and kept up the rituals associated with royalty in the other two cities, Bhaktapur and Lalitpur. Nowadays, though he is rarely present himself, the sword of the king must always be brought along. Some of the festivals centre around the royal palace of each city, in particular the autumn festival known as Dasaiṃ in Nepali, Mohanī in Newari, Durgā Pūjā or Navarātrī in Sanskrit. This is at the same time an archetypal family ritual, observed in every house in the country: all offices close and absent relatives return home. Theologically the festival celebrates the victory of Durgā over the buffalo demon; this myth is given vivid expression by the sacrifice of hundreds of buffaloes to the king's tutelary deity, Taleju, a form of Durgā, who is at the same time a Tantric deity and whose *mantra* is believed to guarantee the king's power. Thus while this is a nation-wide, indeed *the* nation-wide and state festival, it is also above all the festival of the ruling and warfaring (Kṣatriya) class. Other festivals in which the king has an important role are Ghoḍe (horse) Jātrā and Indra Jātrā in Kathmandu (the presence of the Vedic god Indra is another sign of the antiquity of the Newars' religion), Bisket Jātrā in Bhaktapur and the Matsyendra Jātrā in Lalitpur.

In many festivals dancers impersonate gods; when they put on their masks they begin to tremble as a sign that the god has entered them. The most famous of these are the Nine Durgās from Bhaktapur who dance for nine months of every year, visiting twenty-one quarters of the city and the nineteen towns and villages which used to comprise the kingdom of Bhaktapur. There are many other such dance groups: the Eight Mothers of Lalitpur (danced unusually by Buddhists); a similar group from the village of Theco nearby; the dancers attached to the Naradevī temple in Kathmandu; and many more. Lākhe (demon) dancers circulate in association with many festivals. There is a special set of dances in Lalitpur over many nights during the month of Kārtik. These include farces and devotional dances, culminating on the final night in the dance of the half-man half-lion Narasiṃha (an incarnation of Viṣṇu with royal connections) who is acted nowadays by a Brahmin, destroying the demon Hiraṇyakaśipu, acted by a man of the painter caste. In the old days, people say, the painter was really killed; now he merely becomes unconscious and is revived with holy water.

Optional Religious Practices

For the pious individual there is a vast panoply of ways to invest his or her energy. One of the most popular with women is the one- or two-day fast. For Buddhists and those with Buddhist priests, this means above all the *aṣṭamī vrata*, a fast in the name of Bodhisattva Amoghapāśa Lokeśvara, which occurs each month on the eighth day of the waxing moon. Often a group will form, sponsored by one or more rich men who wish to earn merit, and undertake to perform the fast at each of the twelve holy bathing places in the Valley. Another Buddhist fast involves performing the same rite at eight Hindu temples of Viṣṇu and Śiva, who are classed as *bodhisattvas* in the Buddhist scheme of things. Once a year a popular fast is performed to the Buddhist goddess Vasundharā and there are many *guthis* to ensure that it takes place without fail.

Hindus fast for the god Nārāyaṇa (Viṣṇu) on the eleventh day of the waxing moon, and also often perform a fast over several days called the *Satya Nārāyaṇa pūjā* when they have some special reason to celebrate or a particular wish to be fulfilled. At the end of the holy month of Kārtik a few women undertake a five-day fast to Karuṇāmaya or Nārāyaṇa and at the end of it are fetched by their husband and led home in triumph with a band playing. In the old days this fast was often undertaken for a whole month with the women consuming nothing except the holy water in which the deity had been bathed. Every year in the month of Māgh (January–February) Hindu women, both Newar and non-Newar, observe the fast of Svasthānī, a uniquely Nepali goddess identified with Śiva's wife Pārvatī.

Even if they cannot fast they read the stories associated with the fast and the goddess every evening. This practice, like of that of Gai (cow) Jātrā, has spread from the Newars to other groups in Nepali society and is almost universal throughout the middle hills of modern Nepal.

A less taxing but longer-term practice is simply the service of a deity, visiting his or her temple every day for a month, or even a year. This is undertaken by both men and women, though men predominate. Some treat this as little more than a regular morning walk; but in the month of Kārtik, when it is both dark and very cold at 5 am, rather more commitment is required. At certain important shrines regular devotees join in the recitation of Sanskrit prayers every morning, a form of devotion which is open to all and highly valued. On holy days, in the morning, and sometimes also in the evening just for the fun of it, groups of men gather to sing hymns: the ancient style is highly percussive and the words are usually in old forms of Maithili and Bengali, imported from the plains of India centuries ago; the newer style, introduced in the last sixty years or so, makes use of the accordion and in this style new hymns, composed in the local vernaculars (Newari and Nepali) are sung. These hymn groups are usually organised as a *guthi* with certain fixed duties and an annual feast, but membership is optional.

Those with money have numerous possibilities for approved forms of merit-making: donating a fitting or decoration to a temple, founding a Buddhist *caitya* or Hindu Śivaliṅga, building a wayside shelter, establishing a *guthi* for the annual performance of a ritual to one's favoured deity. In recent times more modern forms of religious activity have received sponsorship: publishing religious pamphlets (usually in the name of a dead parent or relative), writing for religious magazines, establishing health clinics, religious schools and other types of social service. Buddhist meditation camps and Buddhist, Hindu or interdenominational conferences have become regular events.

Another way of dividing up religious practices is to consider the individual's motivations. Where compulsory religious practices are concerned the motives are obviously diffuse: there is no need for an individual to ask him or herself why it is being done and the practice goes on out of a general desire to satisfy the gods, perpetuate tradition and avoid any ill consequences (divine retribution, social obloquy) which might follow the evasion of one's religious duty. Optional religious practices on the other hand are undertaken with more precise aims in mind. Sometimes this is merely to win religious merit and peace of mind: it is very widely felt that religious practices protect one from domestic disasters while omissions and mistakes, particularly in the ritual due to a powerful deity, incur misfortunes sooner or later. But other rituals and practices are undertaken with a very specific aim in mind: the birth of a son, success in an exam, new job or business, to cure an illness, or to ensure a safe return from a long journey. Such rites vary in the extent to which such personal and specific desires are explicitly acknowledged: Buddhist fasts or the reading of the text, *The Perfection of Wisdom in Eight Thousand Lines* (Aṣṭasahasrika-Prajñāpāramitā-Sūtra), are officially carried out 'for the good of all beings', and it is only within that framework that one may ask for a particular favour. Other rituals, which some priests perform, or which women (and a few men) possessed by goddesses such as Hariti, the Buddhist goddess of smallpox, recommend to their petitioners, pretend even less to an altruistic motivation: everyone knows what they are for and there are few who have never patronised this type of ritual, though many outwardly condemn them.

One final type of optional religious practice which is equally important in Buddhism and Hinduism is initiation into the cult of a given Tantric deity. In one way this is the most onerous practice of all, for henceforth come what may one must perform the required ritual and say one's prayers every day before eating. Tantric initiations are restricted to high castes and to certain closely defined groups within other castes (e.g. men of the painter caste, who must be allowed into Tantric shrines in order to paint images and wall-hangings). The deities associated with Tantric practice are strictly secret; their shrines are enclosed rooms on the first floor of a monastery or of special god-houses, or on the second floor if in a private home. It is widely believed that looking at a Tantric deity whom one is not entitled to see causes blindness or madness. But for those who are entitled, and who fulfil faithfully their obligations to their deity, a good controlled death, and the attainment of liberation in this life, can be hoped for.

Tantric deities are usually represented in coitus with a female partner and sexual symbolism is central to Tantric ritual. It cannot be too heavily emphasised however that, though everyone knows of their existence, these deities and rituals really are secret: only thus is it possible for them to coexist with the highly moral and ascetic tendencies of exoteric (non-Tantric) Buddhism and indeed Hinduism. Through the use of meat, alcohol and sexual symbolism, which in other contexts are forbidden or disapproved of, the secret truth is taught that everything is emptiness (for Buddhists) or Śiva (for Hindus). Tantric deities are taken to be the highest, innermost and ultimate nature of the divine, of which other divinities and indeed the whole world are just outer forms. Thus it is that, though for most of the population their significance is opaque, the whole of Newar religion is permeated by Tantric symbols. And priests invoke the presence and protection of Tantric deities on behalf of their clients as part of almost every ritual, whether or not the client himself has initiation.

The Relation of Hinduism and Buddhism and the Problem of Belief

Many questions will occur to the Westerner confronted by this religion: what role does religious belief have for Newars? Is not this mass of ritual and worship just a confused jumble, a syncretistic pottage? What kind of Buddhism is it that encourages ritual, hierarchy and secrecy? Do we have anything to learn from such a completely different attitude to the sacred and the 'meaning of life'?

I have indicated the role which respect for tradition plays in the religious life of the Newars, and I have tried to show that this relates primarily to rites and practices. Newar children are taught no catechism nor to read their own scriptures (unless they come from the priestly castes). Rather, from an early age, they participate in festivals and undergo life-cycle rites under the instruction of their family priest and helped by their mothers. Young girls learn to help their mothers and the other young women of the household in making offerings, and themselves teach their younger siblings how to make obeisance to deities. As they grow older both men and women, particularly (though not only) of the upper castes, learn to recite prayers in Sanskrit and often make use of them in their daily ritual. But they are far from understanding them word for word; the point is not to analyse them but to recite them in an attitude of devotion. Reciting prayers, whether or not a manuscript or printed book is used to jog the memory, is also an activity, not a confession of faith. When fasts and some other rites are performed at a certain point the priest reads out the 'story' which goes with the practice; but it is written in an archaic style, he reads it out fast and the participants know the broad outline already; consequently, attention is lax and this too is simply another ritual.

While ritual is carefully codified and maintained by specialists, belief is not: there are no institutions for collective expressions of given articles of faith. Belief is an individual concern. Providing one conforms outwardly to the rites traditional to one's family, one can, if one wishes, believe things apparently in opposition to it. Some Buddhists privately prefer Hindu deities, and I know one prominent Buddhist intellectual whose family background is strongly Hindu. Women on the whole restrict their interest to rites and to the moral stories recited on various occasions by the learned priests of the two religions. Men on the other hand, particularly as they get older and begin to retire from worldly affairs, often take a lively interest in theological matters. It is not uncommon for them to discuss them amongst themselves. But the opinions they express represent their own reflections on past experience, with scraps they have heard from priests or their own older relatives. Doctrine is not codified and the only way to solve a dispute is to ask a priest. And since the organisation of priests is weak and consensual, and in any case concerned with ritual matters rather than doctrine, there is no authority empowered to decide such questions as there is in Western churches. Consequently it is ritual, and not belief, which determines whether one is a Buddhist or a Hindu.

According to one definition, the definition which tends to be given by priests themselves, all those with a Buddhist (Vajrācārya) family priest are Buddhists ('followers of the way of the Buddha'), and all those with a Brahmin family priest are Hindu ('followers of the way of Śiva'). For all compulsory rituals one must call one's traditional family priest and he, on his side, is obliged to come or send a substitute if he cannot. At optional rites however one may invite whomsoever one wishes; and one consequence of this is that certain families, and some castes, which are traditionally Buddhist, that is, have a Vajrācārya family priest, nevertheless invite Brahmins to perform rituals for them whenever they have the chance. The main reason for this is that the rulers of Nepal have been Hindu for a very long time and therefore Hinduism has higher social prestige; further, it is widely felt that Hindus have a better chance than Buddhists of obtaining government jobs, even though there is no systematic prejudice against them and the official view is that Buddhism is just a 'branch' of Hinduism.

Newar Buddhism is unusual in lacking a celibate monastic order. (As a result of recent influence from Tibet and South-east Asia there are now both Tibetan Mahāyāna and Theravāda monks in the Newar community; but these exist as an adjunct to traditional Newar religion and need not be considered here.) Instead of a celibate monkhood Newar Buddhism is led by a caste of *married* monks, made up of two subsections, one being the Buddhist priests, the Vajrācāryas, and the other, somewhat larger, called Śākyabhikṣu ('Buddhist monk') or Śākyavaṃśa ('of the Buddha's lineage'). The idea of married monks may seem strange but it is in fact one of the marks of Mahāyāna, as opposed to Theravāda, Buddhism to put less stress on celibacy and formal monasticism. This is equally true of Japanese Buddhism and of the un-reformed Tibetan schools.

The menfolk of this Buddhist caste, the Vajrācāryas and Śākyabhikṣus/Śākyavaṃśas, all pass through a rite as boys in which they spend four days as monks. In this way they become members of a particular monastery in which they have certain rights and duties for the rest of their life. The immediate neighbourhood of the monastery is inhabited by its members, though many also move, e.g. to set up as gold- or silversmiths elsewhere. In that case they return for important festivals and to fulfil their obligations in the monastery. (Only in the last thirty years have members who have lived for generations many days' travel away from their monastery started to break away and found new monasteries.) Other Newars respect them as a holy order and at certain festivals come to give them gifts as monks. It could be argued that such gift giving, *dāna*, is characteristically Buddhist; though conceptually not very far from worship, *pūjā*, it does seem to play a greater role in Buddhism than Hinduism.

The Buddhist monk caste has control of monastery deities, a category which includes some of the most popular gods in Nepal. As Buddhist priests they also have much the same position for Buddhist lay people as Brahmins do for Hindus. As monks, however, they tend to think of themselves as the only true Buddhists. And herein lies an important difference of values between them and Hindus: Hindus would never say that Brahmins are the only true Hindus; Hindus are inclusive and will tend to accept Buddhists as Hindus, although they assign them a rank lower than Buddhists would ascribe themselves. Buddhists on the other hand tend to define anything which is not on a strict definition Buddhist as non-Buddhist, and therefore as Hindu.

This explains how Buddhists can acquiesce in certain castes who have Buddhist priests being defined as Hindus. In fact, however, most Newars are neither clearly Buddhist nor clearly Hindu. They worship all deities with equal fervour; they carry out all the rites that tradition prescribes; if they have definite opinions this is a personal matter and not one which implicates anyone else. It is only the priestly castes at the top of the hierarchy, and one or two others immediately below them, who are careful not to allow themselves to be defined as members of the other religion. For all other Newars, perhaps 70 per cent of the total, the question of which religion they belong to is rather academic. This does not mean that they cannot tell the difference: they know very well what it is, but they say: 'We honour all deities equally, we respect both Brahmins and Vajrācāryas, we have our traditional practices as every caste and every nation does. There is no need to denigrate one religion and praise another, but one should keep up one's own traditions and respect what is good in all of them.'

There are two reasons why this is a tenable attitude for them. Firstly there is the fact that neither religion denies the existence or forbids the worship of the gods of the other. The Buddha is recognised as an incarnation of Viṣṇu; and Buddhists worship Viṣṇu and Śiva as *bodhisattvas*. One of the most popular gods of Nepal is known to outsiders by his Hindu name Matsyendranāth; but Buddhists, as I have already pointed out, call him Karuṇāmaya, an epithet of the Bodhisattva Avalokiteśvara; and most ordinary Newars, who are all enthusiastic worshippers, call him simply 'the god of [the village] Buṃga', thereby avoiding the question of whether he is a Hindu or a Buddhist deity. For them he is simply a powerful protector, who sends the monsoon rains, and the question of which religion he belongs to is irrelevant. They see the fact that he is worshipped equally by all tendencies of both religions as proof that such distinctions are academic. At the highest level of the pantheon then, the two religions offer competing explanations of the same divinities. But as with the social hierarchy, which has a clear distinction between Buddhist and Hindu at the top, but not at the bottom, the divine hierarchy is also clearly distinct only at the higher levels. Lower down where 'blood-drinking' gods such as the Eight Mothers or Gaṇeśa are concerned, it is not necessary to have alternative names. Both religions accept them as lower deities, though—again, as in the social hierarchy—Hinduism's inclusive tendency makes it more enthusiastic than Buddhism in doing so.

The second reason for the ordinary Newar's attitude to questions of religious attachment I have already described: it is that the primary religious activities are worship and ritual (which is just elaborate worship). This means that doctrine, polemic and even myth are 'second-order' activities; that is, they start from the fact of worship and on the whole reflect rather than determine it. This broad truth applies to both religions, so that a single act of worship to a deity of itself aligns one with neither religion. It is only by systematically worshipping Viṣṇu and Śiva, and avoiding Buddhist shrines and purely Buddhist festivals, that one defines oneself as a Hindu, and vice versa.

The primacy of praxis has a further consequence. Unlike the catechismal beliefs of religions like Christianity and Islam, which leave a relatively small scope to different interpretations, the simple action of worship is open to a wide variety of meanings. I have indicated how most Newars prefer simply to worship while remaining neutral about the question of whether their worship is Hindu or Buddhist. But even within a given religion the action of worship, which is common to every Newar of whatever background or education, can be seen naïvely as the propitiation of powerful beings; it can be seen as one's religious duty which leads to a better rebirth; or it can be seen as a discipline which calms the mind and produces good results for all concerned. In the Tantric systems, involving initiations and the complex worship of secret deities, it can be seen as a technique for identifying oneself with those deities and thereby with the essence of the universe, thus overcoming the limitations and duality of the ordinary world. Newars do not usually stop to consider which of these views they hold, though most of them will be aware, even if only vaguely, of them all. The peaceful coexistence of these various theories permits all Newars, of whatever background, to participate in the same tradition and religious culture.

It would be wrong to conclude therefore that the Newars' religion is an unsystematic syncretism of different elements and traditions which ought to have been kept separate. It is however held together by principles which are different from those we are familiar with from Western religions; and the way in which Hinduism and Buddhism define their relation to each other is quite foreign to Western religions. Moreover Buddhism and Hinduism, in coexisting as they do, are perfectly consistent and true to their own history.

By putting praxis at the centre of their religion, and making the degree and extent of it so much a matter of personal choice, the Newars' religion exhibits great tolerance—tolerance of different practices, of different viewpoints, of individuals' choices. Struggles with faith and a permanent sense of guilt are entirely unknown to them. At the same time their religion provides a framework, which everyone shares, of festivals, life-cycle rites and consecrated social relationships. One can but admire the simple faith, the far-reaching piety and the sheer enthusiastic enjoyment which such a religion inspires. Unfortunately however for those who might wish to emulate it, the Newars' religion is based on a stable social hierarchy, on respect for hereditary differences and rights and on a powerful belief in tradition, all of which, even in Nepal, are now rapidly being undermined by the inexorable process of Western-inspired change.

Further Reading

Allen, M.R. *The Cult of Kumari, Virgin Worship in Nepal* (INAS, Tribhuvan University, Kathmandu, 1975)

Bennett, Lynn *Dangerous Wives and Sacred Sisters—Social and Symbolic Roles of High-caste Women in Nepal* (Columbia University Press, New York, 1983)

Gutschow, Niels *Stadtraum und Ritual der newarischen Städte im Kathmandu Tal, Eine architekturanthropologische Untersuchung* (Kohlhammer, Stuttgart, 1982)

Lévi, Sylvain *Le Népal, étude historique d'un royaume hindou*, 3 vols. (Leroux, Paris, 1905)

Locke, John K. *Karunamaya, The Cult of Avalokitesvara-Matsyendranath in the Valley of Nepal* (Sahayogi, Kathmandu, 1980)

Slusser, Mary S. *Nepal Mandala, A Cultural Study of the Kathmandu Valley*, 2 vols. (Princeton University Press, Princeton, New Jersey, 1982)

Toffin, G. *Religion et société chez les Néwars du Népal* (CNRS, Paris, 1984)

10 Buddhism in China

Bulcsu Siklós

To many, the idea that Buddhism could, within a few hundred years, become an established, state-supported religion in, say, Europe would be far-fetched to say the least. Yet, almost to its own surprise, the age-old, highly conservative and excessively xenophobic civilisation of China managed to make Buddhism its own within a short period of time. This was perhaps the greatest coup ever pulled off by Buddhism, and one without which the Indian religion would have been restricted to playing a purely peripheral role in world history once its influence in its homeland had waned.

Ignoring certain groundless claims for the earlier introduction of Buddhism, many of Buddhist invention, it seems probable or at least possible that Buddhist monks started filtering in to western and northern parts of Han China during the first few years of our era from Central Asia. Obviously the process must have started before the Emperor Ming (58–75) had his dream of a flying golden deity interpreted by his ministers in a Buddhist light, resulting in the dispatch of several envoys to Central Asia. The implication, of course, is that Buddhism was already known, or rather, known about in China prior to this event, evidence for which can be culled from several sources, notably from the biography of Prince Ying of Ch'u. This states that by the year 65 there was a Buddhist community of some size in at least one peripheral part of western China, one which had possibly existed since *c.* 2 BCE. By the end of the first century CE, a community had likewise been established at Lo-yang, the capital, which even penetrated court circles to a degree where imperial shrines were set up for the worship of the Buddha alongside the deified Lao-tzu. Translation activities were also engaged in under the direction of a Parthian monk, An Shih-kao (arrived in China in 148) who laid emphasis on texts revealing meditational and breathing techniques, while his Scythian co-worker Chih-ch'an concentrated on translations of the *Prajñāpāramitā* (Perfection of Wisdom) literature. The monks of this period were without exception non-Chinese, though undoubtedly Chinese laymen played a considerable role in supporting the new community in various ways.

Buddhism during the Han period (until *c.* 220 CE) was doctrinally somewhat primitive, and not much effort was made to translate texts dealing with basic Buddhist philosophical issues. The central tenets seem to have been an acceptance of the idea of reincarnation and of the concept of *karma* understood in a very literal and moral sense, coupled with a totally un-Buddhist belief in the permanence and indestructibility of the 'soul' (how could rebirth take place otherwise?). Emphasis was laid upon simple meditational and yogic techniques paralleled by similar Taoist practices, although certain traditional objects of meditation, such as corpses in various stages of putrefaction, were considered unsuitable.

In this early period Buddhism's path was smoothed considerably by the Taoist theory of *hua-hu*, the Conversion of the Barbarians, according to which Lao-tzu had, after his disappearance westwards, travelled to India, converted its 'barbarian' inhabitants and become known as the Buddha. This was no more than a Taoist defence mechanism—why become a Buddhist when one could equally well approach the doctrine in its original Chinese form—but it basically backfired by obscuring the distinctions between the two systems. Why not be a Buddhist if Buddhism was just as Chinese as Taoism? It was in fact not until the end of the Han dynasty (220) that Buddhism began to gain, in Chinese eyes, a semblance of independence from Taoism.

Certain doubts concerning the innate superiority of Chinese culture assailed the populace after the fall of the Han which was the beginning of a period of chaos that only really ended with the accession of the short-lived Sui dynasty in 589.

In the south, the Eastern Chin dynasty (265–420) maintained the Chinese heritage they had inherited from the Han, but with a lot less self-confidence, given the loss of the northern heartlands and its traditional culture. There had been no sectarian developments as such during the Han period, but by Eastern Chin times there was a considerable polarisation between those Buddhists stressing the aforementioned Hīnayāna meditational and ritual practices, and those putting emphasis on by now better understood theories and practices based on the *Prajñāpāramitā-sūtras* dealing with the concept of *śūnyatā* (emptiness) and its identity with *rūpa* (form). The latter slowly came to dominate Chinese Buddhist thought in the fourth century, and also became an object of interest to Philosophical Taoists who admired the similarity to Lao-tzu's idea of the material world originating in Non-being. Such concerns naturally led to the frequent use of Taoist terminology to express Buddhist concepts in translation, a method known as *ke yi* or 'matching the meaning'; this disappeared after the authoritative translations of Kumārajīva came into vogue in the fifth century. The Chin court was also affected by Buddhism to no small degree. Courtiers and emperors alike became devoted lay followers, while monks vied with each other for imperial favours. A further development was the establishment by Tao-an (312–85) of a cult for the worship of Maitreya, the future Buddha currently residing in the Tushita Heaven in which devotees could be reborn. In turn Tao-an's chief disciple Hui-yüan (344–416) is credited with the establishment in 402 of the Pure Land (Ching-t'u) school dedicated to the worship of Amitābha, the Buddha symbolising the process of transformation (indicated by the element fire) and discriminative wisdom who is said to be the presiding Buddha of the Western Pure Land, a paradise where the *dharmakāya* (Truth Body) of supreme enlightenment can manifest itself in perfected, non-human form. This early version of the Pure Land school was not noted for the missionary zeal that characterised its later variants, and was in fact highly intellectual in its approach. Hui-yüan's best-known and most controversial disciple, Tao-sheng (*c.* 360–434), categorically stated that such Pure Lands did not exist as such, given that the Buddha-nature existed and could be realised within each individual's consciousness. Tao-sheng was also committed to the idea, later characteristic of Ch'an (Zen), that enlightenment was a sudden experience attained without any gradual progression. Either one is enlightened or one is not.

The course of Buddhism ran very differently in northern areas of China under a succession of non-Chinese dynasties. Acceptance was far easier simply because such dynasties naturally gravitated towards a religious system they considered civilised and yet, like them, 'barbarian'—the very reason why the acceptance of Buddhism by the Chinese themselves was often such a slow process.

In the north, various Altaic and Tibetan groups held power, initially amidst ceaseless fighting, for varying lengths of time over areas of varying size. Their leaders came to value the advice, both social and military, and the magical prowess of the Buddhist monks in their domains, and provided a degree of institutionalised support previously unknown. The most notable Central Asian monk to make the later Ch'in capital Ch'ang-an his home was Kumārajīva (344–413), known mainly as the translator of most of the fundamental texts which became so important in later periods. His pioneering translations of the Madhyamaka (Middle Way) classics of Nāgārjuna (second century) led to the establishment of the San-lun or Three Treatise School which provided a forum for much discussion on 'relativity' (the emptiness of phenomena in view of their dependent origination). Further afield in the kingdom of Pei-liang the fourth century saw the rise of Tun-huang, originally a cave-temple complex at the junction of the main caravan routes from Central Asia which attracted numerous monks especially at times of political and social upheaval. Tun-huang retained its importance for about a thousand years up to the end of the Sung period (1126), and is of particular value because of the remarkably well-preserved Buddhist murals on the cave walls. This era also saw the first of many Chinese pilgrims starting on the long journey to India in search of the original textual sources for their religion.

The Turkic rulers of the Northern Wei (386–535) initially encouraged Buddhism in their extensive northern domains, but soon afterwards the machinations of two of the Emperor Wu's (424–51) ministers, a Taoist, K'ou Ch'ien-chih, and a Confucian, Ts'ui Hao, led to a series of restrictions on the religion which culminated in an anti-Buddhist persecution initiated in 446. The motive for this persecution was quite simply the desire on the part of the nation's rulers to Sinicise their 'barbarian' subjects by eradicating their 'barbarian' religion. The fact that the religion happened to be Buddhism was irrelevant.

The normalisation of attitudes which followed Wu's death and the renewed patronage of the nation's leaders led to the development of two primarily economic institutions unique to Northern Wei Buddhism—the Sangha and Buddha Households. The former consisted of groups of agricultural families who were required to pay a certain amount of grain per year to the local monastic office which stored it ready for immediate distribution in times of famine. The latter were groups of criminals who would be usefully employed performing various household duties for their monasteries as well as cultivating monastic lands. Buddhism under the Northern Wei went from strength to strength, especially after the transfer of the capital to Lo-yang which could soon rejoice in a plethora of the most magnificent temples and pagodas yet seen in China. For the first time too there is evidence that Buddhism managed to exert a strong influence on the lives of ordinary people rather than just on court circles. Academic work on Buddhist topics and newly translated texts also proceeded apace during this era, much of it laying the foundation for the later sectarian developments in the T'ang era (618–907).

In the south a series of short-lived native dynasties followed the fall of the Eastern Chin in 420 during what is known as the Nan-Pei Ch'ao (Northern and Southern Dynasties) period (420–589). Imperial encouragement of Buddhism continued, occasionally reaching new heights as during the reign of the Liang Dynasty's founder, the Emperor Wu (502–49), who seems to have considered himself a Chinese version of the famed Indian Buddhist ruler Aśoka. During this period, one of the most studied treatises was the *Satyasiddhiśāstra* (Treatise on the Completion of Truth) of Harivarman (third century), essentially a Hīnayāna treatise putting forward a reductionist view of emptiness (i.e. the view that objects partake of the nature of emptiness since emptiness is the end result after the object has been reduced to ever smaller component parts), an idea that was successfully criticised by the San-lun school on the grounds that emptiness is inherent in objects of all scales by virtue of their interdependence. This era also saw the introduction of the 'idealist' works of the brothers Asaṅga and Vasubandhu (fourth century), founders of the Indian Yogācāra school expounding the idea that it is the mind (not, however, regarded as a single entity) which is responsible for the nature or character (*tathatā*, literally, the 'thusness') of all phenomena which are as a result objectively unreal. The translator of most of these works into Chinese was the Indian monk Paramārtha (arrived in China in 546), also known by his Chinese name Chen-ti.

Opposition to Buddhism in the south, both Taoist and Confucian inspired, remained at a crudely nationalistic but verbal level. Buddhist–Taoist debate revolving around the question of which religion enjoyed historical primacy was prevalent throughout the sixth century, resulting in large numbers of forged texts emanating from both camps. In the north, after initial successes, the fortunes of Buddhism waned yet again under the Emperor Wu (561–77) of the non-Chinese Northern Chou (557–81) who, like his Northern Wei namesake, seems to have been anxious to ensure the Sinicisation of his state by suppressing Buddhism. The full-scale suppression decided upon by the emperor, involving the forcible secularisation of all monks and the destruction of temples, statues and scriptures, came in the years 574–7. Surprisingly enough the decree was extended to cover Taoism, primarily because of the emperor's acceptance of the various arguments against the native religion put forward by the Buddhists in earlier acrimonious debates between the two religions. Wu's successor repealed the decree, and a few years later both the Northern Chou and the (Southern) Ch'en Dynasties disappeared as Yang Chien reunified the country in 581, establishing the Sui Dynasty (581–618).

Considerable encouragement was given to Buddhism during the few years of Sui rule. Buddhism was looked upon as a national ideology, capable of unifying the populations of the north and south in a more effective way than Taoism could, doctrinally fragmented and uncentralised as it was. The Japanese in particular took the Sui attitude of imperial patronage and bureaucratised support very much to heart during their concurrent importation of Buddhism.

Initially the T'ang Dynasty (618–907), though officially Taoist, espoused a policy of tolerance towards all religions found in the land, primarily as T'ang control extended over large areas of Central Asia inhabited by adherents of Islam, Manichaeism and Nestorian Christianity who in time came to form sizeable minorities in major towns. Buddhism had by this time been an established religion in China for long enough for it to adopt specifically Chinese forms at both ends of the social spectrum. Laymen of all classes intoned the name of Amitābha and happily took part in the mass Buddhist festivals which were such a characteristic of the T'ang. Monks provided instruction in basic Buddhist practices for the populace often through the mediums of drama, story-telling and painting, and also set up charitable organisations to assist the poor, ill and dying. One practice much in vogue was that of *fang-sheng* or the release of living creatures about to be killed for food.

Although most of the Buddhist schools which flourished during the T'ang originated far earlier, hardly any can in any real sense be traced back to pre-existent Indian schools. Sectarian distinctions in China were based primarily on the degree of reliance placed upon specific *sūtras* and Indian commentaries, though, typically, stress laid upon one particular *sūtra* by one school did not preclude the study and appreciation of other texts, even of those uniquely favoured by philosophical opponents. The use of the term 'school' rather than 'sect' reflects more clearly the type of relationship that existed between philosophically opposed groups.

The T'ien-t'ai school, the doctrines of which were first promulgated by Hui-wen (*fl.* 550), Hui-ssu (515–77) and Chih-i (538–97), rose to prominence primarily because it attempted to provide a clear and logically consistent systematisation of the vast corpus of Buddhist doctrine, thereby explaining the philosophical discrepancies which had so troubled earlier Chinese Buddhists. The T'ien-t'ai classification was primarily chronological, relating particular *sūtras* to specific periods in the Buddha's life and providing an underlying justification by referring to the pan-Mahāyānist idea of *fang-pien* or 'skilful means' which stated that the Buddha had provided mankind with a vast range of texts and ideas, sometimes contradictory, to enable each person to find the system meeting his or her own requirements and agreeing with each person's pre-existent philosophical stance. The Buddha, finding that the *Avataṃsakasūtra* (Flower Garland Sūtra), given shortly after his enlightenment, was too profound for most, decided upon a graded system of teachings which culminated in the *Saddharmapuṇḍarīkasūtra* (True Dharma Lotus Sūtra, usually just known as the *Lotus Sūtra*). Though a lot of T'ien-t'ai commentarial literature deals exclusively with the *Lotus Sūtra*, the school managed to provide a place for every text, whether Hīnayāna or Mahāyāna, within its all-encompassing system. Indeed, philosophically, a great deal of T'ien-t'ai thought, notably the stress on totality, the mutual interpenetration of all phenomena and the identification of the whole with its parts, is based on the *Flower Garland Sūtra*. As an independent school the T'ien-t'ai in China did not outlive the Hui-ch'ang persecution of 845.

The Hua-yen (*Avataṃsaka* or Flower Garland) school was, as the name implies, based more exclusively on the *Flower Garland Sūtra*, and stressed the relationship between the underlying universal principle or *li* ('noumenon') and phenomena or *shih*, unlike T'ien-t'ai which tended to concentrate on the interrelationship of the phenomena of the universe with each other. Tu-shun (557–640) is regarded as the founder of this uniquely Sino-Japanese school which eventually disappeared from China after the disastrous persecution of 845. The cosmological ideas of the Hua-yen school have attracted increasing interest in recent times in view of their similarity to certain modern concepts in the field of physics. The holistic view outlined above, coupled with concepts such as the emergence of the phenomena of the physical universe from emptiness ('self-creation') may at one time have been considered both naïve and unrealistic, but the whole system has managed to stand the test of time more successfully than many other ancient philosophical systems, both Oriental and Western.

A school of less prominence was the Fa-hsiang (Characteristics of the *Dharma*) school, based on the works of Asaṅga and Vasubandhu introduced during the Liang dynasty (sixth century CE). The school's concern with the analysis of phenomena was matched by its concern with the mechanisms of consciousness and the multiple mind. The five sense consciousnesses are complemented by a mental consciousness which sorts the sense data and provides conceptions for the volitional mind to select from, deal with and analyse. The volitional mind also looks inwards into the (subconscious) store-consciousness wherein all thoughts and karmic effects are automatically stored without discrimination, thereby providing a mechanism for the operation of *karma*.

The main ideas of *Tantra* have been mentioned elsewhere; suffice it to say that an independent Tantric (Chen-yen or *mantra*) school existed in China for a short period, imported by three Indian worthies, Śubhakarasiṃha (Shan-wu-wei, arrived in China in 716), Vajrabodhi (Chin-kang-chih, arrived in China in 720) and Amoghavajra (Pu-k'ung chin-kang, ?–774). Confucian orthodoxy was bound to object to the sexual practices encouraged by certain kinds of Tantrism, and the school as a result disappeared totally after 845.

Several less important schools are also of interest. The San-chieh (Three Periods) school, founded by Hsin-hsing (540–94) during the Sui era had as its main tenet the idea, found in many other schools, that the Buddha's doctrine passes through three historical stages, each stage lasting 500 or 1,000 years (opinions differed). During the first stage, the true doctrine exists in unaltered form. The second stage sees the appearance of a 'counterfeit' doctrine merely approximating to the original. During the third stage, the doctrine begins to decay and disappear. As an aside, it is surely praiseworthy that Buddhism in most of its forms remained faithful to its fundamental theory of impermanence by including itself amongst all phenomena subject to this law, thereby avoiding the historically wrong-headed insistence found so consistently in other religious systems that no process of decay or dissolution could possibly affect the expression of their own eternal truths. The San-chieh school firmly held that the third stage was already at hand, and its resultant pessimism led to a dissatisfaction with all traditional methods of reaching enlightenment. However, regarding the age as corrupt and the populace and authorities of the time as inferior to those of earlier eras hardly endeared the school to the imperial authorities, and resulted in the school's proscription in 713, with what little remained of it disappearing in 845.

The Lü (*Vinaya* or Disciplinary) school, also known as the Nan-shan (Southern Mountain) school was founded by Tao-hsüan (596–667) and was, as its name indicates, concerned almost exclusively with the clarification and exegesis of monastic rules, primarily of those of Hīnayāna origin. Never enjoying a wide following, it ceased to exist as an independent school in 845.

The Chu-she (*Kośa* or treasury) school was in effect founded by Paramārtha with his translation of Vasubandhu's *Abhidharmakośa* (Treasury of the *Abhidharma*), an essentially Hīnayāna treatise. The school essentially maintained that the basic phenomena or *dharmas* of the universe, both physical and mental, actually existed, with only the objects constructed from these *dharmas* being subject to the law of impermanence. By the eighth century the school had for obvious reasons merged into the related Fa-hsiang school, only to perish along with it in 845.

Though many of the T'ang emperors actively encouraged Buddhism, at certain times attempts were made to ensure the prominence of Taoism and to subject Buddhism to various controls. These measures were often advantageous to Buddhism itself—the defrocking of careerist monks and the limits put on monastic wealth enabled the religion to maintain the adherence of its Chinese followers. The atmosphere of relative tolerance came to a sudden end in the 840s and culminated in the well-known persecution initiated by the Emperor Wu-tsung in 845. The persecution was Taoist-inspired, although undoubtedly other factors, primarily economic, played a part in influencing the emperor. Strict controls were introduced in 843 to limit the authority not merely of Buddhism but of Manichaeism as well. In 844 all minor temples were closed or destroyed and all unregistered monks along with all monks under the age of 50 were ordered to return to lay life. In 845, all temples and monasteries, with one exception per prefecture, were destroyed and all temple and monastic wealth confiscated by the state. Happily, no effort was made to exterminate systematically the practitioners of Buddhism, though localised abuses undoubtedly occurred. Wu-tsung died in 846 (probably as a consequence, it should be said, of excessive consumption of Taoist elixirs of immortality) and his successor, Hsuan-tsung, re-established the principle of tolerance characteristic of the early T'ang.

The monastic community had, however, been fundamentally damaged by the events of 845 and did not manage to recover. More ritualistic and scholastic schools were unable to survive without their monasteries and scriptures, especially as their organisational continuity and financial base had disappeared. The only two schools to survive the destruction of the Buddhist infrastructure were Pure Land and Ch'an (Zen)—Pure Land because it was, and still remains, essentially a popular devotional form of Buddhism, and Ch'an because of its anti-intellectual and contemplative emphasis, as well as its clear conscience in face of the charges of economic parasitism levelled against other schools.

The beliefs of Pure Land Buddhism—and the word 'beliefs' is used deliberately—are in the main quite simple and are mostly derived from the *Sukhāvatīvyūha-sūtras* (Pure Land *Sūtras*) originally researched in the early fifth century by Hui-yüan. As mentioned earlier, the Pure Land is presided over by the Buddha Amitābha; invoking his name results in the believer's rebirth from a lotus bud in the paradise from where progression to a state of enlightenment is far easier. Emphasis is thus uniquely placed on reliance on an external deity—a feature almost without parallel in Buddhism, but one which enabled the religion to spread to the proverbially illiterate peasant, as well as to those from all social classes who quite simply had neither the time nor the inclination to meditate for the many years required for attaining enlightenment in more self-reliant systems.

The word *ch'an* is the Chinese equivalent of the Sanskrit term *dhyāna* ('contemplation'), and is sufficient indication of where the Ch'an school places its emphasis. The origins of this school are traditionally traced back to the Indian master Bodhidharma who, after arriving in the Northern Wei kingdom in 520, reportedly sat in contemplation for nine years facing a wall, impervious to the imprecations of his eager disciple-to-be, Shen-kuang, who at last resorted to cutting off his own arm in order to prove his earnest desire for the doctrine, but was rewarded by becoming the second patriarch of Ch'an after his master's death. When in the seventh century Ch'an started to enjoy some degree of popular support, a question arose concerning the legitimacy of the claim of Shen-hsiu (600–706) to be the sixth patriarch of Ch'an. The resultant acrimonious debate led to the division of Ch'an into Northern and Southern Schools, and the disappearance of the former when the primacy of the Southern School's candidate, Hui-neng (638–713), was established. The entire disgraceful episode, of much greater complexity than may be apparent from the above sketch, clearly shows that Ch'an, despite its claims to the contrary, was just as prone to worldly involvement as any of the other more ritualistic schools.

The anti-intellectualism of Ch'an, smacking of Philosophical Taoism, stemmed from the belief that since enlightenment was a state obviously beyond common experience it was also beyond rationalisation. Any rational planned activity (including devotion, *sūtra* recitation, and indeed structured meditation) is therefore useless—in fact, worse than useless since it hinders the ability of the mind to function in a purely natural, unconstrained and spontaneous manner. When it does so function, it is possible for the individual to achieve an awareness of underlying reality, an experience known as *wu* (*satori*, the Japanese term, is perhaps better known), usually translated as 'enlightenment'. It is at least possible to wonder whether the Ch'an experience of sudden enlightenment is quite the same thing as the experience of *nirvāṇa* achieved using more conventional graded methods.

The main techniques employed by the Lin-chi (in Japanese, Rinzai) branch of Ch'an are well known. The master will try various methods—beating and shouting seem to be popular—to jolt the disciple out of the rut of his conventional modes of thinking; alternatively, the master will provide the disciple with a *kung-an* (in Japanese, *kōan*), a paradox of sorts, the answer to which once again necessitates recourse to something other than normal intellectual ways of tackling a problem. Ch'an activities and dialogues can seem peculiar:

> When Shih-lin Ho-shang saw the Layman P'ang coming, he raised up his whisk and said: 'without falling into Tan-hsia's activities, try saying something.'
> The Layman snatched away the whisk and held up his own fist.
> 'That is precisely Tan hsia's activity,' said Shih-lin.
> 'Try not falling into it for me,' returned the Layman.
> 'Tan-hsia caught dumbness; Mr P'ang caught deafness,' rejoined Shih-lin.
> 'Exactly,' said the Layman.
> (The Recorded Sayings of Layman P'ang, pp. 68–9.)

The Ts'ao-tung (in Japanese, Sōtō) branch of Ch'an is far more conventional, relying on graded instruction, reasoned logical argument and seated meditation for attaining the 'truth beyond words'.

After the fall of the T'ang, the country was once again unified under the Sung in 960. Pure Land and Ch'an struggled on much as before, though the country was in dire financial straits. Military and domestic expenditure was inordinately high, and one government fund-raising scheme, that of selling monk certificates (a system introduced under the T'ang in 747), contributed to the decline of the remaining monastic community. A monk was exempt from the taxation and corvée which was such a burden on the average citizen, and hence a monk certificate, apart from being an absolute necessity for every monk, was a desirable commodity for many others. The Sung bureaucracy obviously felt that the advantage of such a ready source of income outweighed the disadvantages of a monastic community full of unqualified monks only nominally Buddhist. Furthermore the Buddhism of the Sung, dominated as it was by Ch'an and Pure Land anti-intellectualism, was in no fit state to counter the arguments of neo-Confucianism, the major intellectual movement of the era which spent much of its time objecting to Buddhism's other-worldly and unfilial concerns. Concurrently, Buddhism was disappearing in India, thereby bringing to an end centuries of fruitful contact between the two countries.

The Mongol Liao Dynasty (907–1125) which controlled much of north China, Mongolia and Manchuria encouraged Chinese forms of Buddhism in its domains, as did the later Manchu Chin (Jurchen) Dynasty (1115–1234). The Mongol Yüan Dynasty (1206–1368), while itself espousing Lamaism, did not discourage specifically Chinese forms of Buddhism in its empire, although during the initial stages of the Mongol conquest of

China, the material damage to the remaining temples and monasteries was considerable. A special relationship developed between the Mongol administration and the Lin-chi subschool of Ch'an after the monk Hai-yün (1201–56) was appointed religious advisor to the khanate. At the imperially arranged debates between Taoists and Buddhists during the mid-Yüan period, Ch'an masters were also asked to put forward the Buddhist view alongside Tibetan lamas. In China itself, politically motivated Buddhist societies flourished, whilst Buddhist intellectual life continued to deteriorate.

The Chinese Ming Dynasty (1368–1662), the founder of which played on the soteriological hopes of the populace awaiting the arrival of the Buddha Maitreya by linking the new dynasty to the concept, initially promoted the activities of the two surviving schools. A Taoist–Buddhist system of granting merit/demerit points for specific charitable and uncharitable acts was much in vogue; at this time, also, attempts were made to show that Buddhism and Confucianism were philosophically compatible. Efforts were likewise made to syncretise Ch'an and Pure Land and to spread the end result amongst the laity. The success of the lay movements of this period led for the first time to a situation in which the leadership of Buddhism in China started passing from monastic to lay hands.

Chinese Buddhism under the pro-Lamaist Ch'ing (1662–1911) was just as inactive as it had been under the Ming, suffering yet another major blow during the pro-Christian and disastrously iconoclastic T'ai-p'ing (Great Peace) rebellion. The rebels as a matter of policy destroyed all Buddhist temples, libraries and works of art in areas under their temporary control; so thorough was the destruction that a large percentage of Buddhist canonical and commentarial literature had to be reintroduced from Japan and privately reprinted and distributed. The names of Yang Jen-shan and Wang Hung-yüan should be mentioned in connection with this re-introduction; it has been reported of the former that he was responsible, almost single-handedly, for the redistribution of approximately one million Buddhist treatises throughout China.

The Republic of China, established in 1911, barely tolerated Buddhism in its efforts to 'modernise' the country, whilst the spread of Marxism caused even more concern to the beleaguered Buddhist community. Although the monk T'ai-hsü (1889–1947) tried to counter such ominous developments with a comprehensive programme of reforms designed to make Buddhism more palatable to the country's new rulers, the age-old religion, barely recovered from the battering it received at the hands of the T'ai-p'ing rebels, charged with social and economic parasitism as well as philosophical wrong-headedness, finally succumbed to Maoism. It remains to be seen if it can survive this latest assault.

Further Reading

Bary, W.T. *et al.* (eds.) *Sources of Chinese Tradition* (Columbia University Press, New York, 1960)
Chang, G.C.C. *The Buddhist Teaching of Totality—The Philosophy of Hwa-Yen Buddhism* (Allen and Unwin, London, 1972)
Ch'en, K.S. *Buddhism in China—a Historical Survey* (Princeton University Press, New Jersey, 1964)
Welch, H. *The Practice of Chinese Buddhism 1900–1950* (Harvard University Press, Cambridge, Mass., 1967)
—— *The Buddhist Revival in China* (Harvard University Press, Cambridge, Mass., 1968)
Wright, A.F. *Buddhism in Chinese History* (Stanford University Press, California, 1959)
Yang, C.K. *Religion in Chinese Society* (University of California Press, Berkeley, 1961) a study of contemporary social functions of religion and some of their historical factors
Zürcher, E. *The Buddhist Conquest of China* (Leiden, 1959)

11 Buddhism in Japan

Bulcsu Siklós

The images of traditional Japan that spring to mind are almost all Buddhist inspired. Shintō, it is true, has its part to play, but the quiescence of the Tea Ceremony, the artistry of the swordsman or flower arranger, the skill of the Nō actor or the haiku poet all have their basis in Buddhist or more precisely Zen practice. These images, so unlike the ones connected with Buddhism elsewhere in Asia, would also lead one to believe that Japanese Buddhism is somehow more Japanese than it is Buddhist, that it has been altered more than any other type. There is perhaps some validity in this view but, even though the Japanese initially adopted Buddhism as an aspect of Chinese culture rather than as an independent religion, in its fullest expression it remains as canonical and hence as Indian as any other type.

Probably in the year 552, the king of the Korean kingdom of Paekche, hard pressed by the expansionist desires of the two neighbouring kingdoms of Koguryō and Silla, decided to send a bronze image of the Buddha, accompanied by several volumes of scriptures in Chinese as well as a letter highlighting the beneficial effects of Buddhism, to the Japanese court. This hardly had much of an effect; in short it was presumably the loss of the Japanese outpost of Mimana on the Korean coast that led to a certain degree of realisation concerning the political, economic and indeed cultural backwardness of Japan when compared to the continent, and which rapidly led to a desire for all that their great neighbour China could offer. Resistance to Buddhism during this initial period was considerable, the traditionalists objecting to the worship of the Buddha on the grounds that it would offend the native deities who would (and, let it be said, did) respond by causing various epidemics and droughts throughout the land.

The responsibility for promoting the new religion fell to Prince Umayado, better known as Shōtoku Taishi (Crown Prince

Shōtoku, 572–622), son of the Empress Suiko (593–628), whom Japanese Buddhists generally regard as the founder of their religion. Doubtless Buddhism would have made little headway without imperial support from the earliest times; support which was generously provided since it enabled the court to present a unified front replete with continental sophistication to the traditionalists of the Mononobe and Nakatomi clans desperately trying to maintain the status quo. The doctrine was no longer proffered by Paekche but was imported by the Japanese court itself directly from the north Korean kingdom of Korai which maintained close contacts with the Chinese Sui dynasty.

The Buddhism of this period was of course non-sectarian and hardly considered inimical to the Japanese spirit as its native practitioners took due care in keeping to the required Shintō observances. Indeed Buddhism was thought of merely as a superior form of magic, its superiority obvious in view of its architectural, artistic and ritual complexity—certainly a provincial noble on his first visit to the imperial capital would have been left in no doubt as to the deficiencies of the autochthonous faith. This said, the commentaries attributed to Prince Shōtoku suggest that at least some Japanese in this early period felt attracted to Buddhism because of its philosophical subtlety and vast range of meditative techniques, although such appreciation was limited to those with a good knowledge of Chinese since no Buddhist text had yet been translated into Japanese.

The first permanent capital at Nara, established in 710, rapidly became the nucleus from which Buddhism spread to the rest of the country. The forty-fifth emperor, Shōmu (701–56, reigned 724–49), ordered the construction of two Provincial Temples (*kokubunji*) in each province, one for monks (*kokubunsōji*) and the other for nuns (*kokubunniji*) who were required to perform observances to ensure the continuity of the state and successful harvests. The *kokubunji* were regarded as branches of the Tōdaiji in Nara, founded in 745, the central hall of which is even today the largest wooden building in the world, housing an immense bronze statue of the Buddha Vairocana (in Japanese, Dainichi nyorai or Biroshana), extremely popular because of the belief that the Shinto solar deity Amaterasu was no more than a local manifestation of this Buddhist divinity.

During this period, six separate schools of Buddhism managed to establish themselves at Nara, all of them equivalents of contemporary Chinese schools. Prior to the Nara period, the year 625 had seen the official establishment of two schools, the Jōjitsu (Chinese, Ch'eng-shih) school based on Harivarman's Hīnayāna treatise, the *Satyasiddhiśāstra* (Treatise on the Completion of Truth) much studied in China during the Liang Dynasty, and the Sanron (Chinese, San-lun or Madhyamaka) school. The Hossō (Fa-hsiang or Characteristics of the *Dharma*) school was introduced in 654, followed by the Kusha (Chinese, Chu-she or Treasury) school in 658. The eighth century saw the introduction of the Kegon (Chinese, Hua-yen or Flower Garland) school and the Ritsu (Chinese, Lü or Disciplinary) school.

As one might expect, corruption was rife in the Nara monasteries; unlike in China there was no Confucian bureaucracy imbued with anti-Buddhist sentiment ready to expose the most glaring abuses of monastic privilege. It was partly to escape the crowds of sycophantic monks that the Emperor Kanmu (782–805) decided to transfer his capital from Nara to Heian (present-day Kyōto) in 794 after a ten-year unsuccessful relocation to Nagaoka.

The Heian period (794–1185) saw the introduction of the Tendai (Chinese, T'ien-t'ai) and Shingon (Chinese, Chen-yen or Tantric) sects, with the word 'sect' being rather more appropriate here than 'school', as we shall see. The eclectic and universal approach of the former enabled it to gain rapid support soon after its official introduction by the Nara monk Saichō (Dengyō Daishi, 767–822), who had been sent to China by the Emperor Kanmu expressly for the purpose of finding the most suitable branch of Buddhism to propagate in the new capital. Saichō's initially close relationship with the importer of Shingon, Kūkai (Kōbō Daishi, 744–835) led to Tendai assuming certain distinctly tantric characteristics, further emphasised by Ennin (Jikaku Daishi, 794–864), absent in the parent form, while the eclecticism of Tendai in time spawned the Lotus Sūtra-based (and uniquely Japanese) Nichiren sect.

A dispute in 993 over the succession to the abbotship of the main Tendai monastery, the Enryakuji on Mount Hiei, led to the establishment of an alternative branch of Tendai at the Miidera in Ōtsu. This was no mere scholarly dispute; in time both monasteries came to maintain large numbers of 'warrior monks' (*sōhei*, also appropriately known as *akusō* or 'bad monks'), little more than mercenaries in priestly garb. The practice grew quickly, with most major monasteries realising the advantage of having a force of no mean military capability under their control which could—and frequently did—attack, loot and reduce to ashes the monasteries of opposing sects. In times of governmental instability successful attacks could also be launched on the imperial capital itself, if a particular claim, usually material, needed pressing.

The main Shingon monastery on Mount Kōya, tranquilly located further from the capital near Ōsaka, was less prone to indulgence in such activities. The sect's political influence was accordingly smaller, but its religious influence was considerable, and not merely on philosophically similar sects such as Tendai. In fact, no post-Nara sect is entirely free of Shingon influence, given that Kūkai's short two-year stay in China resulted in an inevitable simplification of tantric ritual (for example, Shingon recognises only two main *maṇḍalas*, both presided over by Vairocana—one can compare this to the Lamaist situation with literally hundreds of *maṇḍalas* and a far larger range of presiding deities). For other sects there was thus no great difficulty in adapting esoteric ideas to their own needs.

A short-lived and little-known twelfth-century sub-sect of Shingon, the Tachikawa, is of interest as numbered amongst its practices were activities such as ritualised sexual intercourse. One might think that this indicates that the Indo-Tibetan Highest Yoga Tantras (the *Anuttarayogatantras*), replete with sexual symbolism and methods for sublimating sexual energies, had secretly found their way to Japan, but it seems that Tachikawa sexual ritual was based on Taoist practices involving the unification of the male *yang* (in Japanese, *yō*) and female *yin* (in Japanese, *in*) principles.

The confusion, corruption and strife reigning at the end of the Heian period (eleventh to twelfth centuries) led to an outbreak of religious pessimism and an explanation in terms of the Buddhist concept of *mappō* (the End of the Doctrine) or *mappōji* (the Period of the End of the Doctrine), the last and most degenerate of the three eras into which Buddhists often divide the history of their religion after Śākyamuni (see for example the San-chieh school of sixth-century China). Certain Tendai monks felt that the time had come to begin the active proselytisation of the cowed and illiterate populace and for the emergence of a broad-based, popular form of Buddhism worlds apart from the scholasticism, elaborate ritual and political intrigues of the established sects. Drawing on the experiences of Chinese Pure Land proselytisers, the main method popularised was the *nenbutsu* (recitation of the Buddha Amitābha's name) with the aim being rebirth in the Pure Land (*jōdo*). It took a while for these beliefs and practices to form the basis for a new sect *sensu stricto*, though even prior to the Kamakura period (1185–1333) when the capital was relocated to Kamakura by the first shogunal family, the Minamoto, certain individuals had widely and exclusively recommended the *nenbutsu*. The itinerant preacher Kūya (903–72) taught the invocation through the medium of popular songs, while the less unorthodox Chingai (1091–1152) saw it as an adjunct to standard Shingon practice (in other words, he still felt that meditation was of prime importance), though he encouraged simple recitation if there was no viable alternative given the circumstances of the practitioner.

The unwitting founder proper of Japanese Pure Land Buddhism was Hōnen (Genkū, 1133–1212). His dissatisfaction with Buddhism as it then was, along with a wide reading of the works of his visionary precursor Genshin (Eshin sōzu, 942–1017) enabled him to come to the conclusion that the only worthwhile practice was the *nenbutsu* itself (meditation, always the corner-stone of Buddhist practice was, to him, pointless). His emphasis on *tariki* ('other power'), the power of Amitābha (in Japanese, Amida) to save, and his abandonment of another key concept, that of *jiriki* ('self-power' or 'self-reliance') brought him perilously close to monotheism and left him open to the various charges that were levelled against him by the other sects. For example, a petition presented in 1205 to the Retired Emperor Go-Toba asked for the movement to be halted on the grounds that it 1. was not an imperially recognised sect, 2. used uncanonical images which showed monks of other sects failing to reach illumination whilst even criminals were represented as illumined if they recited the *nenbutsu* correctly, 3. ignored Śākyamuni, 4. condemned practices other than the *nenbutsu* wholesale, 5. rejected the Shintō gods, 6. condemned practices other than the *nenbutsu* which did actually lead to the Pure Land, 7. used the *nenbutsu* without the accompanying meditation, 8. rejected the codes of monastic discipline and 9. was a threat to stable government due to its popular base. The Pure Land sect in time showed itself to be, quite clearly, guilty on all counts.

Hōnen was no intellectual match for individuals like Kūkai or Saichō, yet he comes across as a far more reasonable—and indeed Buddhist—personage than his chief disciple Shinran (1173–1262), for whom one sincere invocation was enough to ensure rebirth in the Pure Land. The Pure Land sub-sect he founded, the Jōdo Shinshū (True Pure Land Sect, often known simply as the Shinshū or 'True Sect') abolished monasticism totally, permitted the marriage of its priests (thereby establishing a blood succession to the patriarchy) and became, perhaps predictably, increasingly militant. The eighth True Pure Land patriarch Rennyo (1415–99) did much to encourage intolerance and fanaticism amongst his followers, often disaffected peasants who, in the utterly chaotic political situation of the sixteenth century, frequently rebelled against local feudal lords or took to attacking the monasteries of other sects. When one of the most powerful of these *daimyō*, Oda Nobunaga (1534–82) attempted the military reunification of the country the armies and temples of the True Pure Land were obvious targets for annihilation.

A marginally more sophisticated and contemplative form of Pure Land Buddhism, the Ji ('Time') sect, founded by Ippen (1239–89), was also influential from the mid-fourteenth to the early sixteenth centuries, before losing much of its support to the True Pure Land. The tenets of the Ji sect betray Shingon influence; for example, the *nenbutsu* is regarded as complementary to visualisation with the end result being the identification of the practitioner with the physical form (and thus the mental state, so to speak) of Amitābha himself.

Zen (Chinese, Ch'an) ideas and methods were introduced into Japan in the seventh century by the Hossō monk Dōshō (638–700) as part of Hossō practice, and certain Chinese masters, notably Tao-hsüan (in Japanese, Dōsen, 596–667) visited the country to discuss Ch'an ideas with representatives of the Nara sects. The Tendai founder Saichō was instructed in Zen by a disciple of Tao-hsüan and was apparently impressed enough to include the techniques of this particular Chinese form of Buddhism among the wide-ranging practices of his new sect. Just as in the case of Pure Land, however, it was not until the Kamakura period (1185–1333) that Zen managed to establish itself as an independent sect.

The Rinzai (Chinese, Lin-ch'i) sub-sect of Zen was formally introduced into the country by the (originally) Tendai monk Eisai (Zenkō kokushi, 1141–1215) after his return from China in 1191. Initial opposition from the Tendai sect disappeared once the Shōgun Minamoto Yoriie (1182–1204) gave his approval and protection to Rinzai Zen. He also requested that Eisai found a new monastery (the Jūfukuji) in the shōgunal capital Kamakura, thereby initiating a fruitful and long-lasting relationship between Zen and the increasingly important military class (the *samurai*).

The Sōtō (Ts'ao-tung) sub-sect of Zen was introduced by the (once again) Tendai monk Dōgen (Buppō zenji/Shōyō daishi, 1200–53) after his study trip to the continent lasting from 1223–7. Eisai, under whom Dogen reportedly studied for a short period, had always been willing to compromise with the other sects (it is even reported that he regularly performed Shingon rites), but Dōgen on the other hand was so convinced of the superiority of his *zazen* ('seated Zen') techniques that he felt no need to encourage any other practice and further expressed particular hostility to the *kōan* (Chinese, *k'ung-an*) method of Rinzai Zen. The Sōtō *kōan* is something entirely different. Dōgen simply defined the term *genjō kōan* ('manifestation and achievement of *kōan*') as if it were a synonym for the ultimate present reality, the *dharmakāya* (principle or 'body' of truth). Just as the bird flies in the air without being concerned with or understanding the air, so the practitioner should act naturally and limit himself to existing in the present without worrying about the ultimate. The present moment or in other words the practitioner's present state is itself the ultimate and is therefore the basis of enlightenment. Dōgen also avoided such Rinzai concepts as the *busshō* or 'Buddha Nature' to make his disciples realise that there was of course no actual abiding permanent essence to be sought out within one's mind. The Buddha Nature is simply impermanence.

The wholesale adoption of Zen by the warrior class, a process initiated and promoted by Musō Soseki (Musō kokushi, 1275–1351), spiritual mentor of several shōguns and emperors, led to a widespread secularisation of Rinzai methods. The harmony of nature in miniature was expressed in landscape and rock gardening, the plastic equivalents of monochrome ink painting (*sumie*) and calligraphy, all of which were objects of contemplation for the practitioner. The *samurai* applied Zen to the martial arts and were responsible for the popularisation of the Tea Ceremony (tea itself had been reintroduced to Japan from China by Eisai). Literature also adopted specifically Zen forms. Haiku poetry attempted to capture the simplicity and harmony of the rock garden or ink painting in a mere seventeen syllables, with the best of these poems often being used as objects of contemplation much on the lines of the Rinzai *kōan*. Probably the most original Zen-inspired cultural innovation of the Muromachi period

(1336–1598) was the Nō drama. Nō developed from the *sarugaku* ('monkey music') of early feudal times into a highly stylised and unremittingly gloomy form of drama in which the actors wore elaborate costumes and masks and chanted their lines to the accompaniment of music on a bare stage.

Zen was to the *samurai* all that Pure Land was to the peasant. Each inspired new forms of art and literature, each provided a behavioural code moulded to the needs of its practitioners and each became thereby more purely Japanese.

The last major Japanese Buddhist sect to develop, the Nichiren sect, is also the only one with no continental equivalent whatsoever and further is probably the only Buddhist school or sect anywhere to take its name from its founder. Nichiren (1222–82), a man of humble origins (as he himself always stressed), initially studied Pure Land doctrines at a small provincial Tendai temple until some unknown traumatic event (legend states it was the sight of his Pure Land master dying in agony) turned him against Pure Land and brought on his almost insane hatred for Hōnen. This, along with his increasing admiration for the Lotus Sūtra, led to his pilgrimage in 1242 to Mount Hiei where he hoped to find 'true' Buddhism, true according to the criteria he devised. Any sect based not upon a canonical text but on an independent Indian treatise was ruled out as a repository of 'true' Buddhism—primarily the Sanron, Hossō, Kusha and Jōjitsu. Further, Zen was ruled out on account of its claim to have a separate transmission outside the scriptures. Pure Land was dismissed on personal grounds, while Kegon and Shingon he considered inferior to Tendai which he eventually chose as the nearest approximation to his ideal. According to Nichiren, it was the abandonment of the Lotus Sūtra (the final expression of the Buddha's teaching in the Tendai view) by the Japanese nation which had led to the state of political chaos, to the increasing Mongol threat and to the ruination of the imperial family following the exile of the Emperor Go-Toba (1180–1239) after his unsuccessful attempt to reassert imperial supremacy.

Nichiren's feelings about the other sects are neatly summed up in his *Essentials of the Honmon Sect* (*Honmon-shūyōsho*):

> The followers of *nenbutsu* will fall into the lowest hell,
> Followers of Zen are devils,
> Shingon destroys the nation,
> The Ritsu are national enemies
> And Tendai is an outdated calendar.

According to Nichiren, only by relying on the Lotus Sūtra can equal emphasis be laid upon each of the *sanshin* or Three Bodies (Sanskrit, *trikāya*) of the Buddha. The *hosshin* (Sanskrit, *dharmakāya*), the 'body' or state of ultimate reality manifests itself as, or rather is symbolised by Vairocana, the central object of worship in Shingon; the *hōjin* (Sanskrit, *sambhogakāya*), the 'Enjoyment Body', the 'body' or state enjoyed by an enlightened being in higher realms (e.g. the Pure Land) manifests as (among others) the Buddha Amitābha, stressed as we have seen to the exclusion of everything else by the Pure Land sects, and finally the *ōshin* (Sanskrit, *nirmāṇakāya*), the 'Emanation Body', the intrusion of the *dharmakāya* into our realm has as its prime example the historical Buddha, much revered in Zen.

The method advocated by Nichiren to reach the state of Buddhahood was the *daimoku* ('Great Title'—the title of the Lotus Sūtra) recitation in the form *namu myōhō renge kyō* ('homage to the wondrous Lotus Sūtra'). This is less banal than it may at first sound, since title exegesis, on the premiss that the title of a canonical text should in itself be a summary of the text itself, had long been a concern of most of the Chinese schools of Buddhism, given that the range of meaning of the individual characters making up the title could be so large. Hence according to Nichiren the absolute manifests itself as the five-character title (*myōhō* meaning 'wondrous', descriptive of the absolute; *renge* meaning 'lotus', signifying the universal law of cause and effect; and *kyō* or '*sūtra*' signifying the text's origin from the *nirmāṇakāya*, Śākyamuni), while the subject (i.e. the practitioner) is present in the initial homage (*namu*).

Nichiren's initial preaching activities hardly endeared him to the government or indeed to any of the other sects. His total intolerance led to the promulgation of views so extreme that they are almost without parallel in the Buddhist world. Just as an example, Nichiren seriously proposed on several occasions the physical eradication of his Buddhist opponents. Quite simply he did not consider the killing of Pure Land followers a sin.

With the breakdown in law and order particularly in the fifteenth century, Nichiren followers, perhaps predictably, also took up arms with as much enthusiasm as the followers of Pure Land. These *hokke ikki* (Lotus Rebellions) were especially frequent during the period 1532–6, when Nichiren armies dominated Kyōto until their annihilation by a huge force from Mount Hiei.

To the outside observer, the Nichiren sect seemed a well-disciplined, unified organisation but it was in fact far more prone to internal dissension than the Pure Land sects. Disagreements mainly centred around the question of exactly how tolerant the sect should be—less tolerant groups led by purists such as Nichijū (1314–92), Nichijin (1339–1419) and Nisshin (1407–88) adopted the principle of *fuju-fuse* ('no giving and no receiving', in other words, no compromise whatsoever with anyone not a member of the sect) which gradually came to provide the name for a new sub-sect led by Nichiō (1565–1630). The Fuju-fuse sect became an object of persecution during the Tokugawa period (1600–1867), remaining officially prohibited until 1876.

The popular view often portrays the six Nara schools along with Tendai and Shingon as having nothing more than reactionary and corrupt roles during the Kamakura and Muromachi periods; yet all of them responded, sometimes successfully, sometimes not, to the new developments of Pure Land, Zen and Nichiren by introducing old practices to the population at large. To counter the worship of Amitābha, the worship of Shaka (Sanskrit, Śākyamuni) was encouraged; likewise the worship of Miroku (Sanskrit, Maitreya, the coming Buddha), of Monjushiri (Sanskrit, Mañjuśrī, the Bodhisattva of wisdom), of Kannon (Sanskrit, Avalokiteśvara, Bodhisattva of compassion) and of Jizō (Sanskrit, Kṣitigarbha, the Bodhisattva of the earth, regarded as the protector of children). In the intellectual and doctrinal field, efforts were made to combine Sanron (Madhyamaka) concepts with those of Shingon, notably by Myōhen (1142–1224), resulting in the disappearance of the Sanron as an independent school. A lot of work was also done on the monastic code (the *Vinaya*) to counter its wholesale rejection by the popular sects, while the esoteric sects, Shingon and Tendai, continued to flourish, the latter especially maintaining its political and military influence.

In 1600 the Tokugawa family managed to establish unified effective military rule over all Japan, and followed this by moving the capital to Edo (present-day Tōkyō). The first Tokugawa shōgun, Ieyasu (1603–10), was totally determined to ensure that Tokugawa rule could endure unopposed into the foreseeable future, and as a result decided to limit contact with the outside world, and especially with Christianity which was regarded as a social menace. Christianity was stamped out with military thoroughness by Ieyasu's successors Hidetada (1616–23) and Iemitsu (1623–51), much use being made of the ingenious *fumie* ('treading picture'), usually a brass plaque with a representation of Christ engraved on it which the suspected Christian was required to defile by stepping on it. Refusal usually meant a slow death.

The Tokugawa government was of course fully aware of the divisive and rebellious nature of certain Buddhist sects, but since the military effectiveness of these sects had been severely curtailed by the weapon confiscation programme of Ieyasu's predecessor Toyotomi Hideyoshi (1536–98), it decided that a system of temple registration along with the encouragement of learning was sufficient to maintain discipline and governmental control. The Tokugawa themselves were members of the Pure Land sect, so this sect flourished; the other sects kept themselves busy by rebuilding and refurbishing temples and monasteries damaged in the preceding era. Certain shōguns were in fact noted for their religious enthusiasm, the best-known of whom is the fifth shogun Tsunayoshi (1680–1709) who, amongst other things, issued various Buddhist-inspired edicts protecting animals in general and dogs in particular. His conception of Buddhist morality was perhaps unusual; on one occasion he had a man executed for injuring a dog.

The new-found peace and prosperity of the Tokugawa period was welcome, but in the long run the price Buddhism paid for the advantage of political stability was stagnation.

Zen was the exception, mainly as a result of the activities of Hakuin (1685–1768), a man perhaps more mindful of canonical literature than the Rinzai ideal demanded. Hakuin was particularly concerned with revitalising the *kōan* but his fame also extends into the fields of calligraphy and poetry. The Huang-po (in Japanese, Ōbaku) branch of Chinese Zen also entered the country with the arrival of the Chinese priests Yin-yüan (in Japanese, Ingen, 1592–1673) and Mu-an (in Japanese, Mokuan, d. 1684) and was much respected by the Tokugawa authorities.

Confucianism and Shintō were both much studied during the later Tokugawa period with most men of letters expressing a strong nationalistic interest in the latter. Buddhism's close association with the shogunate as well as its general deterioration left it in a vulnerable position when imperial power was restored and the country opened up to the West at the beginning of the Meiji period (1868–1912). Shintō was established as the state religion in 1870 under the name of *daikyō* ('Great Religion'), and the Shintō-inspired and fortunately short-lived *haibutsu kishaku* ('destroy the Buddhas and discard the scriptures') movement was initiated, resulting in considerable material destruction to Buddhist temples and monasteries and in the secularisation of many priests. An interest amongst the Japanese in all things modern and Western further resulted in an interest in Christianity, another threat to the Buddhist establishment.

Various sects sent representatives to Europe and America to study the methods and organisation of Christianity and also to study new developments in Western thought. Soon after, however, once the constitution of 1889 had assured Buddhism's equality with all other religions found in the land, there was a certain degree of Buddhist-inspired realignment between Buddhism, Shintō and Confucianism against Christianity.

In modern times, at a popular level dissatisfaction with Buddhism became widespread and resulted in the proliferation of 'new religions' drawing their often carelessly formulated ideas from Buddhism, Christianity and Shintō. Three of the better known new religions are recognisable as vaguely Buddhist: the Reiyūkai ('Society of Friendship with Souls'), based on simple morality and the Confucian concept of filial piety; the Risshō kōseikai ('Society for the Establishment of Correct and Friendly Relations') founded in 1938 and concerned with repentance; and last but by no means least the somewhat cultish and intolerant Sōka gakkai ('Value-Creating Study Group') which claims that happiness is dependent on 'profit', goodness and beauty, the three of which can only be understood through detailed study, recitation of the *daimoku* (the title of the *Lotus Sūtra*) and the donation of large sums of money to the organisation.

Further Reading

Eliot, C. *Japanese Buddhism* (Routledge & Kegan Paul, London, 1935)
Matsunaga, D. and A. *Foundation of Japanese Buddhism*, I–II (Los Angeles–Tokyo, 1974–76)
Sansom, G.B. *Japan—a Short Cultural History* (New York, 1943)
Saunders, E.D. *Buddhism in Japan with an Outline of its Origins in India* (University of Pennsylvania Press, Philadelphia, 1964)
Suzuki, D.T. *Essays in Zen Buddhism*, First Series (1927), Second Series (1933), Third Series (1934), London
Takakusu, J. *The Essentials of Buddhist Philosophy* (University of Hawaii Press, Honolulu, 1947)
Tsunoda, R. *et al.* (eds.) *Sources of Japanese Tradition* (University of Columbia Press, New York, 1958)

12 The Religions of Tibet

Tadeusz Skorupski

Tibetan Buddhism or Lamaism

Historical Perspectives

It was in the seventh century CE that Tibet emerged as a formidable military and political entity on to the world scene. The same century also witnessed the formal introduction of Buddhism and the beginning of historical records. Our knowledge about religious beliefs and historical events in Tibet prior to the seventh century remains very limited and it is derived mainly from legendary and quasi-historical accounts. The earliest literary sources suggest that the Tibetan Plateau was first occupied by semi-nomadic groups of people who in the course of time formed into rival factions. These factions were led by chieftains who established their headquarters in fortified strongholds in the major valleys of the central and eastern tributaries of the Tsangpo River (i.e. Brahmaputra). To the north of those valleys a nomadic pattern of life seems to have persisted up to modern times. The darkness of legends began to yield to apparently more historical accounts when some of those local chiefs joined together to recognise the chief who controlled the Yarlung Valley as their leader. This valley is situated to the south of Lhasa which later became the main city in Tibet.

It was the confederacy led by the chief of Yarlung that became the nucleus of Tibet as a country. He was known by the title of Pugyal Tsangpo (sPu-rgyal btsan-po) and his kingdom became known as Pugyal-Bod. The exact meaning of the word 'bod' (? 'native land') is not easily discernible but it has become the name applied by Tibetans to their own country ever since. We possess several versions of a legendary account, first recorded in the fourteenth century, which describes how the first king descended on the sacred mountain of Yarla Shampo (Yar-lha sham-po) in Yarlung. He was greeted by people who according to different accounts are said to have been sages, chieftains or simply shepherds. Since he descended from the sky, they resolved to make him their king. The first king, Nyatri Tsanpo (gNya'-khri btsan-po or, in Tun-huang documents, Nyag-khri) and his successors were considered to have been endowed with a distinct sacral quality, and they were referred to by such titles as 'Divine Mighty One' (Lha-btsan-po) or 'Divine Son' (Lha-sras). They were supposed to have descended from the highest point of heaven by way of a 'sky-cord' (dmu-thag) which passed through the various intermediate levels between the sky and the earth. As they were of divine origin they did not die but at the end of their earthly sojourn they returned to the sky by means of the same 'sky-cord' without leaving behind any mortal remains.

In the sixth generation of the first king's family, during the reign of the king called Drigum (Dri-gum, 'Slain by Pollution' or Gri-gum, 'Slain by Sword'), there took place the change to the normal mortality of the kings. Endowed with immortality and magical powers, Drigum became arrogant and proud, and constantly challenged his entourage to fight with him. Finally, one man called Lo-ngam consented to confront the self-confident king on the condition that the king would not make use of his magical weapons. On the agreed day, the king's opponent attached spear-points to the horns of one hundred oxen and loaded their backs with sacks of ashes. As the oxen became annoyed and struggled together the bags with ashes burst open and the ash-dust clouded the air. Amid the general confusion and poor visibility the king was killed; or in another version he cut his 'sky-cord' and was compelled to remain on earth. From that time onwards the kings left their mortal remains on earth and were duly entombed in the royal burial grounds at Chonggye ('Phyong-rgyas) in the Yarlung Valley.

According to the Buddhist tradition, it was during the reign of the twenty-eighth king, Lhatho Thori (Lha-tho-tho-ri) that a sacred object in the form of a *stūpa* and a Buddhist text were lowered from the sky and deposited on the top of the king's palace; but at that time no one was able to discern the symbolism of the sacred object or to read the text.

The thirty-second king, Namri Lontshan (gNam-ri slon-mtshan), who ruled at the time of the Sui Dynasty (581–618), is the first Tibetan ruler to be referred to by name in Chinese records. When Namri was assassinated (*c.* 627) his young son Srongtsan Gampo (Srong-btsan sgam-po, 627–50) succeeded to the throne. It is with this famous king that Tibet sets foot on the firm ground of history. Srongtsan Gampo initiated a period of military aggression and expansion that continued till the ninth century. A rapid and successful conquest of immediate neighbouring lands such as Zhang-zhung to the north-west and other parts of the vast territories to the north, east and south, brought the Tibetan military troops into contact with various principalities of Central Asia, China and India. Srongtsan Gampo married several noble ladies, of whom one was a Chinese princess (Wen

Ch'eng) and one a Nepalese princess (Bhṛkutī). These two princesses are given much credit by the Buddhist tradition for bringing Buddhist images with them and for supporting the propagation of the new religion. It was for their benefit that the king erected Buddhist temples in Lhasa: the Jokhang and the Ramoche.

There exists a popular legend among the Tibetan people which informs us that the Tibetan race originated from the copulation of a monkey and an ogress. The later Buddhist tradition made use of this legend to demonstrate that it was a predestined plan that the Tibetans were converted to Buddhism. The Bodhisattva Avalokiteśvara, who is regarded as the patron of Tibet, decided in the remote past to convert the 'Land of Snows' (i.e. Tibet) to the Buddha's doctrine. Assuming the form of a monkey he went to meditate in solitude on a mountain summit. He was duly induced to copulate with a rock-demoness and from their union were born the ancestors of the Tibetan people; during the course of their evolution their monkeyish tails shrivelled and the hair of their bodies disappeared.

It was during the reign of Srongtsan Gampo that the time finally came to convert Tibet. The king himself is regarded as an emanation of Avalokiteśvara, and his Chinese and Nepalese consorts as emanations of Tārā in her white and red manifestations. Buddhist temples were erected at different places geomantically determined so as to peg down the demoness prostrate on her back beneath the whole expanse of the Tibetan land. The symbolic implication of this operation indicates the beneficial impact and civilising force of the newly introduced religion. The pinned-down demoness was seen in some respects as Tibet itself, whose ancestral inhabitants were described as red-faced demons, flesh-eaters and blood-drinkers. It is alleged that at death the king and his two wives were absorbed into the statue of Avalokiteśvara installed in Jokhang, the main cathedral at Lhasa which became one of the holiest places of worship and pilgrimage. Srongtsan Gampo is credited with the promulgation of a code of civil laws, some religious instructions and a prophecy about the permanent establishment of Buddhism in Tibet in later generations.

Although the pious Buddhist tradition in Tibet looks upon Srongtsan Gampo as the greatest king and champion of Buddhism, more critical scholarship does not attribute many religious activities to him. It is, however, agreed that Buddhism was introduced or recognised formally at this time, although on a rather limited and moderate scale. A few temples were certainly built and Buddhism was allowed to put down its initial roots as a recognised religion amidst the strong indigenous religious beliefs and practices. There is no evidence in contemporary sources to suggest that the king became a convert. On the contrary, there are strong and convincing indications that he remained faithful to his ancestral religion which cherished the cult of the kings as divine beings. He was buried in the traditional manner in the Yarlung Valley in an elaborate ceremony which included the ancient rituals of animal and probably human sacrifice. The true motives for introducing or rather recognising Buddhism seem to have been, in the first instance, the acquisition of cultural and educational elements from the neighbouring and more sophisticated civilisations in order to develop and govern the country with efficiency. It was during the reign of Srongtsan Gampo that the Tibetan script is said to have been invented by Thonmi Sambhota on the pattern of the contemporary Indian Gupta script.

It was during the reign of the fifth monarch after Srongtsan Gampo that Buddhism appeared in official records. The king, Trisong Detsen (Khri-srong lde-brtsan, 740–*c.* 798), considered as the second 'Religious King' and an emanation of Mañjuśrī, was inclined favourably towards Buddhism which he sponsored and defended against the indigenous priests and the ministers at the royal court who supported them. After a period of internal intrigues and bitter struggles within the royal court, the king and the supporters of Buddhism emerged victorious over opponents who represented the interests of the ancient beliefs and practices.

Trisong Detsen invited to Tibet the Indian *paṇḍita* Śāntarakṣita, who inspired the construction of the first Buddhist monastery in which Tibetans were trained and ordained as monks. The monastery which was built at Samye (bSam-yas) is said to have been modelled on the renowned Buddhist monastic university of Odantapuri in northern India. The Buddhist tradition suggests that opposition from the indigenous religious factions and the local deities still persisted, causing obstructions and evil omens. Padmasambhava, a great tantric master and magician from Oḍḍiyāna, was therefore invited to confront and convert the powerful local deities. These two masters, Śāntarakṣita and Padmasambhava, represented two different forms of Buddhist practices. While Śāntarakṣita taught the conventional monastic and scholastic theories and practices based on the *Vinaya* and the Sūtras, Padmasambhava was a tantric master and a *siddha*, who specialised in mystical and ritual exercises, and the magical coercion of demoniac powers. These two forms of Buddhism permeated each other and have constituted ever since a characteristic feature of Tibetan Buddhism. Padmasambhava encountered innumerable difficulties but overcame them by means of his magical abilities and brought to submission various demoniac powers, forcing them to swear an oath to become the protectors of the new religion. Over the years Buddhism in Tibet has succeeded in the elimination of various indigenous practices, such as animal and human sacrifice. It did not eradicate the local deities but rather absorbed and accommodated them within the already well-populated pantheon brought from India by placing them among the lesser or mundane deities (*laukika*) as sworn-in protectors (*dam-can*).

Trisong Detsen and his court took an oath to protect and to support the Buddhist religion. Members of the ever-increasing monkhood, mostly those from noble families, received important state positions.

The monastery of Samye was exempted from tax and given material support. The monks were outside civil legislation and were granted immunity from bodily punishment.

It seems quite certain that the initial Buddhist inspiration did not come exclusively from India, as the later Buddhist tradition in Tibet suggests, but also came in considerable force from Central Asia and from China. The somewhat contrasting teachings brought from India and China led to a formal debate held at Samye under the patronage of the king. The debate was to produce a conclusive decision as to whether Indian or Chinese practices and teachings should be followed. The Indian group was led by Kamalaśīla, a disciple of Śāntarakṣita, who was invited on the recommendation of his master. The Indian party argued in favour of the conventional Mahāyāna which propounded the theory of the gradual progress of a *bodhisattva* towards the final attainment of Buddhahood. According to this teaching, it is necessary to accumulate vast quantities of both knowledge and merit during the course of innumerable world-ages in order to succeed in one's progress towards Buddhahood. Such a method was seen as being beneficial not only to oneself but also to all living beings. In general terms it was a doctrine that favoured the conventional pattern of philosophical pursuits and moral training that required the stability of monastic life and the practice of morality. The Chinese party led by Hwa-shang, an adept of Ch'an (Zen in Japanese) Buddhism, assumed the position that the absolute nature of Buddhahood can be realised by anyone who was able to acquire, and to abide in, a state of complete equanimity. Conventional morality and philosophical speculations were seen as unnecessary or even harmful because they could impede one's pure contemplation of emptiness (*śūnyatā*). After a period of two years the final verdict was passed in favour of the Indian party. Hwa-shang and his companions were expelled from Tibet and their scriptures were eliminated. However, according to the sources found at Tun-huang, it was the Chinese party that won the argument. The acceptance of the Indian form of Buddhism may well have been motivated by political reasons, for we know that Tibet and China were in constant military struggle.

In the reign of the seventh king, Ralpachen (Ral-pa-can, 815–38), who is also remembered as the third 'Religious King', intense efforts were made to produce a systematic translation of Buddhist scriptures into Tibetan. A number of trained Tibetans who worked side by side with Indian scholars translated many canonical works and philosophical treatises from Sanskrit and from other languages in which the scriptures were recorded. The system of translation was standardised and a Sanskrit–Tibetan dictionary of technical terms, called *Mahāvyutpatti*, was compiled to aid the translators in using the same Tibetan equivalents for the Sanskrit terms. Unfortunately for Buddhism, Ralpachen, who had sponsored the work of translating Buddhist scriptures generously, and had subsidised the building of religious establishments, was assassinated by his older brother Langdarma (gLang-dar-ma, 838–42) who was opposed to Buddhism and supported the indigenous beliefs and practices. The Buddhist tradition looks upon this king as the epitome of an anti-Buddhist ruler. During his short rule the monastic establishments are said to have been damaged and the monks were unfrocked, killed or exiled. Langdarma himself was finally assassinated by a Buddhist monk. It was with him that a glorious period of Tibetan history ended. The claimants to the throne fought each other, political unity collapsed and the great Tibetan empire disintegrated within a short period of time. The whole period of Buddhist history in Tibet from the time of Srongtsan Gampo to Langdarma is generally known as the 'First Diffusion of the Doctrine'.

The next period of Buddhist history in Tibet is known as the 'Second Diffusion of the Doctrine'. After a period of over one hundred years of being eclipsed and limited to isolated communities, Buddhism received a new and decisive impetus for revival in the territories to the west of central Tibet. The defeated and exiled descendants of the royal dynasty established the three kingdoms of Maryul (sMar-yul), Guge (Gu-ge) and Purang (sPu-hrang) in the vast lands of west Tibet. One of the rulers of west Tibet is particularly renowned for his zealous and ardent propagation of Buddhism. He was Yesheö (Ye-shes-'od), the king of Purang who sent a group of young men to Kashmir and India to study and to bring back Buddhist scriptures and teachers. One of the young men sent abroad was the famous Rinchen Zangpo (Rin-chen bzang-po, 958–1055). Having spent seventeen years in Kashmir and India, he made himself competent in the monastic discipline (*Vinaya*) and the Mahāyāna doctrines. After returning he translated many Buddhist works and re-established monastic discipline and the monastic life. He is also credited with the foundation of many monasteries and temples throughout the whole of west Tibet, two of which, Tabo in Spiti and Toling in Purang, still survive. Through the activities of Rinchen Zangpo and his collaborators Buddhism grew quickly and expanded through the whole of west Tibet.

Another inspiring stimulus resulted from the invitation to Tibet of Atiśa from India. Atiśa (982–1054) was one of the most prominent teachers of his time. He was well-versed in the conventional Mahāyāna and in the Tantras. During his sojourn in Tibet he conferred tantric initiations on Rinchen Zangpo and on his own followers, including his chief Tibetan disciple Dromten ('Brom-ston, 1008–64). Although Atiśa taught the Tantras, he also stressed the need for a life according to the monastic discipline. Thus he introduced, along the lines of the great monastic centres of learning in India, a well-balanced situation in which tantric studies and practices were pursued within monasteries whose members were obliged also to observe the monastic discipline according to the *Vinaya*. Atiśa propagated the cult of Avalokiteśvara and Tārā, stressed the importance of the conventional Buddhist morality and the pursual of the gradual path as represented by a *bodhisattva*'s career. It is under Atiśa's inspiration that there developed the general pattern of Tibetan Buddhism that was practised within the monastic context.

The revival of Buddhism in the eastern parts of Tibet is epitomised by the activities of three men who left the central parts of the country and escaped to the east during the persecution that started with Langdarma. It is said that they carried with them the *Vinaya* books. In due course a number of men from central Tibet came to them and were ordained as monks. The newly ordained monks returned to their native localities or dispersed throughout the country and established monastic centres.

During the period between the tenth and the thirteenth centuries many Tibetans travelled to India in search of Buddhist scriptures and spiritual masters. After returning to Tibet many of them lived as solitary or wandering *yogins*; some of them dedicated their time to translating Buddhist texts and only a few established monastic orders. By the beginning of the fifteenth century all the major religious orders of Tibetan Buddhism were established, four of which survived and played a dominant role in the religious life of Tibet till its loss of independence in 1959. As the monastic establishments grew in number and became populated by large groups of monks, the different heads of the religious orders acquired more and more political power and eventually control over the country. By the seventeenth century the descendants of the royal family and different princes who attempted to gain control over Tibet were defeated or eliminated.

The major religious orders developed simultaneously, each order following a particular tradition while accepting in principle the totality of the Buddhist heritage brought from India. The followers of Atiśa became known as Kadampas (bKa'-gdams-pa, 'Bound by Command'). Dromten, Atiśa's chief disciple, founded the monastery of Reting (Rva-sgreng) in 1056, which became the main centre of this order. It followed a strict monastic discipline, observing in particular the rules of celibacy, abstention from intoxicants and from the possession of worldly wealth. Great stress was placed on receiving a direct instruction from one's teacher. It is said that when Dromten once asked Atiśa which was more important, the scriptural text or the teacher, Atiśa replied that personal instructions received from the teacher were more important. Such an attitude was to guard against false teachers and to preserve the continuity of the lineage of teachers and their oral instructions; it also became a feature of other religious orders and traditions. The Kadampas led a rather secluded pattern of life, passing their time in study and meditation. Their main teachings and practices aimed in the first instance to achieve the purification of the mind (blo-sbyong), and then to produce the realisation of moral and esoteric aspirations. The adepts were trained to understand the nature of their own minds and to achieve spiritual maturation as represented by the highest levels of emptiness (*śūnyatā*) and compassion (*karuṇā*). The concept of enlightenment as viewed from the point of absolute truth was equated with emptiness, and considered from the viewpoint of conventional or relative truth, was seen as compassion; emptiness represented the 'Body of Essence' and compassion the 'Body of Form'. The Kadampa order played a crucial role in Tibetan Buddhism because of its insistence on and practice of the *Vinaya*. By the fifteenth century this order had declined to some extent and was later transformed, or rather absorbed, into a new religious order founded by Tsongkapa.

Drogmi ('Brog-mi, 992–1072) was the founder of the Sakyapa (Sa-skya-pa) order. He travelled to India and spent some eight years at the monastic university of Vikramaśīla where he studied the *Vinaya* and the *Prajñāpāramitā* texts. He pursued the study of the Tantras under the guidance of Śāntipa and Virūpa who were renowned as *siddhas*. He received initiation into a number of Tantras, among them into the *Hevajra Tantra*, which he translated into Tibetan and which became the chief tantric text for the Sakyapas. On his return to Tibet, he founded the monastery of Myugulung (Myu-gu-lung) in 1043. His disciple Konchog Gyalpo (dKon-mchog rgyal-po) founded the monastery at Sakya (Sa-skya) in 1073. It was this monastery that gave its name to the whole monastic order. Konchog Gyalpo was a member of the powerful 'Khon clan and it was this family that produced the successive abbots or chief lamas (bla-ma) of Sakya who have continued as the heads of this order until the present time. The succession of abbots within the family was established on the uncle-to-nephew pattern. While the abbot remained celibate, his brothers or close relatives continued the family line and controlled the monastery's worldly affairs. When the abbot died, he was succeeded by one of his nephews. The Sakya monastery, strategically positioned and lying on a trade route to Nepal, flourished and became powerful within a very short period of time.

The apex of Sakya political power was reached in the thirteenth century. The Mongol ruler, Godan, attempting to gain some control in Tibet, summoned the Sakya abbot to his court in 1244. The abbot expressed a formal submission of Tibet to the Mongol khan and in return he was appointed as the regent of Tibet. The next Sakya abbot, Phagpa ('Phags-pa, 1235–80), won the confidence and favour of Kublai Khan, the Emperor of China. Phagpa was appointed as viceregent of Tibet and personal chaplain to the Emperor. The monasteries in Tibet received exemption from taxation and various other privileges. It was at that stage that Tibet became subject to a single political head for the first time since the collapse of the monarchy in the ninth century. Phagpa developed a 'priest-and-patron' relationship with the Emperor. The abbot provided spiritual instruction and the Emperor gave his powerful support to the Buddhist religion. In the fourteenth century the Sakya power in Tibet dwindled away with the decline of the Mongol dynasty in China.

During the thirteenth century a new school branched off from the Sakya order. It became known as the Jonangpa school after the monastery of Jomonang founded by Thugje Tsongdru (Thugs-rje brtson-'grus). The philosophical teachings of this school were considered by many Buddhist masters as unorthodox and extremist. It was opposed with great vigour by the Fifth Dalai Lama. The Jonangpa possessions and monasteries were taken over by the Gelugpas and their writings became prohibited.

Marpa (Mar-pa, 1012–96) is considered retrospectively as the founder of the Kagyupa (bKa'-brgyud-pa) order. At the outset of his religious career Marpa became a disciple of Drogmi from whom he learned Sanskrit. He made three journeys to India, where he studied for sixteen years. While in northern India, he became a disciple of Nāropa from whom he received the teachings known as the Six Doctrines of Nāropa (Nāro chos drug). He also studied with Maitripa from whom he received the transmission of the meditational practices known as *Mahāmudrā*. On returning to Tibet he settled in his native land, Lhobrag, and led what appeared to ordinary people to be the life of a married householder, taking care of his fields and possessions. To those who became his intimate followers, Marpa was known as an accomplished master of tantric practices, qualified to bestow initiation into the most advanced esoteric practices. He traced back his spiritual lineage to the Indian *siddhas* and through them to Vajradhara, the personified principle of Buddhahood. He attracted a handsome group of disciples of whom Milarepa (Mi-la-ras-pa, 1052–1135) became the most famous for his saintly life and his esoteric songs. Milarepa lived an ascetic life, passing many years in solitary meditation in caves on the slopes of the Himalayas. It was to him that Marpa bequeathed the so-called 'lineage of practices' (sgrub-brgyud) that comprised the various yogic exercises brought by Marpa from India. Neither Marpa nor Milarepa were ever ordained as monks. They represented a type of yogic and tantric practice which was different from Atiśa's teachings and practices taught within the monastic context. They represented the esoteric practices that were pursued along the pattern of the Indian *siddha* tradition. They introduced a new genre of religious literature to Tibet and a type of religious poetry that combined the Indian *dohā* tradition and their own spontaneous contributions that reflected their spiritual feelings.

Milarepa had many disciples to whom he imparted his spiritual heritage. One disciple played a crucial role in the formation of this tradition into an organised religious order. He was Gampopa (sGam-po-pa, 1079–1153) of Dvagspo. During his youth, prior to joining Milarepa, Gampopa studied medicine (hence his nickname the 'Doctor of Dvagspo') but at the age of twenty when his wife died suddenly, he turned his thoughts towards religion. He entered the Kadampa order and received monastic ordination. Later on he became Milarepa's disciple. It was through his efforts and writings that he was able to formulate a unified tradition which combined the teachings and practices inherited from Milarepa with the monastic discipline acquired from the Kadampas. He reinterpreted the *Mahāmudrā* teachings in order to adjust them to the monastic life. Thus the whole yogic tradition brought by Marpa became organised into a religious order. It was Gampopa who became the real founder of the Marpa Kagyupa school. All the Kagyupa schools collectively became known as the Dvagspo Kagyupa because of the reforms introduced by Gampopa. Gampopa passed on the monastery that he founded to his nephew, Dvagspo Gomtshul (sGom-tshul or Tshul-khrims snying-po, 1116–69). The Dvagspo Kagyupa proper was identified with Gampopa's monastery and lineage. The founders of the four major branches (che-bzhi) of the Dvagspo Kagyupa were disciples of Gampopa or of his nephew Gomtshul.

The Tshalpa Kagyupa branch was established by Gomtshul's disciple Zhang Yudrak (Zhang-g.yu-brag-pa brtson-'grus 'grags-pa, 1123–93) who founded the monastery of Tshal Gungthang ('Tshal-gung-thang). This branch reached its peak during the early Yuan period in China when the Tshal Gungthang monastery became the centre of an influential myriarchy. Its strong political position was lost when one of its myriarchs opposed Tai-situ Changchub Gyaltsan (Byang-chub rgyal-mtshan). The discovery by Dungtsho Repa (Dung-mtsho ras-pa shes-rab rgyal-mtshan) in 1315 of a *terma* (gter-ma, 'treasure'; see below, p. 259) text—the Sems-khrid—that apparently had been concealed by Gampopa, brought the Tshalpa branch closer to the Nyimapas.

The Kamtshang (Kam-tshang) or Karma Kagyupa branch, the leading sect of the Kagyupa order at the present time, was established by Dusum Khyenpa (Dus-gsum mkhyen-pa, 1110–93) who built the monastery of Tshurpu (mTshur-phu) in 1189 which became the head monastery. It was in this sect that the tradition of reincarnating lamas was introduced for the first time. This system of reincarnation of particular lineages of teachers or lamas was soon adopted by other religious traditions in Tibet and became one of the permanent features of Tibet's religious and political life. The Karmapa sect played a dominant role in the affairs of Tibet from the late fifteenth to the early seventeenth centuries. The sect lost its power to the Gelugpas. There are several important reincarnations that come from the Karmapa branch. They are the Gyalwa Karmapa (considered as the head of this sect), the Zhamar (Zhwa-dmar, 'Red Hat'), the Zhanag (Zhwa-nag, 'Black Hat'), the Gyaltshab, the Situ, the Pabo (dPa'-bo) and the Trebo *tulkus* (*sprul-sku*). The Karmapa sect has produced two sub-sects: Zurmang and Nedo Kagyupas, both of which developed close relations with the Nyimapas.

The third branch of the Kagyupa order became known as the Baram ('Ba'-ram) Kagyupa and was founded by Darma Wangchuk (dBang-phyug). This sect enjoyed some popularity in Khams, the eastern province of Tibet. During the later decades of the nineteenth century this branch became almost completely absorbed by the Nyimapas through the *terma* practices discovered by Chogyur Lingpa.

Gampopa's fourth disciple Phagmo Trupa Dorje Gyalpo (Phag-mo-gru rDo-rje rgyal-po, 1110–70) founded the monastery of Densathil (gDan-sa-mthil) and established a new branch which almost immediately split into eight sub-sects. The main Phagmo Trupa Kagyupa tradition became closely associated with the Densathil and Tsethang (rTse-thang) monasteries which acquired power and wealth through the patronage of the noble family of Lang (rLangs). This family soon began to provide the Densathil monastery with abbots and lay administrators on the uncle-to-nephew basis. As secular affairs gained a predominant importance over religious concerns, the Phagmo Trupa teachers became patrons rather than religious practitioners. The actual teachings transmitted to Dorje Gyalpo were put into practice by his disciples who, as already mentioned, established eight distinct sub-branches (chung-brgyad or zung-bzhi ya-brgyad), issuing from the main Phagmo Tru tradition. Some of the eight branches of this tradition are as follows. The Drigung ('Bri-gung) Kagyupa was initiated by Drigung Kyobpa Jigten Gompo ('Bri-gung skyob-pa 'jig-rten mgon-po, 1143–1217). It is one of the more interesting sub-sects because of its particular body of teachings and its political involvement in Tibetan affairs during the Chinese Yuan and Ming dynasties. It has survived till now and within its own sub-sect it has produced several further sub-sects, of which Lhapa Kagyupa became the most prominent. This sect became the main contender with the Drugpa Kagyupa for dominance in Bhutan.

Tsangpa Gyare (gTsang-pa rgya-ras ye-shes rdo-rje, 1161–1211) who founded the monasteries of Namdrug (gNam-'brug), Longdol (kLong-rdol) and Ralung (Rwa-lung) is considered to be the founder of the Drugpa Kagyupa tradition which became the predominant sect in Bhutan. Many spiritual teachings preserved by this sub-sect were passed to Tsangpa Gyare through Lingrepa (gLing-ras-pa Padma rdo-rje, 1128–88). The teachings that are considered to be the most important for the Drugpa sub-sect focus on the Ronyom Kordrug (ro-snyom skor-drug, 'One Flavour Six Cycles') which employed different practices to achieve the same goal, which is a *terma* instruction concealed by Milarepa's disciple, Rechung (Ras-chung) and rediscovered by Tsangpa Gyare. Another interesting system of spiritual precepts introduced by Tsangpa Gyare was the Tendrel (rten-'brel), an esoteric presentation and interpretation of the *pratītyasamutpāda* (Conditioned Origination). All the major monastic centres established by Tsangpa Gyare were passed on to his nephew Sangye Bonre (Sangs-rgyas dbon-ras dar-ma seng-ge, 1177–1238). The members of the Gya (rGya) family continued as the heads at Ralung until 1616, when Nawang Namgyal (Ngag-dbang mam-rgyal, 1594–1651), a reincarnation of Padma Karpo (Padma dkar-po, 1527–93), was forced by his enemies (the house of gTsang) to flee to Bhutan, thus becoming the founder of the country. The Ralung monastery, along with its affiliated establishments, was taken over by the Tsang authorities and given to Pagsam Wangpo (dPag-bsam dbang-po), Nawang Namgyal's rival for recognition as Tsangpa Gyare's and Padma Karpo's reincarnation. Prior to the dispute Ralung remained at the centre of the Bar ('Middle') Brug School. The unresolved dispute as to who was the true reincarnation of Padma Karpo led to the division of this school into the northern (Byang-'Brug) and southern (Lho-'Brug) branches of the Drugpa. The Drugpa produced several minor traditions which did not develop to the extent of gaining much recognition. The two major traditions that produced important religious works are the Todrug (sTod-'Brug) founded by Gotshangpa (rGod-tshang-pa mgon-po rdo-rje, 1189–1258), and the Medrug (sMad-'Brug) established by Lorepa (Lo-ras-pa dbang-phyug brtson-'grus, 1187–1250). Of the remaining six sub-sects established by Tsangpa Gyare's disciples it will suffice to mention here the Talung (sTag-lung) tradition initiated by Talung Thangpa (sTag-lung thang-pa bkra-shis-dpal, 1142–1210). This tradition, like the Drigung Kagyupa, became strongly influenced by the Nyimapa teachings.

The Kagyupa tradition as a whole, like all the other traditions, has produced a vast body of religious literature. The doctrinal differences between the various Kagyupa branches are not of any great significance, nor are they sources for dispute. Their differences are limited mainly to emphasising certain spiritual practices, following particular texts, and especially to preserving their own lineages. The Kagyupa order played a powerful role on the political scene. The Phagmo Trupa family subdued the political strength of the Sakya abbots and assumed the rule of Tibet. It efficiently controlled the political affairs of the country during the fourteenth and fifteenth centuries, and it retained, at least nominally, the title of the rulers until the seventeenth century. The Phagmo Trupa leaders lost their power to the Karmapa sect which in turn was superseded after a short period by the Gelugpa order.

A similar but quite distinct tradition known as the Shangpa (Shangs-pa) Kagyupa originated with Khyungpo Nalchor (Khyung-po rnal-'byor, eleventh century CE). This sect took its name from the valley in which Khyungpo founded the monastery of Zhong-zhong. Before travelling to India, Khyungpo studied the Dzogchen traditions and the *Mahāmudrā* precepts of Nirūpa. The principle teachings of this sect centre around the Six Doctrines of Nāropa (see below, p. 801). However, those teachings were received by Khyungpo not from Nāropa, as was the case with Marpa, but from the Ḍākinī Niguma, the sister of Nāropa, who received direct inspiration from the Buddha Vajradhara himself. This tradition assumed a definitive form in the fourteenth century through the activities of Barawa Gyaltshan Pelzang ('Ba-ra-ba rgyal-mtshan dpal-bzang). In later centuries it almost disappeared as a separate school but its teachings can still be found persisting among other religious traditions.

The next religious tradition in Tibet to be described

here is the Nyimapa (rNying-ma-pa) order which presents a completely different case. This order developed without any centralised leadership or systematically organised hierarchy. It avoided becoming involved in the political quarrels pursued by the other orders, and its religious centres remained small and scattered for a long time. The Nyimapa order was established as a kind of reaction to the other religious traditions that came into existence with the Second Diffusion of Buddhism in Tibet. The Nyimapas (the name means 'The Ancient Ones') claimed that their religious traditions went back to the royal period when Buddhism was first introduced to Tibet. They were in possession of the scriptures translated during the early period, especially a set of Tantras which had been translated by them before the Second Diffusion. They took the person of Padmasambhava for their archetype and founder. They soon elevated him to the status of a divine figure, a second Buddha who assumed various manifestations of which eight are recognised as principal. In theory he was considered as equal to Śākyamuni Buddha, who was seen as one of Padmasambhava's manifestations, but in practical terms he eclipsed him completely. The Nyimapas attributed to Padmasambhava and his immediate disciples all their teachings in one form or another; their doctrines stand apart from those of the other orders. The Nyimapas recognise two kinds of transmission of their doctrines and scriptures. The Kama (bka'-ma) or Oral Tradition (which is also recorded) is considered to be an uninterrupted continuation of teachings passed on from master to pupil from the time of Padmasambhava. The second form of transmission is represented by a sort of visionary or revelation-like transmission that can occur at intervals in time. This transmission can take the form of a mind-transmission (dgongs-gter) from a departed master to the visionary or a pure-vision (dag-snang). The form of transmitting teachings which is especially developed and highly valued among the Nyimapas is the tradition of the so called *termas* (gter-ma, 'treasure') or rediscovered treasures, usually in the form of texts or objects. The Nyimapas suggest that during his visit to Tibet, Padmasambhava, foreseeing the persecution of Buddhism, had hidden a number of texts in various places with the intention that they should be discovered at an auspicious and appropriate time in the future. The period of treasure-discoverers (gter-ston) began in the tenth century with Sangye Lama (Sangs-rgyas bla-ma). The most important and valuable period of the rediscovered texts evolved between the eleventh and fourteenth centuries. The tradition of rediscovering texts continued in subsequent centuries until the twentieth century and it has always remained open to new discoveries.

The systematisation of the philosophical and religious doctrines of the Nyimapas was initiated on a large scale in the fourteenth century by Longchen Rabjampa (kLong-chen rab-'byams-pa, 1308–64), who produced seven works known as 'Seven Treasures'. It was he who produced the doctrinal bases for the Dzogchen (rdzogs-chen) or 'Great

Perfection', an esoteric system of teachings and practices, whose origins are difficult to trace, and which are valued as the most important among the Nyimapas. The Dzogchen teachings were somehow traced back to Vairocana who lived in Tibet in the eighth century and who is said by the Nyimapas to have been Padmasambhava's disciple. The Nyimapas were severely attacked and criticised by other religious orders for the Dzogchen teachings, especially for possessing scriptures whose origins could not be traced back to India. This criticism applied in particular to the *terma* texts and to certain Tantras. Some more radical critics rejected those texts completely as nothing more than mere fabrications. However, objective research has shown convincingly that considerable portions of those texts contain very ancient materials. By the seventeenth century the Nyimapas succeeded in gaining respect for their tradition as a valid form of Buddhist teachings and practices. For a long period a great majority of the Nyimapas were married men, many of whom acted as 'village priests' (sngags-pa). They pursued yogic and tantric practices on which they embarked without any theoretical preparation. For them the mystical experience always remained the chief goal. In the eighteenth century a reform movement began in eastern Tibet which stressed the necessity of studying the doctrines in a systematic and scholastic manner, and also the practice of the *Vinaya*. Among the Nyimapas there are thus men who take tantric vows and receive various esoteric initiations and consecrations, and live as married men or *yogins*, and those who live in monasteries following the *Vinaya*.

In the nineteenth century a new movement arose known as Rime (ris-med) or 'ecumenical approach' which attempted to formulate a non-sectarian approach to the presentation of the Buddhist doctrines. Generally speaking, the Tibetans were always eclectic and non-aligned in many respects, especially in the sense of following renowned religious teachers rather than particular schools. But this time an attempt was made to unify all religious systems and to eliminate sectarian differences and quarrels. The broad orientation of this movement was a return to the original sources and teachings that were recognised by all schools. The participants of the Rime movement came from several orders but it was from among the Nyimapas that there came the most important personalities such as Kontrul Lodro Thaye and Khyentse Wangpo.

Whenever it refers to religious orders in general, the Tibetan religious tradition speaks of four orders: Sakyapa, Kagyupa, Nyimapa and Gelugpa. The Gelugpa (dGe-lugs-pa) order was founded as the last of the four major sects, but within a short space of time it became the most powerful in political terms. It was founded by Tsonkapa (Tsong-kha-pa, 1357–1419). In his youth Tsongkapa travelled from monastery to monastery, mainly in central Tibet, and pursued his studies with competent teachers of various schools. Being exceptionally gifted he acquired a profound knowledge of the *Vinaya*, the Mahāyāna philosophical doctrines and the teachings of the Tantras. By the age of forty he had become influential as a religious master. At the same age he entered the Kadampa monastery of Reting. His main ambition was to revive the strict monastic life which is said to have become relaxed by this time: many monks abandoned the celibate life and indulged in worldly affairs. Tsongkapa emphasised the religious ideals of strict monastic discipline, the life of celibacy and abstention from intoxicants. In his philosophical and doctrinal instructions he based himself on Atiśa, and in particular on the great Indian thinkers such as Nāgārjuna, Asaṅga and Diṅnāga. He produced a masterly exposition of Mahāyāna Buddhism in a work entitled *Lam-rim-chen-mo* or 'The Great Exposition of the Gradual Path' which was composed as a commentary on Atiśa's *Bodhipathapradīpa*. The tantric doctrines were explained in another work entitled *Ngags-rim-chen-mo* or 'The Great Exposition of the Tantra Stages'.

In 1409 Tsongkapa founded the monastery of Ganden (dGa'-ldan). Two other very important monastic centres, Drepung ('Bras-spungs, in 1416) and Sera (in 1419) were established by his disciples. Within a short time, he gained a considerable following and his school constantly expanded to receive overt support from many monks of other orders, and particularly from lay people who were tired of religious people who involved themselves in politics and worldly affairs. In 1408 he established the annual New Year religious function, called the Great Prayer, in the Jokhang at Lhasa, which was to serve as a yearly rededication of Tibetan people to Buddhism. His learning and saintly personality inspired such a distinct religious movement that the Kadampa monasteries in which his followers lived became completely absorbed and ceased to exist as a separate order. In the initial stages Tsongkapa's followers were called the New Kadampas but soon they became named as the Gelugpas or 'Those of the Virtuous Order'. The Gelugpas attempted to maintain strict monastic discipline and follow scholastic pursuits without themselves engaging, like the other orders, in political disputes. The support of political factions was often represented by aristocratic and princely descendants of the royal families. Very soon, however, they too became involved in political games. The third successor of Tsongkapa, Sonam Gyamtsho (bSod-nams rgya-mtsho, 1543–88), visited Mongolia in 1578 and conducted a series of teachings. He gained the sympathy of Altan Khan from whom he received the title of Dalai Lama. This title was applied retrospectively to his two predecessors and a reincarnation lineage was established. The political supremacy over Tibet by the Gelugpa order was assumed during the life of the Fifth Dalai Lama (1617–82) who received military assistance from Gushri Khan of the Qosot Mongols. The civil and military administration of the country became the responsibility of a regent (sde-srid) appointed by the Dalai Lama, and the khan assumed the role of a 'Religious Protector'. Later on a somewhat similar system was maintained with the Manchu emperors of China. From the Fifth Dalai Lama until 1959 when the Fourteenth Dalai Lama fled to India, the rule of Tibet remained with the Gelugpa order. The Fifth Dalai Lama bestowed the title of Panchen Lama on his teacher, the abbot of Tashilhunpo monastery (bKra-shis lhun-po). The reincarnating lamas of this lineage gained a powerful position and wealth, and they often played an active role in the political and religious life of Tibet.

Main Characteristics of Tibetan Buddhism

The numerous texts that were brought from India during the two diffusions of Buddhism were eventually translated into Tibetan and divided into two major groups: *Kanjur* (bka'-'gyur) and *Tanjur* (bsTan-'gyur). The *Kanjur* included the works which contained the 'Buddha's Word' and the *Tanjur* comprised numerous commentaries and treatises composed by Indian masters. The *Kanjur* resembles the classical *Tripiṭaka* only in a very general manner. Apart from the *Vinaya* and a number of the early *sūtras*, it contains many Mahāyāna *sūtras*, the *Prajñāpāramitā* literature, the *Ratnakūṭa* collection, the *Buddhāvataṃsaka* and the texts belonging to the four classes of the Tantras. It consists conventionally of 108 volumes. The *Tanjur* has no evident Indian prototype. It consists of 225 volumes and, apart from philosophical and exegetical texts concerned with doctrines, it contains works on medicine, crafts, iconography and the like. The *Kanjur* and *Tanjur* jointly contained more than 4,500 works of various lengths. The systematisation and classification of the canonical texts were largely done by Buston (Bu-ston Rin-chen-grub, 1290–1364). In deciding which texts should be included in the Canon, Buston took a firm position that only those works which could be related to their Indian originals should be included. Such an assumption led him to exclude from the Canon a large number of texts, particularly the tantric works translated during the earlier period. The Nyimapas who cherished those Tantras claimed that they were transmitted through a *ḍākinī* (mkha'-'gro-ma, a class of female deities) or that they were found as *termas*. The old Tantras, being rejected by the 'New Buddhist tradition' (gsar-ma-ba) were made by the Nyimapas into a collection known as the 'Old Tantras' (rNying-ma'i rgyud-'bum). Similarly they assembled their *terma* texts into several collections. While the Nyimapas recognise the authority of the *Kanjur* and *Tanjur*, their teachings and practices are based mainly on the collections of their own. Apart from these, the religious masters of all traditions in Tibet produced a bewildering number of works, individual or collective (gsung-'bum), that were concerned with various aspects of Buddhist doctrines and practices.

Tibetan Buddhism has produced a large number of original thinkers but still the Tibetans generally assume that their contribution to the doctrines is limited to classification and clarification of obscure or difficult points. Practically all the doctrines, not always with convincing proof, are referred back to Indian texts or masters. The broad and fundamental doctrines of all Tibetan schools have the same Indian foundation. They all derive their philosophical orientation from the philosophical schools of India, in particular the Mādhyamika, the Vijñānavāda, the Vaibhāṣika and the Sautrāntika. The differences between the schools are not rooted in contradicting or opposing doctrines, although disputes happened, but rather in their allegiance to particular exegetical or philosophical traditions, or again, as is the case particularly among the Nyimapas, in their attachment to textual transmissions or a body of practices. The division into sects should not have pejorative implications but should rather be seen as the result of separate religious traditions, similar to the Christian orders of the Middle Ages.

Indian Buddhism produced many teachings and practices, especially in its later stages, which could not easily be preserved as a living tradition by one religious order. All the Buddhist schools in Tibet recognise the authority of the canonical texts except for the excluded texts mentioned above. The Mūla-Sarvāstivāda *Vinaya* is the only *Vinaya* that has been translated into Tibetan and that constitutes the foundation of the monastic life of all the religious orders. The ultimate goal is the same for all adherents to Buddhism. It is deliverance (thar-pa) from *saṃsāra*'s bonds and passing into *nirvāṇa*. The notion of *nirvāṇa* and its relationship to *saṃsāra* was not firmly defined during the early period of Indian Buddhism. As the philosophical theories evolved, especially among the Mahāyāna schools, the concept of *nirvāṇa*, which had previously been conceived of as 'an escape' from *saṃsāra*, was gradually replaced by a 'positive' interpretation of an 'Absolute'. This was variously perceived as pure light or luminosity, as pure consciousness in which discursive thinking which differentiates subjects from objects does not exist, or as 'emptiness' (*śūnyatā*). However, one does not arrive at these highly advanced concepts of pure mind or consciousness, or of absolute emptiness, during the early stages of one's spiritual career. Nor does one attempt to understand them or put them into practice at this stage. The whole training begins with some more general and yet fundamental assumptions. The Buddha's *Dharma* is not something just to be accepted without reservations but above all it is to be understood, reasoned out in one's own mind, and mystically experienced. The path of liberation begins with a correct vision of the nature of things, and with appropriate conduct. This conduct will be suitable to reach the final goal which is the awakening of one's spiritual entity to the highest truth that transcends the phenomenal world of illusive appearances and dichotomic concepts. One becomes aware that all things are impermanent in the sense that all things perceived in this world and all concepts cannot be thought of as real but as being without any true nature and value. Having understood the deceptive character of all phenomenal appearances, one gains a further awareness of a state that reaches beyond transitory phenomena. In order to free oneself from the bonds of this world and to reach beyond its limits, one embarks on the path of appropriate practices.

Tibetan Buddhism follows the path of the Mahāyāna ideals. One takes a vow to attain the supreme state of Buddhahood. It is the *bodhisattva* career that one attempts to pursue. The goal is not just one's own personal deliverance but also the deliverance of all living beings. The doctrinal position of this career is defined and advocated in the *Prajñāpāramitā* scriptures. The long path towards enlightenment begins with accumulation of merit and knowledge. One must acquire moral purification and intellectual alertness in order to separate oneself from worldly impurities and to become a receptacle for the supreme enlightenment. The *bodhisattva* path is graded into ascending levels, usually conveniently divided into ten stages of spiritual progress centred around the Ten Perfections (*pāramitā*). The process of cultivating the thought of enlightenment (*bodhicitta*) is thus presented by the Mahāyāna as a long and arduous path that is pursued for two or three incalculable world-ages (*asaṃkhyeya*).

The Mahāyāna introduced some other important concepts of which the notion of the three Buddha-Bodies is one of the most important. While phenomenal existence on the level of conventional truth appears to be real, in reality it is false. Through the acquisition of an intuitive knowledge that enables one to abolish all concepts of duality and erroneous perceptions of phenomena, one approaches the level of absolute truth which, as already mentioned, can be expressed by several technical concepts. This highest truth or the quintessence of all things constitutes the nature of the supreme Buddhahood which can be conceived of as the self-abiding Buddha-Body (*svabhāvikakāya*). Such an inconceivable state may assume a threefold manifestation: Absolute Body (*dharmakāya*) which is beyond all forms and concepts; Glorified Body (*sambhogakāya*) which becomes manifested in numerous Buddhist paradises, the abodes of Buddhas and Bodhisattvas; Manifested Body (*nirmāṇakāya*) which corresponds to a Buddha manifestation in a human body. This concept of a threefold and cosmic manifestation of the supreme Buddhahood gave rise to a great variety of Buddhas described in scriptures and depicted iconographically. The same concept became a doctrinal foundation in Tibetan Buddhism for numerous lineages of reincarnating lamas. It is asserted that different Buddhas or Bodhisattvas can become manifest in different people. A particular Buddha or Bodhisattva may 'reveal' himself in one person or in several. Furthermore, several people can become emanations of different aspects of the same Buddha; emanations of his Body, Speech, Mind or Activities. The principle of reincarnating lamas is interpreted in two ways. While a particular lama represents a Buddha emanation, at the same time he is also considered to be a reincarnation of his predecessor who also represented the same Buddha emanation. The reincarnating lamas are called *tulkus* (*sprul-sku*, emanated-body). When a *tulku* dies, a search is made to find a child that possesses certain established indications of being a reincarnation of the departed predecessor. There are numerous lineages of reincarnating lamas among the Nyimapas and the Kagyupas. The Gelugpas have two prominent emanations: one is the line of the Dalai Lamas who are emanations of the Bodhisattva Avalokiteśvara, and the other is the line of the Panchen Lamas as emanations of Buddha Amitābha. The reincarnations can appear at any time, discontinue or become suspended.

To avoid certain discord and to justify various practices, Tibetan Buddhism adopted the Indian classification of doctrines and practices into three vehicles (*yāna*). This classification asserts that the Hīnayāna was taught for people who are endowed with average intelligence. The Mahāyāna was destined for those of superior capacities, and the Mantrayāna or Vajrayāna was devised for people with the highest intellectual and spiritual abilities. Such a gradation of teachings and practices enables people of different mental categories and walks of life to embark on a suitable path. The lower vehicles are recommended for the lay people and in particular for the religious as a preparatory stage for the most advanced practices. Thus stress is placed here on the necessity and utility of the gradual path. One must accumulate merit and knowledge, and acquire a gradual purification through many reincarnations. Within monastic training it is this general orientation that constitutes the core of intellectual studies and daily practices of meditation.

The tantric practices and meditation which are styled as the rapid path towards the highest goal that may be achieved in one life-span are justified and accessible only to those who are sufficiently prepared to understand them and to execute them. So far as the philosophical doctrines are concerned, the Tantras accept as their foundation the doctrines of the Mahāyāna, in particular those of the Mādhyamika and the Vijñānavāda schools. The Tantras are not preoccupied with speculation. Their chief goal is to induce and acquire a mystical experience. In a general way, one could say that the Tantras represent a ritualised and yogic application of the Mahāyāna philosophical concepts. Two of those concepts, *saṃsāra* and *nirvāṇa,* stand at the centre of tantric considerations. The Tantras assert that a mystical experience of their non-duality leads to the realisation of the supreme Buddhahood. The duality of concepts and appearances is seen as remaining at the root of all imperfections and through its elimination one achieves the highest spiritual perfection.

To the two concepts of *saṃsāra* and *nirvāṇa,* we may add some other pairs of concepts which also portray the same state of reality from somewhat different angles. These are 'means' (*upāya*) and 'wisdom' (*prajñā*), 'compassion' (*karuṇā*) and 'emptiness' (*śūnyatā*). The concepts of 'wisdom' and 'emptiness' refer to absolute truth, and the concepts of 'means' and 'compassion' may be conveniently seen as parallels of relative or conventional truth. Various activities and practices within *saṃsāra* that lead to the supreme wisdom are seen as the means towards it. The same means pursued out of compassion for all living beings are referred to as the compassion that induces the dawn of emptiness. It can be asserted, in a general way, that *saṃsāra* as a whole is the means for achieving *nirvāṇa* for it is within it that the various practices of purification, meditation and intellectual training are pursued. The ascent towards the supreme goal is not merely a one-way effort but rather it should be viewed as a mutual merging of the two extremes, as it were, represented by the pairs of concepts just mentioned. As one's inner disposition becomes more purified one becomes a receptacle for the highest perfection that begins to unfold itself.

Thus the Tantras propound that it is a merging of these dualistic or dichotomic assumptions that should be experienced and retained within oneself through meditation and yogic practices. For the purpose of tantric exercises, the Tantras made use of a large variety of symbols to represent those abstract concepts: the *vajra* (means) and the bell (wisdom), the moon and the sun, the vowels and the consonants, the male and the female. Similarly the same concepts can be personified as deities. Different deities can be seen either as embodying the totality of Buddhist perfection or a part of it. Thus for instance Vajrasattva or Samantabhadra represents the supreme state of Buddhahood, while the Five Tathāgatas of the Yoga Tantra represent a fivefold manifestation of Buddhahood. Once united in a tantric embrace the deities represented as male (means) and female (wisdom) symbolise the non-duality of all concepts and manifestations.

A *maṇḍala* which represents a cosmic diagram is perhaps the best example of tantric ideals and aspirations. If we take for instance the *maṇḍala* of Vairocana, the deities are distributed as follows. At the centre of the cosmos is Vairocana with his female partner. To the four cardinal points of the compass are distributed the other four Buddhas (Akṣobhya etc.) with their goddesses (Locanā etc.). The subsequent circles of the diagram are occupied by a group of Bodhisattvas and lesser deities. As the deities become more distant from the centre, they assume a lesser importance. Each deity is attributed a particular aspect of Buddhist perfection and is conceived of as counteracting certain aspects of human imperfection. A *maṇḍala* can be depicted iconographically and used as an aid in meditation or, in the case of more advanced practitioners, it can be visualised directly. The meditational exercises of visualisation are called evocations (*sādhana*). During an evocation one first imagines or creates mentally the foundation of the *maṇḍala* diagram or the cosmic palace which symbolises the physical world. Next one envisages the deities which are distributed to their assigned places. So far this performance has recreated the illusory world of phenomena. The next stage consists of emanating rays of light from one's heart by means of which the divine manifestations that pervade the envisaged deities are summoned from the absolute sphere and are known as the knowledge-deities. The meditational state has now succeeded in uniting as it were the phenomenal and transcendental spheres. The next moment leads to identifying oneself with the deities of the *maṇḍala*. One attempts to assume and to retain the transcendental perfection of the deities. At the end of such an exercise the *maṇḍala* is dissolved. The practice of evocation can be performed by visualising a group of deities or just concentrating on one particular deity. It can be performed as a meditational practice or it can be expressed externally in a ritual with recitations, chanting, music and presentation of offerings.

Another practice based on the same principle is to think of one's own body as a *maṇḍala* or as being endowed with different mystic levels (*cakra*) or channels which can enable one to achieve meditational trances. This kind of practice is derived from the common lore of Indian yogic tradition. Yet another method makes use of a female partner. In such trances the *yogin* (means) identifies himself with a particular Buddha while his female partner assumes the role of the Buddha-Goddess (wisdom). While the *vajra* and the lotus are united (which here means during sexual intercourse), the jasmine drop (semen) representing the thought of enlightenment (*bodhicitta*) must not be lost but should ascend through the *yogin*'s body to the summit of the head where the culminating moment of esoteric trance is achieved. This kind of practice can only be performed by well trained *yogins* and their chosen partners, both of whom are required to possess absolute control over their bodies. Such practices are never performed within monasteries, and the monks who take monastic vows perform only tantric meditations which do not impede the vow of celibacy.

The various tantric methods, and especially the mystic experience to which they lead, cannot be easily communicated or conveyed to others mainly because such practices are liable to misconceptions and misuse. In all tantric practices stress is placed on the continuation of living transmission of teachings and practices. The mere knowledge of tantric texts is said to have no value. A suitable master is required to guide his disciples in their meditational and ritual exercises, to instruct them and to bestow initiations upon them. So that the tradition may become efficient, the disciple must first receive a direct textual transmission (*lung* or *upadeśa*) from his master; this is often done by reading the text aloud. An oral transmission of texts is regarded as important for two reasons: it is a formal permission to study the texts and it produces a certain spiritual capacity for understanding them. After a period of studying and listening to instructions, the disciple receives tantric initiations (*dbang*, *abhiṣeka*). The tantric consecrations vary in number and nature. Some of them are preliminary and general, others are highly advanced; the higher Tantras have four major consecrations.

The recognition of the superiority of mystical experience over intellectual speculation led to the admission of the possibility of many forms of individual experience. Such an assumption allowed the tantric practitioners to make use of various yogic practices available in India, and of magical performances that they considered appropriate and suitable to their personal taste. However, all those yogic practices and magical skills had to be interpreted within the context of Buddhist ideals. The tantric tradition, like other Buddhist schools, has produced a vast body of texts known as *Tantras*: hence the name Tantric Buddhism. The Tantras are often divided into four classes: Action (*kriyā*, *bya-brgyud*), Performance (*caryā*, *spyod*), Yoga (*rnal-'byor*) and Highest (*anuttara*, *bla-na-med*). The Action Tantra is characterised by external practices such as ritual offerings to deities, recitation of *mantras*, magic rites and rituals whose chief aim is to acquire certain spiritual but also mundane benefits. The Performance Tantra makes use of the elements contained in the previous category but it adds the practice of mental concentration and meditation. The Yoga Tantra, which stands at the centre of all the tantric practices, makes use of psycho-physical yogic exercises and meditation. The external rituals are not essential but they are used as additional aids. It is in this class of Tantras that the methods of evocation and identification with deities have been fully developed. The Highest Tantra is considered to advocate the most advanced esoteric practices in which the experience of non-duality of phenomenal and transcendental spheres and the illusory character of their duality are mystically achieved through the aid of a female partner. This category of Tantras very often speaks of the highest spiritual experiences as the Great Bliss (*mahāsukha*, *bde-chen*) which represents a transposition into mystical level of the joy experienced in the tantric union. Many people are puzzled by the tantric practices that involve sexual yoga. In the case of Tibet one general observation can be made here. During the initial period of Buddhism in Tibet there existed it seems a considerable number of yogic adepts who made use of sexual yoga. We have written evidence, a letter of the king of Purang, which condemns such practices. In due course, when the monastic orders and discipline became established, such practices were limited to individuals who pursued their practices outside monasteries. There are still today married lamas among the Tibetan orders, especially among the Nyimapas; those people do not follow the *Prātimokṣa* rules (the *Vinaya*) but take tantric vows. It should be said that the Tibetans have a great respect for the Tantras as a means of mystical experiences and especially as a source of powerful magic rituals which can be employed to achieve various results. In the monasteries life flows according to the *Vinaya* rules, the doctrinal outlook is that of the Mahāyāna, and the rituals are often of the Tantras; very often tantric deities are depicted on the walls of monasteries.

So far we have considered the features of Tibetan Buddhism which are largely applicable to all the religious orders. There exist certain differences between the orders. The major differences amount to following particular traditions of texts and practices. The Sakyapa order, as far as the tantric tradition is concerned, gives a predominance to the *Hevajra Tantra* and related texts. The doctrinal and exegetical assumptions are centred around the teaching which places in apposition the practical path towards the supreme goal and its fruit (*lam-'bras*). While one advances along the path of religious practices, one at the same time acquires the fruits of one's efforts in proportion to those efforts. Like the Gelugpas, the Saskyapas study the Mādhyamika philosophy. The Gelugpas are the greatest champions of the Mādhyamika doctrines. They attach importance to dialectical studies and intellectual training. The writings of Tsongkapa and his two chief disciples, Khedrub and Gyaltshab (mKhas-'grub-rje and rGyal-tshab), provide a general framework for intellectual training. Among the Tantras, the Gelugpas specialise in the *Kālacakra Tantra*. The Kagyupas present a more complex tradition. Apart from the traditions brought by Marpa and the eclectic systematisation of Gampopa, they have also adopted certain Nyimapa practices. The practices systematised by Gampopa centre around the *Mahāmudrā*—'Great Seal'—teachings. The Great Seal stands for the ultimate non-duality. The teachings were brought from India but Gampopa reinterpreted them within the general and wide context of Buddhist philosophy and practice. The Six Doctrines of Nāropa are of course a particular feature of this order, but they also spread to other traditions. The first of Nāropa's doctrines making use of the haṭha-yoga techniques explains the practice of meditation used to acquire the ability to sustain or retain bodily heat in adverse and cold circumstances. The second doctrine explains visualisations that lead to becoming aware of the illusory character of one's body. The third doctrine centres on the illusory nature of dreams and related states. The pure light nature of absolute reality is taught in the fourth doctrine. The transference of consciousness is the subject of the fifth doctrine. Here one learns how to transfer one's consciousness at the moment of death into one's chosen deity or to dissolve it into the universal luminosity. The sixth doctrine is similar. It teaches how to animate dead bodies. The transmission of the sixth doctrine discontinued with the sudden death of Marpa's son.

The Nyimapas have produced their own most interesting body of literature. They do not preserve the classical tradition of scholastic training nor group their teachings on the Indian pattern. They emphasise spiritual practices in preference to intellectual pursuits; one learns as one experiences is the general orientation. Their doctrines are not systematised into three vehicles but into nine. The *Śrāvaka*, *Pratyekabuddha* and *Bodhisattva* Vehicles (*yāna*) are classed as the three lowest vehicles. The first three Tantra classes (*kriyā*, *caryā*, *yoga*) constitute the three lower vehicles of the Vajrayāna. The three highest vehicles *Mahāyoga*, *Anuyoga* and *Atiyoga*, consist of the tantric texts belonging to the Highest Tantra, the old Nyimapa Tantras rejected by Buston, and other similar texts. As the highest and most valuable body of teachings the *Atiyoga* explains the doctrines and practices known as *Dzogchen* (*rdzogs-chen*, literally 'Great Perfection'). The *Dzogchen* teachings, introduced by Vairocana, centre around the Tantras that do not have *maṇḍalas* containing numerous deities to be contemplated. The practice focuses on luminosity-emptiness, that is uncreated, without beginning or end, a primordial self-existence named as Samantabhadra (Kun-tu-bzang-po). Samantabhadra represents a state even beyond the Buddhas, the most refined and pure intelligence of which all beings are possessed. Deliverance from the phenomenal world is gained through the elimination of all impurities caused by the projections of the mind. One must therefore eliminate all mental activities. The actual practice often involves regular periods of meditation on Light which is frequently performed by gazing at the sun. A successful effort should culminate in becoming completely absorbed and dissolved bodily into the Light, assuming the form of a rainbow ('ja'-lus). The *Dzogchen* practices were criticised and condemned by many masters of other schools as being a disguised form of Chinese Ch'an (Zen).

Certain practices introduced in Tibet survived as living traditions through different masters but without belonging to any particular order. Of those the Chö (gCod, 'cut off') practices are perhaps the most original. They were brought to Tibet by Phadampa Sangye from India, it is alleged, along with related practices called *Zhi-byed*. The Chö school in Tibet was established by a woman-*ḍākinī* called Macig Labdron (Ma-gcig lab-sgron-ma). Its philosophical and doctrinal foundation is grounded in the *Prajñāpāramitā* literature. Thus its final goal is the same as that of other orthodox traditions. The practices, however, are very different. They centre around the terrifying aspects of human nature and phenomena in general. Its practitioner wanders off to places such as dreadful cemeteries, awesome mountains, haunted crossroads and so on. While meditating one evokes and then provokes the spirits and wrathful demoniac powers around one and then one tries to control them. The culminating moments of such meditational sessions involve the act of cutting up one's own body into pieces and offering it to the host of terrifying beings around. At the end of meditation one reabsorbs within oneself all the hallucinatory apparitions born from one's own mind. The ultimate goal is to become aware of the illusory nature of phenomena, the non-existence of one's self, and to gain the supreme Wisdom.

Interaction with Popular Religion

Apart from the orthodox and monastic Buddhism as represented by the different religious orders and traditions described in the previous pages, there exists in Tibet a popular religion, totally garbed in Buddhist attires, but in truth constituting a mixture of Buddhist and non-Buddhist elements. The general and overall attitude of ordinary people is Buddhist. They place their trust and take refuge in the Three Jewels (*Triratna*): Buddha, his *Dharma* and his *Saṅgha*. They practise Buddhist morality and accumulate merit through various actions such as charitable deeds, prayers, prostrations before images and sacred constructions, circumambulations of temples and *stūpas*, donations to monasteries and going on pilgrimages. Some more educated people read sacred texts and many Tibetans dedicate their lives completely to religion at advanced stages in life when they pass all their worldly responsibilities on to their children.

For the Tibetans at large, the world of everyday life is crowded with various categories of spirits and demoniac powers. Some of the more important deities are referred to by their proper names but a large majority of them are reduced to generic appellations. Each place, village or town, valley or plot of fields has its own local deity (*sa-bdag*, 'master of the earth') who controls it. This class of deities, like others, must not be provoked or made angry for it can cause diseases, death or loss of property. Another category of spirits called *lu* (*klu*) controls underground waters, lakes and rivers. They too must not be disturbed by polluting water. Some deities considered to be very powerful inhabit mountain passes or the summits of numerous mountains. Some of the mountains are dedicated to different Buddhas or Bodhisattvas but the majority of them are in the control of deities whom the Buddhist tradition classes as *laukika* or belonging to this world. Many of the most powerful local and mountain gods were converted to Buddhism and made into 'Religion-Protectors' (*chos-skyong*, *dharmapāla*). On occasions of crossing mountain passes, or near the places where the local deities are said to dwell, people make food offerings and recite prayers which are Buddhist in nature. There exists a great variety of rituals for propitiating the different categories of lesser deities, for offering ransoms or even fierce rites to eliminate them altogether. The entire life of Tibetan people is orientated towards self-defence and constant efforts are made to appease and to placate the powers that surround them. Each individual is accompanied by some deities. On one's right shoulder is the enemy-god (*dgra-lha*) who protects against enemies and who is a remote echo of the primitive period of nomadic hunters. The right armpit carries the paternal-deity (*pho-lha*), the left armpit the maternal-deity (*mo-lha*) while the uncle-deity (*zhang-lha*) rests in the heart. These three deities represent the continuity of the family. They seem to represent the paternal and maternal ancestors who watch over the safe continuity of the family lineage. The hearth is inhabited by the hearth-god (*thab-lha*), the storeroom by the abundance-god (*bang-mdzod-lha*), and the house-god (*phug-lha* or *khyim-lha*) dwells in the central pillar of the house. The house itself can be interpreted in cosmological terms. Thus, for instance, the central pillar represents the world's axis and the ladder connecting the ground floor with the upper storey, having thirteen rungs, symbolises the thirteen levels of heaven. The personal deities are also attributed different parts of the house as their habitations.

The Buddhist doctrine of the non-existence of a soul is generally accepted but popular belief firmly asserts that each individual has a soul which is called *la* (*bla*) which has a definite form. The *la* resides in the body and it can become separated from it on certain occasions, such as moments of fainting, mental disorder or death. It can also be abducted by evil spirits. There are special rituals to recall the *la* that wandered astray or to regain it from a malevolent spirit. Another element resting within the body is called the life-force (*srog*) which is identical with the duration of one's life. It penetrates the whole body, flows through with the breathing and its main seat is the heart. It represents the life-principle as opposed to the state of death. Certain astrological forces are represented by the so-called wind-horse (*rlung-rta*) on which depend one's health and prosperity.

The oldest Buddhist doctrines in India maintained that one was reborn soon after death. The sum of one's good and bad actions (*karma*) conditioned the next rebirth. The later Buddhist tradition introduced the concept of an intermediate period between death and rebirth. It was asserted that during that period the departed ones could be aided to gain, if not a complete deliverance, then at least a better rebirth than the one imposed by the rule of *karma*. In Tibet this period, reckoned as lasting for forty-nine days, has become associated with some very ancient concepts, especially that of a soul as comprising the whole person. This type of soul-concept is not easily discernible because, once again, it is garbed in Buddhist terms. The ancient term itself is not employed but it is subsumed in the Buddhist technical term of consciousness (*vijñāna*, *rnam-shes*). At the moment of death, or soon after it, one receives instructions called *phowa* (*'pho-ba*) which describe to one the process of death and the immediate events that follow it. Through those instructions one should understand that there is nothing to be feared and that the only successful conduct to assume is to confront with calmness the manifestations that appear before one. It is assumed that immediately after death one has a vision of a beam of light. If one follows this luminous vision one should be able to cut off all the successive rebirths and to reach the supreme state of deliverance. If one hesitates, even for a moment, one begins to fall back into one's next rebirth. The luminous beam is paralleled with a similar beam of darkness which becomes predominant as the intermediate period evolves. The moment of death is considered as extremely important. One must not be disturbed for one's consciousness might be perturbed and become an evil ghost or take possession of another man. There are special exercises that teach how to perform by oneself the act of dying when the death cannot be avoided. Those who acquire this knowledge very frequently die while fully aware. Usually they assume the bodily posture of their chosen deity and then transfer their consciousness directly into the heart of the deity or to the sphere of pure consciousness or luminosity. In the case of ordinary people, once physical death is ascertained the consciousness receives instructions through the reading of a text known as *Liberation through Listening in the Intermediate State* (*Bar-do-thos-grol*), better known in the West as *The Tibetan Book of the Dead*. This text explains what happens at each successive day of the intermediate period. Once the consciousness begins to relapse into the world, it passes through a series of visions consisting of seeing various deities both peaceful and terrifying, traversing dangerous abysses, enduring attacks of all kinds and meeting ordinary people and members of the family. As the fall becomes deeper and deeper, the beam of light gradually dwindles away and with it the last chances of following it. Finally the consciousness becomes aware that it needs a body to act like all other people around it. It perceives copulating people and desires to unite itself with the seed of life, gaining thus its next rebirth.

The Tibetans, like many other civilisations, make use, but on a very much larger scale, of divination and astrological calculations. They employ many techniques to discern various omens and events. Most of the divination methods are contained in special books and their astrology includes Indian, Chinese and Tibetan materials. There exist people who specialise in divination and astrology. The more simple methods are used by people at large. While engaged in trading, travel or a particular enterprise, the Tibetans often consult specialists to find out whether there are any obstacles arising from demons or evil people. The difficulties are overcome by the use of amulets, ransom offerings presented to demons or by appropriate rituals. The Tibetans also make use of oracles, who act as media and become possessed by different deities. A particular deity will take possession of its medium, who goes into a trance during a seance. Oracles are found not only in villages but also in monasteries. The Dalai Lamas have always consulted the state oracle at Nechung near Lhasa.

The aspiration towards the Buddhist *nirvāṇa* is certainly present among ordinary people, but in general they aspire to gain a better rebirth. The high religious aspirations of people are often expressed in their desire to reach the legendary country of Shambhala, the land of abundance, peace and freedom from all suffering. Shambhala is believed to lie to the north of Tibet beyond impenetrable mountain ranges. Its rulers continue the line of pious kings who, of course, profess Buddhism and know the most advanced esoteric teachings. When the time will come, the king of Shambhala, like the epic hero Gesar, will lead his armies to destroy evil and establish a universal kingdom of just and virtuous happiness on the earth. The land of Shambhala can only be reached by those endowed with spiritual purity, for only good people have a chance to traverse the dangerous mountains and snares that separate Tibet from Shambhala. Some more sophisticated accounts speak of Shambhala as being in the hearts of people who live a moral life.

Indigenous or Pre-Buddhist Beliefs

There are two distinct, somewhat opposed, and yet similar religious traditions in Tibet. One is represented by Buddhism, brought from India, and the other is Bon, which claims different origins but in fact represents a heterodox form of Buddhism from the eleventh century onwards. Both these religions claim—and are followed in this by some Western scholars—that Bon and its followers, called Bonpos, represent the ancient religious beliefs of Tibet. Critical scholarship has proved decisively that such an assumption does not portray the true situation. Ever since Buddhism was introduced in Tibet, it gradually eliminated the ancient beliefs, especially those that were in a direct contrast to its doctrines. Some of the more acceptable practices, and especially myths as we have seen, were subsumed into both Buddhism and carried forward by Bon, in both religions under an appropriate terminology. Thus all the materials in Tibetan religious sources that contain or refer to the ancient beliefs are given a suitably transformed interpretation. The description of the ancient beliefs, therefore, can only be limited to generalities and certain accounts that appear almost certainly to have existed in Tibet before the introduction of Buddhism in the seventh century; some of the ancient elements have already been mentioned above.

The oldest indigenous Tibetan beliefs seem to have centred around the sacral and divine character of the very early kings. The transition to the earthly mortality of the kings did not eliminate their sacral nature but it necessarily introduced new elements which were largely connected with funeral rites. The interment of the kings, from Drigum onwards, involved elaborate ceremonies to assure their peaceful stay in the realm of the dead. The kings were buried with a whole set of worldly possessions, including animals and probably their companions. The funeral rites included special ransom ceremonies which aimed to prevent evil powers from disturbing the dead, and also, it seems, to seal off, as it were, the world of the dead from the living. On such occasions animal sacrifices were performed and suitable verses were recited. The belief in the realm of the dead led to the cult of ancestors which was expressed through periodical offerings made by families to their departed forefathers. It seems quite certain that bloody sacrifices were still practised on special occasions, such as the swearing of solemn oaths or the instalment of the kings, even during the initial stages of Buddhism in Tibet. A great number of the ancient practices seem to have been concerned with divination and astrological calculations to determine the causes of people's misfortunes and ailments, and to procure suitable cures to eliminate them. The sources of people's troubles were often attributed to local gods and demons of all kinds. The usual manner of counteracting and preventing harmful influences of various evil powers was achieved through the use of ransom offerings.

The specialists who performed the funerary rites, divination or made offerings to different categories of spirits were known as *bon* or *shen* (*gshen*). Those priests engaged by the royal court were credited with various magical powers, skills in ritual sacrifices and abilities to perform spectacular feats such as flying in the air. The religion, as such, seems to have had no name but at times it is referred to in texts as 'divine conventions' (lha-chos) in contrast to 'human conventions' (mi-chos), or again as 'the custom of heaven and earth' (gnam-sa'i-lugs). Some scholars assert that it was called *tsug* (gtsug) or *tsuglag* (gtsug-lag). The origin of the world is attributed to a category of celestial beings called *cha* (phyva). The heavenly dwelling consisted of thirteen levels and the earth had nine. The *cha* gods, presided over by a leader (sku-lha), controlled the cosmic events according to the Law (tsug). The harmonious rule of the universe was retained by the Law with some gods remaining in heaven and other gods taking residence on the earth. The universal order was disrupted by a demon released from the ninth subterranean level. Moral decay evolved and only some people sustained the Law. The general immoral chaos will end and good people will regain the control epitomised by the Law but, in the meantime, they remain in a peaceful state in the abode of the dead.

Another discernible feature of the ancient beliefs is the cult of mountain deities. Certain mountain peaks were treated as sacred and it seems that the early Tibetan tribes had their separate mountains. The deities living on those mountains belonged mostly to the group of the most powerful category known as *tsan* (btsan, 'mighty'). Even today there are many mountain peaks which are considered sacred.

Bon Religion

The Tibetan word for religion is *chö* (chos). It had its particular meaning in the ancient times but with the introduction of Buddhism it was employed to translate the Sanskrit technical term *Dharma*—the Buddha's doctrine. The ancient interpretation of this term dwindled away and only certain aspects of it continue among popular beliefs. The term 'Bon', which in the ancient times referred to a category of priests, was employed from the eleventh century onwards to denote a whole body of religious teachings in the same way as the Buddhist *Chö* (*Dharma*). Both Buddhist *Dharma* and Bon traditions are fundamentally the same so far as the philosophical doctrines are concerned. The Buddhist tradition traces itself to India while Bon asserts its origins in the country to the west of Tibet which it calls Tazig (sTag-gzig, asserted to be Iran). The Bon religion, it must be pointed out, incorporates a large portion of ancient beliefs but in a completely transformed manner; so, too, does the Buddhist tradition, as already mentioned.

The Bon teachings were first propagated on earth by Shenrab Mibo (gShen-rab mi-bo), whose historicity is not attested; the name itself is an epithet. His life story is patterned on that of Śākyamuni but it incorporates many original accounts. Shenrab was born in Olmo Lungring ('Ol-mo lung-ring) situated in Zhang-zhung (the western part of Tibet near Mount Kailasa) or in Tazig, depending on different accounts. Olmo Lungring, designed as an eight-petalled lotus with the sky above it in the form of an eight-spoked wheel, had a mountain at its centre which consisted of nine successive levels symbolising the 'Nine Ways of Bon'. From the four sides of Mount Yungdrung (g.Yung-drung) there flowed four rivers towards the cardinal points. To the south of the mountain there was a palace in which Shenrab was born. The palaces to the west and north were inhabited by Shenrab's wives and children. Olmo Lungring was separated from the rest of the world by an impenetrable mountain range and access to it was gained by an arrow-path (mda'-lam); once Shenrab shot an arrow thus creating a passage. In the past ages, Shenrab and his two brothers studied with a Bon sage. When they had completed their training, they went to the supreme lord of compassion, Shenlha Ökar (gShen-lha 'od-dkar), who advised them how to help beings living in misery. The oldest brother guided living beings during the previous world-age. The second brother, Shenrab, became the teacher of the present world-age and his younger brother will teach in the future.

At the age of thirty-one, Shenrab renounced the world and lived in austerity teaching his doctrines. His propagation of Bon was constantly obstructed by a powerful demon Khyabpa. On one occasion, while pursuing Khyabpa who stole his horses, Shenrab arrived in Tibet; it was his only visit. Before leaving Tibet, Shenrab pronounced a prophecy foretelling Tibet's conversion and gave some instructions to local people on how to placate various deities and exorcise demons. Having returned to Olmo Lungring he died after a period of illness and passed into *nirvāṇa.* Shenrab's son Mucho (Mucho ldem-drug) continued to teach the doctrines, put them on record and then translated them with a group of translators so that they could be propagated in many countries. The tradition that spread to India became the origin of the Śākya clan from which issued Śākyamuni Buddha as an emanation of Shenrab; other sources assert that Shenrab and Śākyamuni were brothers.

Bon was propagated in Tibet (the name of Tibet or Bod is seen as being derived from the term 'Bon') well before the arrival of the first king. The Bon scriptures were brought to Zhang-zhung by Mucho's six disciples and translated first into Zhang-zhung languages and then into Tibetan. The first diffusion of Bon in Tibet ended with the death of Drigum who died in retribution for suppressing Bon. The Bon doctrines were revived during the reign of Drigum's son Pude Kung-gyel (sPu-lde gung-rgyal) and continued to flourish until the reign of Trisong Detsen as the religion of Tibetan people. With the conversion of Trisong Detsen to Buddhism and his support of it, Bon began to be persecuted. The Bonpo adherents were forced to become Buddhists, many were exiled and some killed. Dranpa Namkha (Dran-pa nam-mkha'), one of the chief Bonpo figures of the eighth century, deliberately became Buddhist in order to preserve Bon. With the help of his companions he recorded many Bon scriptures and hid them in different places for future rediscovery by his successors. As evil omens occurred and Trisong Detsen became ill, the Bonpos were allowed to resume some of their practices in certain parts of Tibet.

The period from the eighth to the eleventh century is submerged in darkness and silence. The Bonpos speak of a third diffusion of Bon in the eleventh century which coincided with the second propagation of Buddhism. The Bonpos assert that as far as the continuation of monastic ordinations was concerned, both Buddhists and Bonpos went to eastern Tibet to receive monastic vows from the same group of people. From the eleventh century onwards the Bon tradition often refers to itself as the New Bon (Bon-gsar). The first Bonpo texts were rediscovered by three laymen at Samye. A large number of texts were rediscovered by Shechen Luga (gShen-chen klu-dga', 996–1035), a married man who practised asceticism. Shechen found so many *terma* texts that some of his Buddhist contemporaries accused him of plagiarism. He acquired a good number of followers who spread Bon. Three of Shechen's disciples were entrusted with the continuation of three different traditions. To Druchen Namkha ('Bru-chen nam-mkha'), whose family came from Gilgit ('Bru-zha), he entrusted the study of metaphysics and cosmology. The Druchen family patronised the Bon religion until the nineteenth century. Then it ended its male line, when for the second time the Panchen Lama's reincarnation was found in this family. The second disciple, Zhuye Legpo (Zhu-yas legs-po), continued the Dzogchen teachings, while the third one, Paton (sPa-ston dpal-mchog), upheld the tantric tradition. In the course of the following centuries, the Bonpos built a number of monasteries all over Tibet.

The Bonpo scriptures were systematised in the fifteenth century by Sherab Gyaltshan (Shes-rab rgyal-mtshan), who classified them into two major groups, the *Kanjur* (bka'-'gyur) and the *Katen* (bka'-rten). The *Kanjur* texts attributed to Shenrab consist of 116 volumes and include doctrinal expositions. The *Kanjur* also includes texts that narrate ancient cosmogonic myths and three biographies of Shenrab. The *Katen* group of 131 volumes, like the Buddhist *Tanjur*, contains commentaries, rituals, works on arts and crafts and so on. One text that is particularly cherished by the Bonpos is called *Zhang-zhung Nyengyu* (Zhang-zhung snyan-brgyud) and represents an uninterrupted tradition of *Dzogchen* teachings.

The fundamental teachings, like those of the Buddhist, propound the nature of impermanence, the law of karma, and the path towards enlightenment. The Bonpos recognise the *bodhisattva* ideal and the three Buddha-Bodies. The technical terminology differs from the Buddhist one but it expresses the same concepts. On the whole the Bonpo doctrines as recorded in their scriptures represent an amalgamation not only of texts that parallel those of the Buddhists but also of a vast quantity of magical rituals, various legendary accounts and cosmogonic myths, some of which echo old Iranian and Central Asian cosmogonies.

The Bon doctrines are classified in two different ways. One classification divides them into five categories under the name of 'The Four Portals and the Treasury as Fifth' (sGo-bzhi mdzod-lnga). The second classification includes all the elements of the first one and is called 'The Bon of the Nine Successive Stages' (Theg-pa rim-dgu'i bon) or simply the Nine Vehicles of Bon.

The first vehicle, 'The Vehicle of the Shen of Magic', deals with different methods of prediction such as astrology, divination, examination of omens, medical diagnosis and with ransom rituals. 'The Vehicle of the Shen of Worldly Appearances' explains the origins of gods and demons, exorcism and different ransom rituals to gratify or to subjugate gods. The third vehicle, 'The Shen of Magical Illusion', deals with fierce rituals that aim to destroy completely the adverse powers. Some of those rituals include a *linga* (effigy) which represents the enemy to be eliminated. The person or demon concerned is summoned to reside in the *linga* and then ritually destroyed. The fourth vehicle, 'The Shen of Existence', is concerned with funeral ceremonies. The next vehicle, 'The Vehicle of Lay Followers', refers to the religious practices to be performed by lay people. Stress is placed on pursuing life according to the ten virtues and the six perfections. The monastic life is dealt with in the sixth vehicle. It describes in detail the monastic discipline and ordinations. The last three vehicles deal with tantric teachings and practices. The 'Vehicle of Pure Sound' propounds higher tantric practices, theories of spiritual realisations and rituals. 'The Way of Primeval Shen' explains different states of meditation, circumstances of tantric practices, the manner of choosing masters and tantric partners, and various tantric requirements. 'The Supreme Vehicle' is represented by the *Dzogchen* teachings that have very much in common with those of the Nyimapas.

The Bonpos survived until the present time. In Tibet they were greatly outnumbered by the Buddhist population. The Tibetan Buddhists have always frowned upon the Bonpos and considered them to be dangerous magicians. However, on the whole they were left in peace, apart from a few open attacks on them, and a number of them studied in Buddhist monasteries. Some Tibetans speak of white and black Bonpo magic. White magic refers to harmless magical activities and black magic to fierce and demoniac performances. The Bonpos themselves know these terms but do not retain a living tradition of such practices. It all seems to be a mere echo of the remote past.

Further Reading

Hoffmann, H. *The Religions of Tibet* (Greenwood Press, London, 1961)
Karmay, S.G. *The Treasury of Good Sayings: A Tibetan History of Bon* (Oxford University Press, Oxford, 1972)
Nebesky-Wojkowitz, René de *Oracles and Demons of Tibet* (Graz, 1975)
Snellgrove, D.L. and Richardson, H.E. *A Cultural History of Tibet* (Weidenfeld & Nicolson, London, 1968)
Snellgrove, D.L. *The Nine Ways of Bon* (Oxford, 1967; reprinted Boulder, Colorado 1980)
—— *Indo-Tibetan Buddhism, Indian Buddhists and their Tibetan Successors* (London, 1987)
Stein, R.A. *Tibetan Civilization* (Faber & Faber, London, 1972)
Tucci, G. *Tibetan Painted Scrolls*, 3 vols. (Rome, 1949)
—— *The Religions of Tibet* (Routledge & Kegan Paul, London, 1980)
Waddell, L.A. *Buddhism and Lamaism of Tibet* (London, 1895; reprinted New Delhi, 1974)

13 Buddhism in Mongolia

Bulcsu Siklós

It may come as a surprise to some to discover that the religion most prevalent in areas inhabited by Mongolians was, and to an extent still is, Buddhism. Other types of Mahāyāna Buddhism, the types practised in Tibet, China and Japan, are easily distinguishable both from each other and from the parent Indian form, while Mongolian Buddhism, even when its existence is acknowledged, is usually treated as identical to its Tibetan antecedent, and hence subsumable under it.

The Mongols were relative latecomers both to Buddhism and to the historical scene. It is true that Mongolian tribes, often in alliance with other Altaic peoples, had made numerous inroads into China itself from early in Chinese recorded history, but even so, the sense of historical continuity relating the Mongols to world events and enabling them to be treated independently of other (in Chinese terms) 'barbarian' groups in matters of religion dates only from the thirteenth century, after Činggis (Jengiz, Gengis, etc.) Khan's unification of the Mongol tribes into a cohesive whole. The religion of the Mongols of this time and earlier could be classed as Shamanism, although it is hardly possible to treat all the Mongolian tribes together, the distinction between the majority nomadic groups and the more northerly sedentary tribes being particularly important to bear in mind. It has been suggested that Central Asian nomadic nations in general came quite late to Shamanism, perhaps borrowing most of their shamanic concepts from the forested areas further north.

The Mongols also came into contact with various Iranian religious concepts during this early period, primarily through their association with the Uighurs, a Turkic-speaking people who had converted to Manichaeism in the eighth century. The number of religious terms and divine appellations taken over from Iranian languages and still in use is quite considerable—for example the chief of the traditional shamanist grouping of the 33 *tngri* or 'gods' is known as Khormusta in Mongol, and is equivalent to the problematic Zurvanite deity Ohrmazd, principle of light, and to the Mazdean Ahura Mazdā. In fact, looking at the various *tngri*, whether in the above grouping of 33 or in the commoner grouping of 99 (44 'eastern' and 55 'western') or indeed looking at Mongolian shamanic practice in general, it is almost impossible to sort out all the various Iranian, Taoist, Manchu-Tunguz shamanist and, later, Buddhist ideas which might have come into play in forming what might be called the Mongolian shamanic synthesis.

During the thirteenth century, whilst Mongolian armies were busy laying most of Asia waste, the Mongol emperors were encouraging a great number of foreign administrators and religious practitioners to come to the Mongol court, with the delegation of various tasks to these non-Mongols being done fully on the grounds of suitability, and not on the grounds of supposed cultural superiority. It is probably on similar grounds that the Mongols decided to adopt the Uighur alphabetic script (derived ultimately from Syriac through Sogdian), rather than the more prestigious and unsuitable Chinese script, the adoption of which would have drawn the Mongols into the Chinese cultural sphere and led them down a totally different religious path from the one they eventually followed.

The numerous Tibetans at the Mongol court were in the main representatives of the most influential political and religious force in Tibet at that time—the Sakya (Sa-skya) sect of Tibetan Buddhism. Although in time the Sakya lamas came to be regarded as religious specialists at the court, much as Uighurs were regarded as administrative specialists, the initial contacts of the Mongols with Tibetan Buddhism were exclusively political, and stemmed from the extremely wise Tibetan decision to submit unconditionally to the Mongols. Any other decision would surely have led to the near-total destruction of Tibetan civilisation and of that particular form of Buddhism which is now associated so strongly with Tibet. The loss would have been compounded by the fact that the North Indian antecedent of Tibetan Buddhism was at this time systematically being extinguished by the Muslims.

The Sakya monks at the Mongol court managed to arouse a considerable amount of interest in Buddhism, especially during the reign of Khubilai (Kublai) Khan (1260–94), who seems to have taken a personal interest in the new religion. This was in the main due to the practical instruction he received in Buddhist practice from the most important figure in the history of this, the 'First Conversion' of the Mongols, a certain 'Phags pa blo gros rgyal mtshan or, for short, 'Phags pa (1235–80). His adroitness in arousing Khubilai's interest in Buddhism led to the initiation of Kubilai himself and his consort, Camui, into the tantric cycle of Hevajra, and to the conversion of the whole imperial court. Numerous honours were heaped upon 'Phags pa, who was also asked to create a new script in which, hopefully, all the main languages of the Mongol Empire could be written. Known as the 'phags pa or dörbelǰin ('square') script, it was rather cumbersome and did not outlive the Yüan (Mongol) dynasty.

Just as during the Second Conversion of the Mongols to Buddhism, which dates from the time of the later Ming dynasty, the worship of Tantric deities in their wrathful aspects was much more prominent than any other aspect of Lamaism in Mongolian religious life. Apart from Hevajra, mentioned above, and other major meditational deities assigned Buddha rank, several of the protector deities (of Bodhisattva rank, considered responsible for safeguarding the Doctrine) were extremely popular. Such wrathful deities, bedecked with ornaments of human bone, spattered with human blood and fat, and often portrayed in a state of sexual union with female partners, seemed to have appealed to the Mongol court and high-ranking military—certainly these deities were considerably more terrifying and licentious than the old shamanic gods. It should also be mentioned that the practice of Tantra in many ways stands very close to that of Shamanism. There is not too much difference between the tantric assimilation of one's 'body, speech and mind' to those of the deity, achieved through visualisation, and the shamanic assimilation of the deity into oneself, in other words, the attainment of possession. Naturally, tantric practice precluded the social function of the shaman, and added certain soteriological, eschatological and indeed philosophical ideas to the world-view of the Mongol practitioner. This last aspect should be stressed, since it is commonly stated that the Mongol court limited itself to misunderstanding, and consequently indulging in, the violent and sexual side of Tantra. This side of Tantra certainly was part of the appeal of Buddhism, but the closeness of a large part of its basic practice to Shamanism and its more elaborate imagery helped ensure the victory of this very special form of Buddhism over the various other religions competing for support at the imperial court—Taosim, Nestorian Christianity, Manichaeism, Islam and even Catholicism.

The First Conversion of the Mongols to Buddhism did not go very deep, and was confined almost exclusively to the Mongol aristocracy and military. The average Mongol still worshipped the old gods, the gods of natural phenomena, the god Eternal Blue Heaven and many others, and had probably never seen a lama or even heard of Buddhism. So, although by the time of the last Mongol emperor, Toγan Temür (1333–68), part of the *Kanjur* (the first section of the Tibetan Canon) had been translated into Mongolian and several monasteries founded, Shamanism remained the characteristic religion of Mongolia at large.

The eclectic and analytical studies of that most learned of Tibetan mystics, Tsonkapa (Tsong-kha-pa, 1357–1419), provided the inspiration for the development and growth of the first indigenous

Tibetan school of Buddhism, the Gelugpa (dGe-lugs-pa). Throughout north China in the early Ming period considerable interest was shown in this highly esoteric and 'magical' form of Buddhism, and the resultant presence of large numbers of Gelugpa lamas caused considerable resentment in orthodox Chinese and imperial circles. This resentment culminated in the anti-Buddhist persecutions of the late Ming, in the face of which lamas fled in large numbers to the more congenial environment of south and west Mongolia, initiating the Second Conversion of the Mongols to Lamaism, this time in its Gelugpa form. The fragmented political nature of Mongolia at this time ensured that certain Mongol groups, initially seeking political support from a mostly unified Tibet, managed to make Buddhism their own within a few decades, whilst other, more isolated groups remained shamanist and had to wait until the nineteenth century for their first proper contact with Lamaism.

During the early stages of the Second Conversion in the mid-sixteenth century, south-east Mongolia had a true *cakravartin* (universal—and pious—monarch) in the person of Altan Khan. His meeting with bSod nams rgya mtsho resulted in the rapid conversion of all south-east Mongolian tribes to Lamaism, the outlawing of certain shamanistic practices (notably sacrifice) in the area, the consolidation of Gelugpa authority in Tibet itself and the conferral of the title Dalai Lama on bSod nams himself. The title 'Dalai Lama' is an abbreviation of the Mongolian *bilig-ün dalai lama*, 'Ocean-of-Wisdom-Teacher'. Since bSod nams conferred the title of 'Dalai Lama' posthumously on two of his predecessors, he counts as the third in the lineage of *rgyal-bas* (lit. 'victors' i.e. Dalai Lamas). After the death of the Third Dalai Lama, the Gelugpa returned these favours by accepting a newly-born relative of Altan Khan as the reincarnation of the Dalai Lama—a privilege indeed.

The process of conversion continued in similar ways until all Mongol territories were affected. One of the most common methods employed was straightforward bribery:

> In order to begin the spread of the Buddha's doctrine . . . the Tüsiyetü Khan of the Khorchin lets it be publicly known that he will give a horse to whoever learns by heart the summary of the Doctrine, and a cow to whoever can recite the *Yamāntaka-dhāraṇī* by heart.
> (From a biography of Neyiči Toyin (1557–1653); quoted from Heissig, pp. 36f.)

Gelugpa authorities frequently objected to this sort of activity, especially as it encouraged tantric practice without prior training or initiation, but in the long run it was probably to their own advantage that their warnings were scarcely heeded.

Merely teaching *mantras* and various invocations at a popular level would hardly have ensured Lamaism's lasting success in Mongolia. Institutions for the study of the doctrine, monastic training, translation, printing and so forth were soon established in most Mongol territories. Most characteristic were the numerous unattended temples known as *süme*, prevalent in nomadic regions, at which nomadic lamas would assemble only on festival days to perform specific rites before once again rejoining their herds.

Before we go on to discuss Ch'ing times, one individual of considerable interest should be mentioned, Öndür gegen (1635–1723), the first in the reincarnation lineage of the *rJe btsun dam pa khutuγtu*, who was primarily responsible for the ground gained by the Gelugpa in Khalkha ('Outer') Mongolia at the expense of other Tibetan schools. It may indeed have been a gesture of reconciliation on the part of the Gelugpa that Öndür gegen himself was recognised as an incarnation of the historian Tāranātha who had belonged to the heterodox Jo nang school of Tibetan Buddhism. The Jo nang pas were considered aberrant by all other schools for holding the concept of a type of 'emptiness' which was non-relative. Their monasteries were taken over by the Gelugpa in the seventeenth century.

The Manchu emperors of the Ch'ing dynasty saw in Lamaism a useful means by which to pacify the Mongols, arch-troublemakers that they were, and took on the role of chief patrons of Lamaism in all Mongol areas under their control (collectively known as Inner Mongolia). Lamaism flourished as never before, especially from the time of the K'ang Hsi Emperor (1654–1722) onwards. K'ang Hsi himself seems to have taken a personal interest in the alien religion, and was instrumental in summoning Ngag dbang blo bzang chos ldan (1642–1714, the first in the reincarnation series of the *lCang skya khutuγ tus*) to Peking to take up permanent residence there as the chief incarnate lama of Inner Mongolia. This encouraged the growth of his capital as a Lamaist centre and prevented Mongols being drawn to the natural headquarters of the Doctrine, Lhasa. The Manchus were concerned about the possibility, real in their eyes, of the development of a lamaist 'state' directed from Lhasa with the Mongols supplying the military wing. They even went so far as to construct a smaller version of the Potala, the Dalai Lama's Lhasa palace, at Jehol, the emperor's summer residence.

The Yung Cheng Emperor (1723–36) was by all accounts an ardent Buddhist with an interest in Zen as well as Lamaism. He turned his childhood palace into the famous Yung-Ho-Kung, which soon became the major Lamaist temple in Peking where the *lCang skya khutuγtus* would, with Imperial co-operation, pick the names of prospective reincarnations of high-ranking lamas from a huge golden urn.

More and more high-ranking incarnates were being drawn to Peking throughout the seventeenth and eighteenth centuries, out of the many who had been newly confirmed by the Manchu Court. This honour was freely given to any lama who had rendered some service to the court or to Lamaism in general, and so the number of incarnates grew to almost unmanageable proportions. By 1900 there were 14 incarnate lamas in Peking itself, about 160 in Inner Mongolia, some 120 in Outer Mongolia and 35 in the Kokonor region, a total of some 326—more than the total number of Gelugpa incarnates recognised by the Manchu court for Tibet itself.

Perhaps the most remarkable figure of eighteenth-century Lamaism in Mongolia was the *mergen lama-yin gegen*, bLo bzang bstan pa'i rgyal mtshan, who was single-handedly responsible for the compilation of what could be termed a Mongolian national liturgy incorporating elements both of Buddhism and of Shamanism. A scholar of considerable ability, he tried to amass as many authentic texts relating to Shamanism as he could, and produced vast numbers of liturgical texts treating the worship of shamanistic deities in Buddhist guise.

The end of the eighteenth century marked the beginning of the decline of Mongolian Lamaism. Literary and religious activity still continued, though in Inner Mongolia it was becoming increasingly difficult to finance large-scale projects because of the impoverishment and instability of the Ch'ing (brought about in part by increasing European intervention). The situation was better in Outer Mongolia; it was from here that Lamaism started spreading northwards to Buryat Mongolia which was still fully shamanist in the early nineteenth century—indeed, many parts of Buryat Mongolia remained exclusively shamanist until the establishment of Soviet rule.

With the formation of the Mongolian People's Republic after the death of the eighth and last *rJe btsun dam pa khutuγtu* in 1924, both Shamanism and Lamaism were constitutionally prohibited in what had been Outer Mongolia. In Inner Mongolia after the fall of the Ch'ing in 1911, Lamaism managed to hang on, even though it was officially unsupported and frowned upon. The political and economic situation in Inner Mongolia was utterly chaotic during the first half of this century—monasteries owed vast amounts of money and were liable to be sacked or destroyed by any number of roving bands of marauders. Worries were compounded by reports of persecutions of Buddhists in both the Mongolian People's Republic and in Buryat Mongolia, especially after the so-called 'Lama Risings' of the 1930s, and Inner Mongolia, just like Tibet, was unable to escape the inevitable destruction of all its cultural institutions during the Chinese Cultural Revolution of the 1960s.

Further Reading

Heissig, W. *The Religions of Mongolia* (Routledge & Kegan Paul, London, 1980)

Lessing, F.D. *Yung-Ho-Kung—An Iconography of the Lamaist Cathedral in Peking*, vol. 1 (Stockholm, 1942)

Buddhism in Mongolia

Miller, R.J. *Monasteries and Cultural Change in Inner Mongolia*, Asiatische Forschungen, vol. 2 (Wiesbaden, 1959)

Pozoneyev, A.M. *Religion and Ritual in Society—Lamaist Buddhism in Late Nineteenth-Century Mongolia*, ed. J.R. Krueger (Bloomington, Indiana, 1978)

Index

Abhidharma 68–9, 97, 99, 103, 107–8
Abhinavagupta, Śaivite scholar 154, 158, 163–4, 167, 168–9, 171
Achaemenid dynasty 27–8
Ādi Granth, Sikh scriptures 188–9, 191
Advaita Vedānta 42, 111, 119, 124, 126, 177–8
afterlife,
  in Hinduism 173
  Vedic concept 50
Ahura Mazda, chief god of Mazdaism 20, 22–32, 280
Akali Dal, Sikh party 192–3
alchemy,
  in Indian religions 87, 119
  in Tantrism 123
  in Taoism 15–18
alcohol, Buddhist ban 64
Ālvārs 40, 92, 111–12
Amar Das, Sikh Guru 186–7, 189
Amitabha Buddha,
  in China 226, 228, 232
  in India 98, 101
  in Japan 239, 240, 243–4
  in Tibet 265
Amritsar, Sikh centre 188, 193
Anāhitā, Mazdean deity 26, 28, 29, 31
Ānandavardhana, Hindu poet 85, 92, 112
anātman (Sanskrit) = *anatta* (Pali), in Buddhism 99, 204, *see also ātman*
ancestor cults, Tibet 279
Angad, Sikh Guru 186, 189
animism, and Buddhism 200
antinomianism 42, 94, 116, 122, 123–6
  and Tantrism 118
Āraṇyakas 43, 47
Arjan, Sikh Guru 187, 188, 189
art, Buddhist 241–2
Āryas, in India 39–41, 43–5, 51, 71, 73–5, 86–7
Asanga, Buddhist scholar 102, 228, 230, 262
asceticism,
  in Indian religions 50, 57–8, 60, 86, 125
  in Mazdaism 32
  in Theravāda Buddhism 198, 205
  see also Śaivism
Aśoka, Maurya Emperor 69, 71, 195, 197, 227
astrology, in Tibet 278, 279
Atharva-Veda 43, 46, 48, 50, 52, 54
atheism,
  and Buddhism 78
  and Hinduism 78
  and Jainism 78
Atiśa, Buddhist scholar 252–3, 255, 261
ātman (self) 52–3, 65, 99, 108, 110–11, 163, 179 , *see also anātman/anatta*
atomism, in Hinduism 107
Aurangzeb, Mogul Emperor 190
Avalokiteśvara 101, 103, 244, 249, 252, 264–5
avatāra, in Hinduism 81–2, 90, 93
Avesta, Mazdean scriptures 21, 23, 28, 32, 34

Bādarāyaṇa 54, 110, 111
Bahaism 35
Bāṇa, Hindu poet 85
baptism, in Sikhism 190, 192
Basavaṇṇa, Indian poet 125
Bāüls, India 125
Bhagavadgītā 54, 75, 79–80, 91, 92
Bhagavān, in Hinduism 79–83, 86, 93, 111
Bhāgavata-Purāṇa 40, 76, 80, 91, 92
Bhairava Kāpālika Śaivism 136–7, 138, 140, 143, 152, 162
bhakti (devotion) 91, 92, 93, 97, 115–16
Bhāve, Vinobā 180
bodhi (enlightenment) 60–1, 64, 66, 100–1, 226, *see also* enlightenment

bodhisattva (Mahāyāna ideal) 100–1, 121, 251, 264, 269, 277
Bodhisattva (the Buddha Śakyamuni in a past life) 100–1
Bodhisattva (the Buddha Śakyamuni in a past life) (heavenly) 103, 121, 210, 216, 221, 264
see also Avalokiteśvara
Bon religion 273–4, 275–8
Boyce, Mary 24, 35
Brahmā, in Hinduism 78–9, 84
Brahma-sūtra 54, 110–11, 112
brahman,
in classical Indian religions 47–9, 60, 65, 73, 108–12, 123–4
in modern Hinduism 173, 176
in Upaniṣads 52–5
Brāhmaṇas 43, 47–9
brahmin,
and antinomian movements 124
and Aryan heritage 41
and Buddhism 200
and epic-purāṇic religion 72–3, 77, 91
in Nepal 208, 211, 214, 216, 220
and Śaivism 170–2
and Vedic religion 47–8, 55, 183
Brahmo Samaj 173–4
Bṛhadāraṇyaka-Upaniṣad 52, 53
Buddha (Prince Siddhārtha) 60–1, 98, *see also* Śakyamuni
Buddha-Bodies, *see trikāya*
Buddhaghosa, Indian monk 103–4, 195–6, 205
Buddhas, celestial 101, 121, 255, 269, 281, *see also* Amitābha; Vairocana
Buddhism,
Amida 239–40, 538, *see also* Amitabha Buddha
early history 51, 56–71, 116, 123
expansion 70–1
and gods 200
Pali Canon 68–9, 70, 96, 194–6, 200
popular 69–70, 200–1, 239
Tibetan Canon 262
see also atheism; Hīnayāna Buddhism; Mahāyāna Buddhism; monasticism; Tantrism; Theravāda Buddhism; *and under individual countries*
Burma, Buddhism 198–9, 200
Burrow, Thomas 22, 26
calligraphy in Japanese Buddhism 241, 245
Cambodia, Theravāda Buddhism 198, 199
caste system,
India 41, 55, 94, 125–6, 176, 179, 183, 186, 832
Nepal 208–9, 211, 214, 218
celibacy,
in Buddhism 220, 253, 254, 261, 267
in Jainism 57–8
Ch'an (Zen) Buddhism 18, 226, 231–3, 234, 251, 270, 283, *see also* Japan, Buddhism; Zen Buddhism
Chāndogya-Upaniṣad 52
Chang Tao-ling 15, 16
Chen-yen Buddhism 122, 238, *see also* Tantrism
China
Buddhism 95, 103, 224–34
early history 17, 122, 224–9
modern history 234
monasticism 225, 228, 231, 233
schools 229–33
Christianity 234
Confucianism 10–11, 16, 227, 228, 230, 233, 245
Islam 228
Tantrism 17–18, 230
Taoism 10–19, 225, 228, 231, 232, 234, 239
see also Buddhism; Confucianism: Hīnayāna Buddhism; Taoism
Chö (gCod) practices, Tibet 270, 275
Christology and Hinduism 175, 176
Chu-she school of Buddhism 231
Chuang-tzu (Chuang Chou) 11, 13–14, 15
colonialism and Buddhism 199
Confucianism 10
and Buddhism 228, 230, 233, 245
consciousness,
in Buddhism 230, 263, 269, 272
in Hinduism 53–4
in Tantrism 143–5, 151, 161–3, 165
cosmology,
Buddhist 229–30
Hindu 107, 108–9
Jain 59
creation,
in Hinduism 176
myths 48, 74, 82

culture, Chinese 225

daēva in Mazdaism 21–2, 25–6, *see also deva*
Dalai Lama 261–2, 264–5, 273, 282
Damascius 11, 29
darma (cosmic law) 49, 55, 59, 92, 108
darśana 105–6, 108–10, 112
deva,
  definitions 21–2, 537–8
  in epic-purāṇic literature 70, 78–9, 81–3, 84, 86
  folk and regional beliefs 52, 81, 82, 88
  in Jainism 57
  in Vedas 44–6, 47–8, 52–3
Devīmāhātmya 84, 86, 91
Devīpañcaśataka 151–2, 164
devotionalism in Hinduism 42, 86–94, 102–3, 183–4
dharma (Buddhist: smallest component of reality) 69, 99–101, 103, 231
Dharma (*Dhamma*) (teaching of Buddha) 66–8, 69, 71, 98, 100, 195–6, 203, 263, 275
Digambara Jainism 56, 114
divination, Tibet 273, 274
Dobbin, Christine 34
Dogen, Buddhist monk 241
Drogmi, Tibetan scholar 254, 255
Dromten, Tibetan scholar 252–3
dualism,
  in Hinduism 112
  and Mazdaism 25, 32–3
Duchesne-Guillemin, Jacques 31
Dumezil, Georges 21, 22–4, 26, 28, 31
Duperron, Anquetil 34
Dzogchen teachings, Tibet 259–60, 269–70, 277, 278

education, in Hinduism 174–5, 179–80
enlightenment,
  in Buddhism 232, 263–4, *see also bodhi*
  in Tantrism 166–7
  in Tibetan Buddhism 253–4, 263–4, 267, 277
Entities in Mazdaism 23–4, 26
Epics, Hindu 72, 73–8, 110–11
essence of religion 178
ethics,
  in Buddhism 64, 67, 69, 196, 202–3, 244, 252
  in Hinduism 75, 109, 175, 179
  in Jainism 57–8
  in Mazdaism 25
evil, in Mazdaism 20, 32, 36
experience, religious, *see bhakti*: enlightenment (*bodhi*); liberation (*mokṣa, mukti*); meditation

Fa-hsiang school of Buddhism 230, 231
fasting,
  in Jainism 58
  in Nepali religion 216–17, 218, 219
festivals,
  Buddhist 228
  Hindu 89, 90–1, 93, 119
  Nepali 210, 211, 214–16, 219
fire,
  in Mazdaism 26, 27, 29
  in Vedic religion 44, 45, 46, 52, 87
Fischer, Michael 35
Flower Garland Sutra 229
Frye, R.N. 24, 27, 29
Fuju-fuse, Buddhist sect 243

Gampopa, Buddhist scholar 255–7, 269
Gandhi, Mahatma 178–9
Ganges 87
Gāthās (Mazdean hymns) 23–6, 32
Gauḍapāda, Hindi writer 111
Gelugpa (dGe-lugs-pa) school of Buddhism 255–7, 260–1, 264, 268–9, 281–3
Ghose, Aurobindo 177
Gignoux, Philippe 36
Gnosticism 30
Gobind Singh, Guru 190–1, 192
God,
  in Asian religions, *see also daēva; deva; kami*
  as neutral 537
  as personal 79, 176, 183
  see also Bhagavān; monotheism; theism; *and under individual deities*
Goddess, in Hinduism 82, 84–6, 88, 92, 93, 210, *see also* Śaivism
government, and modern Hinduism 180
grace, in Hinduism 111–12, 116, 125
Guhyakālī, cult 152–4
guru, role 93, 150, 167, 187, 189
guthi in Nepal 211, 213, 216, 217

Haiku poetry 236, 241
Hakuin, Buddhist writer 245

Han dynasty, China 224, 225
Harivaṃśa 75, 80
Harivarman, Buddhist scholar 103, 227, 237
haṭha-yoga 183, 269
Heissig, W. 238
henotheism 24, 25, 27, 30, 32, 47
Herodotus 27
Hīnayāna Buddhism 71, 95, 100–1, 103, 237, 265
  in China 225, 227, 231
  see also Theravāda Buddhism
Hinduism,
  and Christianity 175–6
  diversity in 42, 539–40
  early history 533
  epic-purāṇic,
    God and gods in 78–86, 111
    literature 72–8
    worship 86–94
  and Islam 173, 176
  modern 173–80
  and Sikhism 183–4, 191–2
  see also Epics; monotheism; philosophy; Purāṇas; theology; Vedānta; Vedas
Holy Spirit 25
Honen, Buddhist scholar 239–40, 242
Hosso school of Buddhism 237, 240, 242
Hua-yen school of Buddhism 229–30, 238
Huang-po, Zen sect 245
Humbach, Helmut 22, 25

I Ching 10
'idolatry', in Hinduism 88, 90, 173–8, 184
immortality, in Taoism 15–16, 17
Incarnation, in Hinduism 175, *see also avatatāra*
India,
  Christianity 40
  religions 39–42
  traditional religions 42, 79–80, 87–8
  see also Buddhism; Hinduism; Jainism; Parsees; Sikhism; Tibet, Indian influence
Indonesia, Buddhism 533
Indra, Vedic *deva* 45, 79, 215–16
initiation, in Tantrism (*dīkṣā*) 128, 130 137
  and consecration (*kaulādīkṣā*) 150
  and cult of Yoginīs 139
  Kashmiri tradition 159–60
  Mongolian traditions 282
  and Newars 210, 211, 218, 222
  Tibetan traditions 255, 267
Iran,
  Islam 31–2
  Revolution 35
Islam, and Sikhism 183

Jainism 51, 77, 90, 107–8, 124, 129
  early history 56–9, 60
  later history 114–16
Japan,
  Buddhism 220, 228, 236–45
    links with China 236–7
    monasticism 238–9, 240
    schools 237–44
    threats to 245
    see also Zen Buddhism
  Christianity 244, 245
  new religions 245
  Shintō 236–7, 240, 245
Jātaka stories 196, 203
Jayadrathayāmala 142–6, 150–1, 153–4, 162–3
Jesuits 209
Ji ('Time'), Buddhist sect 240
Jīva, see soul, in Jainism
Jodo Shinshu Buddhist sect 240
Jojitsu school of Buddhism 237, 242
Jonagpa, Buddhist order 255

Kadampas, Buddhist order 253–4, 255–6, 262
Kagyupa, Buddhist order 255–60, 264, 269
  Kālī cult 121, 137, 138, 140, 142–6, 163, 164, 166–7, 176
  and Kaulism 150–2, 162
  sects 256–8
Kanjur 237, 267, 282
Kāpālika tradition 138–43, 146–8, 150, 159, 162, 168
karma,
  in Buddhism 71, 200, 203–4, 225, 272
  in Hinduism 52–3, 55, 62, 109, 128, 161, 230, 277
  in Jainism 57–9, 116
Kashmir,
  non-Tantric traditions 169–72

Śaivism 131, 147, 149, 151, 157
post-scriptural traditions 158–72
Katen, Tibetan texts 277
Kaulism, *see* Śaivism, Kaula
Kegon school of Buddhism 238, 242
knowledge,
in Buddhism 251, 264, 265
in Hinduism 50, 52–3, 106, 112
in Jainism 50, 116
in Tantrism 118, 140, 159–60, 171
see also Gnosticism
Krama system, Tantrism 131, 145, 150–1, 152, 153, 158, 162, 164–7
Kramasadbhāva 151–2, 164
Kṛṣṇa, Hindu god 74, 75–6, 79–80, 81–2, 92–3, 112
kṣatriyas (warriors) 55, 56, 73, 208, 215
Kṣemarāja, Śaivite teacher 167, 168–9, 171
Kubjikā cult 131, 154–6, 167, 169, 171
Kubjikāmata 154–5
Kublai Khan 254, 280
Kundakunda, Jain teacher 56, 116
Kusha school of Buddhism 237–8, 242

laity,
in Buddhism 100, 234, 270
in Jainism 58
see also religion, popular
Lamaism,
China 233–4, 238–9, 283–4
Mongolia 280–4
Tibet, *see* Tibet, Buddhism
lamas, Tibet, reincarnation 256, 261–2, 264–5, 277
Langdarma, Tibetan king 251–2, 253
language,
and Hinduism 40, 106–8
and Jainism 114
see also Pali; Sanskrit
Lao-tzu 10–14, 16, 224–5
Laos, Theravāda Buddhism 198, 199
law, *see dharma* (cosmic law)
liberation (*mokṣa, mukti*),
in Buddhism 60, 61, 63–5, 101
in Hinduism 50, 52, 55, 106–10, 112, 116, 268
in Jainism 56, 57–9, 107
in Tantrism 121, 130, 131–5, 141, 149, 159–67, 171, 218
Lin-ch'i, Zen sect 233, 241
Lingayite movement 125
literature,
Buddhist 68–9, 71, 77, 95–7, 146, 229, 241–2, 262, 269
Hindu 40, 73–8, 92–3
Jain 114–15
Sikh 185–6, 188–9, 191
Lotus Sūtra 97, 103, 229, 238, 242, 245, 938–9, 941
Lü (*Vinaya*, Disciplinary) school of Buddhism 231, 238
see also Vinaya
Mādhyamika school of Buddhism 102, 226, 237, 263, 265, 268–9
magic, in Tantrism 117–18, 129, 157–8
Mahābhārata (Hindu scripture) 75–6, 80, 81, 115
Mahāmudrā (Great Seal) 255, 256, 258, 269
Mahānayaprakāśa 166
Mahāpurāṇa, Jain 77, 114
mahāsāṅghikas 71
Mahāvastu (Buddhist scripture) 71, 77, 90
Mahāvīra (Prince Vardhamana) 51, 56–7, 59, 73, 115
Mahāyāna Buddhism 17, 66, 71, 95–104, 105, 124, 198, 229, 261
early sources 95–7
philosophy 101–4, 111, 263–4, 265
revivalism 97–101
tantric approach 119, 121–3, 129, 268
in Tibet 251, 252
Maitreya 17, 98, 199, 226, 234, 244
Maitreyanātha, Buddhist scholar 102
man, divinity of 177
Mānbhāv (Mahānubhāvas) movement 124–5, 126
maṇḍala,
in Japanese Buddhism 238–9
and pursuit of power 119–20
and Śaivism 138, 140, 141–3, 145, 149
in Tibet 266–7
Manichaeism 29–32, 228, 231
mantra, tantric,
in Newar religion 215
and pursuit of power 119–20
and Śaivism 130, 133, 140, 152, 164
types 117–18, 119
Mantrapīṭha cults 136, 137–8, 140, 143, 146, 168
Manu 55
Mao Shan (Shang Ch'ing) sect of Taoism 17

Maoism 234
Marpa, Buddhist scholar 255–6, 269
Marxism, and Buddhism 234
Mata system, Tantrism 150–1, 152, 162
maṭha (*āśrama*) 91, 93–4
Mazdaism ('Zoroastrianism') 20–36
  deities 21, 25–6, 29, 31–2, 279, *see also daēva*
  and evil 20, 32, 36
  and historicity of Zarathushtra 23–6
  history 21–4, 27–31
Mazdakism 30–1
meditation,
  in Buddhism 64, 101, 201, 205–6, 225, 237, 239–40, 265–70
  Indian religions 50
    in early Buddhism 60
    in epic-purāṇic tradition 86
    in Hinduism 109–10, 112
    in Jainism 58, 116
    in Upaniṣads 52–3
  in Taoism 11–12, 15–16
mediums, spirit 273
merit,
  in Buddhism 98, 196, 198, 200, 202–4, 205, 234, 251, 264, 265
  in Hinduism 111–12
  in Jainism 115
  in Nepal 213, 216–17
Milarepa, Buddhist scholar 255, 257
millenarianism, Buddhist 199
Mīmāṃsā 107, 108, 130, 159
Mitra, god of Mazdaism 26, 27–9, 31
Mogul Empire 189, 191
mokṣa, see liberation
Mole, Marijan 22, 25, 30–1
monasticism,
  Buddhist 66–7, 69–70, 97–8, 220, *see also* Sangha
  Hindu 111, *see also maṭha* (*āśrama*)
Mongol dynasty 233–4, 242
Mongolia,
  Buddhism 279–84
  Tantrism 280–2
monotheism,
  and Buddhism 239–40
  in Hinduism 51, 79–81, 83, 92, 111, 124–5, 173, 175
  and Indian religions 54
Morony, Michael 31, 32
mukti, see liberation
mysticism,
  Buddhist 250, 260, 265
  Eastern, *see* Taoism
  Hindu 112, 174, 176–7
  and Śaivism 148
myths, Vedic 45–6

Nāgārjuna, Buddhist scholar 102, 226, 260
Nānak, Guru 125–6, 182, 184–5, 188–9
  successors 186–8, 189–90
  teachings 185–6
Nārāyaṇa-guru 126
Nāropa, Buddhist teacher 255, 258, 269
Nātha-yoga 90, 125, 183, 184
Nāthas, *see Nātha-yoga*
nationalism,
  and Buddhism 197, 199
  and Hinduism 175–6
nature, in traditional religions 44
Nāyaṉārs 40, 92, 112
nenbutsu (recital) 239–40, 242
Nepal,
  Buddhism and Hinduism 207, 209–10, 212–16, 218–23
  history 207–8
  modernisation 209
  monarchy 207–8, 215
  religion as worship 210–18, 222
  Tantrism 210, 211, 215, 218, 222
Nestorianism, in China 228
Newars 131, 208–16, 219–23
  and Tantrism 152–3, 218
Nichiren, Buddhist sect 238, 242–4
nihilism and Buddhism 65, 97, 103
nirvāṇa,
  in Chinese Buddhism 232
  in early Buddhism 66, 69
  in Mahāyāna Buddhism 97, 99–100, 103
  in Śaivism and Tantric traditions 129, 145, 166
  in Theravāda Buddhism (*nibbāna*) 201–2, 203–5
  Tibetan Buddhism 263, 265, 273
Nityāsodaśikārṇava 157–8
Nō drama 236, 241
Nyāyādarśana 106, 108
Nyimapa, Buddhist order 256, 258–60, 262–3, 264, 268–9, 278

öndür gegen 283
ordination, Theravāda Buddhism 196, 197–9, 201, 276

Padmasambhava, Tibetan Buddhist 250, 259–60
Pali, Theravāda Buddhist scriptures written in 194–6, 200, 203
Pāñarātra school of Hinduism 89, 111, 112, 121, 128, 146, 162, 169
Parā, goddess 141–2, 149, 155, 164, 169
Parbatiyes (service caste) 208–9
paritta texts 202, 203
Parsees 20, 33–5, *see also* Mazdaism
persecution,
  of Buddhists 227–8, 229, 231, 245, 282, 284
  of Jains 114
Phagpa ('Phags-pa), Tibetan abbot 254, 280
philosophy,
  Buddhist 99–100, 101–4, 108, 237, 263–5, 274
  Hindu 105–13
pilgrimage,
  in Buddhism 204–5
  in Hinduism 90
polytheism, and Hinduism 47, 78–9
possession, in Tantrism 150, 237, 278
power (*śakti*) 119–20, 123, 141, 148
Power Tantras (*Śakti-tantras*) 140–2
priesthood,
  in Mazdaism 31–2, 33–5
  in Vedic religion 46–9, *see also* brahmin
Prithvi Narayan Shah 208
Purāṇas,
  Hindu 41, 73–8, 83, 110–11, 115, 30–1, 174
  Jain 114–15
purdah 179
Pure Land (Ching-t'u) school of Buddhism 226, 231–3, 234, 239–40, 247–9; *see also* Amitābha Buddha

Rādhakrishnan, Hindu philosopher 177, 178
Ram Das, Sikh Guru 186–7, 188–9
Rāma, Hindu god 74, 76, 79, 81, 93
Rāmakantha, Tantric scholar 158, 159, 161
Rāmakrishna, Hindu mystic 176
Rāmānuja 111
Rāmāyaṇa 76, 81, 93, 115
Ramprasad Sen, Hindu poet 85, 93
rationalism and Buddhism 98, 232
realism,
  and Buddhism 99, 102, 103, 108, 121
  and Hinduism 108, 111
reason in Eastern religion 173, 199
Recognition, doctrine of 163–4, 167, 168
reincarnation,
  Tibetan lamas 256, 261–2, 264–5, 277
  see also transmigration
Reiyukai (Association of Friends of the Spirit) 245
relativism 14, 226
relics in Buddhism 204, 205
religion, popular, and Buddhism 270–8
religions,
  folk 200
  tribal 51, 532
renouncer traditions 49, 50–71, 78, 86, 108, 203, *see also* Buddhism; Jainism; Upaniṣads
revelation,
  in Hinduism 43, 175
  in Tantrism 128, 129, 130, 137, 160, 167, *see also smṛti, śruti*
revivalism, Buddhist 96, 97–8, 100, 259
Ṛg-Veda 43, 46, 48, 52, 106, 130
Ṙime movement 260
Rinchen Zangpo, Tibetan scholar 252
Rinzai, Zen sect 233, 241, 245
Risshokoseikai (Establishment of Righteousness and Friendly Intercourse) 245
Ritsu school of Buddhism 238
ritual,
  Buddhist 101, 121, 203, 212–15
  Hindu 89–91, 93–4, 112, 125, 130, 212–15
  in Mazdaism 30–1, 32, 36
  tantric,
    in Japanese Buddhism 238–9
    in Nepal 212, 218
    and righthand/lefthand Tantra 122–3
    and Śaivism 128–30, 136, 138, 141, 148, 149–50, 152, 158–71
    types 119–20
  in Vedic religion 44, 45–8, 58, 108
Roy, Rammohan 173–4
Rudra, Vedic deity 132–6, 139, 143, *see also* Śiva

Sacraments, Hindu 93

sacrifice,
in Mazdaism 30, 33
in Nepal 210, 213
in Tibet 279
in Vedas 44–8, 50, 54, 86
Sadyojyoti, Kashmiri scholar 158, 161
Saicho, Buddhist monk 238, 240
Śaiva-siddhānta 92, 112, 131, 146, 147, 158
Kashmiri 159–61, 167–71
Tantras 136, 138
Śaivism 89, 119
asceticism 119, 131, 132–5, 138, 147, 149–50
Atimārga 132–5, 139
Lākula division 133–5, 138
Pāsúpata division 132–3
and the Goddess 128, 136, 139, 143–5, 152, 155, 166
Kaula 134, 147–58, 159, 167, 170, 172
Mantramārga 132, 134, 135–8, 139, 142, 157, 158, 171
and Tantrism 121, 124, 128, 131
domesticated cults 158–72
see also Krama system; Trika
Śāktism 86
Sakya sect, Tibetan Buddhism 254–5, 260, 268, 280
Śākyamuni 17, 239, 240, 243–4, 259, 274, 276, *see also* Buddha
Sakyapa, *see* Sakya sect
salvation,
in Buddhism 199, 200
in Hinduism 174, 184
in Sikhism 185–6
in Tantrism 159–63, 171
see also liberation
Sāma-Veda 43, 46, 52
Śāmbhava system 155
Saṃhitās 43
Sāṃkhya *darśana* 54, 108–9, 110–11
saṃsāra,
in Buddhism 63, 99–101, 200, 263, 265–6
in Hinduism 85, 106, 107–10, 116
in Tantrism 159, 163
samurai, and Japanese Buddhism 241–2
San-chieh school of Buddhism 230–1, 239
San-lun (Three Treatise) school of Buddhism 226, 227, 237
Sangha, Buddhist monastic community 195–9, 202–3, 206, 227
Śaṅkara 42, 111, 155
Sanron School of Buddhism 237, 242, 244
Sanskrit,
and Buddhism 96
and Hinduism 48–9, 106–7
and Jainism 59, 114
Śāntarakṣita, Tibetan Buddhism 250–1
Sants, India 92, 116, 125–6, 184, 185
Saraha, *Dohākośa* 124, 125
Sāramati, Buddhist scholar 102
Saravatī, Dayāmanada 175–6
Sarvāstivāda school of Buddhism 103
Sautrāntika school of Buddhism 102, 103, 263
self, *see ātman*
Sen, Keshab Chunder 174–5
sexuality,
in Buddhism 244
in Indian religions 55, 66–7
in Tantrism 120, 134, 145, 148, 149–50, 166, 218, 239, 267–8, 281
shamanism 30, 33
Mongolia 279–82, 283–4
Shenrab, religious figure 275–6, 277
Shingon school of Buddhism 122, 238–9, 240, 242, 244
Shinto 236–7, 240, 245
Shotoku, Prince 237
Siddhārtha, the Buddha 57, 60, 61, 64, 65–6, 68, 71, 73, 203
Sikhism 182–93
and antinomianism 125–6
contemporary 192–3
early history 182–5
Khalsa 190–1, 192
leaders 185–8
reform 191–2
Śiva 45, 78, 79–83, 88, 92, 121, 124–5, *see also* Śaivism
smṛti,
in Buddhist meditation 64
secondary revelation 77, 128, 130–1, 169
society, cohesion of 41
Soka gakkai ('Value-Creating Study Group') 245
Somānanda, Tantric scholar 163
Soto, Zen sect 224, 241
soul 13, 107, 112, 225
in Buddhism 65–6, 225, 271–2
in Hinduism 107, 108–9, 111–12, 173, 177

in Jainism 57–9, 65, 116
in Mazdaism 26, 36
in Taoism 13
in Tibet 271–2
see also ātman
Spandakārikā 162–3
Sri Lanka, Buddhism 61, 68, 70–1, 95, 103–4, *see also* Theravāda Buddhism
Śrīvaiṣṇavism 111–12, 121, 125
Sronggtsan Gampo, Tibetan king 248–50, 252
śruti (direct revelation) 128, 130, 169
Sthānakavāsins 115
stūpa cults 69–70, 87, 96, 204, 248
súdra, caste 55
suffering,
in Buddhism 61–2, 64–6, 100–1, 200, 201–2
in Tantrism 132
śūnyatā (emptiness) 100, 225, 251, 253–4, 263, 265
sūtra (concise philosophical formula) 107, 109–10
sūtra (Mahāyāna treatise) 96–7, 101, 103, 229, 250
sūtra (Sanskrit; Pali: *sutta*) (the Buddha's sermons) 68–9, 96
Svacchandabhairava cult 137–8, 140, 146, 168–9
Svasthānī, fast of 211, 216–17
Śvetāmbara Jainism 56, 58–9, 114, 115
Śvetāśvatara-Upaniṣad 54, 79–80

taboos 118–20, 121–2, 123
Tachikawa school of Buddhism 239
Tagore, Devendranāth 174
Tagore, Rabindranāth 176–7
Tanjur (Tibetan Buddhist texts) 262
tantras, classes 273, 274
lefthand/righthand 123
texts 131, 132, 134, 136, 140–4, 150–3, 164
Tantrism 17–18, 42, 116, 117–23
and Buddhism 119, 121–3, 129, 146, 265
decline 130
diversity 128–9
and Hinduism 119, 120–1, 122, 123, 130, 174, 210
Vaiṣṇava 128–9, 162, 169, 186
and Vedic tradition 130–1
see also Śaivism
Tao Te Ching 10–14
Taoism,
and Buddhism 17–18, 225, 228, 231, 234, 239
canon 18
philosophical 10–14, 18, 225–6, 232
religious 14–18
Tea Ceremony, Japan 236, 241
Tegh Bahadur, Guru 189–90
temple,
in Buddhism 90
in Hinduism 77, 88–90, 91–2, 93–4, 125
in Jainism 90, 115
in Sikhism 188, 192–3
Tendai school of Buddhism 238, 239–41, 242, 244
termas (treasures) in Buddhism 256, 257, 259–60, 262, 277
theism 26–7, 30, 32, 106, 112
popular, *see* Hinduism, epic-purāṇic
theology,
Buddhist 249
Hindu 75, 78–9, 89–93, 105–13
Nepali 215–16, 219–20, 221–2
Sikh 185–6
Theosophical movement 34–5
Theravāda Buddhism 61, 71, 95–6, 99, 101, 103–4
early history 194–7
fundamental 199
in India 194, 197
modern 199–206
popular 200–2
in Sri Lanka 194–5, 197–9, 200–1, 205
Tibet,
Bon religion 278–83
Buddhism 21, 95, 122–3, 129, 220, 280–1, 282–3
characteristics 262–70
history 247–62
Indian influence 250–1, 252–3, 262–3, 267, 270, 273–4
and popular religion 250, 252, 270–3
sects 253–61
monarchy 247–52, 274
monasticism 250–3, 255–6, 260–1
Tantrism 254–5, 259–60, 265–9, 278
T'ien T'ai Buddhism 18, 229, 238
toleration, religious, in Hinduism and Buddhism 94, 221–2

tradition, oral 43, 259
traditions, esoteric, *see* Tantrism
trance, in Tantrism 150, 278
transcendence 50–1, 52–3, 71, 78, 107, 110
transmigration 50
in Buddhism 61–3, 202–3, 225, 272–3
in Jainism 57–8
in Kashmiri Śaivism 160, 163
in Sikhism 186
Trika Tantras 131, 137, 140–1, 145, 146, 157–8, 171–2
Kashmiri 160–1, 163–4, 167, 169
Kaula form 149–50, 151
trikāya (Three Buddha-Bodies) 101, 121, 242–3, 264, 277
Trinity, Hindu 78, 82
Tripurasunāri cult 131, 155, 156–8, 169, 171–2
Trisong Detsen, Tibetan king 250–1, 276
truth,
in Buddhism 263, 265
in Hinduism 178–9
Ts'ao-tung, Zen sect 224, 241
Tsongkapa, Buddhist scholar 254, 260–1, 269, 281
Tulsīdās, Hindu poet 81, 93

Umāsvāti, Jain teacher 56, 59
Union Tantras (*Yāmalātantras*) 137, 140, 143
Upaniṣads 43, 44, 51–6, 57, 60, 73, 106, 108, 110–11, 174
Utpaladeva, Tantric scholar 163–4, 168

Vaibhāṣika school of Buddhism 263
Vaikhānasa school of Buddhism 89, 263
Vairocana Buddha 146, 237, 239, 242, 260, 266, 269
Vaiśeṣika *darśana* 108
Vaiṣṇavism 88–90, 92, 121, 128–9, 162, 169, 186
vaiśya, trader caste 55
Vajrayāna Buddhism 95, 122, 129, 219, 265, 269
Varuṇa, Vedic *deva* 45, 47
Vasubandhui, Buddhist scholar 102, 103, 228, 230, 231
Vasugupta, Tantric scholar 158, 262
Vedānta (Hinduism) 54, 93, 106, 110–12, 173, 175, 177, 215–16
Vedānta-darśana 110
Vedānta-sútra 54, 110–11
Vedāntadeśika, Hindu poet 92, 111
Vedas 43–9
and Buddhism 64
and daily life 50, 169
and epic-purāṇic religion 72, 77–8, 80
and Jainism 58
and Śaivism 169–70
scholarly study 43, 108
and Upaniṣads 51, 54–5
see also Hinduism
Verethraghna, god of Mazdaism 26, 29, 31
Vibration, doctrine of 162–3, 165
Vidyāpīṭha 136–7, 148, 149
Vijñānavāda school of Buddhism 102, 263, 265
Vinaya 67–8, 69, 70
in Japanese Buddhism 244
in Theravā-da Buddhism 196–7
in Tibetan Buddhism 250, 252–4, 260, 263, 268
Vīra-Śaivite (Lingayite) movement 125
Vīryakālī cult 151
Viṣṇu,
avatāras 81–2, 90, 183
as Bhagavan-figure 79–80, 111
and monotheism 111–12, 124–5
in Nepal 216
in Tantrism 128–9, 154
and temple worship 90, 92
in Vedas 45, 78–9
Visuddhimagga 195–6, 205–6
Vivekānanda, Hindu philosopher 176, 177–8

women, in Indian religions 116, 179
worship, *see* Nepal; ritual

Yajur-Veda 43, 46, 52, 130, 133
yoga,
in Buddhism 225, 255–6, 266, 267–9
in Hinduism 53, 91–2, 109–10, 176–7
in Tantrism 123, 141, 170–1, 268
in Taoism 15
see also haṭha-yoga; Nātha-yoga

Yoga-darśana 106, 109
Yogacārā school of Buddhism 102, 228
yogī, Tibet 253, 260, 267
Yoginīs, cult 139–41, 142, 146–7, 165–6
reformation 147–58
Yu Chi 16, 17

Zarathushtra 20, 22, 23–6, 33–4
Zen Buddhism 236, 240–4, 245, *see also* Ch'an (Zen) Buddhism
Zurvanism 28, 29–30, 32–3, 279